REBELLIONS

Memoir, Memory and 1798

For
Clare, Fiona, Deirdre, Oisín, Fergus, Seán

REBELLIONS

Memoir, Memory and 1798

TOM DUNNE

THE LILLIPUT PRESS
DUBLIN

First published 2004 by
THE LILLIPUT PRESS LTD
62–63 Sitric Road, Arbour Hill,
Dublin 7, Ireland
www.lilliputpress.ie

1 3 5 7 9 10 8 6 4 2

ISBN 1 84351 039 1

The Lilliput Press receives financial assistance from
An Chomhairle Ealaíon / The Arts Council of Ireland.

Set in 10.5 on 14 Bembo by Susan Waine
Printed in Middlesex, England, by Creative Print and Design Group

CONTENTS

Prologue   I

PART I   *The Historian: An Intellectual Memoir*

CHAPTER I   The Child   13
CHAPTER 2   The Christian Brother   32
CHAPTER 3   University College Dublin   45
CHAPTER 4   University College Cork and Cambridge   56
CHAPTER 5   The Academic   78

PART II   *Understanding 1798: Historiography, Commemoration*

CHAPTER 6   Histories of 1798: from Musgrave to Cullen   101
CHAPTER 7   Commemoration: Comóradh '98   115
CHAPTER 8   Commemorationist History?   130

PART III   *5 June 1798*

CHAPTER 9   Sources   151
CHAPTER 10   Background: Old Quarrels and New Politics   161
CHAPTER 11   Rebellion: The Background to the Battle
      of New Ross   187
CHAPTER 12   5 June 1798: The Battle   214
CHAPTER 13   The Killings at Scullabogue   247
CHAPTER 14   New Ross: The Aftermath of the Battle   265

      Envoi   275

APPENDIX A: The Gaelic Poetry of Micheál Óg Ó Longáin:
      A Case-Study in Politicization   279
APPENDIX B: The Ballads of Thomas Dunne   284

      Notes   289
      Bibliography   315
      Acknowledgments   325
      Index   327

ILLUSTRATIONS

My parents' wedding photograph, January 1942 19

Courtdale, with the remains of the Norman tower 22

South Street, New Ross, with our house and shop 23

My first Communion, by Annie Brophy, Waterford 1949 26

A family photograph, again by Annie Brophy, 1955 30

The Novice, August 1959 39

Desmond Williams with Taoiseach Garret FitzGerald, Belfield 50

Maureen Wall 50

Oliver MacDonagh 57

John A. Murphy 83

Planning The Irish Review, *Belfast 1986* 87

Making last-minute changes to my paper on Wolfe Tone, 1981 90

The Heritage Industry 119

The Wexford Echo, *11 June 1998* 120

The significance of Scullabogue for Comóradh '98 129

John Rice's gravestone, St Stephen's Cemetery 159

New Ross *in* 1796, *drawn by G. Holmes, engraved by J. Walker* 169

New Ross *by W.H. Bartlett* 170

Musgrave's map of the area around New Ross 200

Edward Foran's statue of Michael Furlong and his flag of truce 218

Early eighteenth-century map of the town, used by Musgrave 220

George Cruikshank's version of The Wig Cannon 228

General Henry Johnson 233

The Tholsel, New Ross: in 1798 the ground floor was an open arcade 237

George Cruikshank's notorious drawing of the Scullabogue massacre 254

John Rice's house, Irishtown, still occupied by the family 272

'On Vinegar Hill, o'er the pleasant Slaney':
Private Grief and the Public Sphere

On a cold bright winter's day, early in 1995, I stood for the first time on Vinegar Hill overlooking the town of Enniscorthy, Co. Wexford, and the solitary hour I spent there affected me deeply. I was surprised at how small the area was and tried to imagine it thronged with people when the hill served as a major rebel camp for three hot summer weeks in 1798. Harder still to imagine were the scenes that marked the last bloody battle for the hill, when 'terraced thousands died, shaking scythes at cannon'. This striking image of Seamus Heaney's[1] portrayed the rebels as country people, like my paternal ancestors, farming just south-west of the town in that panorama of rich agricultural land visible from the summit. My own initial sense of 1798, however, was an urban one, from beyond the southern horizon in my home town of New Ross. It came above all from my mother, Joanna, the first historian I knew. Her mental map of the county, where she spent her whole life, consisted of generations of complex interfamily connections, radiating out from her own family, the Rices. She had a particular pride and interest in her great-great-grandfather, John Rice of the Irishtown in New Ross, killed in the aftermath of the horrific battle for the town on 5 June 1798, and in his cousin, Edmund Ignatius Rice, who founded the Irish Christian Brothers four years later in nearby Waterford.

I had climbed the hill that day not out of historical curiosity, but to recover from an unsettling visit with my mother in a nearby nursing home. She had suffered a series of strokes four years earlier at the age of eighty-two, and had borne confinement to a wheelchair with her usual fortitude and good humour. That day, the gradual deterioration in her speech and slow fading of her memory reached some kind of crisis for her, and she became distressed at her inability to communicate with me. That in itself was a shock. She had always kept from her children, and particularly from me, the eldest, the true extent of her suffering. When my father died sixteen years earlier, for example, she hid her intense and constant fear of living alone, admitting it fully only in the security of the nursing home she had chosen to move to before it seemed necessary. She had a fierce independence, and would not be a burden on any of her six children, scattered widely in Ireland and overseas. Now she could not conceal her condition, and this was part of her distress.

The inability to communicate properly involved the diminution of her greatest resource for coping with her environment and making sense of her world. An ease with language had long been at the core of her remarkable charm, partly natural, partly the product of her many years in business. 'She could sell sand to an Arab,' was my father's regular and not altogether admiring comment. For her, business often seemed less about profit than conversation; her customers were for the most part neighbours, friends or lifelong acquaintances. She sold them footwear almost as a postscript to leisurely discussion of family and relationships, often involving stories of childhood about which she had an intense nostalgia.

Now that flood of talk had dried to a trickle and instead, when I visited I retold the stories as I remembered them, she would smile or say the odd word. Gradually I became aware of other aspects of the loss involved in her enforced silence; I remembered so few of her stories, and could trace family connections only to a limited degree. As we went through her old photograph album, it was already too late to fill the gaps in my knowledge. Also, we were at cross purposes – mine concerned fact and meaning, hers the shards of memory. More separated us than age. While, like her, I make sense of my life through stories, I am trained to interrogate other people's stories in the light of the knowledge and understanding of the past that academic history has developed. For her the 'historical' 1798 – the Catholic nationalist account encapsulated in the ballads and statues of the centenary of the Rebellion, a decade before my mother's birth – and the family story of the death of her great-great-grandfather were seamlessly joined. He died for Ireland and in defence of the weak, a heroic death comparable to the heroic life of his cousin Edmund, as she saw it.

Standing on the rocky summit of Vinegar Hill that day, and seeking distraction from the sadness of her enforced silence by imagining the bustle of the rebel camp, I was struck by the conflict between the popular or communal memory of 1798 and how historians like myself write about it. It is not simply that we are impelled to historicize that memory, explaining it as a product of historical developments, but that we are also constrained and limited by the surviving evidence and by the debates to which we contribute. History has little to say about the ordinary people caught up in that cataclysm, whether as rebels or as innocent bystanders. The record, and the debates, put the focus instead on the leadership and their ideology. Thus, for example, while I had written about the contemporary ballads surviving from the Rebellion, my focus had been on contrasting them with the genteel versions used by the bourgeois United Irishmen in their attempts to politicize the poor.[2] It now struck me, with some unease, that my criticism of the United Irish failure to understand popular culture could be applied to myself, and indeed to modern historians in general. Academic history all too often lacks empathy with the individual stories that both constitute and reflect communal memory. The nature and even existence of such memory is contested and problematic, not least because of politically inspired attempts to shape or manipulate it.

Before I left the hill, I read the text of the monument erected in 1989 by Comóradh '98, the official body set up by local politicians to manage the celebration of the upcoming bicentenary. While the monument in the town centre depicts a priest leading a peasant rebel and requires no text other than '1798', this one stresses the importance of the largely Protestant and secular-minded United Irishmen, and, linking the Rebellion to the bicentenary of the French Revolution, claims that 'the '98 insurrection established a revolutionary spirit and that the republican ideology of Tone and the United Irishmen inspired a new form of patriotism. This ultimately led to a democratic system of government in Ireland.' This version is, in essence, as traditional as the other, but I recognized the echo of a new emphasis in the historiography of the Rebellion also. One of its main proponents was later to write that 1798 'never passed into history because it never passed out of politics',[3] and certainly previous commemorations, especially in 1898 and 1948, produced versions that had more to do with the politics of those times than with the actual events of 1798. The bicentenary clearly would be no different, but in 1995 I could not anticipate that the interaction of a new political context with emerging trends in history-writing would give new life to an old-fashioned nationalist account.

Nor did I realize fully then that my hour on Vinegar Hill made new connections for me between a number of related interests and concerns, and between my private and professional lives. It led me to question the kind of history I had been writing, and to wonder if I could accommodate the family story I had heard from my mother, and other stories like it, in an attempt to understand the Rebellion in more human terms as a sum of the individual experiences of ordinary people. What motivated the rebels to such acts of both courage and cruelty as this hill witnessed? Given how little evidence they left behind them, can we ever know? How were they viewed by the tens of thousands of Wexford people whose lives were changed irrevocably by the violence of those weeks? What was their experience of the chaos and confusion that historians, from the beginning, have reduced to the false neat categories of military engagements?

In the months that followed I developed my own small project for the bicentenary, initially to please my mother. Beginning with the family tradition of how my great-great-great-grandfather died, it focused also on the world of the country men who had attacked New Ross with extraordinary courage, and massive fatalities. They came mainly from the area north of the town, from the barony of Bantry, where my father's family had farmed since the mid-seventeenth century.

I next climbed Vinegar Hill three years later, in January 1998. Once again the sun shone and it was bitterly cold on the summit. It was the morning of my mother's funeral and soon the cortège would leave, bringing her home to New Ross for the funeral mass, following the characteristic detailed instructions she had written out years before. For a week her six children had gathered around her bed as her body closed down with a slow, dignified finality. We talked to her and about her, retelling her stories, reminding one another of episodes in our childhood, hearing from one another memories unique to each. It was a week of much laughter as well as sadness, and if she was conscious of it, that would have pleased her. Her death, when it came, ended years of pain and distress and had been long anticipated, even longed for by her, ever since her beloved Art had died nearly twenty years before. Acknowledging this helped us to accept her passing, but did little to prepare us for the void that it left in our lives. This is something we all have had to learn for ourselves.

Now that the voice that had been my first guide in the world was finally silenced, there would be no more stories: so much folklore was lost with her, the last of her family. More than ever it was to seem important to me that I try to fit her story to mine. I had already published an article that tried to give a context and explanation for John Rice's death, and to understand the background of the Bantry rebels. It also took issue with Comóradh '98 for 'presenting a sanitized and politically correct version of the rebellion that is in tune with the common nationalist perception of the current "peace process", a lost dream of "United Irishmen", which we can still make a reality'.4

I knew my mother was pleased that I had written about John Rice and had used some ballads written by my paternal grandfather. I also knew, of course, that her view of '98 had been closer to that of Comóradh than to mine, and that this highlighted an interesting tension for me. By now, professional concern (and indeed some anger) at the crudities of the official line began to loom larger than the sense of family *pietas* with which I had begun my research. Even that day of private grief offered several reminders of the willingness of a diverse range of interests to exploit (as I saw it) the dead of two hundred years before. Vinegar Hill was daubed with Sinn Féin, IRA, and INLA graffiti, including crude anti-British sentiments. A mass rally was soon to be addressed there by Gerry Adams, and Comóradh '98 was already distancing itself from the anticipated identification of the IRA's thirty-year war with 'the United Irish Revolution'. The whole point of the bicentenary, after all, was to distance revolutionary ideology from its real consequences. Others saw a business opportunity. That evening, after a meal in the town, I was given an advertisement for 'Cream of '98: Irish cream liqueur' as a souvenir. It carried the Comóradh '98 logo, and featured Edward Foran's romantic painting, for the centenary, of the battle of Oulart Hill. Thus, art and advertising combined to package and sell the Rebellion, with official approval.

Making my way to Vinegar Hill the morning of the funeral, I bought the *Irish Times* and read it on the summit. It carried a report of the launch by the Taoiseach of the official programme for the bicentenary. Mr Ahern declared: 'We are commemorating the most sustained effort in Irish history to reconcile and unite what were the three communities with different religious beliefs and ethnic backgrounds – Protestants, Catholics and Dissenters.' He spoke on behalf of 'a sovereign Irish government' that, he claimed, 'can trace its political lineage back to 1798 when the first republics in Wexford and Connaught were declared'. Linking the commemoration to 'the peace process', he put forward the achievement of 'a new lasting and peaceful end' to the Northern Ireland conflict as the best way to crown the bicentenary and 'fulfil some of the ideals of the United Irishmen'. A feature article in the same issue of the *Irish Times* quoted the historian Kevin Whelan on the unprecedented involvement by successive Irish governments in the commemoration of historical events during the previous four years, in contrast to its failure in 1991 to support efforts by prominent republicans to highlight the seventy-fifth anniversary of the 1916 Rising (which attracted little public support). However, the remarkably popular (and politically less contentious) commemoration of the Great Famine, starting in 1995 and lasting several years, was orchestrated and funded by the government, who 'did a pretty good job on it', according to Whelan. (Modestly, he made no mention of his own prominent role.) Now, as part of 'a maturing process', in his view, 'the state is taking responsibility for this' (i.e. the 1798 bicentenary). He added: 'After all, the State that doesn't respect its own history is a bankrupt one.' He was identified as a member of the 'National Commemoration Committee'.

Both press conference and interview raised interesting questions. How does the state *know* 'its own history'? Given that history is a matter of interpretation rather than some agreed objective reality, how did the state come up with the version of 1798 articulated by the Taoiseach? Assuming that Mr Ahern was not emulating his predecessor, Dr FitzGerald, and finding solace from the burdens of office in historical research, did that version come from the 'National Commemoration Committee'? And if so, where did *they* get it? What is the proper role of the academic historian involved in official commemoration and its inescapably political agendas? Recognizing that interpretation involves ideological bias, academic history aspires to correct this by immersion in the full range of the surviving evidence. Some contributions to the bicentenary, however, had already raised the question whether ideology had not more bearing on their interpretation than the witness of the historical record. It is impossible to read that record and not be reminded endlessly that the Rebellion in Wexford was an event soaked in blood, and marked more by cruelty and fanaticism on both sides than by the ideals of the United Irishmen. In its brief course, many thousands of people died in this relatively prosperous corner of Ireland, the vast majority of them ordinary Wexford people – whether rebels, their followers or innocent bystanders.

This overwhelming fact had already led me to disagree publicly with Kevin Whelan's view that, in commemorating the Rebellion, 'we must relinquish our obsession ... with pikes and deaths, murder, mayhem and martyrdom. We should instead stress the living principles of democracy and pluralism which the United Irishmen formulated.'[5] To demur at this emphasis, of course, is to invite the criticism that one is against 'democracy and pluralism', just as to call attention to the sectarian dimension of the Wexford outbreak is to run the risk of accusations of being sectarian. Thus, a week after the funeral, on a national radio programme, I was to be accused by a fellow historian of 'playing the Orange card' when I took up the presenter's request that I talk about the rebel atrocity at Scullabogue. This was a defining moment for me, and led ultimately to the present work. It also encouraged me into further public controversy, mainly in the pages of the *Irish Times*.[6] Now, after the high tide of the commemoration has receded, the basic questions remain, and the only answers that should count, at least for historians, are those that relate to the evidence, whatever their implications for contemporary politics.

My contribution involves a focus on the most bloody and the most decisive day of the Rebellion, Tuesday, 5 June 1798, when the remarkable run of rebel successes ended at New Ross, leaving perhaps 1500 dead in its narrow streets (roughly half the population of the town) in one horrific day. Nearby on that same day occurred the most infamous rebel atrocity, the burning of over a hundred men, women and children, almost all Protestant, in a barn at Scullabogue, a half-mile from where I was born. My starting-point was one of my mother's stories – indeed, perhaps the master story of her linked narratives. A piece of oral history, handed down through five generations of her family, it described the death of her ancestor, John Rice, of the Irishtown in New Ross, in the bloody aftermath of the battle. The version written down by my cousin, Bride Roe, in a marginal note to her excellent layout of the Rice family tree, corresponds to what I remember hearing from my mother:

> He was executed by a group of English soldiers because he had sheltered some women and children in a loft behind his house during the battle of Ross. The hiding place was discovered and all were killed. Finally John Rice was dragged outside his door and a Hessian officer drew his sword to cut off his head. However, John Rice caught the sword in his teeth and would not let go. Then, he was dragged down the street and shot at the cross of the Irishtown.

What began as an attempt to contextualize this vivid story historically, and to understand its basic folk motifs, led me to an analysis of the accounts we have of the battle for the town and of the linked atrocity outside it. My initial window into the motivation and world view of the rebels, for which so little evidence survives, came through the notebooks of my paternal grandfather, after whom I was named: Thomas Dunne, a farmer of Courtnacuddy, near Enniscorthy, part of the old barony of Bantry. The rebels who attacked New Ross came mainly from this area, as did their leaders, John Kelly 'the boy from Killanne' and Thomas Cloney of Moneyhore, who wrote the only account of the battle from the rebel side. They did not, it appears, include my great-great-great-grandfather, Arthur Dunne, and trying to understand why he stayed at home highlighted some aspects of his community and its culture, just as the ballads written seventy-five years later by my grandfather highlighted others.

While my starting-point thus involves the faint and problematic records of two unimportant non-combatants, and while my focus is on one day, the questions I am raising and seeking to answer are major ones for the Rebellion as a whole. The attempt to provide a historical context for my mother's story (and for others that have survived in the local folklore) also highlights some of the problems of dealing with memory historically. Most sources used by historians involve memory, and all memory is itself shaped by historical conditioning. First-hand accounts, even when written almost immediately – like the depositions, or evidence at trials, which are crucial here – all reflect that conditioning. They have to be checked against one another and probabilities established, but the historian is always aware of being short-changed or manipulated, and of needing to find the truth often in the cracks rather than the surfaces, in the silences rather than by separating or harmonizing the voices. Of course, the idea that the historian is a dispassionate, detached observer, a scientist weighing the evidence, while a useful ambition, and perhaps a necessary pose, cannot be taken too far. The historian is also part of history and describes the past in terms of the perceptions and the needs of the present. Simultaneously looking forwards and backwards, the historian is inextricably political and fundamentally compromised. Like Walter Benjamin's image of 'the angel of history': 'His face is turned towards the past … But a storm is blowing from Paradise … This storm irresistibly propels him into the future to which his back is turned, while the pile of débris before him grows skywards. This storm is what we call progress.'7

In searching through the débris, the historian must be aware that what survives by way of evidence comes mainly from those that 'progress' has favoured. The old Marxist cliché that history is a record of barbarism, written by and for the winners, has a particular resonance in a colonial context like that of Ireland, in which the voices of the losers are not only difficult to find, but are difficult to understand when heard, because they speak in a different language, and one to which most historians are deaf. The voices of the Irish poor are buried not only in the accounts, but also in the language of the colonial power. They are also inaudible for the most part in nationalist accounts, which mimic colonial culture and use its language. This is particularly true of the late eighteenth century, when English was replacing Irish at all social levels, and when a complex web of bilingualism effectively disguised the process and the trauma involved. The record is almost entirely in English, and the Irish-language element of that complex culture remains largely invisible and inaudible, although it is crucial in any understanding of the politics of the poor.

I found that the sources even for the official side in the Wexford Rebellion are remarkably thin and incomplete; the state archive on the battle of New

Ross would fit comfortably into one of my mother's shoeboxes. Those on the rebel side are dominated by the proclamations of the bourgeois or gentry leadership; the voices of the rank and file have to be excavated from the unsympathetic records of courts-martial, the depositions of 'suffering loyalists', and the accounts of loyalist prisoners and other victims of the Rebellion; they echo in contemporary ballads in English, more clearly in poetry in Irish, and both invoke a particular communal memory as a basis for practical or political concerns. In this book I use such sources to reconstitute, to the very limited degree possible, the *mentalité* of the ordinary rebel, and to test the current orthodoxy that this had been transformed by politicization from above by the United Irishmen.

A different kind of invisibility obscures the conformist, assimilationist middle-class Catholics of the period like John Rice. Their business was carried on largely outside the Protestant monopolies of corporation and guilds, especially in an old Norman town like New Ross; their leases, often short term, and sublettings usually went unrecorded; the records of their Church in this era are few; even the records of Catholic political associations normally include only the socially prominent. Thus a small-town 'rising' Catholic like John Rice left little mark on the official record, and we can only project onto him what we know of his class and infer what we can from his relationship to the much wealthier Rices downstream in Waterford.

Two other elements, apart from the problematic surviving evidence, profoundly shaped my search for meaning behind the family and communal memories of a traumatic time, and their recasting in narrative form. It demanded intense engagement with previous writing about 1798, from contemporary accounts to the latest historical findings, and particularly with the political basis of these interpretations. This in turn led me to confront my own social, cultural and political formation, and I decided to discuss this openly here, rather than allow silently for it as my training dictated. My life has not been extraordinary, nor my work of any great significance, but a brief account of both may help to illuminate a period of profound change in Irish society and culture. This experiment of linking together elements of autobiography, historiography and history, while not initially planned as such, may also have value as a case-study of how our understanding of the past is formed. Thus, it may be seen as part of the current trend of what French historians have called *ego-histoire*, but it was written without specific reference to such writing.[8] It may be regarded instead as a further example of a new awareness among historians worldwide of the linkages between autobiography and history writing, and of the ideological and literary dimensions of their professional enterprise. But it all began with my mother's stories. Some of these, as I was to discover, were not only celebrations of family and place, but offered ways of coping with a threatening world.

PART I

The Historian: An Intellectual Memoir

'Before you study the history, study the historian … Before you study the historian, study his historical and social environment.'

E.H. CARR, *What is History?*

… This is the use of memory:
For liberation – not less of love but expanding
Of love beyond desire, and so liberation
From the future as well as the past. Thus, love of a country
Begins as attachment to our own field of action
And comes to find that action of little importance
Though never indifferent. History may be servitude,
History may be freedom. See, now they vanish,
The faces and places, with the self which, as it could, loved them,
To become renewed, transfigured, in another pattern.

T.S. ELIOT, 'Little Gidding'

CHAPTER I

The Child

My mother was a romantic, at least in relation to the story of her family and her childhood. She had an intense nostalgia for 'the old days', when people were happy even though poor, when neighbours constantly visited, doors weren't locked, and life was simple. When her own children moved away and settled elsewhere she warned that the friendships formed in these new surroundings could never be as important or as lasting as the ties of family. Her stories of her own family were vivid and exciting. Leaving aside the ancestor killed in 1798, and his relationship to Edmund Rice, these focused mainly on her father, John. Born in Melbourne, Australia, in 1850, shortly after his parents emigrated there from New Ross, he was brought back to Ireland, aged eight, by his mother, on the death of his father. The rest of his long life, he told stories of kangaroos and Chinamen, of the six-month voyage back, and of gold nuggets his father had acquired in the goldfields and which his mother is said to have used later to set him up on an independent basis. His parents hardly emigrated, as my mother believed, 'for an adventure', but because his father was the third son and had to make his own way. The widow returned with her three sons, aged eight, four and two, to a family dominated by their grandfather, who lived for another five years and who had himself been eight years old when his father was killed in 1798. The longevity of her father and his grandfather brought the Rebellion very close to my mother – who was, in effect, at just one remove from the boy who had seen his father killed.

I remember no stories of her father's life after his return to Ireland until he married at fifty, nor is it clear how they lived. His mother (formerly Margaret Murphy, with her own connections to 1798, being a grandniece of the famous Father John Murphy) had, seemingly, bought house property in the Irishtown of New Ross and elsewhere, and it was, perhaps, because this ensured the future of her eldest son that his younger brother Michael inherited the family's share of the grandfather's property and business. In any case, when my grandfather married in 1900, he lived first on the farm at Ballymacar, just outside the town, which, according to family tradition, his mother had purchased with gold, and which also had 1798 associations, having been then the house of the parish priest of Cushinstown; there is a tradition of rebels getting Communion there before the battle of New Ross. When my grandfather's unmarried brother Michael died fourteen years later and added heroically to a family reputation for charity by leaving a considerable part of his property in trust for the poor of the town, my grandfather was able to purchase part of it back. It was to be his last positive contribution to the family's fortune. Shortly before that, he had inherited his mother's property, and then the portion of his brother's not left to charity.

In his mid-fifties, therefore, he was a man of considerable wealth, owning three farms and (according to my mother) thirteen houses. When he died, forty years later, most of it was gone. A man of great charm, he kept open house, did no work, and, it was said, drank a bottle of whiskey a day. My mother, always protective of him, was open about his alcoholism, but stressed that he 'never got drunk', was foolish but always kind and good-humoured. Only in her final years did she hint at the grimmer reality of his occasional violence and the fear in which they all lived of this lovable patriarch turning suddenly and unpredictably into a monster. This was the untold story that shaped her life, and still shapes mine. I believe that it was this that led to such a powerful emphasis on family and to such insistence on a romantic memory of childhood, and that made her so determined to achieve independence and control in her own life. Only in recent years, as her children became more aware of the hurt, vulnerable child she had been, did we come to terms properly with the complex way she had related to us: immensely supportive of our ambitions and independence, and at the same time finding it hard to accept that this would give us different attitudes and values from her own. In particular, the religious faith that had been the main consolation of her life took the form of a dogmatic orthodoxy. She was the most literal-minded and traditional Catholic I've ever known; her moral universe was black and white, and shaped by pre-Vatican II certainties. Yet, while often shocked at the criticisms we voiced, she was respectful of the choices we made and very supportive, for example, when I, my brother John and my sister Rosaleen in turn left the various religious orders we had joined. But we also felt strongly that there were limits to her tolerance, and a number of us concealed from her our break with Catholicism. The greatest legacy of her father's alcoholism may have been some stunting of the ability to express negative emotions, and most of us found it impossible to confront her on any emotive issue. Challenged, she became hurt and withdrawn in a way I found devastating. My family thus lacked the emotional safety valve of the usual rows and conflicts, and it was to take me many years to realize that it is better in one's personal life to express anger and explore difference than to suppress such feelings.

Perhaps I also inherit from my mother not only a fascination with the past, but the urge to redefine it. She reinvented a father who was a benign presence and much-loved local character (perhaps after he had reinvented himself). His old age became the second romantic period of his life and the other subject of her stories, featuring his dapper, youthful appearance and his remarkable health up to his death at ninety-five. 'If he hadn't gone out into the yard on a frosty night and caught pneumonia, he'd be alive to this day,' she once told me, waving aside my calculation that that would have made him 130 years old. What I didn't then understand was that he never died in her mind; up to the time she herself died, his memory and his legacy shaped her view of the world.

By comparison, her mother was a shadowy, saintly figure, whose father, James Gantley, a member of the Royal Irish Constabulary, seemed more vivid to me as a child. His story features another heroic legend: his death, also from pneumonia, being ascribed by my mother to his attempts to help a poor woman who had run away in the depths of winter to escape an abusive husband. Why this story may have appealed so strongly to her only strikes me now. She was very pleased when I told her that a discussion at a conference of Irish historians I had attended had revealed that virtually everyone present had an RIC ancestor. 'They were very go-ahead,' was her astute comment.

Her father's legacy made her successfully independent, from an unpromising start, when she left school early to 'serve her time' in a shoe shop. Twelve years later, aged twenty-seven, she opened her own shop with a £100 bank loan guaranteed by an uncle. This was an unusual step for a young woman at that time, even one who was already, though secretly, engaged to a 'strong' farmer. After she married and my father joined her in the business, it continued to operate under her name, J. Rice. 'We didn't want to confuse the customers,' was her explanation, but that name over the door was always a matter of pride to her, a sign not only of her own success, but of continuity with the family tradition of business in the town since the late eighteenth century.

Remaining so publicly a Rice linked her also to Ballymacar, her childhood home, which we visited regularly and heard about daily. So powerful was its meaning for her that when her brother in his old age sold it to a neighbour, and not to another family member as she had wished, she didn't speak to him for years. By then she was not only retired from business but had sold the shop, after accepting stoically that none of her six children wanted to take it over.

My father's story seemed less glamorous, rooted as it was in a rural community where his ancestors had farmed for over three hundred years. He had little interest in the family history and no nostalgia for his childhood. Indeed, as it appeared in the stories told by himself and his brothers, it was a life of physical hardship and dour duty, presided over by an authoritarian and remote father. I am named after him as tradition dictated. When my father was sixteen his mother died, and with a father who seemed unable to communicate except to give orders he came to rely on his older sisters, May and Peg, and to form an intense friendship with his brothers, Jim, John and Nick, which was to last all of their lives. Their father, Thomas Dunne, also had other resources. He had always been bookish and will appear later in this account as the author of romantic nationalist verse, celebrating the 1798 heroes that came from his district. Up to his death, he spent every Sunday in a back room, drawing and writing in a series of notebooks, only two of which survive. He was, his sons agreed, a hopeless farmer, despite his meticulous field maps and his records of crop rotation. In the wider community, however, he was different: gregarious, and prominent in local politics, he was secretary of the local Land League and ultimately a Poor Law Guardian. Even in his old age, he was known to his sons, as well as his neighbours, as 'the Guardian', a name that suited their image of him.

He in turn was ruled by his brother John, a formidable cleric, ultimately parish priest of Castlebridge and known to all, including his brother, as 'the Canon'. He still lives in the folklore of Curracloe as a blackthorn-wielding guardian of public morality, beating courting couples from the sinful shadows and warning against the depraved habits of summer visitors from Dublin. But he was also a founder of the Gaelic League in the county, and, more surprisingly perhaps, one of the group that started the Enniscorthy paper, *The Echo*.[1] He was the real head of the family, seemingly following a tradition going back several clerical generations. By his nephews' accounts, he decided what they should do with their lives, and their father informed each in turn of his fate.

My father was told on a Friday, when he was sixteen, that he was to leave the Christian Brothers School he was attending in nearby Enniscorthy and start to serve his time in Burke-Roche's Drapery on the following Monday. He obeyed, lived over the shop in an attic with other apprentices, and was fed scraps by a sanctimonious employer, whose parade every Sunday with family and large prayer book to a front pew in the cathedral he could recall to the end of his days, always with a flash of anger. The only fellow-employee he talked about was a man from Clare, sacked for trying to organize the staff in a trade union. A similar sense of social injustice featured in his stories of the Carews of Castleboro. His family had been tenants on the Castleboro estate since the seventeenth century and had bought out their farm under the Wyndham Act in 1906, the year my father was born. Yet he recalled the annual visit of Lady Carew to his primary school as an experience of being patronized, and he would wax indignant every time he told of farmers who still did occasional work at the Great House being given rubber shoes for their horses lest they spoil the lawn.

It was an anger felt even more keenly by his older brother Jim, bringing him into the IRA and into conflict with his Redmondite father. In 1921, he was one of those who burnt the great Palladian mansion of the Carews, despite their long record as liberal landlords and the sale of the land to their former tenants.

While my father thus grew up in an intensely nationalist environment, he had little time for such politics, always mocking gently the die-hard republicanism of his elder brother. His one political story summed it all up. He was fourteen and forking corn on the threshing-mill at home when two RIC men arrived, looking for Jim, who was on the run. My father shouted 'up the IRA' ('just acting the eejit') and was instantly hauled down and frogmarched toward New Ross, fifteen miles away. Coming near the town, they stopped at a little pub at Ballyanne, where his captors had a few pints and bought him a lemonade. Then, as they left the pub, they turned him towards home, booted him in the backside and told him to behave himself. A different outcome might have made him, and me, a nationalist.

My father spent ten years as a shop assistant in Enniscorthy, the last few in a shoe shop on the Square. That, together with his farming background, must have been part of the initial attraction of this quiet humorous man for my mother. For them to meet, however, a dramatic change in his fortunes had to occur: Enniscorthy, though only eighteen miles away, was remote from her world. In 1931 his Aunt Biddy died, at Courtdale, under the shadow of Carrigbyrne Rock and eight miles from New Ross. It was a farm she had married into, and in her will the bulk of her estate was left to the Maynooth

Mission to China, and the farm was put up for sale. The Canon as executor facilitated the sale to his brother on behalf of my father – presumably to keep it in the family. And so my father, thrilled to escape the town and his menial position, suddenly found himself the proud possessor of ninety acres and of an undreamed-of independence. Not that he got things too easy. The Canon, in order to raise money to compensate the family who had previously owned the farm had sold off every animal, every piece of farm machinery, and all seed and fertilizer leaving only the farm buildings and the land. He also insisted that he keep on his aunt's ancient maid, who slept in the house, and this meant that propriety (and the Canon) dictated that my father should sleep in the stables! With the Canon's death in 1932, he gained the house as well as the farm. I was born there ten years later.

According to his brothers, my father was a very good farmer – not that they ever said so to his face, but instead teased him for opting eventually for a soft life in the town. The only thing I ever heard him take pride in was coming through the 'economic war' with no debts, and never failing to sell the butter he made himself during times when it was impossible to sell animals. 'I made the best butter in County Wexford,' he told me shortly before he died, and such an uncharacteristic boast commanded instant assent. In fact, his time in farming was dominated by de Valera's 'economic war' with Britain over the land annuities, which massively depressed an already sluggish agricultural economy and made most relatively prosperous farmers, like my father, intensely anti-Dev. Unlike most of them, however, this did not make him a supporter of Fine Gael (though he did regard James Dillon as the best-ever Minister for Agriculture); instead, as far as I know, he was a Labour supporter, perhaps from his earlier urban experiences. His stories of farming were of hardship overcome; of leaving home at 3 a.m. to walk his animals to the fair at New Ross in order to get a good 'stand', and of walking them home unsold twelve hours later, having failed on one occasion even to give calves away; of being refused a loan of £100 from the bank that had financed my mother, despite his much greater equity. But there were funny stories also, of 'characters' and encounters in pubs, of waking up wet and hungover in his trap outside his front door, his pony waiting patiently, having got him home unguided.

He met my mother during his trips to the town shortly after he settled in Courtdale, and several years before she started her own business. They were engaged secretly for nearly ten years before marrying in 1942, my mother wearing her engagement ring out of sight on a chain. I never learned the reason for the secrecy, but the delay was to allow each of them to become

*My parents' wedding
photograph, January 1942.*

better established economically. Their wedding was also mysterious, taking place not in New Ross, but in Newman's University Church in Dublin. My father's brother, John, officiated; his brother Nick and my mother's sister Nancy were the only witnesses. Afterwards they all walked across Stephen's Green and had breakfast in the Wicklow Hotel. It was the first time in Dublin for both of them and neither had any connection with the university. My mother next visited the University Church after my graduation twenty-five years later and we walked across Stephen's Green to the soon-to-be-demolished Wicklow Hotel for lunch. I asked her why they had got married in that way. 'Well', she said with uncharacteristic vagueness, 'you know how your father hates fuss, and your Uncle John arranged it.'

He was thirty-six and she was thirty-three. Before driving back to Wexford in his brother's Ford (John was a regular traveller to Dublin to see the latest films, a lifelong passion), they had a studio photograph taken by J.E. Stanley Ltd. My mother sits demurely in an ornate chair (its plush arm badly frayed); my father stands leaning against a table. Neither looks at the camera and neither is smiling, but both seem quietly pleased with life. Or so I read it, inevitably seeing it in the light of my experience of their relationship and searching it for clues or confirmation. To me, now, their lack of any overt sign of affection or intimacy seems appropriate; they were rarely demonstrative, at least in front of their children. What my siblings remember about my leaving home at fourteen to join the Christian Brothers is the remarkable sight of them sitting for a long time on the settee silently holding hands. The reluctance to express emotion was doubtless common enough in their generation, and may explain why mine has taken so enthusiastically to continental habits of embracing and kissing. Yet the sensitive antennae of childhood registered no sense of tension between them, and they were affectionate, supportive parents who succeeded in creating the kind of stable, happy environment neither had experienced as children.

While my mother appeared the dominant personality – the buyer for the shop, the authority figure for her children – she still deferred to my father on the rare occasions he expressed a strong or contrary preference. To us he seemed more indulgent, less demanding, and above all less dogmatic, particularly on religious matters. A daily Mass-goer, he took Communion only once a year and then to obey a basic requirement of the Church. There seemed to be a theological basis for this: typical of his generation, he had Jansenist views of a basic unworthiness to partake. More fundamentally, perhaps, he was too modest to make such regular public demonstration of piety. He sat always at the back of the 'men's' side-aisle; unlike his early employer, he seemed determined not to make his church-going an occasion for social display. She, on the other hand, had a more orthodox, unselfconscious religious sense; she taught us to take Communion always as part of Mass, and sit well up in the centre of the church.

The memory of her unaffected piety that stays with me most is of her warbling hymns as she baked bread in the evenings, while we did homework or listened to the radio. A lifelong member of the Children of Mary, she favoured Marian hymns: 'I'll sing a hymn to Mary', 'Bring flowers of the rarest', 'Oh, Mother I could weep for mirth' and many more. (Her secular repertoire was also highly sentimental, featuring the *Melodies* of Moore and the drawing-room songs performed by John McCormack.) For her, faith remained central, simple and certain, and included reverence for the official Church. He shared the anti-hierarchical instincts of his priest brother, John, who at the end of his days got permission to continue saying Mass in Latin, according to the old rite, in a gesture that combined his conservative theology with a robust individualism. My parents were united, however, in viewing Father John as the possessor of great spiritual and healing powers. It was this and his remarkable charm, rather more than his status, which made him *the* authority and source of comfort when problems arose.

With their marriage, my parents' stories combined, and the construction of their story, as well as the basis of their shared life, began to take shape. As an adult and an aspiring historian, I became fascinated by the differences in their accounts of key aspects of that life, and in particular of the major decision they made in the early years of their marriage to move from the country to the town and, within a decade, to sell the farm, Courtdale.

Her account betrayed a sense of impatience with his basic quietness or shyness. The decision to move and later to sell was his, she maintained, and was due to a deep-seated unease about owning a farm that had, in a sense, come to him though the marriage into it of his aunt. He was, she believed, over-sensitive to the views of neighbours, ascribing to them a lack of acceptance of him as an outsider. (Given the circumstances of the original sale, however, it may well have been resented locally.)

His version, never so explicitly stated, or elaborated, was that she wanted to move to give their children greater opportunities. Being closer to him, and intensely aware of how much he disliked shopkeeping and urban life, I had long been of the view that his version was the 'true' one and had imagined the move as a source of conflict between them that had endured, though unstated and normally invisible. But, after her death and listening for the first time to a tape of her reminiscing to my sister shortly before her stroke, I heard a version that made sense and combined elements of their antagonistic versions, as I'd regarded them for many years. It was wartime, and petrol was unobtainable. Lacking confidence in their flighty young mare, my mother cycled the eight miles to and from the shop every day rather than take the pony-trap. She did that journey in all weathers while carrying me, and was back in the shop a few days after my birth. Six months later, with another child coming, simple convenience and practicality determined the move. Added to which, as she often told me, the shop was making far more than the farm, and life on the land was hard. Thus the move suited my father also; his nostalgia for farming only came later. What she regarded as his oversensitivity to the views of neighbours in the late, taped version only related to his difficulties years later in letting the land; 'his neighbours formed a ring and wouldn't bid against each other'. Once again, it was a practical decision to sell: 'He never regretted it until land got dear.' Before he died in 1978, land in that area was getting £3000 an acre – more than he got for his ninety acres in 1952.

The move to the town was momentous for all of us, but particularly for my future. As the eldest son, brought up with a strong sense of duty, I would never otherwise have envisaged any life for myself other than farming. Some

Courtdale, with the remains of the Norman tower-house just visible.

years ago, I sat in my car outside the garage in Ballinaboola, the nearest village to the farm; a crossroads rather, containing only Sutton's grocery-cum-pub and Davy Byrne's garage. Davy, like so many of his old neighbours, remained a good customer of my father's until he retired from business, and I was waiting to make myself known to him. He was talking to a man about my own age, who sat high in his tractor, and as I envied the leisurely, neighbourly lifestyle their chat epitomized, it struck me with sudden force that, in an alternative life, I might have been the man on the tractor, with a very different experience behind me – essentially a different person. Later, seeing photographs of the Carrigbyrne Pikemen, one of the best known of the local groups who dressed up in period costume and added greatly to the pageantry of the '98 bicentenary, I had the same thought, and resolved (not altogether successfully, as will become clear) to be more sympathetic to the sense of local pride to which 'Comóradh '98' appealed.

Although we moved to the town within a year of my birth, I went regularly to the farm with my father until he sold it, and my memories of it are of my mother's brother James and his wife Cathy living in the house, and my father and James involved together in the farmwork. I remember standing on a bank and watching him plough with a horse so huge that my legs could not encompass his wide back when my father swung me on to him. I had long treasured a story of my first year, told by my mother, which involved an eagle

South Street, New Ross, with our house and shop in left foreground.

swooping down from the high rock behind the farmhouse and carrying off a chicken only feet from where I lay on a rug on the lawn. When I reminded my mother of this during a visit to the nursing home at a time when her problems with speech had not yet become acute, she denied all memory of it. 'Perhaps it was a barn-owl,' she offered, to mollify me. 'There was a very large one in the old castle beside the house.' How did the owl become an eagle? Did she embroider the story to please a small boy, or did I do so in turning my life into something more interesting? Or was there in fact an eagle whose image, like so many others, was wiped out by the stroke?

It was a relief to discover in 1998, on my first visit to Courtdale since I was ten, that there really was an old castle beside the house where I was born, though its present owners had reduced its height to a little below that of the house for safety reasons. An early Norman tower-house, it is one of many in south Wexford, and possibly the Castle of 'Hoel of Karrathobren' first mentioned in Earl Marshall's charter of the forest of Ross (1231-4), which gave the name Courhoyle (Cúirt Hoel) or Courtdale to the immediate area and, colloquially, to the farm.[2] There was, therefore, a very old connection between Courtdale and New Ross, itself founded by Earl Marshall in 1190. I was also gratified to find from Seamus De Vál's informative article on Wexford place-names that 'Cúirt Óil' was also mentioned in the sixteenth-century Bardic compilation, the *Leabhar Branach*, or *Book of the O'Byrnes* – the subject, in part, of my first scholarly publication.[3] Too much should not be made of such coincidences, yet our sense of place may have a meaning and significance beyond rational calculation, and it may not be too fanciful to speculate whether my birthplace, and my early years in an old Norman town, may have contributed to my ultimate choice to be a historian – or indeed that they shaped the kind of historian I have become, with a particular focus on the Irish experience of colonialism. The old 'castle', or more precisely the gap between it and the farmhouse, produced a more tangible benefit for my father when my uncle James shared with him the contents of a small bag of gold sovereigns he found there. While of less romantic origin than the nuggets brought back from Australia, this gold was also put to practical use, in the purchase of the larger shop and house in the middle of South Street in New Ross to which we moved after a period in Bridge Street. This eighteenth-century house (then part of the Tottenham Estate, possibly one of those finished just before the Rebellion and used to house loyalist refugees), freezing in winter and cool in summer, had been turned into a 'department store' in the 1870s by a P. O'Kelly, whose name was carved three stories up, at roof level, so that to some old residents it remained Kelly's, to most customers Rice's, and only to family and friends Dunne's. If my father felt any irritation at being addressed regularly as Mr Rice, he never showed it.

The local world I was born into seemed to differ little in its fundamentals from that which greeted my parents, and indeed their parents. It remained overwhelmingly rural, its social conservatism dictated in large part by the economics of the small family farm. Its Catholicism also reflected and reinforced these social imperatives and remained traditional, unquestioned and all-enveloping. However, the outside world impinged more and more through the radio, newspapers and cinema; my parents, it seems, were addicted to all three before they married.

The day I was born, the United States announced a major breakthrough in the development of the atom bomb and the Allies condemned Nazi atrocities against the Jews; such news would have come to them crackling over the airwaves or in the paper (always the *Irish Independent*) brought daily from town. But neutrality in the war had added to the isolationism that was already such a feature of the Gaelic Catholic Free State, and the Cold War was soon to bring a new dimension of fear and suspicion of the outside world. Balancing the sense of that world as alien and threatening were the stories every family had from the Irish diaspora, like those of my Uncle Jack driven home from Chicago by the Depression and taking over the farm at Ballymacar. Even more exotic were Father John's tales of his years in New Zealand, a temporary mission after ordination. These included fishing for tuna with Zane Grey, ever afterwards his favourite author. Grey's romantic macho stories of the Old West in their lurid covers were passed on to my father, as were detective stories by such as Ellery Queen, Raymond Chandler and the Catholic writers Ronald Knox and G.K. Chesterton.

Efforts by Church and State to keep out filthy, modern and foreign tides operated only at the level of high literature or pornography. The Ireland of my childhood was saturated in English popular culture. Our comics were the *Beano* and *Dandy*, until we graduated to the *Hotspur* and *Bunty*; the *Our Boys*, brought home monthly from the Christian Brothers School, offered little competition and then only when it modelled itself on English school stories. We listened to *Life with the Lyons* and *The Clitheroe Kid* on the BBC, though *Listen with Lynch* came to offer an exciting Irish alternative. The popular songs I remember are a similar *mélange* of English and American, with those of the Walton's programme, introduced by the memorable voice of Leo Maguire, competing remarkably well in retrospect.

By and large, the life of the imagination was focused elsewhere, but I don't remember any sense of conflict between the life I lived and what I read or listened to – which was also, of course, largely conservative and traditional in its way. I saw no incongruity between my absolute passion for the game of hurling, and my collection of cards featuring English cricket and soccer players – though I had never seen either of those games. Of course, there were no cigarette cards of GAA players, and no scrap album available to me in 1953 other than one featuring the coronation of Queen Elizabeth, which I happily filled with newspaper clippings about Wexford hurlers. And life did imitate art. When I went to boarding school, which the Christian Brother Juniorate essentially was, I was already familiar with its ethos of muscular Christianity from reading stories of English public schools, even though the school's language was Gaelic. Irish people have been comfortable with such inter-penetration of cultures for centuries.

Irish Catholicism determined my sense of the world – and not just its theology, but its liturgy, ceremony, music and art. Becoming an altar boy in the parish church, aged about nine, confirmed a piety and conformity that was already marked and increased my exposure to Church culture. I was taught

*My first Communion, by
Annie Brophy, Waterford 1949.*

enough Church Latin to make and understand the liturgical response. Wearing
the soutane and surplice, involved in the great rituals of the high altar, gradually being inducted in the use of thurible and incense and the higher myster-
ies of Easter ceremonies and formal sung masses – all added to the sense of
being special, chosen, apart. Going silently in and out of the sacristy, all wood
panelling and sumptuous vestments, seemed more mysterious and privileged
even than serving on the altar. Thrilling also was our banishment (even from
the sacristy, where there was a loudspeaker) for certain sermons given by visiting and exotic clerics to the separate men's and women's annual missions.
Then, as generally after any normal Mass or Benediction, the discipline and
decorum so foreign to small boys was abandoned in boisterous games in the
shrubberies around the church, featuring rivalries between 'uptown' and
'downtown' boys. All of us were middle class, respectable, but I was aware that
being a 'downtowner' involved an extra social cachet (or, in the eyes of our
enemies, made us snobs).

The Church was also the focus of my main musical education. The Ferns
diocese was unusual in the extent to which Gregorian or plain chant was
taught in all schools, culminating in annual regional competitions and thrilling
mass choral ceremonies. To be thus made part of a great European musical tradition was a privilege and, however dimly, we were taught to feel that. Again,

Church Latin was involved and the reading of simple musical notation, but above all the transformative magic of the 'Gloria' from the 'Missa de Angelus', or the 'Salve Regina'. The visual Church art of that time now seems dull and banal, but to a child's eyes the stained-glass figures of saints, the array of angels in the sanctuary mural, and the elaborately carved altars in the magnificent parish church (by Patrick Pearse's father) were all part of what made the church special, and engaged eyes and minds during the more tedious aspects of the liturgy. The Church also offered an exciting window to other worlds through the missions to Africa, China and the Far East especially. My mother subscribed to many missionary magazines, and I dreamed of being a missionary in the Phillipines, riding from one remote station to the next on a white horse – a knight in shining armour.

While the Church offered a range of stimuli for the budding romantic, the countryside around my town offered others. As I ferry my own children around the relatively peaceful and safe city of Cork, I sometimes wonder at the remarkable *sangfroid* of my parents' generation. So long as we were home for meals, we had the freedom of the countryside and there seemed to be little apprehension of danger. This applied even to the river: the magnificent, tidal and deadly Barrow. Everyone knew the legend of the Crutched Friars driven out of the town in the fourteenth century and putting a curse on the inhabitants, that three people would be lost to the river every year. Drownings were indeed a regular occurrence, and were always related to the legend. They included my first cousin and contemporary, John Rice of the Irishtown, a gentle, unassuming boy, lost coxing a rowing eight at twenty-one. As he was the only son of the only remaining Rice family in the town, his premature death also meant the dying out of the name locally after two hundred years with the passing of my mother's generation.

I could see the river from my bedroom and was always aware of the level of the tide, and the play on it of wind and rain. I learned to swim in it at the end of a rope from the Boat Club landing-stage, and at an age that amazes me now took out the heavy rowing boats on my own, with no knowledge of life-jackets, and went upstream with the flowing tide to the meeting with the Nore, coming back again on the ebb, scrabbling for the safety of the landing-stage at the end, to avoid being swept under the bridge and downstream towards Waterford. It involved a heady mixture of freedom and responsibility – and, remarkably, nobody fussed. It was as if the town had some kind of fatalistic accommodation with the river, which more than anything else had shaped its history. It was a far cry from the early centuries of the town's foundation, when it was the busiest port in the kingdom, but ships continued to come, mainly coasters collecting grain or bringing coal, but occasionally something more exotic, when the streets would echo to the speech of foreign sailors.

Its normal life, however, was more prosaic. Sean O'Faolain, who visited the town with Hubert Butler a few years before I was born, described New Ross in *An Irish Journey* as 'a town with a great past, a small present and but slight promise of any future in proportion to its former greatness'. He enjoyed the 'modest bourgeois pride' of a shopkeeper (possibly our neighbour Mr Haydon):

> a nice melancholy man, who praised New Ross with a melancholy, judi-cial, hand-rubbing reluctance … 'The town is a little pinched' (I loved that euphemism 'pinched'). 'We're all a little pinched! Still!' Nodding, hand-rubbing, deciding.'I'll tell you how it is with us. The commercials coming to New Ross tell me this – that *they get paid.*'

It was a pride my mother expressed regularly. In that, and other ways, she epit-omized what O'Faolain imagined as 'the local mind', seeing in 'its traditions an empirical rule of life, preserving continuity with all that there is of value in the racial genius'. Looking at the town's rundown quay and old maltstores, O'Faolain wondered 'what it would be like to be born here in these tor-mented days of war'.4

For a child it had a great deal to offer, a sense of security combined with remarkable physical freedom, but also a sense of belonging. We were conscious that the town had a particular history, that its coat of arms, featuring two hounds bringing down a stag on a bridge, went back to its foundation by the Normans; that the remains of its gates and walls also harked back to that remote past, when it seemed a kind of Camelot. There were the ruins of the great medieval Abbey of St Mary's, with its scary vaults, skulls visible through the grilles; and, on the way to Duncannon, the even greater Abbey of Dun-brody, whose abbots had sat in parliament. But our sense of the town's history was dominated by the battle that had taken place there in 1798, when the tide of the Rebellion turned and 'the gold sun of freedom grew darkened at Ross'. This is how it was described in the ballad 'Kelly, the Boy from Killanne', which we learned with others like it in school and heard sung at concerts and played by bands at hurling matches. When we sang 'The Boys of Wexford', we did it with real pride and passion: 'We are the boys of Wexford, who fought with heart and hand, / To break in twain the galling chain and free our native land.' For us then, as for many in Wexford today, the 1798 rebels and the heroes of the county's hurling team were part of the same culture and continuum. In

1955, when Wexford won their first All Ireland hurling title since 1911, the team went in triumphant procession from town to town, led by pikemen and pipe bands.

I was six during the 150th anniversary of the Rebellion, and dimly remember the enactment of the battle of New Ross in the GAA field, Barrett's Park. The Urban Council commissioned a series of plaques, featuring maps of the town, showing where various aspects of the battle took place. I knew where they were all situated and copied their texts in a notebook. Every day I passed and repassed the town's only secular statue, just down the street opposite the Tholsel. We knew that the heroic pikeman it depicted was carrying a flag of peace, and was shot in cold blood (for O'Faolain it was 'merely a comical bit of Victorian Ireland'). It was literally, and imaginatively, the centre of the town and indeed where the centre had been from the town's foundation, its ancient market place. The image of it that I retain from the depressed 1950s also features quiet groups of unemployed men leaning against the Tholsel, or in the summer, sitting on the surround of the pikeman's plinth, smoking and playing cards, as we went to and from school – aware, however vaguely, that we were privileged. For all its rich past and the beauty of its setting, my home town offered little future indeed for many of its citizens.

The main use to which put we put our now unimaginable freedom was hurling, for which we had an insatiable appetite. There were daily informal games with a sponge ball in Murphy's Yard, and more formal weekly sessions during school term in Barrett's Park with proper boots and togs and the initially fearsome leather *sliotar*. It gave me another particular role, again essentially a romantic one, in that I was a goalkeeper, aspiring to heroics and coping with disaster and derision. What made us especially fanatical was the example of the Wexford team, in this golden age of the Rackards, Keoghs, Nick O'Donnell, Ned Wheeler and my own particular hero, the diminutive goalkeeper Art Foley.

From about the same time as I trained as an altar boy, I started going to matches with my father, by crowded excursion train to Dublin, forming a special bond with him and sharing a communal excitement that rose to fever pitch each summer. Cork were the great enemy and Christy Ring their evil genius. The routine on these, my first visits to Dublin, was Mass at Westland Row and lunch at the Mont Clare Hotel, followed by a walk across town, with a pause for a pre-match pint at the Shakespeare Bar, Parnell Street, for my father and his friends, while I drank a warm orange in the street outside, warily eying other small boys who were similarly employed, especially if they sported

To the left of a family photograph (again by Annie Brophy), 1955.

the rival colours. Some of those who had come on the train stayed comfortably in the bar and listened to Micheál O'Hehir's vivid commentary on radio, but we joined the queue at the canal end, and stood always at the same place on the terraces. That Wexford team were straight out of *The Hotspur*: romantic heroes, overcoming impossible odds, and always, it seemed, snatching victory from the jaws of defeat.

All my old hero-worship came flooding back twenty years later when the unmistakable, slightly stooped figure of Bobby Rackard emerged from the gloom of his pub in Killanne to serve a group of us, including my father and his brothers Jim and Nick. Part of the mystique of the Rackard brothers in the 1950s was that these modern Bantry heroes were said to have grown up in the very home occupied by Kelly 'the boy from Killanne'.

Although hurling helped to make it bearable, for the most part school was a grim, brutal and frightening experience. After my years as a Baby, Junior Infant and Senior Infant, spoiled by nuns and senior girls in the Mercy School, the Christian Brothers Primary School in New Ross was bound to be a shock. I remember still the fear with which I peered around the mobile blackboard at the intimidating rows of small boys on the first day, while my mother talked to the Brother. There had been a dozen or less in the convent class; here there were over seventy. Previously my classmates had been gentle downtowners; here were uptown roughnecks and big lads from the country. There had been no corporal punishment (that I remember) in the convent; here it was incessant and remained so for the next six years. To survive I became a diligent student and even more polite conformist, and very rarely got beaten. But every day had its quota of fear and every beating of another boy was traumatic. The schoolyard held even greater terrors, because there my defence mechanisms were counterproductive and made me a target. It took me many years to realize that I led a comparatively charmed life because my best friend, Michael Hanrahan, was as tough as anyone and a good hurler: I had protection. There were compensations, especially the annual pantomime, and there were days away, supporting the team in games against other Christian Brothers Schools in Wexford, Enniscorthy and Gorey; travelling in ancient buses, with school benches in the aisle to take the maximum number of excited boys, sporting red and white colours.

Moving to secondary school (in the same buildings) brought some improvements – fewer beatings, smaller classes (a large cohort left after primary school) and more variety, with exotic new subjects, especially science and Latin. The science teacher, Brother 'Matty' Lennon, was a genial, accident-prone enthusiast, his lab coat testimony to minor explosions, small fires and chemical spillages. As headmaster, he encouraged people to pursue their enthusiasms, whether my friend Larry Murray in his unlikely passion for pole-vaulting, or my religious vocation. But academic standards, generally, were poor (two-thirds of my class were later to fail the Intermediate Certificate), and the small town library offered more stimulus for the minority of committed students than the school did. Yet when I left it at the end of second year, it was to join the Christian Brothers, with a strong sense not only of religious vocation, but of the desire to become a teacher. As the Brothers themselves recognized, the home and not the school was what formed character and ambition or, as they put it, 'fostered vocations'.

CHAPTER 2

The Christian Brother

Our home was certainly pious, with the family Rosary every evening and regular church-going, far beyond any formal obligation. My parents' bedroom had an altar, with statues of the Sacred Heart, the Blessed Virgin and Saint Anthony on a linen ornamental cloth. There were regular visits from Father John, to us a Father Christmas for all seasons, occasionally bearing gifts of an extravagance that I now recognize as the prerogative of childless uncles and aunts. Apart from family photographs and some romantic landscapes in ornate frames (a wedding gift), the art on our walls was religious, and perpetual lamps burned in front of pictures of the Sacred Heart and the Immaculate Heart of Mary. But perhaps the most significant spiritual presence for me was that of Edmund Ignatius Rice, founder of the Christian Brothers a hundred and fifty years before, and cousin, as we all knew, of our ancestor John Rice. My mother had great devotion to his memory, and prayed for his canonization – as we did daily in school. Having this heroic, inspirational figure in the family was a matter of pride to us; it was also known in the school, and thus to the 'postulator' who visited when I was fourteen, seeking out boys who felt they might have a vocation to join the Congregation. It was nothing remarkable, then, to contemplate such a step. Large numbers joined the priesthood and religious orders, and others apart from the Christian Brothers recruited at this very young age. It was a time of faith – and a time of poverty – when religious vocations offered a road to spiritual fulfilment and service to others, and for many also, though subconsciously, a way out, to an education and higher social status.

It was only years after I had left the Congregation that it dawned on me that what made me unusual in my group (apart from my relationship to 'the Founder') was that I was from a relatively well-off background. Not that we felt ourselves so, materially: for most of my childhood we lacked not only a car, but a bathroom and carpets, for example. We were *petit* if *bourgeois*, a 'little pinched', in fact, but never short of necessities, secure in a thriving business, and able to manage three weeks' holidays by the sea every year. For mother, in any case, a frugal life was also the ideal; when I first read de Valera's speeches extolling the simple rural lifestyle of his youth, I could hear her voice. Where she was a snob was in her pride in belonging to one of the town's oldest business families, however reduced from her father's inheritances.

There was, no doubt, an element of escape from a cramped environment in my vocation also. O'Faolain had wondered if 'a boy in Ross, awakening to a sense of wider horizons' would find 'scope enough in the tannery, the felt-factory, brewery, the new place for the manufacture of electrical supplies – all small enterprises?' My parents shoe shop may have offered more, but at some level I probably shared O'Faolain's conclusion that no Irish small town 'offers enough scope for Irish energy'.[1] My motivation was undoubtedly mixed – religious certainly, but also romantic and adventurous, and fulfilling expectations that were never explicitly stated but that arose naturally from the clerical tradition of my father's family, and the ghosts of dead Rices. I would join Edmund's order and, like his cousin John, sacrifice myself for others. In the years when I wore the clerical half-collar favoured by the Brothers I was often asked, especially by neighbours on my rare visits home, why I wouldn't 'go all the way', that is, become a priest? One reason, it strikes me now, may have been that, always impatient, I realized that the seminary would not have taken me for another three or four years. Anyway, with two first cousins already fulfilling Dunne expectations in that regard, perhaps I wanted to be different.

While my mother was pleased by my choice, she naturally opposed the idea of taking such a major step at such an early age – I was fourteen, and the year was 1957. In the end she gave in to my persistence, and to the assurances of the postulator that I would simply be a schoolboy for the next two years and not be asked to make any further decisions. She realized that the foreign missions loomed large in my imagination, but for now I seemed content to be immersed in the great adventure of going away in my black suit, with a new fine trunk packed with the prescribed clothes, beautifully labelled by her. Within a few months a new life had begun, in company with boys my own age from all over the Southern 'Province' (the island being divided by a line from Dublin to Galway in the Christian Brothers organization), in the beautiful house and grounds in Old Conna, Bray, Co. Wicklow that had once, we were told, belonged to the Protestant archbishops of Dublin, and in 1798 had belonged to William Coyngham Plunket, the lawyer who defended Henry Sheares; it was now called Coláiste Ciarán.

Arriving in the spacious ornate hallway of the old house I had, for the only time in my life, a powerful sense of *déjà vu*; before being told, I knew there was a ballroom off the hall, now used as a chapel. I had, I felt, been here before. Quickly I came to believe that I had, indeed, come home (it was emphasized strongly that we had left our original families to join a new one), and I was very happy not only in Bray but in successive 'houses of formation'. The contrast with my old school was remarkable. Here there was no corporal punishment and bullying was not tolerated. We were treated fundamentally as adults who had taken on immense responsibilities and as new members of the community, its postulants. The teachers were all Brothers, and were among the best the Congregation had. It was all profoundly civilized, carefully disciplined and impressively caring. Animal spirits were catered for, not only in almost daily organized games, but also in regular 'manual labour', emphasized as part of an ancient monastic tradition. And there was an open-air, unheated swimming-pool, used for much of the year and part of the character-building Spartan regime. It was, indeed, very much as I had imagined boarding-school from the stories of Greyfriars, with its emphasis on games, codes of honour and study. Yet it was also an intensely Gaelic environment. I found myself suddenly coping with doing all my subjects – including science and Latin – through Irish, and from a very poor base, rapidly gaining fluency. In the Christmas Concert, which my parents attended (we were only allowed home for a brief holiday in the summer), I played the lead in a half-hour play in Irish, *An Fear Siúil*. They were impressed and a little lost, having hardly a word of the language. Culturally, I seemed to have moved radically away from them, and during my seven years in the Brothers I lived, indeed, in a bilingual world. It was a great cultural gain, for which I remain immensely grateful. Today, though I work regularly with Irish texts, I speak the language infrequently; yet when I search for a word, it is the Irish version that comes unbidden as often as not.

The use of the Irish language and the passion for Gaelic games were the most visible aspects of an all-pervading nationalist ethos, which was almost as central a part of the culture of the Brothers as Catholicism itself. The history I learned was of the most traditional Catholic nationalist kind, well captured years later in the illustrated history the Brothers produced for schools. Reading the Rev. Patrick F. Kavanagh's *Popular History of the Insurrection of 1798*[2] now brings me back vividly to the intense exposure I then had to his faith-and-fatherland brand of history. And yet the ethos of the Brothers was also internationalist, if not cosmopolitan. They were conscious and proud of being a Papal Congregation, and they were shortly to move their headquarters to Rome. We were familiar with the map of the world that showed the Congregation's missionary activity in North and South America, Australia, Africa, India. We were, in a sense, as conscious of being part of a worldwide empire as the most patriotic British child would have been a generation earlier.

Catholicism itself had also a more international ethos then, with Latin the common liturgical language, and a Cold War solidarity against Communism. The secular libraries in the houses of formation offered an ideologically determined range of fiction that was in marked contrast to my former preference for nineteenth-century English novelists. There were boys' adventure stories in Irish, notably the thrilling detective stories featuring Réics Carlo, and there was a range of Catholic fiction and prose – Canon Sheehan, G.K. Chesterton, John D. Sheridan, and Cold War novels featuring the martyrdom of Catholics behind the Iron Curtain. An older and more generous tradition of the universal Church shone through in liturgy and in music. There was not only a more extensive training in traditional plain chant but also, once we were in the Novitiate, the sung Office.

One of the most remarkable features of the Christian Brothers as a modern 'active' order was their adoption of major elements of the traditional Benedictine rule, more associated with the contemplative life. We sang instead of the full Office a shortened version, the 'Little Office of the Blessed Virgin Mary', but it contained the haunting music of the original. Even later, in communities of Brothers where I lived and taught, where it was spoken rather than chanted, it still retained a certain magic, and reinforced the sense of belonging to an ancient tradition, shared by people from all over the globe. It gave a sense of living in three languages – Latin, Irish and English – as the inhabitants of my home town had done down to the early eighteenth century.

One bitterly cold morning during that first year I was harvesting sprouts in the old walled garden with frozen fingers when I heard my name called and was astonished to see, with the Superior of the College, my uncle Father John and the Provincial. When I reached them, I was even more astonished to hear my uncle berate the two Brothers, and to note their deferential tone. There was no question of my going to India, they reassured him: 'He should never have been asked to volunteer.' Two days earlier, my parents had received a letter from me (like all such during those years, read by the Superior before posting). It had given them the good news that a Brother from the English

Province had spoken to us and looked for volunteers to go to England and ultimately to India. I had given my name, as had a number of others. My parents immediately got on to my uncle, who came hotfoot to remind the Provincial of the promise made to my mother and to tell him most unequivocally that I was going nowhere.

Of all the roads not taken, this proved the most haunting. My good friend, Pat O'Brien from Kilkenny, did take it a few years later, and has spent his life helping street children in Calcutta. If I had gone, would I ever have left the Congregation in the face of such extreme need? The level of commitment involved can only be guessed at. But then, given that my original sense of the missions had been the romantic one of moving benignly through a beautiful landscape on a white horse, I might have fled precipitously from the horrors of urban poverty in India. I'll never know, though I've often thought about it, particularly during the decade my sister Rosaleen spent as a Medical Missionary of Mary in the Turkana desert of Kenya, when I envied the crucial role she played in the lives of some of the poorest people on earth and yet recoiled from her account of what it involved.

Instead I stayed in Ireland, moving the following year to Coláiste Iognáid Rís, Carriglee, near Dún Laoghaire, a new college custom-built to cater for the huge numbers joining the Congregation. There I did the Leaving Cert in one year, taking honours only in Irish. This was the legal minimum for entry to teacher-training college and, as the Brothers had their own at Marino, the minimum was all we needed. It was a foolish policy, reducing the normal schooling of postulants by a year, having forced them already into accelerated development by taking them as young as fourteen.

Again the teaching was through Irish, and was exceptional; the environment was positive and happy, at least for most of us. We played hurling incessantly, helped on the farm, swam almost all year round in the sea, and took long bracing walks. There were stricter rules about 'special friendships', especially with younger boys, which I was so naïve as to understand only in terms of the official line – that the rule was designed to make us charitable to all, and to avoid the hurt caused by cliques. The rigours of Novitiate in the beautiful surroundings of St Helen's, Booterstown, the following year, buried normal adolescent urges yet deeper and there was a cost, emotionally and psychologically, in the culture of celibacy and in the treatment of young boys as small adults, miniature monks. This was the Brothers' name for themselves, and the extent of their commitment to old monastic traditions became ever clearer after you 'took the habit' and became a novice.

Life became even more enclosed; as a symbol of fully leaving the world, and our original families, we took new names. I became Brother Bosco – a controversial choice, allowed only on appeal, because Bosco was the founder of a rival congregation, the Salesians. He was my choice because he had forbidden the use of corporal punishment and relied instead on persuasion. My later attempts to emulate him got me into some difficulty with Superiors.

The Novitiate year was extraordinarily tough. The saintly novice master, Berchmans Cullen, was amiably eccentric in speech, but relentless in testing our vocations. He demanded heroic, unquestioning obedience. We went for walks in the rain without coats or hats, and in hot sun with both. I once spent several periods of manual labour shifting a pile of stones from one place to another – and the following periods moving them back again. The 'discipline', a set of knotted leather thongs, was handed to each at the start of Lent and we were expected to flagellate our bare backs, morning and evening. Most of us chose to beat the pillows instead, safe in the privacy of our cubicles (the celibacy culture had advantages!), and I was shocked to note the weals on a friend's back when we recommenced swimming in the sea in March.

Instead of secular study, we had intensive courses in theology, liturgy, choral singing and scripture; there was daily meditation on readings by a sixteenth-century Spanish mystic, Rodriguez, and formal retreats on lines laid down by Ignatius of Loyola. Again, the staff were excellent, and in scripture studies I had my first exposure to 'revisionism' in a close reading of the gospel of St Matthew, using a modern annotated text that interrogated the sacred word in terms of secular, historical and archaeological scholarship. It was, in a way, a scholarly version of the 'Apologetics' that had been a feature of the Christian Doctrine, even in New Ross, and was designed to equip us to argue the faith rationally, if confronted ('on a train journey' was the proffered scenario) by a non-believer, or even (shock, horror) a Communist. It was, at times, an exhilarating, even shocking experience, sailing, we thought, close to the winds of blasphemy. Even more exotic was the weekly visit by our only secular teacher, the flamboyant Barry Cassin, who taught us elocution and voice projection – the basic skills of teaching – and did it wonderfully well. His elegant clothes and actor's voice brought colour into our lives and the whiff of the outside world we had renounced. I wonder what he thought of the solemn rows of soutaned young men, with their wide range of accents and their earnest attempts to imitate his mellifluous tones.

In the Novitiate my special position as a relative of the Founder's came more into focus because the novice master was an assiduous researcher into his life and collector of folklore about him.[3] To my embarrassment – and pleasure – he regularly referred to my family's relationship to the Great Man. Less pleasurable was the experience of being honoured by him with some of the more difficult and less popular duties, including the regular bleary reading of the first extract from Rodriguez at 6 a.m. I also had the ghoulish task of looking after the clothes of dead Brothers, which were sent to St Helen's from all over and, if good enough still, dry-cleaned and stored in atmospheric underground vaults for the use of the novices. It gave a certain power to be the one assigning working soutanes (we each had a new, tailored one for good use), the old-fashioned Chesterfield coats we still wore, and the wonderful cloaks with velvet collars, worn in the house and grounds in cold weather. I was also in charge of flowers for the altar, which meant I was given the run of the fine walled garden and extensive glasshouses, and an incidental training in flower-arranging. Nowadays, when I hack happily at my wild garden and put together vases of whatever is in flower each weekend, I am reminded that there were some unexpected permanent gains from my experience of monastic life.

Despite such outlets, the pressure to perform and conform was relentless; yet, surprisingly, few gave up that year. When it happened there would be no warning – just an empty place, an absence never referred to. We lived on our nerves; waves of helpless giggles would sweep through the chapel when pigeons in the trees outside cooed more persistently than usual, and hurling and football matches became more frenetic and physical. But, as I imagine is the case in an army, there was also remarkable camaraderie and an intensity of purpose that made the experience worthwhile, even memorable.

When I took my first vows at the end of that year, I was happy and fulfilled, and looking forward to teacher-training. My experience of Marino, however, lasted only two months, two weeks of it in teaching practice in Donnycarney. On Armistice Day 1960 I found myself instead taking over 6B, in Francis Street Primary School off The Coombe in inner-city Dublin. The Department of Education had put pressure on the order to have more of its science teachers properly qualified and so, following a mad logic, the two in my group who had scored highest in (Pass) Maths in the Leaving Certificate were simply taken out of training without any consultation or warning and told we were instead to start full-time teaching, out 'in the community' two days later, while doing the Matriculation that would qualify us for entry to a science degree the following October. When I left the order, I had taught for four years on the strength of my Leaving Cert (Pass), while the other so

The Novice, August 1959.

abruptly chosen spent several more years in a similar role, before being finally sent to university – by night! The Brothers did not always value or treat properly their own members, and the vow of obedience was often pushed to unreasonable limits.

I lived in the Synge Street community while teaching in Francis Street, and later in communities in Tralee and Limerick. Despite a certain rough humour about young monks (known as 'gearcs', possibly from the Irish *gearrcach*, a fledgling), I found the Brothers in community not only welcoming, helpful and supportive – the communities functioned as families in many practical ways – but also often iconoclastic, ironic, even cynical, especially about authority, whether local Superiors, more distant Provincials or the institutional Church. This shocked me at first, but I rapidly adjusted to it as part of the bracing adult world, after the years of 'formation' with their unquestioning obedience and extraordinary good behaviour. Synge Street was a large community and included some highly talented members, like the artist Brother Gilmore and, among younger men, the current Provincial, Mark Mc-Donnell. I was encouraged in my interest in classical music, first stimulated by impromptu music-appreciation classes, listening to *Grand Hotel* on the radio during study periods in Bray. I developed a passion for Kathleen Ferrier and Russian novels, and despite the vow of poverty started to collect records and books. My copy of T.S. Eliot's *Selected Poems* has 'T.B. Ó Duinn, 1961' inscribed on the flyleaf, emblematic of an unconscious cultural eclecticism.

This experience of community life is at odds with the common perception of the Christian Brothers today as anti-intellectual sadists. Certainly they did little to encourage their members to do higher degrees or develop creative talent; the demands of teaching and religious duty were considered too great and important to allow for such activities, which also smacked to many of élitism. It is remarkable that Ireland's premier teaching order, with a worldwide scope and influence, produced no original thinking in the field of education, and little in the academic area. The only publication I remember in my time was J.G. Ó Muimhneacháin's important textbook on Irish grammar,[4] and it seemed somehow appropriate that the first scholarly monograph to appear, years later, was Liam Ó Caithnia's magisterial survey of the history of hurling, written in Irish as *Scéal na hIomána*.[5] Yet in the domestic or community sphere many Brothers followed literary or scientific enthusiasms. In a very enjoyable year in the small community in Tralee, for example, I read through the collected works of D.H. Lawrence, among other finds in the well-stocked library, and had lessons on astronomy from one of the older members. There too I had my first exposure to television, or more precisely to the children's programmes on the new RTÉ, the limit of what the very traditional Superior considered suitable viewing, though an exception was made for coverage of the visit of that good Irish Catholic, President Kennedy.

There was a marked contrast between the normal civilities of life in the Christian Brothers communities (the best-run having many of the attributes of a good old-fashioned gentlemen's club) and the general brutality of the schools the Brothers ran. It puzzled me then, and still does today, how such decent, well-meaning men were the exponents, and even promoters, of a regime of systematic corporal punishment, and continued to operate on these traditional lines long after the general educational system had abandoned them. A year I spent as a lecturer in Mary Immaculate College of Education in Limerick in 1976/7 involved supervision of teaching practice by trainee teachers and showed me how radically the ethos and curriculum of primary schools had changed since I had taught in those run by the Brothers fifteen years earlier. After visiting a series of schools that were bright, happy centres of creative encouragement, I found myself in a Christian Brothers School that resounded to the sound of the leather from early morning, when latecomers were lined up in the hall for punishment. The scene seemed unchanged from that which I had ventured into timidly as a six-year-old, and the principal of this sad place had been a contemporary in the Novitiate. In November 1960, minutes before I had met the pupils of 6B in Francis Street for the first time (one of whom was fifteen on the day I turned eighteen, a month later), I was handed a 'leather' (strips of soft leather stitched together and fitting snugly into a soutane pocket) by the principal, with the age-old injunction: 'Begin as you mean to go on. It's either you or them and they understand nothing else.'

Underprepared as I was for the job in hand – teaching up to forty boys, most of whom would leave school at the end of that year, and who desperately needed the minimal Primary Certificate for passing the state exams in Irish, English and Mathematics – I initially felt I had no option but to follow the principal's advice. I take no particular credit for rapidly abandoning it and finding other methods of persuasion and control (Barry Cassin's lessons being my main resource). With my cossetted background, squeamish, romantic nature and schoolboy experiences, I simply hadn't the stomach for it. It was humiliating to have to resort to it and, being the norm, it had little effect on boys coarsened by the culture. There were other Brothers who rebelled against it, as I did, but it was so much the norm that non-conformity could appear threatening.

In my last year as a Brother, my refusal to impose discipline in the traditional way led the Superior to berate me in front of a bemused class, all but accusing me of being homosexual. I leave room for speculation as to the psychosexual basis of this brutal tradition to those qualified to engage in it. I can only hazard the opinion that it reflected attitudes in society as a whole (parents certainly berated me and others for not 'beating it into him') arising from a long history of poverty, with education seen as the only means of escape and betterment. The cliché regularly invoked was of being 'cruel to be kind'; it was a hard world, and corporal punishment 'made a man of you' as well as encouraging the necessary effort. Like all traditions, this culture of brutality was self-perpetuating and, in the end, a matter of defiant pride. As education became more liberal and child-centred, as society grew more permissive, the old regime appealed to some as a guarantee of discipline and manliness. Resorting to force is, fundamentally, a confession of weakness and fear. The Brothers' training and all-but-cloistered existence certainly inculcated a deep suspicion of the world outside, especially as social and cultural change accelerated. They understood less and less of the culture their pupils lived in, and tended to see it as threatening and corrupting. 'Beating it into them' thus got an extended lease of life.

I have no recollection of any discussion or awareness then of the related problem of sexual abuse, for which a large number of Christian Brothers, some of them my contemporaries, have been charged in recent times. While the obsessions about 'special friendships', especially between older and younger boys in the Juniorate, indicates to me now a concern about the potential for such abuse, I don't think the issues involved were ever addressed directly. Indeed, the whole area of sexuality was largely assumed to be dealt with by its effective denial or sublimation in the vow of chastity. While watching *States of Fear*, the television documentaries that did so much to highlight the abuse of children in residential care, I was shocked particularly by the testimony of a man who claimed appalling abuse by Brothers in the industrial school they ran in Tralee.[6] I had spent several weeks on relief duty there in the summer of 1963, but had subsequently suppressed all memory of that time. Why?

At this remove, I can only recall that it was a profoundly upsetting experience, not because I was witness to any particular horror, but because of the atmosphere of meanness, bleakness and fear. This was a different world from the excellent secondary school where I had taught all that year, and even more from our comfortable, normal life in community. The industrial school was known as The Monastery, and the Brothers who staffed it lived there, apart. I was only dimly aware of its existence before being assigned to help out. My clearest memory is of embarrassment at the harsh demeanour of staff and the cowed servility of the boys, so overwhelmingly grateful for any hint of kindness. While I can recall no abuse (that is, much beyond the norm of corporal punishment that also obtained in the secondary school), I am not surprised to learn now that some of the cases pending relate to experiences in The Monastery. It was a secret, enclosed world, run on fear; the boys were wholly at the mercy of the staff, who seemed to have entirely negative views of them.

I can recall none of the Brothers involved, but it was generally believed in the Congregation that men were often sent to staff such terrible places because they had proved difficult, or inadequate, or had got into trouble in 'normal' schools. They too often felt punished and incarcerated, and the threat of banishment, especially to the more remote schools like Daingean, was often the subject of nervous jokes. While their Juniorates were staffed with their brightest and best, the Brothers, it seems, often left the far more needy boys of their industrial schools to the inadequate or the troubled, who were given no special training and little supervision.

Although the individuals concerned have to bear their own weight of responsibility for wrongs committed, there are clearly also ways in which the whole order was to blame. Founded by Edmund Rice precisely to look after such marginalized and vulnerable children, it had come to define itself by its successful, increasingly middle-class schools, and by a mixture of muscular Christianity and militant nationalism that fitted its dominant culture of physical violence all too well. The corrosive, dehumanizing effects of that cultural mix can hardly be exaggerated. Or so it appears to me now. Then, while uneasy about some of these aspects, I was more focused on the positive attributes of the Brothers as educationalists, like their dedication and enthusiasm, and I was entirely a traditionalist in my passion for hurling. I had found great fulfilment in teaching, and had gained much culturally and educationally (though I was stunted emotionally – something it took me years to acknowledge). Yet I had come to feel more and more out of place.

Perhaps the experience in The Monastery was a factor in my first articulating clearly, in that summer of 1963, the desire to leave the Brothers. I agreed to give it another year, and was moved to the much larger community of Sexton Street in Limerick. Known as 'White City' after its colourful and abrasive Superior, its more authoritarian regime completed my disillusionment. Despite good friends (companions in adversity) and a welter of extracurricular activities, I became more and more convinced that I should go. Clearly, I had a spiritual crisis; not only the loss of a sense of vocation but also, as it emerged eventually, of faith. But inextricably mixed in with that was a sense of alienation from life and important aspects of the culture. In Sexton Street, for the first time in my life, I became troublesome and disobedient, reacting strongly and emotionally to what, I felt, amounted to bullying. I began to take more notice of the world outside, going clandestinely to cinemas, for example, ushered through without payment, like everyone in clerical garb. Finally, a brutal and utterly unsympathetic interview with the Visitor (a member of the Provincial Council on the annual inspection of each house) settled the matter. He made it clear that obedience was to be unquestioning, no matter what the provocation. I was no longer willing to accept that.

I've never regretted my time in the Brothers, nor my decision to leave, but I no longer believe, as I maintained for years, that leaving cost me little emotionally. I was glad to escape and lucky that my parents could and did help me to establish a new life, but I lost a community, and took years to find a new one. And I lost friends with a shocking, abrasive abruptness. My novice master had been at his most stern when expounding on the text, 'He who puts his hand to the plough and turns back, is not fit for the Kingdom of Heaven.' Now I experienced a version of being cast into 'exterior darkness'.

Once my going was certain, I had to swear to tell no-one; when I came to pack the trunk I had left home with a lifetime before, I discovered that my photograph albums, books and records had been confiscated. (I don't know how I held onto my copy of Eliot.) In a reverse procedure, I was forced to abandon the life I had lived as Brother Bosco, just as by taking that name I had turned my back on my childhood and family. The vow of poverty, which I had taken annually for four years, meant I owned nothing. I was called an hour before the community rose and taken to the station to wait a long time for the train to Dublin. There I was taken to Clery's department store and exchanged my cheap black suit and black coat and hat for a cheap grey suit, coat and hat. I was given £50. My trunk was easy to carry, containing only my few clothes and my Leaving Certificate.

Thirty years were to pass before I met any of my old friends from that time. Over three years later, after graduation and when doing the Higher Diploma in Education, I wrote to the Provincial for a reference, and to the Superiors of all the Christian Brothers Schools in Cork for teaching hours. None of them replied. I had ceased to exist.

CHAPTER 3

University College Dublin

It was exciting to re-emerge, a blinking and bedazzled twenty-one-year-old, into the 'real' world and to find it changed over seven years to a degree I had only dimly noticed. There was a new prosperity and sense of optimism; the line of unemployed at the Tholsel in New Ross had dwindled and a Dutch company had opened a modern chemical fertilizer plant. The town had been put on the map by the visit of John F. Kennedy to the quayside from which his grandfather had emigrated, and he had joked about his alternative life, working across the river in the Albatross factory. The event was recorded by the new national television station, which opened windows on the outside world that could not be shut again, or covered in lace curtains. Suddenly, there were teenagers (which I had never been) and pop culture, and my boyhood friends had transferred their energies from the hurling field to the dancehalls. Going to hear the Royal Showband with them in Tramore was a considerably bigger culture shock than joining the Brothers. Even the Church was on the move, and the Second Vatican Council promised changes that kept me, and others like me, interested for another decade.

Attempts to cope with this accelerated experience of modernization were helped by my ambition to get back to teaching – but qualified this time. In Francis Street CBS I had signed a form for the salary I never got every month, and I can still see the designation on top – 'Temporary, untrained assistant teacher'. Wearing the habit and 'owning' the school had compensated, but I had felt ignorant and inadequate. My parents not only accepted my unexpected return with equanimity, but proved willing to pay for university.

Before embarking on that adventure, I was given another important introduction to secular culture, this time by my father. He drank two pints of Guinness every night next door in Gus Kennedy's remarkable establishment, at the back of a shop that now sold televisions. More a club than a normal pub, it opened late and featured the same dozen men (shopkeepers, a Garda Superintendent, a teacher, an engineer, a printer) in the same seats, drinking the same drinks and holding versions of the same conversation every evening. The pub seemed a hobby rather than a business for Gus, who actively discouraged any enlargement of his clientele, and the fact that I was allowed to join this magic circle was a tribute to my father; they even broke the strict (and only) house rule – no treating – and he was allowed to buy my drinks. I learned the important art of slow, moderate pint-drinking and the value of ceremonial and good conversation. It was an excellent preparation for university life, as once again my trunk was replenished and I headed off in October 1964 on a new adventure, joining the swelling throngs at University College Dublin.

UCD was then a city-centre university, and the streets, pubs, restaurants, cinemas and dancehalls around and beyond St Stephen's Green were a permanent distraction from, but also an essential part of, our liberal education – at least as we applied Newman's philosophy, taught as a set text in first year English and still a major influence. Earlsfort Terrace was both overcrowded and intimate, with endless streams of students flowing up and down stairs and through the wide corridors, and all ending at some point in the maelstrom of the Great Hall, with its checkerboard flagstones and constant roar of conversation. Its slow emptying after the last lecture on Saturday morning betokened the start of an often lonely weekend for country students in the flats and bedsits of Rathmines and Ranelagh. There was a constant mingling of students from most faculties, rare in modern campuses, and a sense of excitement from the Great Hall's role as a departure lounge, as people met and exited into the anonymity of the world outside the big doors. For some, doubtless, the sixties did swing, and university is remembered mainly as the occasion for sex and rock 'n' roll, but for most, I suspect, there was little if any of the former, and the latter was experienced mainly in the still-decorous environs of alcohol-free ballrooms where the ritual dress dance emphasized the strongly bourgeois flavour of student life. In my first year I felt inadequate and overawed and made few university friends, finding an alternative social life among the Mater Hospital nurses and doctors I met through my sister Mary. The next year, immersed in the life of the highly sociable group of History departments, was dramatically different.

In my memory, history students were intensely serious, with a remarkable *esprit de corps*. Our lives ruled by the weekly essay, we spent most of most days in the History Library, leaving it *en masse* for lectures, and in smaller groups for tutorials, coffee or meals. We were absorbed in our courses and the life of the departments, and our friendships often had an edge of rivalry. We were also intensely interested in politics, and the Terrace was a microcosm of the political world in nearby Leinster House.

The Students' Union was still dominated by the 'machine' politics introduced by the Fianna Fáil tyro Gerry Collins; Fine Gael radicals like Vincent Browne, gratefully accepting James Dillon's dismissive epithet of 'Young Tigers', offered an exciting alternative; in my final year Christian Marxist activists, later associated with *Grille*, promoted the politics of Liberation theology, and were to feature in the 'gentle revolution' the following year. Already prominent was John Feeney, the most flamboyant past pupil of the new Jesuit school, Gonzaga. While I supported Labour, I never joined the party, although my classmate and fellow-townsman Tom Powell was a member of the National Executive and I did help to stuff envelopes during the 1965 general election, when Labour made a major breakthrough. We had little interest in Northern Ireland. The few Northern Catholics among us were exotics from what seemed then a far-off land, though we subscribed to the notion that it was really part of our national territory. We were entirely unsuspecting of its imminent tragic future.

We were conscious of civil rights – but in the United States of America – and we were particularly exercised by the response to student protests against the Vietnam War. UCD also had a number of American students who were avoiding the draft. But the war dragged on and one by one they left, sucked inexorably into the American military machine. A history student who appealed personally to the College President for an extension of his stay claimed he was told not to be a coward, but to go and fight for his country. We watched him board a plane after a new kind of 'American wake'.

The most common subject taken with history then was politics (a new department), and in our second year a number of us founded the Politics Society, with Christina Murphy as first auditor, and myself as secretary. Our model was the long-established History Society, though not its tradition of rowdy sessions of 'private business'. The people that we invited to speak included the old parliamentarian James Dillon (who evoked the memory of Tom Kettle in an oratorical style that had some of the theatricality of Micheál Mac Liammóir), the urbane and radical-seeming Chief Justice, Cearbhall Ó Dálaigh and the shy, combative political columnist John Healy, the *Irish Times* 'Backbencher'. That newspaper was in the process of transformation, from its old Ascendancy image (the only copy sold in New Ross in the 1950s was to the Protestant bank manager) to the paper of a new urban intellectual and professional class. Reading it became a daily ritual, and the best days featured the Myles na gCopaleen column, more wickedly subversive of the old pieties than anything thrown up later by revisionist historiography. If we had a hero (not a concept we'd have endorsed) it was Noel Browne, the conscience and living martyr of Irish radicalism. I have a vivid memory of listening to him in a packed Liberty Hall, straining to hear his passionate whisper, experiencing almost physically the white heat of his anger as he lashed out at Catholic control of health and education.

I had gone to UCD intending to study English and Irish but did history instead, mainly because it seemed excitingly relevant to the changing world around us. History had teachers who communicated not only their passion for the subject, but also their sense of it as an instrument to understand and even manage that change, not in any programmatic sense (there wasn't a hint of Marxist historiography), but in encouraging dispassionate, critical thought.

Robin Dudley Edwards – Dudley to everyone – Professor of Modern Irish History, seemed every inch the eccentric professor, an effect largely calculated. Carrying his still-handsome head rather as Robespierre described St Just, 'as if carrying the Blessed Sacrament', his wild bunches of hair, occasional flamboyance of dress, excitable fluting voice and theatrical lecturing and social styles all created a persona much loved, sometimes feared, but hard to ignore. His lectures began and ended abruptly (even, seemingly, in mid-sentence), ranged far and wide to no discernable pattern, and were bravura extempore performances without notes. What stayed in the mind – and it was a waste of time to try to take notes – was that history mattered, and each one of us was entitled, indeed expected, to have an opinion. The style was dictated in part by his serious eye problems, occasionally necessitating an appropriate black patch: Dudley was a pirate. He was also a true egalitarian, who made every student feel a colleague, and this was especially clear in one of his characteristic enthusiasms, the Irish History Students' Association. Its annual conference was 'the recurrent stage on which many of his more fabulous exploits were set',[1] and on these occasions he could be offensive as well as outrageous. But when not performing, or drinking, he could also be immensely courteous and encouraging, and that is how I remember him best.

T. Desmond Williams – Desmond to some – was equally theatrical. He too had a self-conscious and well-worked persona as a man of mystery, an *éminence grise*, behind an air of disarming ineptitude. Whereas Dudley declaimed,

Desmond mumbled; when he left the lecture hall abruptly, it was because he had run out of cigarettes. Often he didn't turn up for weeks, but then would hold a class for three hours instead of the scheduled one. I was never very interested in the already old-fashioned diplomatic history he taught, and never felt his brilliance or understood his awesome reputation, then or since, as a 'world-class mind'.[2] The little he published still reads like he sounded then, low-key, impressionistic, yet a little ponderous. What he was still best known for (in a history school highly conscious always of its own folklore) was his glittering undergraduate performance, and he epitomized the Oxbridge cult of the 'starred first', also one of the less attractive aspects of UCD history. We knew that he had been at Cambridge and was highly regarded by Herbert Butterfield, one of the great stars in our firmament. It was said that he was involved in the Nuremburg trials, and had unrivalled knowledge of the archives of Nazi Germany. More prosaically, as his obituarist James McGuire put it, he had 'nominal military rank' as part of an international group editing the papers of the German foreign ministry. Despite this 'unrivalled opportunity to work on primary material' he published nothing of substance; his appointment to the Chair of Modern History aged twenty-eight did him a great disservice by removing any pressure to publish.[3] He epitomized glamour, however, and gave, if obscurely, a sense of history's political role. Those comparatively few who came under his influence clearly experienced a rare intellectual charge and were devoted to him. One of my last glimpses of him was at a function in the UCD History Boardroom in Belfield, his former student and then Taoiseach, Garret FitzGerald, down on one knee by his chair, deep in conversation as the room emptied.

The best teaching came from more junior staff, particularly in Irish history, where Art Cosgrave, Margaret MacCurtain and Donal McCartney offered challenging new approaches to old problems and controversies, whether Poyning's Law, the 1641 rebellion or the 1916 Rising. There was no dogmatism, but independent, critical thought was encouraged and complexity and the marshalling of evidence insisted upon. If the general mood was what came to be called revisionist, it was neither iconoclastic nor anti-nationalist. This was especially true of Maureen Wall.[4] Her lectures were models of structure and clarity, but what made them memorable was that they were fresh, lively reports on research in progress, bringing the archives into the classroom, making the undergraduate a privileged participant in exciting and as yet unpublished new work. As well as taking her documents course on the Catholic middle class in the eighteenth century, I had the privilege of having

*Desmond Williams with Taoiseach Garret
FitzGerald, Belfield.* [Photo: Michael Laffan]

Maureen Wall.

her as tutor in my second year and in that role she was encouraging, not only of our feeble efforts to write, but also about our future role in society and the broader value of the training we were receiving.

Cormac Ó Gráda's judgment that the record of the history departments at UCD in the 1940s and '50s was relatively poor in publishing terms, but strong in teaching and postgraduate research, is valid also for the '60s.[6] The ideas underlying our education were summed up in 1967 in Geoffrey Elton's influential book *The Practice of History.* The emphasis, as he recommended, was on 'the proper techniques of the trained professional', who must 'train himself to his trade'. I can recall no-one echoing Elton's belief that 'a philosophic concern with such problems as the reality of historical knowledge or the nature of historical thought only hinders the practice of history', yet there was no systematic study of the theoretical basis of history or its relationship to the social sciences, much less to literature. There was, however, occasional encouragement to reflect on the nature of the subject, particularly from Hilary Jenkins, and it was this, perhaps, that inspired me to struggle through Collingwood's *The Idea of History* (1946). I liked its stress on 'the historical imagination' rather than history as science, and on the history of thought as the core of the subject.[7] While largely innocent of theory, however, we were conscious of tradition, and in particular the professionalization of Irish history since the 1930s and its consequent political and cultural role, critical rather than celebratory of official and traditional orthodoxies.

Brendan Bradshaw has recalled his alienation from the ethos of the history departments when he was an undergraduate at UCD some years before me. He had felt that the approach of his teachers was relentlessly hostile to the strongly nationalist and republican ethos of his own background.[8] This was not my experience. Doubtless my own intense nationalist conditioning had been weakened by my rejection of the ethos of the Christian Brothers, but it seemed to me (or seems in retrospect) that even the younger lecturers operated largely from *within* a basic nationalist position, anxious, in part, to rehabilitate it by putting it on a better scholarly footing.

For example, the main reinterpretations (or what might nowadays be called revisionist accounts) of the 1916 Rising came from UCD historians, and the most radical of them from Maureen Wall. This detailed with scrupulous clarity the key role of the IRB faction, who planned the Rising not only as a blow against British rule but as a coup within militant republicanism, puncturing the romantic myth of 1916, as articulated in the proclamation of 'the Provisional Government' of 'the Irish Republic'. Yet Wall's tone was essentially positive and admiring. She concluded with a defence of the plotters as 'the leaders of a submerged nation', and of 'the Dublin Rising, with its flags, its proclamation of the Republic' as 'a dignified protest', and 'a success'. The foreword of the volume in which Wall's essay appeared explained that it had been commissioned by the official 1916 commemoration committee, chaired by the then Taoiseach, Seán Lemass, and that advantage had been taken of the fact that the actual publication had been delayed until 1969, the anniversary of the meeting of the first Dáil, to publish the 'formal Declaration of Independence' of that body, including its legitimizing of the Rising.[9]

The conclusions drawn by their undergraduates (who heard much of this material in lectures) were often more negative. My own revulsion at the messianic, blood-sacrifice message of Pearse's *The Singer*, put on by the Abbey Theatre for the commemoration, was, as I recall, shared by others. That experience seems in retrospect a defining moment, what Joyce called an 'epiphany' or a sudden 'revelation of the whatness of a thing'.[10] I had taken my seat high up in the gods of the old Queen's Theatre in great anticipation, having been brought up to reverence Pearse only to be chilled, literally, by what I heard as the short melodrama unfolded, with its eerie prefiguring of Pearse's own death. I recoiled at the perversion of the teacher's role to that of rabble-rouser, leading those who trusted him to certain death.

The megalomania of the final message – 'One man can free a people as one man redeemed the world' – seemed to sum up the psychology of those who believed that any amount of human suffering could be justified in the name of the 'people'.[11] When this mindset resurfaced in the propaganda of the Provisional IRA in the 1970s, it intensified the sense of revulsion at the blood-sacrifice ideals of 1916 that the fiftieth anniversary celebrations had, paradoxically, evoked for many.

We were trained (in so far as undergraduates can be) in the rigorous tradition of historical scholarship epitomized by *Irish Historical Studies*, the journal founded by Dudley Edwards and Theo Moody of Trinity thirty years before and dedicated to 'the advancement of Irish historical learning on scientific principles'.[12] Too much emphasis should not be placed on this use of 'science', which was essentially an aspiration couched in the language of German empiricism. I don't remember any such emphasis, nor what Bradshaw was to criticize as the flawed 'interpretative principle of value-free history', which masked 'unacknowledged bias'.[13] Indeed, the opposite was the case. We were taught history as a series of debates, of rival interpretations; we were trained to sniff out bias, and to highlight it. If value-free history was put forward as an attainable idea, I certainly never believed in it, and the reading that influenced me most made me suspicious of all interpretation, and aware that history was a 'slippery discipline'.[14]

Two small, heavily recommended books influenced me particularly. Herbert Butterfield's brilliant essay on the dominant nationalist interpretation of the English past, *The Whig Interpretation of History* (1931), showed 'that it studies the past with reference to the present' and was busy 'dividing the world into the friends and enemies of progress'; taking 'a short cut through complexity', it focused on those elements that cumulatively produced the Glorious Revolution and made the English Constitution the envy of the world.[15] For 'Whig' read 'Irish nationalist' and for 'The Glorious Revolution' read 'The 1916 Rising' and the continued appeal in 1960s Ireland of this iconoclastic youthful revisionism was understandable. Its influence will be clear in my analysis of Comóradh '98 and the historians most associated with it.

But the great liberating text of my undergraduate reading was another slim volume by a very different Cambridge historian, the chronicler of Soviet Russia, E.H. Carr. His *What is History?* appeared in paperback in 1964, the year I went to UCD. Its focus on the historian as 'part of history' led to its key injunction: 'Before you study the history, study the historian ... before you study the historian, study his social and historical environment.' His key belief that 'history means interpretation' owed a debt also to Collingwood, and he was aware that this emphasis on the role of the historian could be pushed 'to rule out objective history at all'. Carr did not believe that 'the facts of history are nothing: interpretation is everything'; instead he saw the historian as engaged in 'a continuous process of moulding his facts to his interpretation and his interpretation to his facts' – a formulation many historians would probably still agree with.[16]

In my undergraduate history training we studied neither Marx nor Freud. This was, more surprisingly, even true of my other subject, politics. This had as a core component, taught over the two years, 'Political Theory', which began with the Greeks and ended with Kant! Our professor, Conor Martin, also lectured on Karl Popper, so that we were encouraged to read his attacks on the Marxist and Freudian systems we had not studied. We were dimly aware of the eccentricity of this, and of the Catholic ethos of the department, with its odd official name, 'Ethics and Politics', and its priest-professor, one of five such, who I now know were essentially nominated by Archbishop McQuaid.

Things were already changing, with politics overshadowing ethics, and new lay staff being appointed, beginning with John Whyte in 1961. Students did not know that during our second year Conor sought to stop Whyte's research on Church-state relations at the behest of the archbishop, effectively forcing him to resign. Yet Whyte was a devout Catholic and his seminal study, later published as *Church and State in Modern Ireland*, 'is now commonly seen as a moderate defence of the Catholic stance'.[17] I don't remember Whyte's lectures, but was glad of the greater focus on modern Irish politics by new appointments, Maurice Manning and Brian Farrell. In retrospect, it seems that part of the attraction of this department was that it mirrored my sense of flux, and mediated the huge changes taking place in my own life and in society as a whole in a safe and basically a conservative way. This was even true of the remarkable lectures of Fergal O'Connor. I have no memory of their formal designation, only the crowded lecture theatre, with bona-fide politics students vastly outnumbered by gatecrashers from every faculty, come to hear frank meditations on public and private morality, on the state, war, the media, the duties of citizenship; on the family, relationships, sex, selfhood – a particular version of the 'liberal agenda' argued passionately by a frail Dominican priest in an old fashioned dog-collar.

E.H. Carr's criticism of Cambridge history as narrow and conservative could, therefore, also be applied to much of the training I had in that discipline at UCD. Far from being confined to an unreal value-free approach, we were exposed to a range of approaches and interpretations, though without a systematic grounding in their theoretical and methodological bases or even in the development of historiography. Above all, it was too conventional in its view of sources.

The worldwide trend towards social and economic history was slow to reach Ireland and any sustained focus on cultural developments even slower, so that the insights of cultural anthropology or historical geography, for example, were not available. On the other hand, there were considerable strengths in the traditional approach to 'the practice of history', particularly because undergraduates were treated seriously as trainee historians, expected to read widely, encouraged to develop their own interpretations, and shown how to construct and defend them. We were also offered such a range of courses, and such diversity within each, as to allow us to develop interests outside the mainstream and in effect to design our own degree course if we wished.

My attempt to do this was based on Collingwood's proposition that 'all history is the history of thought'.[18] While it was easy to study modern European history in terms of competing ideologies, the exciting new research on Ireland and Britain was heavily focused on the nineteenth century and was more Namierite (i.e. focused on élite power-play) in approach. I found most scope in the medieval period, following particularly the work of two more Cambridge historians, David Knowles and Walter Ullmann. A related focus was the scientific revolution, and here Butterfield's *Origins of Modern Science* (1965) was a revelation, not least because, like Ullmann, he argued for continuities between the medieval and modern world-views. The strongly religious flavour in these writers was also an attraction, again providing continuity with my earlier experiences and interests.

Such specialization had its dangers when it came to final exams, and this was confirmed particularly by Dudley's paper on the Tudor period, which was heavily political and included, it seemed, not a single question I could attempt. I 'dried' completely, fighting rising panic as the first hour ticked away and I had not written a word. Allowed five minutes outside and given some calming advice by Tom Garvin, who was invigilating, I returned and wrote furiously, proving Carr's maxim that 'the historian will get the kinds of facts he wants'. When, a month later, I had the equally traumatic experience of being called for a 'viva' before the assembled staff and a number of external examiners, it was my 'remarkably original' answers on Tudor policy that seemed to impress most! As I could remember none of them, further improvisation was called for before, to my astonishment, I was awarded not just a first, but *the* first. Folklore told us that there was never more than one, and preserved the names of many of the elect, back to the awesome, unimaginable figure of the young Desmond Williams. It was all part of the theatricality which Dudley especially loved.

I was all too conscious of the role that chance had played in my own particular case. And yet, it changed my life. I had come to college with the limited and utilitarian aim of qualifying as a teacher and getting back to the classroom. Now the expectation was that I would do research, as was made clear to me after the results were announced by my tutor, Peter Butterfield. His quiet insistence on practical skills had been as important to me as his father's writing, and his encouragement mattered now. Messages from him and others continued to reach me in Cork, where I had moved immediately after my finals in 1967, having been lucky enough to get a full-time teaching job while also enrolled for the Higher Diploma in Education. Over the following five years I also did a Masters thesis while teaching in a dynamic new secondary school, Coláiste an Sprid Naoimh.

The choice of Cork was determined by the fact that my wife-to-be, Mary O'Callaghan, lived there; the prize awarded on my degree result bought an engagement ring. Oliver MacDonagh's arrival in Cork from Australia a year later gave the unexpected privilege of working with this major figure, and the unexpected ambition of an academic career. Then, in the final stages of my Masters, came the eruption of violence in Northern Ireland. It was to overshadow all our lives, and to influence profoundly the kind of history my generation would write.

CHAPTER 4

University College Cork and Cambridge

I was delighted to be back teaching, and my sense of a fresh beginning was enhanced by the fact that Coláiste an Sprid Naoimh was a new school and we were still in temporary accommodation. It had a young, lively staff, with better academic backgrounds than the majority who entered secondary-school teaching at the time. This was a key element in the ambitious plans of its charismatic founder, Brother Bonaventure (Murphy), a Presentation Brother. Devious at times and difficult to work with, he still inspired the sense of difference and destiny that was to make it in time one of the leading schools in the country. I was so anxious for the job that I agreed to teach Irish and (old) maths to Leaving Cert in my first year, and was happier in following years when able to concentrate on history and English. There were some exceptional students, well-read, keen to argue, and interested in current affairs, and I learned a lot from them. There is no job in the world like it on a good day, but twenty hours or more a week of intensive teaching is exhausting, and those academics who have done it tend to have a greater sense of realism (and privilege) about their lighter workloads. I also went back to being an enthusiastic trainer of hurling teams, and had as captain of the under-fourteens one Jimmy Barry Murphy; for some Cork friends, this is my main claim to fame. I was active in the Association of Secondary Teachers of Ireland, and a supporter of the traumatic strike that was finally to give teachers a decent salary scale. The fact that I also found time for research after I finished the teaching diploma, and, indeed, came to enjoy it more than anything else I did, was due to two remarkable men: my supervisor, Oliver MacDonagh,[1] and my subject, William Ewart Gladstone.

Shy and diffident in manner, peering with quizzical humour through thick glasses, Oliver was difficult to get to know at first. When teaching,

Oliver MacDonagh.

however, he was transformed. His remarkably resonant voice took on both power and passion; he was fluent and uncompromisingly intellectual. These qualities were also evident in the provocative, original short survey of modern Irish history he had just published, the book that first made me aware of the importance of literary style in history writing.[2] Indeed, he had a great love of literature, particularly that of the nineteenth century, and was to publish widely in that area, beginning during my first year with him.[3] Some colleagues found him intimidating and rather remote, but his students found great warmth, empathy and a sense of fun. He was, it later emerged, a great sports enthusiast (especially for Munster rugby) and had supplemented his allowance while an undergraduate at UCD by working as an occasional racing tipster for the *Irish Times*. When we first met I was aware of his early research on the Famine but only gradually came to realize that the book of his Cambridge PhD on the growth of the nineteenth-century British state, had already made him a major international reputation.[4] It was a great thrill to find a copy one Saturday morning in Sean Daly's Aladdin's cave, the much-missed Tower Books, then a major resource and meeting place for Cork academics and researchers. After ten years' teaching in Cambridge and five in Australia, Oliver had returned to Ireland to be near his elderly parents and father-in-law, but he clearly enjoyed other aspects of being back, teaching and re-immersing himself in Irish history and society at a time of major political change.

After the bustle and intensity of my undergraduate experience I found University College Cork rather slow and easy-going. Small and intimate on its beautiful riverside campus, its students (or at least those I met through Mary, still an undergraduate) seemed cheerful and relaxed, their lives focused on the convivial student bar and restaurant rather than the small library. But, in fact, it was undergoing rapid growth and modernization under an inspirational president, M.D. McCarthy, and Oliver was soon playing a significant role in this, as well as developing the range and resources of the Modern History department. A major attraction of Cork for Oliver was its excellent holdings in nineteenth-century British history, making this fertile ground for research students, then very few in number.

When I approached Oliver about doing an MA he was enthusiastic and suggested some broad reading on the Home Rule issue in British politics, beginning with Gladstone. This was then an area of lively debate, after major publications on Butt by David Thornley, and on Parnell by Conor Cruise O'Brien and Leland Lyons.[5] The second (1965) edition of Nicholas Man-sergh's *The Irish Question*, with its emphasis on ideology and its sympathetic treatment of Gladstone, particularly influenced me. Oliver was not surprised that I never got past my starting-point, and the thesis submitted three years later was on 'W.E. Gladstone: The evolution of the Home Rule policy'. He was a great motivator, intervening little but to great effect. His ideal was complexity of argument allied to clarity of style, and he made it clear that the latter depended mainly on restraining a tendency to excess in the former. His own writing was, and remains, a benchmark. I could not anticipate how important he was to become in all I was to attempt as a historian, as well as being a great friend and support. His death in 2002 was a profound loss.

I was entranced by the reach of Gladstone's mind, and particularly by the tensions between his increasingly liberal rhetoric and pragmatic politics, and between his claims of consistency and movement across the political spectrum from ultra-Tory to near-Radical. A rich range and variety of source materials were available: letters, journalism and speeches, though not at that time, unfortunately, his remarkable diaries. UCC proved to have virtually all the printed material, and a summer in the British Library working on the Gladstone Papers completed the research. There was also, at this time, the beginning of a strong Namierite assault by John Vincent and A.B. Cooke[6] on the old liberal view, exemplified by J.L. Hammond's *Gladstone and the Irish Nation* (1938).

Whereas this had linked the conversion to Home Rule with Gladstone's well-known earlier support for romantic nationalism in parts of Europe, the new interpretation claimed that it owed nothing to ideology and everything to a pragmatic, even cynical response to the complex balance of forces between and within parties after the 1885 general election. I had found, in short, a marvellous research topic, the kind that could become something of an obsession and cause a change in priorities, even for someone working full time.

Gladstone, as I came to portray him,[7] was neither romantic nor cynic, but a conservative who came to believe that liberal policies offered the best guarantees of the social cohesion under the leadership of an enlightened aristocracy that was always his aim. Likewise, he was a strong imperialist who came to see the concession of limited self-government in some cases as the best guarantee of empire. Thus, his Irish reforms, culminating in Home Rule, had as their ultimate aim the rehabilitation of the landlord class and the salvation of the Union, by making landowners and 'unionists' of the Catholic majority. They were also designed, of course, to gain or keep political power at Westminster. Ideology, articulated mainly through an often flamboyant rhetoric, was both a political weapon and an expression of deeply held beliefs, and like most people Gladstone saw no contradiction between proclaimed idealism and evident self-interest.

One thing, above all, emerged from this first research project: despite the rhetoric and even, on many levels, the reality of the Union, Ireland was seen throughout the nineteenth century as a colonial/imperial problem, and this was true of all shades of political opinion in Britain. The bitter conflict over Irish Home Rule was, fundamentally, a conflict between two views of empire. Whereas Gladstone proposed to treat Ireland on the model of the white, self-governing colonies such as Canada, his opponents compared it more and more to India. What Oliver MacDonagh had called 'the element of colonialism in Ireland's situation'[8] has been the focus of all my research and writing since, making mine a rather lonely, even eccentric voice among Irish historians of the modern period. Over the past twenty-five years, as I've moved from trying to understand the Irish Question in British politics to working on aspects of the Irish experience of colonialism, I've tried to develop a nuanced view of what that term means in the Irish context and how it relates to other core elements in our history. While I never became a 'Gladstonian' in the sense of accepting his liberal rhetoric about Ireland, I was persuaded of his sincerity and the potential for a new, more consensual politics, lost in the wreck of his Home Rule initiative.

This latter view doubtless was coloured by the fact that my thesis was a product not only of the research involved but of a period when an escalation of the Northern Ireland crisis emphasized both the complex meaning of the colonial basis of Irish historical experience and the lethal consequences of a polarized politics. During the thirty bloody years it has taken to find a viable basis for consensual politics and for ending violence, 'the Troubles' have had a profound effect, not only on politics, but also on historical consciousness. History has been a weapon in the conflict; thousands have been victims, in effect, of competing versions of the past, often cited to legitimize their deaths. Awareness of this certainly influenced some to believe, with Ronan Fanning, that the writing of Irish history demanded a particularly direct 'confrontation with mythologies designed to legitimize violence as a political weapon in a bid to overthrow the state'.[9] It took the debate on revisionism over the past decade to make me understand and acknowledge fully this aspect of the 'political unconscious' in my own writing.

Like most people in the Republic, I knew little of Northern Ireland and few Northerners, apart from the middle-class Catholic students I'd met at UCD. My future parents-in-law had been on a caravan holiday there; it was becoming a fashionable destination, a foreign holiday needing no plane or ferry. While I would have then unhesitatingly endorsed the idea of eventual Irish unity, I would have equally unhesitatingly repudiated the use of force to achieve it. I remembered the IRA border campaign of the 1950s, and had learned from my father (and, of course, the Church) to reject the cult of Sean South of Garryowen (killed during an attack on an RUC barracks and the subject of a well-known ballad); indeed I was to find the same cynicism about South among some Christian Brothers who had taught him in Limerick. The nationalism of the Brothers, like that of most Irish people, was mainly rhetorical, and any appeal such rhetoric had for me was further eroded by my undergraduate training and the grosser inanities of the 1966 commemoration of the 1916 Rising. So, in 1969, while still a mainstream, if largely unthinking, constitutional nationalist, I was unhesitatingly and indeed vehemently opposed to republican violence. Though the provocation was certainly great, that response seemed regressive, barbaric and an exacerbation of the problem. The civil rights movement, which came to prominence in 1968, by contrast seemed modern and admirable, led by students and young graduates like myself, and applying the slogans and tactics used against racism and war in the United States to the patent injustices of the Stormont system and the discrimination practised against the Catholic minority. When state collusion in sectarian attempts to suppress the movement led to an escalation of violence and the emergence of the hardline Provisional IRA at the end of 1969, the focus began to shift for me, as for many others, away from the issue of civil rights (which, it could be believed, would now be addressed over time) to the rights and wrongs of armed struggle, and the revival of the blood-sacrifice ideals of 1916 that the Provisionals claimed to represent in the interest of the Republic then declared.

If, as Conor Cruise O'Brien has argued, 'the 1966 commemorations in Dublin favoured a recrudescence of the IRA',[10] we have seen that they had also caused some to query those aspects of the nationalist tradition that 1916 represented, and that the state and educational systems continued to promote, or more accurately, to pay lip-service to. When that rhetorical tradition erupted in its most extreme real-life form in Northern Ireland, many apart from myself were thus quicker to repudiate it than they might otherwise have been. The Provisionals could sweep aside protests at their methods or lack of mandate with the claim – absolutely true, as Maureen Wall's essays had shown – that they were in the tradition of the signatories of the 1916 Proc-lamation, the self-styled 'provisional government' of the proclaimed Republic. This was part of a historical mindset which, while only one factor in the situation, was bound to be of particular concern to me as an apprentice historian and even more as a teacher of history working with idealistic teenage boys.

From early on I was forced to articulate my own feelings about republican violence in classroom discussions. Personally and politically I felt it to be repel-lent, but my main argument was historical: that it reduced the long, complex history of Anglo-Irish relations and its particular outcome in the polarized statelet of Northern Ireland to a travesty, offering a simplistic solution that was not only obscenely wrong in itself, but utterly counter-productive in terms of the development of democratic politics or normal community relations. Some of the boys thought my views shocking and extreme, especially when I tried to represent the viewpoint of Ulster unionists. Most were confused, and in that they reflected the views of their parents and of mainstream political culture.

The confusion in public opinion in the Republic arose largely from the fact that the Provisionals articulated not just the rhetoric of 1916 but that of contemporary politics, and in particular of Fianna Fáil, the party of govern-ment. This continued to emphasize routinely the evils of partition, the com-mitment to unity, the culpability of the British, and the responsibility of nationalists to complete the work of the dead generations of patriots. Thus, for example, the Belfast republican John Kelly could quote a recent statement of the Fianna Fáil Minister for External Affairs during the 1970 trial of his former cabinet colleagues, charged with importing arms for supply to the IRA: 'The claim of Ireland, the claim of the Irish nation to control the totality of Ireland has been asserted over the centuries by successive generations of Irishmen and women and it is one which no spokesman for the Irish nation could ever renounce.'[11] The ambivalence over many months of the Taoiseach, Jack Lynch, on the one hand sacking Provisional supporters in his Cabinet, and on the other echoing their rhetoric and continuing to rely on their support in the Dáil, epitomized a key aspect of the public mood in the early years of the Troubles. Because we had all shared the rhetoric and its assumptions, we all felt complicity in the tragedy that was unfolding, and for that reason, perhaps, some of us also felt emotional and angry at the invocation of *our* name to justify murder.

I was not involved politically, but by chance had a long conversation with Jack Lynch around the time of the Arms Trial. He had performed the official opening of the new Coláiste an Sprid Naoimh building that morning and returned for a concert in the evening, effortlessly charming the audience with a song from the stage and working the hall like the consummate populist he was, very much at his ease in his political heartland. His request that his Garda driver should be given some quiet hospitality before they left meant that the Taoiseach, in his turn, had to accompany the driver/bodyguard. The headmaster, ever inventive, dragooned a small group, including the two senior history teachers, Dennis Kennedy and myself, to entertain the Taoiseach while he sat with his driver in the headmaster's study. One whiskey turned into several (at least for the Taoiseach and his hosts; the driver was mindful of his duties) and a conversation that, in my memory, lasted several hours. I expected to dislike him, as I had long disliked his overt appeal to the Catholic voter and his general conservatism. Used to the black-and-white television image, which gave him the spaniel-eyed look beloved of cartoonists, I was surprised at his sharp blue eyes, and was soon won over by his great charm and sense of humour (and, doubtless, by such unexpected proximity to power).

The conversation featured stories of hurling, and of Cork characters, but returned several times to recent events, on which he seemed to us remarkably unguarded and outspoken. I remember his vehemence against Neil Blaney and Charles Haughey, and his analysis of the crisis mainly in terms of personalities and power – and sport. It was him or them, and he had no option but to sideline them, 'take them out'. If there was talk of nationalism, I don't recall it. The ideological emphasis instead was on democracy; that the IRA threatened it, and that he had acted to save it. History will very likely judge in his favour on that score.

I remember being involved in only one public (or semi-public) political action at this time. At one of the crowded meetings of the ASTI, which gradually moved its conservative membership to strike action, a proposal came from the floor that the Cork branch should make a donation to 'An Cumann Cabhrach'. The proposer, a well-known republican activist, claimed this was a purely charitable organization and that the money would go only for the relief of distressed Catholic families in Northern Ireland. This was a popular cause, and part of the brief of the government committee established by Lynch that was at the centre of controversy over claims that it also supplied arms.

I'd read or heard somewhere that 'An Cumann Cabhrach' was a Provisional front organization and opposed the motion, surprised by my own vehemence in arguing against any contribution that might be used to purchase weapons. After some debate the motion was dropped, and for weeks afterwards I had nightmares, fearing the midnight knock and retaliation. This was fanciful, as I knew even then, but such was the atmosphere of the time, and the hostility of a section in the hall to what I'd said. As Conor Cruise O'Brien found around this time in opposing a 'release the prisoners' motion at a Trade Union Congress, I was seen 'to refuse the *minimum* Republicans expected of *all* Irishmen, and thus to risk exclusion from the Irish nation, in one way or another'.[12]

Quoting Conor Cruise O'Brien in this way, now, and identifying with his stance at that time, will likely offer a shorthand form of dismissal for some readers of everything I've written. 'Unionist', for example: old smears are best. Like many of his admirers, I regret that O'Brien's deepening pessimism about Northern Ireland should have eventually become so dark as to carry him outside the broad consensus behind the Good Friday Agreement, and to support diehard unionism. There is a sad irony in this, because O'Brien was, in effect, one of the main architects of that agreement. His clear, unflinching dissection of nationalist rhetoric from the late 1960s and his courageous, dogged re-education of Irish public opinion in relation to the North made a significant (perhaps indispensable) contribution to the painfully slow process that has finally led to the abandonment of the territorial claim to Northern Ireland, together with much (if not yet all) of the old, discredited paraphernalia of what has passed for republican nationalism in Ireland. So much of what he wrote twenty to thirty years ago is now such common currency that it is difficult to remember how radical and important it was. But the effort should be made, and a true estimate of his contribution be formed to challenge the current caricature.

At the very time that the crisis in Northern Ireland seemed to plunge us back into the old nightmare of Irish history, an escape route was opening up as it had for James Joyce in his exile on mainland Europe. The overwhelming 'Yes' vote in the 1972 referendum on joining the EEC seemed to me a decisive turning away from a traditional narrow nationalism, which might also in time dissolve the intractable problems of Northern Ireland and of Anglo-Irish relations. The expectation that this might happen quickly has proven over-optimistic; the escalation of the Troubles, the divergence between Britain and Ireland in their acceptance of Europe, and the slow pace of European integration saw to that. But the hopes of a quarter of a century ago are at last proving well-founded, and shared European experiences and concerns have played a major role in the evolution of new consensual political structures in Northern Ireland.

The year 1972 was also marked by a widening of horizons in my own life, with the move to Cambridge to pursue research for a PhD. Not long before that a very different path had opened up briefly before me. My father's deteriorating health and the clear choice of all six of their children to pursue careers elsewhere (on traditional lines initially; the boys teaching, the girls nursing) left my parents with a dilemma. Having built up a successful business, they no longer had the same incentive or energy to run it, yet no-one wanted to take it over. 'Children are an insurance for your old age,' was one of my father's many sayings (though offered increasingly with his own wry irony), and they had both grown up accepting that the duties of children extended to fulfilling their parents' expectations about succession and continuity. Yet, to their great credit, they made no such demands on us, or even voiced disappointment. They were proud of our education and achievements. In their eyes, of course, a family shop was not like a family farm; the emotional investment was less, as my mother's estrangement from her brother over his selling of Ballymacar was soon to show. Nevertheless, the shop was both their life's work and a good living, and they made a suggestion – no more than that – to each of us in turn, beginning with me as the eldest. Would I consider moving to a teaching job in the town, or nearby, with the shop as a lucrative sideline, run by a manager, and with a share of the profits also supporting their retirement? I thought long and hard about it, conscious of what I owed them and concerned about their future. Mary, by now my wife, had her own reservations but would have quite liked to return to living in a small town, like those that her father's bank job had brought her to in childhood. I felt I had the wrong temperament for business, even at a remove, and no interest in returning to teach in a school where I had been unhappy. Less clearly understood then, but subconsciously important, was the fact that I'd have found it very hard to live in my mother's shadow, that her ability to let go was in direct ratio to the distance one lived from her. But what determined my response, above all, was that I wanted the opportunity to pursue further research and have an academic career; the very different option of a return to New Ross crystallized that.

The shop – and the family home over it – was sold, and my parents retired to a house they built on the outskirts of the town and named 'Courtdale' after the farm where they had begun their married life. There, for the first time since then, my mother could indulge her passion for gardening, and there too few years later, in 1979, my father died in his sleep. He'd had a number of health problems, but it was a dramatically worsening emphysema (he was a cigarette- and pipe-smoker) that caused him most distress in the months before he died. When I brought him to the pub on his last visit to Cork, he wasn't able to go to the bar and buy his round. As I came back with the drinks he said, tapping his forehead, 'You know, up here I'm still a young chap, but these damn things (tapping his legs) don't do what I tell them any more.' I miss the humour and wisdom of those pub conversations begun in Gus Kennedy's all those years ago.

The decision to pursue research elsewhere and full time was not an easy one. I was nearly thirty, married, and had 'a fine pensionable job' and excellent prospects in the expanding second-level sector (as the new educational journalism was beginning to call it). And I loved teaching more than ever. But I now had an even greater love, which in the end could lead me back to teaching, and I was encouraged strongly by Oliver MacDonagh to follow my instincts. My wife Mary's encouragement was even more important, and characteristically generous. She had just embarked on a law degree and my decision effectively put her career on hold. Looking back, I took too little account of that and, indeed, of the unexpected demands my approach to research had made on our life together. As I remember it, the decision to make the change was taken relatively easily; what was more difficult (and for a time looked impossible) was to get funding and, connected with that, choosing where to go. Cambridge was the obvious choice, with its strong UCD connections, its galaxy from my undergraduate firmament (including Nicholas Mansergh in my research area), and Oliver MacDonagh's long period there; it also offered a range of studentships and scholarships. Oliver encouraged me to think of

Yale, where he had spent a semester; he had been excited by its interdisciplinary ethos, 'much livelier than Cambridge'. I had an offer, but what quickly ruled it out for me was the American PhD system, with its requirement of two years' intensive coursework before beginning research. After the experience of the MA I did not want to go back to what was essentially an undergraduate mode. Given the interdisciplinary way my interests were to develop, I've sometimes regretted this road not taken.

Cambridge seemed more attractive, allowing me to dive straight into research. Also, Mary and I had liked it enormously on a visit during my summer researching in London. And so Cambridge became the goal, with Peterhouse the obvious first choice of college. Acceptance proved easy but funding remained a problem, as it emerged that I was past the age limit for college studentships, and that the scholarships available to me could offer pitiably little money. What made it possible to go, in the end, was the award of a Michael Collins Scholarship, after a tough interview from a board that included a gruff and suspicious M.J. Costello ('Why Cambridge? And why *British* history?') and an urbane James Dooge, and held in the latter's imposing Senate room. While this paid the fees, there was still a substantial shortfall in terms of the minimum income the university required, and this was met by a letter of guarantee from my bank. As my time in Cambridge was marked by rapid inflation, and the decision of the Labour government to treble the fees of overseas students and then to treat Irish students as 'foreign', my PhD was financed mainly by an epic overdraft, and by Peterhouse proving an indulgent landlord.

Gearóid Ó Tuathaigh, who'd recently returned to Galway from Peterhouse, offered to meet me to talk about what I might expect. It was a valuable, stimulating, rather alarming encounter. Gearóid's glorious flood of language and pell-mell of ideas were memorable. His assessment of the Cambridge History faculty and the Peterhouse fellowship was colourful, at times acerbic, and proved to be astute; his advice on broadening my MA research was prophetic; but his depiction of postgraduate life in Cambridge as fiercely competitive proved, to my relief, to be a matter of temperament, and perhaps of age. (I was ineligible for most research fellowships.) Before leaving Cork I had to arrange to meet another postgraduate of Oliver's, Ian d'Alton. He was also on his way to Peterhouse, but trailing clouds of glory as the recent winner of the Royal Historical Society Alexander Prize for his stylish article on Cork Protestants in the dying decades of the Union.[13] The fact that we had never met reflected the part-time nature of my links with the department and my lack of a sense of being part of an academic community while doing the MA. Peterhouse was to make up for that, thanks in part to the presence not only of Ian but also in time, of Joe Bergin and Denis Smyth from UCD.

And so the trunk I had brought to the Brothers and then to UCD accompanied me on yet another quest. Leaving it in the flat provided by the college and setting out in search of basic provisions, the first person I noticed in Trumpington Street was Conal Ó Catháin, also from New Ross. I hadn't seen him since my mid-teens but he was easily recognizable with his shock of red hair, and I learned that he was now an architecture postgraduate. Turning into the little shop, I stepped aside as a distinguished-looking elderly gentleman emerged, carrying a women's magazine, and I recognized Herbert Butterfield, not long retired as master. And so the familiar and the exotic combined in my first impressions of Cambridge, and this proved the pattern of the following four years. I could smile at the cliché of the flagstone under the gate, worn hollow by scholars shuffling through for nearly seven hundred years, but I was somewhat in awe at joining the oldest college in Cambridge. And indeed it was to prove, especially in respect of its fellowship and social occasions, a rather fusty, desiccated environment, in which I was never very comfortable. For years now my University Library Card (the basic Cambridge ID) has described me as belonging to egalitarian Clare Hall, where I have been a visiting fellow and am since a Life Member. Yet, though I may resist it, I remain a 'Petrean', including, doubtless, in ways I don't recognize.

Some of the history fellows were welcoming; Joe Lee, in particular, in his role as tutor. Either from him, or from Brian Wormwold, who had been one of my external examiners at UCD, I heard during those first days a classic Desmond Williams story, which illuminated my dim sense of unease at the UCD-Peterhouse connection. He was a frequent visitor to Cambridge, but this time, just before I arrived, was special because he was on his way back from the German archives, determined to do something substantial at last on his early research topic. He brought with him a small suitcase full of filing cards and this, the story went, had fallen to the floor in his room and burst open, scattering the cards which, alas, had not been numbered. The task of reconstituting their sequence proving too much, Desmond stuffed them back into the suitcase any old way, sighing at the exigencies of fate. 'And, of course, he'll probably never open it again.' So the legend of the lovable, incompetent and unfulfilled genius was added to (mainly, perhaps, by Desmond himself) and, it was to strike me over time, one Cambridge stereotype of the quaint nature of the Irish character reinforced.

[67]

Some months later I was one of the chosen few asked by historian Kitson Clark to stay back for a drink after the weekly seminar held in his wonderful rooms over Trinity's main gate. Now in his seventies, a rubicund, contented Pickwick, he spoke with great fondness of Oliver, *our* mutual friend, but also of Gearóid Ó Tuathaigh, 'so brilliant, so colourful, so very Irish'. I sensed immediately what he was to make clearer on subsequent occasions (we also shared a fondness for good whiskey): that I was somewhat of a disappointment, rather too quiet, almost *English* – 'but then you are from the south-east where the Normans landed'. I think that most Irish students in my time experienced some version of this traditional colonial stereotype, rarely used or intended offensively, but fondly, as a welcome relief from the more prosaic aspects of English national character.

This insider/outsider dichotomy has long been inescapably part of the dilemma of all Irish people living in England, whatever their background. Ian d'Alton's Protestantism, for example, made him feel it in ways hidden from me. Outside charmed circles such as Cambridge, it was a difficult time to be Irish in Britain, with terrorist attacks on the 'mainland' exacerbating traditional anti-Irish sentiment. I experienced little of that, but felt defensive nonetheless, and confused. Once more I was forced to examine my own response to contemporary events even as I researched some of the historical roots of the conflict. Exile always sharpens identity, though not necessarily in the way prescribed by nationalism.

I don't remember the research proposal I made in my original application to Cambridge, only that it involved further work on Ireland and empire. Shortly after arriving I developed an idea for a different kind of focus, a comparative study of British stereotypes of Ireland and India during Home Rule, using literary and visual evidence as well as political rhetoric. Cambridge was particularly strong in Indian history at that time, and I had been very taken by some recent works, like A.J. Greenberger's *The British Image of India* (1969) and Bernard Smith's *European Vision and the South Pacific* (1960), and the ways in which they resonated with L.P. Curtis Jr's *Anglo-Saxons and Celts: A Study of Anti-Irish Prejudice in Victorian England* (1968) and his *Apes and Angels: The Irishman in Victorian Caricature* (1971). The Indian comparison, and a focus on the often unconscious or unstated assumptions behind stereotypes, seemed to offer a way into the still opaque dimension of colonialism in the Irish experience under the Union. My first task, however, was to find a supervisor.

My hope that Nicholas Mansergh would take me on died over coffee in the Master's Lodge in St John's. Burdened with the Mastership on top of his faculty commitments and his punishing publishing schedule (he was then editing the multi-volume edition of documents on the background to Indian independence), he had decided to take on no more postgraduates. I was disappointed, but also a little relieved, finding his patrician reserve at odds with the engaged tone and empathy with popular nationalism of his Irish writings. I met him only one more time, with his wife at a small dinner party in their honour at David Fitzpatrick's house. A third and further revised edition of *The Irish Question* had just appeared, and I expressed my enthusiasm and asked some questions about it. He was clearly embarrassed, and turned the conversation to non-academic matters where, it became clear, he was happier that it remain. It was impossible to know whether this was due to modesty or etiquette, a sense that such conversation was somehow out of place in a social setting, the result perhaps of years at Cambridge 'High Tables', where conversation is so often relentlessly trivial.

And so I was assigned initially to Edward Norman, Dean of Peterhouse and scourge of liberals in the Church of England. Behind the clipped, often dismissive speech and the acerbic humour, he was a caring and compassionate man, who saw himself primarily as a pastor and was to prove a true friend. He was clearly very fond of Ireland, and particularly Catholic Ireland, in an English and High Anglican way. He had got to know the country well when researching his first book, *The Irish Catholic Church in the Age of Rebellion* (1965), enjoying particularly the expansive hospitality of some parish priests. His scarifyingly iconoclastic *A History of Modern Ireland* (1971) had just been published, and while it was, in fact, testimony to his love for the country and his anxiety to be of service in its deepening crisis, it was received, understandably, as anti-Irish polemic. Its basic propositions – that Ireland should be studied as part of British history; that the Republic was as English as the North, only more backward; and that Irish nationalism was both ludicrous and trivial – put it, for many, in the tradition of Sir John Davies, if not Edmund Spenser. James Anthony Froude might be a more interesting comparison. It offered little hope that there would be any meeting of minds between us on the value of examining British attitudes towards Ireland in terms of imperial ideologies and stereotypes. Edward was quick to acknowledge this fact and made no effort to divert me into another channel, but instead went to some trouble to persuade Jack Gallagher, the formidable and colourful Professor of Imperial History, to make room for me, a rather awkward Irish 'garron'* among his stable of thoroughbred revisionist Indian historians. George Steiner memorably

---

* 'A small and inferior kind of horse, bred and used chiefly in Ireland and Scotland.' *OED*.

defined 'a worthwhile university or college' as 'quite simply one in which the student is brought into personal contact with, is made vulnerable to, the aura and the threat of the first class'.[14] Peterhouse, under the brooding presiding genius of Maurice Cowling, met that test for historians; so did working with Jack Gallagher.

Often called 'the living Buddha', Jack was an enigma. His background was Catholic working class and Liverpool-Irish, but his friend Richard Cobb could describe him as 'the most English Irishman I have ever met'.[15] A scholarship boy in Trinity College, Cambridge, his studies were interrupted by the war, during which he saw active service with the Royal Tank regiment, especially in North Africa. His early graduate work was on the British in West Africa, but he was also making research trips to India before independence. The key Egyptian chapters of *Africa and the Victorians: The Official Mind of Imperialism* (1960) by Jack and his collaborator Ronald Robinson were written during the Suez Crisis, and the whole work could be read as an argument that the break-up of the empire was less traumatic than might appear, because there never had been an 'empire' in the way normally understood. It could even be read as a defence, as much as an anatomy, of 'the official mind', yet Jack was famously cynical about officialdom, as he was about the trappings of empire.

A non-conformist, to the extent of being frequently a hell-raiser, he was, nevertheless, elected vice-master of Trinity the year I arrived, and held that position until his death eight years later, a veritable pillar of the establishment. One key to the enigma was the extent to which Trinity was his life and his only family; another, perhaps, a sense of patriotism buried deep, beyond fear of ridicule. That he was a brilliant, mercurial, unconventional revisionist has tended to obscure the fact that he was also a traditionalist, not only a Namierite but, in relation to India, for example, in the mould of James Mill, 'writing up Indian history as 'part of British history',[16] according to Ranajit Guha.

I liked him a great deal, but remained a little in awe of him, and cannot claim to have known him. Perhaps no-one can; 'he always wore a mask and did not reveal much of himself to anyone', according to his friend and collaborator Anil Seal.[17] Cobb thought him, 'with his round face, his round glasses and his unblinking eyes ... rather like the Cheshire cat ... he was always about to be there, but never quite there'.[18] His elusiveness was the stuff of folklore, and becoming his student meant joining the ranks 'palely loitering' on his staircase or after his lectures or seminars, in hope of pinning him down to an appointment. He answered neither the phone nor letters; several times I witnessed him instructing the porter bearing the daily pile of post to dump it straight in the wastepaper basket, after checking for 'any scented lilac envelopes'. I'm sure we all considered, at one time or another, writing under such cover to get his attention. It was obviously all part of a cultivated image but also, it seems, an extreme form of the reluctance many academics (myself included) feel to deal with the mess of real life as represented by tax forms and bank statements. When the deterioration in his health forced him to move some years later to the ground floor, it is said that those helping him found thousands of pounds worth of uncashed cheques, stuffed behind and between books, together with unopened tax claims and court-summonses and invitations to the Palace. Part of the enigma was that this systematic irresponsibility did not extend to his treatment of postgraduates, which was impeccable.

When we met for the first time he agreed to take me on but was clearly unhappy with my proposal on the comparison of Irish and Indian stereotypes: 'Fascinating, no doubt, but the History faculty will never wear it; too many of them would feel it wasn't history.' (This was probably true, but it may also have reflected his own views.) Instead, he urged that I should expand on my MA research to deal with the various strands of opposition to Gladstone's Irish policies and the role of ideology in the Home Rule crisis of 1886. In the end that is what I did, though somewhat grudgingly and never feeling fully engaged by it, except in the argument it involved with the two dominant and related approaches to modern British/imperial history in Cambridge at that time.

My emphasis on the role of ideology in élite politics was at odds with the fashionable extreme of the Namierite tradition, usually called 'high politics', and exemplified in the work of Cowling and John Vincent; similarly, the view that there was an important ideological dimension to imperial policy challenged the all-conquering Robinson-Gallagher thesis. Jack enjoyed and encouraged the argument, and sympathized to a degree with my dislike of the 'high politics' approach, but the dual focus on Ireland and Westminster made it easy to dismiss my argument about empire as peripheral to the analysis of developments elsewhere. While he liked talking about Ireland, he had a Disraelian impatience with the Irish question ('the Pope one day and potatoes the next') and shared the common view that British politicians never took it that seriously, despite the series of major crises it provoked.

I have sometimes regretted that I wasn't encouraged to share the dominant focus of Jack's postgraduates, especially those working on Indian history, which was in local case-studies, testing the role of indigenous collaboration. Such an approach to the eighteenth-century Ascendancy, or to the Home

Rule party under Parnell, might have offered a more effective challenge to a view of empire that diminished both its domestic importance and its impact on its victims.

Instead, I tried to test the Robinson-Gallagher formula by analysing the role of ideology in the major controversies and splits over policy towards Ireland in Gladstone's second administration, when it was also mired in the related crises over Egypt and South Africa.[19] Of crucial importance, it seemed to me, was the emergence of a new, and certainly more aggressive imperialism from the late 1870s, whose focus and model was India rather than the old, now largely self-governing colonies such as Canada, the model for Gladstone's traditionally colonialist Home Rule bill. Home Rule proved such a divisive issue, above all, because of the extreme fears it raised over the survival of the empire itself and because it threatened the core, but rarely explicit, values of English nationalism.

As my focus was on Britain, rather than Ireland, the true extent of my unease with the Robinson-Gallagher model of empire did not then become clear, even to me. Only when I read the 1994 *tour de force* on Indian historiography by Ranajit Guha, a founder of the Subaltern Studies Group, did I feel the delayed shock of recognition and anger. Some of Guha's critique of 'the Cambridge approach' is weakened by old-style Marxist moralizing, but its key argument struck me as incontrovertible. This approach is in itself 'colonialist', he argued, not least because, according to it, 'the colonised ... have no will of their own', no role other than collaboration, no politics other than that structured by the imperial system.[20] The history of resistance to colonial rule is effectively made to disappear, while indigenous elements of solidarity and ideology are denied.

By reducing empire to a series of local arrangements, held to be mutually beneficent, and implying some kind of equality, the Robinson-Gallagher model not only lessens the trauma of its disappearance for Britain but denies the trauma experienced by its victims, denying indeed that there were any victims. That's what I should have been most angry about.

Instead, I fulminated against the 'high politics' version of the Home Rule crisis, which was published as I was writing my thesis but had been well flagged earlier in A.B. Cooke and John Vincent's *The Governing Passion: Cabinet Government and Party Politics in Britain 1885–6* (1974). By portraying the Home Rule crisis as entirely artificial, simply a vehicle for a handful of cynical politicians to promote their own political ambitions and frustrate those of their rivals, and involving *no* political convictions on either side, Cooke and Vincent trivialized not only one of the most significant episodes in British political history but also the troubled and painful history of Anglo-Irish relations under the Union. I tried to challenge the analysis with the evidence of my own research, arguing against the systematic exclusion of ideological factors, their depiction of a hermetically sealed world of 'high politics' concerned only with its own power struggles, and the belief that only the evidence of the private thoughts of politicians, their letters and diaries, explained their actions in the public sphere.

The Governing Passion was remarkably conservative, a perversion of traditional diplomatic history, which it resembled in being largely the reconstruction of a series of secret communications that result in (or are a prelude to) policy. It was mandarin history, the history of what really counted, but it also seemed a musty, arid enterprise, the lighting up of a sealed room uncontaminated by the world outside. Yet it was also a work of immense sophistication, often devastating humour and formidable scholarship within the narrow limits it set itself. The extreme nature of the case made, the contempt behind its dismissal of principle and its denial of prejudice, were deliberate, and basically political, and so was my response.

The Governing Passion represented for me the ultimate in high-Tory nihilism, that mood which is, perhaps, the best barometer of the deflating effects of the loss of empire on a once celebratory nationalism. If there never was an empire, and nothing ever mattered in British politics, then clearly nothing significant has changed and there is no need for self-analysis, much less self-recrimination, now. With its pathological dislike of liberalism, its disdain for 'enthusiasm' and its distaste for democracy, such nihilism carried to their logical (or illogical) conclusion the most negative and extreme views of a more complex historian, and a brooding presence at Peterhouse, Maurice Cowling.

Cowling's career[21] and his own oblique reflections on it offer unique insights into the politics of what I disliked most in Cambridge history, and so are worth considering briefly.

I met Maurice Cowling only occasionally, sometimes summoned for a drink after dinner, sometimes at my request to discuss research. Like Gallagher, he was particularly interested in discussing the most radical and consistent of all Tory leaders, Lord Salisbury. Cowling was only forty-six in my first year, but seemed older, world-weary, semi-reclusive and with a major reputation already, not only for his own extensive publications but as the founder of a new style, even a 'school'. His own description of that style was a 'genial malice', and a sense of threat hovered over all conversations with him. I was

relieved to experience only the geniality, doubtless because of the UCD connection and his hope of some new story about Desmond Williams, which
occasionally I could supply thanks to visits from Michael Laffan, then in
Norwich.

Cowling has always been clearer about what he was against than what he
was for. The reluctant-seeming fragments of autobiography in his continuing
'intellectual history of modern England', *Religion and Public Doctrine in Modern
England* (vol. I, 1980; vol. II, 1985; vol. III, 2001), stressed repeatedly his hatred
of the liberalism that he considered to be pervasive not only in politics but in
academic writing and the Anglican Church. He defined such liberalism as
marked by 'moralism, social concern and concern for human freedom' (the last
two obviously negated by the first) and lacking in irony or subtlety.

He had once considered the priesthood, and a passionate conservative
Anglicanism informed all his work. He hated above all the 'Anglican guilt,
sociological *chic* and Christian capitulation to humanistic liberalism of the prevailing establishments', and remained grateful to the 'Anglican reactionaries'
who taught him as an undergraduate and cured him of 'middle-class guilt,
élitist liberalism and everything that Toynbee stood for'.[22] They may also
explain why, in some respects, he could sound like the intellectual wing of the
anti-liberal mandarins who controlled the Irish Catholic Church. In recent
years he has been seen as a major influence on some of the young Tory 'radicals' who emerged under Thatcher and particularly that not untypical Peterhouse product, Michael Portillo.

Butterfield, rather than Namier, is the historiographical key to Cowling.
Like Namier, Cowling's trilogy of political histories 'reduced the subject
matter to the depiction of named participants across tightly confined periods',
but like Butterfield he has also tackled much larger topics; the perspective has
always been moral and religious, and 'his subject has always been England'.[23]
Perhaps because of his more embattled sense of religion and his direct experience of war in early manhood, Cowling has lacked Butterfield's essential
optimism. The next generation again of Peterhouse historians, notably John
Vincent, has been even less able to relate belief to action, and in that they too
exemplify 'a doctrine about England'.

In retrospect my problems with Cambridge history reflected, at a deeper
political level, a conflict between, on the one hand, an Irish experience in
which the discredited orthodoxy was a narrow nationalism, the established
religion over-dogmatic and the hoped-for future a truly liberal society; and on
the other an English experience little aware of its own nationalism, inimical to

liberalism as the discredited past and seeming (like the Anglican Church) to have no clear idea about the future. More fundamentally still, perhaps, it was a conflict between the perspective of the 'colonized' (which included acceptance of some of what seemed the empire's more positive values) and the view from the imperial centre (which rejected those same values, in part as a cause of imperial decline). I was a post-colonial in a post-imperial world.

My only extensive conversation with Herbert Butterfield took place when I was in the midst of writing up my thesis. We were the only guests at a lunch given by a mutual friend, the Tübingen historian Lothar Hilbert, who had been Butterfield's research student and who idolized him. We met in the ornate gloom of one of Cambridge's grander hotels, and were virtually the only diners. We talked about UCD, and Butterfield was particularly animated when I spoke highly of his son. He listened with apparent sympathy to my fulminations at *The Governing Passion*, but it became clear that he did not really want to talk about history, even to Lothar. Instead he brought the conversation back, time and again, to death, especially his own (he was seventy-five, and was to live another four years). The meal ended in reflective silence.

I never had my PhD thesis published, or any part of it, although I did, perversely, publish a long article on the element that the strict Cambridge word-limit had forced me to cut, the defection of the liberal intelligentsia over the first Home Rule bill.[24] This allowed me to argue for the centrality of empire and ideology, without the tedium and difficulty of relating them to the minutiae of 'high politics'. Like most students, perhaps, I was heartily sick of the thesis by the time it was bound and submitted; like some others, I experienced a hiccup in the loose and leisurely Cambridge examining process, which gave me an anxious six months and alienated me further from my *magnum opus*.

Aspects of what happened to me then seem barely credible now, given my own experiences as a PhD examiner; others illustrate further my odd 'colonial' status. I was told by Jack Gallagher that the History faculty insisted on an Irish external examiner, and was asked for the names of any with a Cambridge background who might be suitable. I objected as strongly as I could that my thesis was entirely on British imperial history, and that there was no obvious Irish examiner. But the faculty held firm to their view and a Dublin-based academic was asked to be external examiner, despite his lack of expertise in my area. I was not too unhappy, as this individual had always been very decent with students and I admired his work.

The internal examiner was Ronald Robinson, although he had moved to Oxford and the *viva* was held there. It seemed to go very well, even though the extern, understandably, appeared to be a little lost on the historiography. A week later I was told that there was a problem; the extern wanted some minor changes to the thesis before passing it, but he hadn't been specific. Several times over the following months he was asked for the details of what was required but failed to provide them. My informant was Edward Norman, who was most supportive in what became a deeply upsetting experience, as job interviews loomed and my debts mounted.

The impasse was broken in a remarkable way. I was summoned to meet Robinson at the house his family still occupied in west Cambridge. When I arrived he was playing cricket on the large lawn with his son, who was bowling to him. I was greeted warmly and invited to 'toss me a few'. As he patted my tentative lobs, he said in his best RAF manner something like this: 'Decent chap our extern. That's what life's about Dunne, you know – chaps.' (Thunk.) 'Seems to be in a spot of bother; think we should help him out, what?' (Thunk.)

Over cucumber sandwiches he gradually made me realize that he was proposing that I should meet the external examiner informally and suggest possible changes to him. Which is what I did, flying to Dublin at my own expense. Towards the end of a pleasant lunch at his club I proffered a short list of changes, asking if he had something like them in mind. He was enthusiastic and indeed the small additions I made did improve the thesis, explaining it better for the non-specialist. After a half-day's work I resubmitted, and was told shortly afterwards that the extern had written a glowing report, recommending immediate publication. It was meant sincerely, I know, and he had intended no harm: he had simply dug himself into a hole, having taken on a role he was not suited to.

The experience left me with a sense of unfinished business, but Cambridge had given me much, not least a challenging intellectual environment and a community of scholarship. Its occasional snobbishness or preciousness is a trial mainly for those who live there all the time. My intense and detailed confrontation with 'high politics' and the new imperial history at Cambridge offered, perhaps, a tougher and more focused experience than I would have had at Yale. It was also one that had something of particular value to offer an Irish historian, being an engagement on a variety of levels with British and imperial culture, and the historiography it spawned. It made me question further my own sense of identity, and recognize more its hybrid nature. It confirmed my interest in the contingent nature of political ideology and its complex relationship with practical politics, and it further opened my eyes to the centrality of colonialism in the Irish experience, especially in Anglo-Irish relations under the Union.

My last six months in Cambridge also involved a different, though related trauma to that of the confusion over my PhD. This arose from the need to sign on for the dole every week, and to apply for housing benefit. The trauma was, of course, less than for many who queued with me every week in the dole office (in Cambridge a more genteel environment than I imagine it was in most places) and who faced, possibly, long-term unemployment. An academic job somewhere, sometime, was virtually guaranteed in those expansive days and at worst I could go back to teaching. But we had a child by now, no money and worrying debts.

We were rescued, ironically, by the generosity of John Vincent, Professor of History at Bristol. We met early on at a conference and maintained some contact; he asked if he could read my thesis. Despite its attacks on his work, he was generous in his comments, and even more in offering me temporary work to begin producing a critical edition of the recently discovered diaries of Gladstone's one-time Irish secretary, Lord Carlingford. I spent a fascinating summer in the air-conditioned chill of Bristol University Library's manuscript room, reading this unique sequence of diaries by a major Anglo-Irish politician which, apart from their great political interest, detailed a love story of such intensity and a bereavement of such sustained and epic grief as to epitomize important aspects of Victorian sentiment and sensibility.

The project foundered shortly afterwards because of copyright difficulties, but by then I was back in Ireland and in a very different academic environment.

CHAPTER 5

The Academic

I n October 1976 I found myself once again in Limerick, where I'd spent my last year as a Christian Brother twelve years before. This second stay was also destined to be for one year only, but it proved an intense and formative experience. I had been appointed a lecturer in History at Mary Immaculate College of Education, long established as a training college for primary teachers and now going through a major transition from the old two-year certification to a three-year degree programme. A recognized college of the National University of Ireland, its degree was validated by University College Cork. It had recently catered for women only, all resident and strictly supervised. The ethos was strongly Catholic, the college being a foundation of the Mercy Order, which still supplied the president and a small number of the academic staff. Its 'manager' (i.e. one-man governing body) was the Catholic Bishop of Limerick, Jeremiah Newman, a combative self-proclaimed reactionary, though one who fancied himself as an intellectual, and who had been an academic.

Optimistic reflections on how much both I and the country had changed in the twelve years had to be adjusted somewhat in the light of my initial experiences of Mary Immaculate. It was still primarily a convent where the students quietly conformed and the rapidly growing lay staff could seem rather loud intruders. In the holidays the staff common room reverted to being the nuns' private chapel; to gain access to their offices academics had to ring the convent bell. The lofty corridors and smell of beeswax had an incongruous familiarity. At the sung Mass in a nearby church which inaugurated the academic year, I listened with mounting horror and disbelief as Bishop Newman thundered from the pulpit that the only function of the college was to train Catholic teachers for Catholic schools, and that academic staff (pointing to our serried, gowned rows) must eschew the arrogance and presumption involved in liberal cant about 'academic freedom'. Here was a man whose pathological dislike of liberalism was more extreme than anything I had encountered at Cambridge.

Luckily Newman proved to be an anachronism, though not an irrelevance. His sermon was, in effect, a tacit recognition of his inability to control the pace and direction of change in the college; all he could do was to delay the necessary reform. Co-education (though men were still a timid minority), a rapid increase in numbers, a new liberal arts curriculum and the recruitment of many new (and young) academics to teach it were transforming the old teacher-training ethos. To their credit the nuns seemed to take to the changes with enthusiasm – not least the powerful figure of Sr de Lourdes, who made the transition from old-style disciplinarian (famous for regular measurement of skirt-lengths) to modern college head with impressive ease but without ever quite relinquishing the airs of a Reverend Mother. My history colleague, Sr Bríd, would have liked a far more radical change, believing that the nuns should revert to their original social roles among the poor. It was a friendly staff room with elements of determined cosiness, shared coffee breaks and lunches being almost unavoidable, if not quite compulsory.

Academic departments were small and rudimentary, apart from Education, which had more than half the total staff and dominated the curriculum. The academics came from a range of backgrounds but developed a common commitment to achieving proper consultative and representative structures. This was not easily achieved, with the administration, a monopolistic education department and the bishop all having vested interests in the status quo. I was on the enthusiastic wing of the reforming tendency (just as, in the wider community, I canvassed for Jim Kemmy, Limerick's populist socialist and a fine local historian), and learned a great deal from having to confront so many basic issues in my first academic job. The charismatic leader of reform was my head of department, Brendan Bradshaw.

A native not only of Limerick but of its medieval core, where his family had lived for many generations, Brendan was also a Marist priest, and the College President clearly expected him to be an ally, and indeed on occasion a back-up chaplain. Instead, as part of a courageous insistence on academic norms, he was ostentatiously secular, an historian who happened to be a priest, 'Dr' rather than 'Fr'. Already an established and highly respected scholar, he was seen as the shining star of the academic staff as a whole, someone who had given up a Cambridge career to help a new academic development in his native city. He had been ahead of me at both UCD and Cambridge; though I knew of him, we had never met. Our research areas were different but related. He had made his reputation in the field of Tudor government. He too focused on policy towards Ireland and had come up against the limitations of the Cambridge model in relation to it. He clearly loved teaching, and with his combination of passion and quiet charm was as inspirational for students as for staff. His practical concerns were the balance of the degree programme and the lack of an academic council or any formal representative body.

Some time ago, moving office, I found a fat file of minutes, memoranda and position papers arising from the many unofficial staff meetings of that frantic time. While the details had receded, the feeling of commitment and excitement was easy to recall, as well as a sense of achievement as changes began to take effect, especially in the curriculum, during that year. By then, however, Brendan had returned to Cambridge, to our shock and dismay.

At a farewell function the History Society, which he'd helped to establish, made him a presentation, an engraving of King John's Castle in whose shadow he had grown up. He made a remarkable speech, full of real regret at a move that to most academics would have been a major career boost. He implied that he had been given little choice (rumour had it that his former supervisor at Cambridge had put intolerable pressure on him), said, disarmingly, that his consolation was that he was moving to his 'second favourite city', then emphasized, paradoxically, that all he'd ever wanted was 'to teach Irish history to Irish students'. Making a different choice, as he did, may have contributed to a different – or, more accurately perhaps, more static – view of Irish history as a whole.

Teaching Irish history to Irish students in an Ireland undergoing unprecedented social and cultural change, and in the shadow of the unchanging horror of Northern Ireland was a challenging experience for those of us engaged in it. It shaped our research and writing as well as what and how we taught, undermining many of the assumptions we began with. It is a striking fact that many historians most identified with the attack on revisionism, including Bradshaw, have either taught mainly abroad, or taught little Irish history anywhere. (Equally, most of the critics of revisionism who are or have been Irish-based are literary or cultural critics, with a different, less empirical approach to historical research.) The reasons for the acute differences that developed between Brendan and myself in the intervening years are, no doubt, various, and relate to background as well as experience; his family tradition was republican, and his father had been Fianna Fáil mayor of Limerick. Our contrasting approaches to Irish nationalism became obvious when I took over his special-option course on that topic. Students were quick to comment, and a debate continued between those who championed his more traditional analysis and those who preferred my more iconoclastic approach. My sense of the challenge of teaching Irish history to Irish students was to be sharpened further by moving back to Cork six months after Brendan's departure, to a department specifically designated 'Irish History'.

It could have been otherwise. History at UCC was then, and for years afterwards, divided into separate departments:Irish, Modern and Medieval. This unfortunate compartmentalization was reinforced by the statutory rights of the three professors, which were interpreted to mean that staff from one department could not encroach on the teaching area designated by the others (research and publication had no such limitations, fortunately). The anomalies were most obvious in Irish History, which had medieval and modern elements but was the monopoly of the named department, so that, for example, Joe Lee, one of the best-known historians of modern Ireland, could not teach Irish history because he was Professor of Modern History. Likewise, our leading medievalist, Donnchadh Ó Corráin, being in Irish History, was debarred from developing wider medieval programmes.

I had applied for two advertised posts, one in Irish History, the other in Modern. I was recommended for both, but the heads of department concerned agreed I ought to be offered the Irish job. As with my parents' decision to move to the town in my infancy, it was a road chosen for me, with major consequences for my development as a historian. In the Modern department, as the British history specialist, I would have drawn more directly on my research work in devising courses and been stimulated to publish and do further research in that area. Instead, teaching Irish history (where I had no research experience), I began to develop new research interests and to take on board different historiographical concerns.

It had been critical to my appointment that I had sufficient proficiency in the Irish language to be able to teach to degree level through it. This need arose from the department's commitment to a new interdisciplinary degree programme through Irish, which could be combined with Irish language and literature by students wishing to take a full Irish-language degree. The new programme, called, awkwardly, 'An Léann Dúchais agus Ábhair Gaolmhara' (literally, native learning and related subjects), was co-ordinated by Gearóid Ó Crualaoich and had a core in Folklore/Ethnography, with supplementary units in subjects like Music, Geography and Economics as well as History. Problems arose, notably too few students combined with too complex a structure, and accountability (never clearly defined) to Bórd na Gaeilge, a statutory body which had, essentially, a political agenda in promoting the Irish language. But the new programme posed interesting challenges and led to new kinds of research by both staff and students.

The course I devised for it combined my existing interest in imperialism and Ireland with a new interest in the nature of the response of the Gaelic élites to conquest and colonization, as revealed in one of the few sources available – bardic poetry and the political poetry that came after it. In part, this also built on my immersion in Gaelic poetry from the colonial period, which was such a feature of my education in the Christian Brothers; indeed my whole experience then equipped me with the language skills that got me the job. This focus on literary sources also gave me the opportunity to teach with texts and to focus on the reconstruction and contextualization of a very particular political ideology. Having to design such a course from scratch was the first stage in a new research interest, and so it happened that my first publication was not on Home Rule but on Gaelic poetry, mainly of the sixteenth and seventeenth centuries.[1]

I was encouraged to offer the course on Gaelic poetry by my departmental colleagues, three remarkable historians. Donnchadh Ó Corráin's wide learning and radical iconoclasm were redrawing the map of Early Christian Ireland; Kenneth Nicholls had an unrivalled knowledge of the sources for Gaelic Ireland in the late medieval and early modern period; while John A. Murphy, the head of department, had not only done important work on the seventeenth-century sources but had also written an excellent two-volume textbook in Irish. All three featured in the Gill and Macmillan History Series launched around this time, and, together with Joe Lee, were largely responsible for making it the popular and scholarly success that it was.[2]

John A. was a supportive head of department and an exciting, engaged teacher, combining some traits of the classical pedagogue (including an extensive repertoire of quotations in Latin, Irish and English) with the gifts of the modern mass-communicator. Coming from a strong republican background in West Cork, his initial historical and political instincts were nationalist, though always with a robust individualist turn. His growing public role, in the media and in the Senate, was shaped mainly by his response as a historian to the deepening of the crisis in Northern Ireland during the 1980s.

His ability to rethink his views, often radically, his willingness to entertain and to honour opposing viewpoints, and to take up unpopular positions, made a significant contribution to the redefinition and repositioning of Irish nation-

John A. Murphy.

alism, and the sea-change in public opinion regarding republican violence. He too has been one of the real architects of the peace process. As a trenchant, popular critic of the dishonesties of traditional nationalist rhetoric, he was probably more influential than Conor Cruise O'Brien, being more main-stream, always recognizably speaking from *inside* the tradition, a man of the people who effortlessly and annually meets Corkery's litmus test of being at home at a Munster hurling final. The fact that 'one of their own' moved so close to O'Brien's position (though largely independently of his influence) made him even more of a target for the venom of ultra-traditionalists.

Over the years I've seen some of the hate-mail, and got some sense of the strain involved; having a drink with him in a pub can still be an alarming experience, with perfect strangers suddenly launching into torrents of abuse. His intellectual honesty and courage have been inspirational. Nobody has better exemplified the political responsibility of the historian in a society still traumatized by its past, and at a time when so much spurious 'history' was being evoked to condone, and even justify, murder and terrorism on all sides.

John A. has, on the other hand, been the custodian within UCC of traditional academic values, particularly as a long-time and highly influential governor, and as the author of a history of the college which managed to be at
the same time scholarly, celebratory and admonitory.[3] I have come to share
strongly his sense of belonging to that university, of it representing my 'little
platoon', to quote Burke, or my 'community', in the language of the Christian
Brothers. Sadly this has not remained true of my new department of History,
created subsequent to John's early retirement in 1990, and the death of the
Professor of Medieval History, John Barry. This effectively absorbed the two
smaller departments into the far larger Modern History department, headed
by Joe Lee. As the only professor in post he was able to insist on remaining
head of the new entity for as long as he chose, which meant until he retired
in 2002 (even when out of the country on extended leave and with two other
professors in post). The benign authoritarian ethos that had long characterized
Modern History now became that of the new department; those new to it,
who continued to express their own views, were marginalized.

It has been a great sadness to feel thus alienated from some colleagues, and
there is a sense of irony in having to cope still with an environment so similar
to that which I found – and rebelled against – in the Christian Brothers forty
years ago. But then academic life, with its strong sense of hierarchy and community, and the opportunities for petty tyrannies that those offer, retains similarities to the monastic life out of which it grew.

Like monks, we academics have a highly developed sense of vocation and
self-worth. We are privileged, paid better than most to do interesting and
varied work, that we largely choose for ourselves, and have dedicated time for
research and writing. But this very freedom and autonomy often makes us
strangely dissatisfied, bad at working together and at exercising authority, and
prone to paranoia. To others – including non-academic university colleagues
– we can appear to lack a sense of proportion, and a sense of humour. I am
conscious that in trying to describe aspects of my academic career I may
exemplify such lacks and, being still involved, that I have not the sense of distance that I have in relation to my time in the Christian Brothers.
Undoubtedly the kind of academic I am has been conditioned greatly by that
early experience. Monks are trained to suppress their individuality in the
interests of their own spiritual development, and of the community at large.
Academics are encouraged to express their individuality to the point that
many lose any sense of community and are content with the satisfying, almost
private world of teaching and research. Coping nearly as badly now, as in my

early days, with the authoritarian mind, I too have tended to retreat into that world, which has its own consolations. In particular I have continued to benefit enormously from working with students, and through them to feel connected to the community of scholarship, which universities at their best still aspire to be. But I have always wanted to develop that sense of community and co-operation with academic colleagues also, and having lost any role in the smaller sphere of my subject area where for many years I was very active, I was lucky to find alternative roles and real collegial spirit in the wider academic community, particularly as faculty dean for six years, and nowadays as a member of the Senate of the National University of Ireland.

An academic community that has also given me an active (and to a degree, political) role is that of historians in Ireland. Throughout the 1980s I served as either secretary or chairman of the Irish Committee of Historical Sciences, the umbrella organization for professional historians in the Republic and Northern Ireland. The role of the ICHS since the 1930s has been to maintain a common approach to Irish history and a trans-border community of scholarship, and it was never more important than during that dark decade, dominated first by the hunger-strikes and then by the appalling and seemingly unstoppable spiral of violence in Northern Ireland. The work of the ICHS was, largely, practical and low-key: the organization of the biennial conference and the publication of its proceedings, the revival of the monograph series, Studies in Irish History, and the continuing production of annual bibliographies. We organized Irish representation at the planning sessions and conferences of the world body to which we were affiliated, the Comité International des Sciences Historiques; we represented the concerns of historians to both governments, whether at the threat posed by quarrying to Eamhain Macha or the opening hours of the National Library. We met for many years, appropriately enough, in the Archives department of UCD, then in St Stephen's Green. This department was the last great achievement of Dudley Edwards, and his bust looked down challengingly at us from the top of a filing-cabinet as we climbed the stairs.

The significance of the North–South basis of the ICHS was, I think, well understood but largely taken for granted. While there was a common professional approach, there was no approved line or orthodoxy. Professionalism and tolerance of conflicting viewpoints summed up the contribution we hoped to make to the wider community, but it was not easy to be optimistic in those days. The fraught political background to one of our meetings comes vividly to mind. Crossing St Stephen's Green, heading for the Cork train after we had concluded our business over lunch, I became aware of a wall of sound different from the usual traffic noise, moving around the perimeter, its source invisible. Puzzled at first, I then remembered the march announced in support of the hunger strikes. The rise and fall of reiterated chants became clearer and more threatening, the one I remember being, 'Gerry Fitt, he's a Brit'.

Emerging from the park at the top of Grafton Street at the same time as the head of the march reached that point, I watched its progress: black flags, grim faces, and those hate-filled refrains. Banners carried the names of the communities and organizations represented, and it became clear that virtually all were from Northern Ireland. This heightened the palpable sense of hostility to the audience of this orchestrated street theatre, the Dublin shoppers, who looked back with blank indifference at this strange, sullen anger, this unwelcome intrusion of Northern realities into their weekend routines. There was a clear social contrast also visible, or so I imagined it, between the prosperous-looking Dubliners and the Northern marchers, mainly working-class, with whose problems most of the onlookers had long since ceased to identify. My own response, as I remember it, was not indifference, but anger, mainly at the exploitation of the dead and the cult of martyrdom, once again, by those who believed their terrorism was justified by Irish history. The routine meeting of Irish historians that had taken place earlier seemed to pale into insignificance, yet I believed then, and believe even more now, that the quiet work of such groups, offered the best hope of ending the nightmare that the march partly represented and reflected.

At that point, like most citizens of the Republic (including, possibly, most historians), I had never been north of the border, and felt ashamed of the fact. What finally brought me to Belfast a few years later, and regularly thereafter, was another cross-border academic venture. A number of us – two literary scholars, a philosopher and a historian – came together to plan a new critical journal, which became *The Irish Review*, and was aimed at that elusive but vital audience, 'the general reader'. Edna Longley, based at Queen's University Belfast, a noted critic and passionate promoter of the poetry of Northern Ireland, was already involved in various cross-community and cross-border cultural initiatives; Kevin Barry, a friend of mine since Cambridge and then lecturer in English in Maynooth, was an eighteenth-century specialist with a wide range of interests and contacts in the contemporary cultural scene, notably the theatre and cinema; Richard Kearney, a continental-trained philosopher lecturing in UCD, already had the remarkable achievement of ten years of *The Crane Bag* behind him. I was the historian, in part because of my friendship with Kevin, in part because of my

Planning The Irish Review, *Belfast 1986. From left: Richard Kearney, Tom Dunne, Edna Longley, Kevin Barry.*

interest in interdisciplinary approaches to literature and history. Over the years, other editors have made important contributions at different times (Clare O'Halloran, Brian Walker and Caoimhín Mac Giolla Leith), and we lost one of the founding editors when Richard Kearney felt he had to concentrate on his own writing and on new commitments in the area of film.

The first number appeared in 1986, and its lead article, Roy Foster's 'We Are All Revisionists Now', sparked off a major debate, still raging, on the writing of Irish history, and was a model of the stylish, accessible, expert writing we aimed to publish in both English and Irish. It is for others to judge what contribution *The Irish Review* has made, academically, culturally or politically. Trying, as we do, to cater for the widest possible range of themes, approaches and views, can give a feeling of serendipity and allow too little scope, at times, to follow through on the full range of debates that have been introduced. Certain core concerns provide the clearest continuity: above all, the problems – and the achievements

– of Northern Ireland, and, related often to this, the interpretation of Irish history and the changing face of Irish literary studies. As a major forum for the debate on revisionism we have published writers from all sides, and on a wide range of topics: Luke Gibbons, Kevin Whelan and Desmond Fennell, as well as Ronan Fanning, John A. Murphy and Hugh Kearney. On the related question of colonialism and Ireland, Brian Walker and Liam Kennedy have argued that this is an inappropriate model, while David Lloyd, Colin Graham and Terry Eagleton have contributed pioneering articles arguing the relevance of post-colonial theories to Ireland.

Some of the articles that I remember best did not have Irish themes; Hubert Butler's haunting essay on the Holocaust, 'The Children of Drancy' (No. 4); Neal Ascherson's stylish account of the left in Eastern Europe (No. 12). Other contributions that concerned Ireland have been outside, or perhaps above, the clamour of debate, like Tim Robinson's profound and magical discussion of Irish placenames in 'Listening to the Landscape' (No. 14) and Christopher Harvie's bravura attempt at doing a literary Braudel on the Irish Sea (No. 19).

As with teaching, I feel that I've gained more from *The Irish Review* than I've put into it. It has made me engage with a range of writing and expertise far beyond my usual interests, and has put me in touch with many talented and remarkable people beyond the staid groves of academe.

A contact I valued particularly was with Hubert Butler. We corresponded occasionally, and I once visited him in his old family home near Bennetts-bridge towards the end of his long life. We'd both written on Wolfe Tone and on Edgeworth (I had done more research but his were the deeper insights), and he talked particularly about Edgeworth, with whom he was connected by marriage. From a profusion of family photographs waiting to be sorted on the dining-room table he produced matter-of-factly a silhouette of her, executed in the 1790s; she still lived for him. Already over ninety, he had the most beautiful head I'd ever seen, and, though he tired easily, one of the sharpest minds; he still wrote every day.

Such encounters more than compensated for the demands of editing a journal, but my main debt to *The Irish Review* was a sense of the complexity of the Irish experience and the value of interdisciplinary approaches to understanding it.

The reader will be able to judge the kind of history I write from the final section of this book, and some, doubtless, will categorize it as revisionist. The question of revisionism has loomed large in Irish cultural debate since the mid 1980s; it was the only contemporary issue featured in the 1991 *Field Day*

Anthology of Irish Writing, for example.4 Criticism of major aspects of modern Irish history-writing has often been fierce, particularly from literary and cultural critics associated with the Field Day enterprise, and the overlapping group of scholars attached to the Irish Studies programme at the University of Notre Dame in Indiana. The response of most historians has been to ignore their critique, or to shrug it off as a basic misunderstanding of what they do, and get on with 'the practice of history'. Some have pointed to the (to them) obvious point that all research and writing about the past inescapably revises our understanding in the light of new evidence, questions or perspectives; to their critics this only demonstrates their lack of understanding of what is at issue. In fact the critique of revisionism has focused remarkably little on what historians have actually written, and has been concerned more with tone than with substance.5 In practice it has been less a critique than an accusation, a charge of political bias. As one of its most prominent targets put it early in the debate, it was used mainly as 'a smear word for those supposedly unsound on the national question'.6 There has been little mutual understanding or development in the arguments, and the debate would now be seen by many as passé and rather arid (though there are still interesting interventions). However, the question seems to be worth addressing briefly, if only because it may affect the response to what I have to say.

So, am I a revisionist? I have certainly been described as such, particularly in relation to two short pieces published early in my career on the ideology of Wolfe Tone and on the politics of Gaelic poetry in the early modern period. In the only extensive critique of revisionism by a historian, Brendan Bradshaw cited the former as an example of the 'invincible scepticism' and 'corrosive cynicism' that marked 'the revisionist enterprise' in its treatment of a 'nationalist hero'. The other piece, he believed, 'sought to demonstrate the archaism of Gaelic mentality ... and, therefore, its inability to develop national consciousness'.7

I dispute these interpretations, while recognizing that my alienation from the traditional nationalism I grew up with has undoubtedly influenced my historical writing at times, most clearly my 1982 essay on Tone. The introductory section mentioned, in passing, 'contemporary tragedy and horror'.8 I accept that my attempt to show that Tone was a complex figure and a product of his own time was also an oblique attempt to complicate the political debate of my own day. I believe that this is a legitimate aspiration for a historian (apart from it being an inescapable, if rarely acknowledged aspect of much history-writing), so long as it was subordinate to the basic scholarly endeavour, as I

Making last-minute changes to my paper on Wolfe Tone, Conference of Irish Historians, Belfield 1981. [Photo: Michael Laffan]

hope and believe it was in this case. My argument that Tone was a 'colonial outsider' alienated from his Ascendancy background, his sense of nationalism poorly developed, his radicalism constrained by strong authoritarian tendencies, was certainly meant to be provocative. But it was based, above all, on a detailed textual and contextual analysis of his political writings, and that analysis still stands up, even after Tom Bartlett's important broadening of the context of Tone's republicanism,[9] and the much greater detail and nuance of Marianne Elliott's massive biography.[10] Or so I like to think.

My article on bardic poetry disputed the claim that its politics was proto-nationalist, and stressed, instead, the localism, pragmatism and traditionalism of the Gaelic world view.[11] My intention was not to 'demonstrate' that Gaelic politics were 'archaic', much less to 'target' Irish 'vernacular culture', as Luke Gibbons claims.[12] Rather, I sought to trace the response of a sophisticated tradition, which had coped remarkably well with the earlier phase of colonization from the twelfth century, to the more radical, sustained and ideologically driven assault of the Elizabethans. The response of the poets, reflecting their masters, was increasingly one of trauma and loss, of nostalgia and fatalism and religious appeal, which all came to focus on the millenarian hope of return and restoration vested, with rapidly diminishing conviction, in the Stuarts. All of this, of course, was ultimately to feed into the Irish nationalist tradition, but it was also in time to be distorted by it. In retrospect I consider that article (and more recent ones I've published on Gaelic poetry and song in the late eighteenth and early nineteenth centuries)[13] as an attempt to rescue the Gaelic tradition from the distortions, which have also had the effect of marginalizing it further and hastening its decline. The real traducers of 'vernacular culture' have been those nationalists who have colonized and exploited it, without bothering to understand it.

Other things I've written have also included a rebuttal of nationalist perspectives and explanations, and this certainly reflects my own politics as well as the response of modern historians generally to crudities of traditional nationalist historiography. But much of my academic writing has had a different focus, being an attempt to see Irish historical experience through the prism of literature (and, more recently, of art).[14] My use of literary sources and advocacy of interdisciplinary approaches has made me unusual among Irish historians, most of whom also reject the colonial paradigm I see as the key context for Irish cultural development. All of this should bring me closer to the position of Bradshaw, and to the Field Day critics of revisionism, but my understanding of colonialism is at odds with the nationalist view that they echo, and I have little empathy with their political traditionalism.

Bradshaw's article is titled, honestly and appropriately, 'Nationalism and Historical Scholarship'. This relationship has also been a major concern of those who have used the language of modern literary and cultural theory to attack some higher-profile Irish historians. Bradshaw's defence of the traditional 'liberation' core of the story of Ireland as representing 'the historical consciousness' of 'the national community'[15] may sound very different from Seamus Deane's proffering of 'nation, nationalism and tradition' as among 'those continuities that make meta-narratives possible',[16] but the impulse and conclusion are shared. Deane's political traditionalism is even more overt (and surprising) in the broadening of his most vehement attack on revisionism (and particularly on Roy Foster) into an excoriation of 'liberalism' and 'its buzz-word … pluralism'.[17] In a similar vein Luke Gibbons has attacked the 'liberal humanist ethic' of 'the revisionist enterprise' in his defence of 'the variegated pattern of nationalism'.[18] Such invocations of fashionable (or once fashionable) Marxist slogans do little to establish a connection between revisionism and liberalism. Terry Eagleton's suggestion of a common 'ethical relativism' is interesting on a number of counts, but his attack (as a 'radical') on 'liberal revisionists', 'liberal pluralists' and 'emancipated Irish liberals' owes as much to Field Day as to Marx. The rhetoric is standard ('What is wrong with these scholars is not that they are revisionists but that they are middle-class liberals'), but the conclusions are strange. Not only is there nothing wrong with being a middle-class 'radical', but middle-class nationalists (a traditional Marxist target) also have right on their side. Nationalism is, perhaps, 'ephemeral', but it is also now for Eagleton a 'radical political aspiration', and 'simply the logical offshoot of the democratic principle of self-determination'.[19]

Nationalism to my mind, is not synonymous with radicalism, or even republicanism. The term 'Irish republican', for example, usually denotes the subordination of 'republican' to a version of 'Irish' at variance with its proper meaning. I'm a republican in that I'm committed to a fully democratic society. I'm also an Irish republican in that I believe that the achievement of such a society in Ireland demands reform of specific structural problems such as the complete separation of Church and state, including public and secular control of education and healthcare. Practical (as opposed to mystical) Irish republicanism has focused in recent decades on breaking the patriarchal system, built by the alliance of Catholicism and conservative nationalism, highlighting issues like contraception, abortion and divorce as important civil rights, especially for Irish women. I have been a supporter and at times an active campaigner on these issues, often described by traditionalists as 'the liberal agenda'.

I am not uncomfortable or unhappy with the term liberal, though it lacks precision and Ireland has not had a liberal party since the mid-nineteenth century. Clearly classic liberalism (the original target of Marxist critique), with its over-facile belief in progress and human perfectibility, has not survived two world wars and the horrors of the Holocaust. Its contemporary use by ultra-conservatives in the United States as 'the political form ... of capitalist production'[20] makes it even easier to use as a dismissive sneer word, as we've seen in the case of those critics of revisionism who claim to be radical but seem most distressed at the damage done to tradition. While some Irish revisionists would, doubtless, reject the label liberal, I accept that it can be used in a way that describes my politics. Terry Eagleton has written about his life as a progression from dogmatic Catholicism to dogmatic Marxism, with no debilitating liberal interlude.[21] My experience of religious dogmatism, rather more intense than his, has left me with a strong aversion to such mindsets.

I identify strongly with Ireland (and even more with Wexford), sometimes fiercely, sometimes no doubt foolishly, often sentimentally. I exist through its languages, relate to the world primarily through its literatures, art and music; I am fully at home nowhere else. However, like Connolly, 'Ireland without its people means nothing to me'. I relate to Irish people, but not to 'the Irish people', at best a lazy way of making large, unverifiable generalizations, at worst a spurious claim to representation or empowerment. Like Captain MacMorris, I don't know 'What ish my nation?' beyond Leopold Bloom's practical definition of 'the same people living in the same place';[22] but as commonly used, it is for me too often either a meaningless platitude, or the catch-cry of a corrupt politics. It has no tangible historical existence beyond the claims of those who purported to define or represent it and the fluctuating, temporary coalitions they assembled to promote some version of it. On the other hand I am fascinated by Irish experience and have given much of my life to trying to understand it; to be more precise, I am interested in the experiences of people living in Ireland and in particular circumstances and at particular times. And it is as a historian, above all, that I judge nationalism so negatively.

Nationalism is notoriously imprecise and various as an ideology. This indeed is part of its strength; it can be tailor-made to fit any situation, and continually re-emerge in different guises. But what all nationalisms have in common is a particular communal story: myths of origin, of persecution or glory that are all posited on a particular view of history. The nation's story validates the national struggle, and to do so has to be simple, romantic and heroic, in a word, inspirational.[23] Its inherent tendencies are to be totalizing (that is, claiming to be all the relevant history there is) and reductionist (that is, eliminating complexity). If the nationalist account is fully accepted, historical research is only relevant in so far as it supports or expands it; contrary accounts are not just wrong historically, they are unpatriotic and harmful, and it is this belief that has given such an emotional charge at times to the attack on revisionism. Thus Desmond Fennell, writing in *The Irish Review* argued that revisionism 'does not serve the well-being of the nation'. People 'need for their collective well-being an image of their national past which sustains and energises them personally', which represents the nation as 'always in some sense right-minded, and right acting and occasionally morally splendid'. This, he believes should be 'the framework of meaning and moral interpretation'.[24]

Bradshaw has also argued that the revisionist stress on complexity, discontinuity and hybridity as key aspects of Irish experience, in place of traditional narratives of a shared 'national past', has been a betrayal of public trust. Positing, more explicitly than Deane, a conflict between professional practice and 'social responsibility', he seems to believe that the latter has to prevail, even to the extent of requiring of historians the promotion of what in his view were morale-sustaining historical myths. His now notorious query 'whether the received version of Irish history may not, after all, constitute a beneficent legacy – its wrongness notwithstanding?'[25] arose from a discussion of *The Englishman and His History* (1944), in which Herbert Butterfield came close to embracing the Whig view of the national past that he had demolished so effectively a decade before. In a series of public lectures celebrating England's 'good fortune' in 'the continuity of our history' in the darkest days of the Second World War, he pondered the public utility of 'a sublime and purposeful unhistoricity', that is, of the deliberate writing of 'history' known to be spurious but believed to be morale-boosting. [26] Bradshaw does not explicitly endorse this, but he certainly proposes it for discussion in what was intended as a provocative challenge to his colleagues to think about the impact of their work. Bradshaw himself has resisted any temptation to follow the path indicated by Butterfield. His writing on sixteenth- and seventeenth-century history continues to be impeccably professional and more complex and dense, indeed, than that of most Irish historians. Unfortunately others have been less professional, and the systematic and unprecedented use of what can only be called a purposeful unhistoricity for clearly articulated political purposes has marked and marred the bicentennial of the 1798 Rebellion. This is a central theme of the second part of this book.

If a committed nationalist can clearly be a first-rate historian, so too someone who rejects its philosophy can be professional and objective in writing about nationalism, as I have tried to be. What is involved in each case (as for all historians) is a recognition of the need to take account of the biases involved, and above all to be open, inclusive and sympathetic in relation to the evidence. In the practice of history Brendan Bradshaw and I have far more in common than divides us, in that each of us is immersed in, and argues from the evidence. However differently we may read aspects of it, no interpretative statement is made by either of us without reference to sources. This indeed is what tends to distinguish historians generally from many literary and especially cultural critics today. I would like to think that nationalism will be less and less relevant as a touchstone of historical interpretation in the future, and that we are truly in a post-revisionist phase. A decade ago, in a special issue of *The Irish Review* (No. 12, 1992), I argued that we had been brought 'beyond revisionism' by 'new histories', dealing for example with women's experience, or detailed local studies, and that this offered a far more radical challenge to old orthodoxies.

While traditionalists, clearly have reason to regard me as 'unsound on the national question', and so in their terms a revisionist, yet in one key aspect of my work, as noted earlier, I am the Irish historian who appears to be closest both to Bradshaw and to the literary and cultural critics of revisionism. I have repeatedly echoed Bradshaw's concern that modern scholarship has down-played the 'catastrophic dimensions of Irish history', and particularly 'the conquest of the Early Modern period [and] the accompanying process of dispossessions and colonisation'. I have also called on historians to engage with theory, and especially with the insights of post-colonial studies. Where I differ is that I reject, as simplistic, nationalist explanations of colonialism; for me, as for a growing number of post-colonial scholars worldwide, nationalism has been part of the problem, not the solution.

Recent trends in Irish writing on the colonial revolution of the sixteenth and seventeenth centuries do tend, as Bradshaw argued, to marginalize 'the history of the dispossessed' and to reduce colonial expropriation and settlement to 'internal British migration'.[28] I have gone further and pointed to similar trends in the writing of eighteenth- and nineteenth-century history, so dominant that any recognition of a colonial dimension appears to be systematically excluded. Instead, Ireland is seen, for example, in terms of standard European *Ancien Régime* patterns, as in recent work by Cadoc Leighton, Sean Connolly and Jackie Hill,[29] or in terms of an evolutionary modernization process, as in the influential models developed by Louis Cullen and Joe Lee.[30] The comparison with the trends in British imperial history discussed above is striking, and it could be argued that a similar conservatism, both professional and political, underlies the denial of the related basic historical experiences of imperialism and colonialism. However, I do not see this trend as a revisionist conspiracy to underpin colonialism in Ireland while at the same time denying its existence, as Deane, again echoing Bradshaw, has charged.[31] It may, though, at a largely unconscious level, be a response to the Northern Ireland crisis at a time when Provisional Sinn Féin were exploiting the charge of colonialism, with considerable success (and I accept that insistence on the colonial dimension of our past has major implications for how we view Northern Ireland). It certainly reflects trends in historiography, especially in Britain and France, and a laudable though still limited willingness by Irish historians to explore comparative perspectives.

But the systematic exclusion of the colonial model has its basis, above all, in the nature of the source materials on which Irish historians rely almost exclusively, that is, official and élite archives. Few use the range of literary sources that are vital to understanding the cultural dimensions of historical experience (and are the basis of post-colonial studies), whether at élite or popular levels; fewer still use the Irish-language sources which give the perspectives of the losers, initially the dispossessed and degraded native ruling classes, and later the Irish-speaking poor who adopted the former's distinctive political culture to fit their own social, economic and cultural needs in the course of the eighteenth century. Not only are these perspectives largely absent from the official sources, but more fundamentally the colonial basis of the Irish experience is systematically obscured and even denied by these sources in their insistence on the legal fictions that Ireland was first a "Lordship", then a "Kingdom", then part of a "United Kingdom".

Ireland's colonial experience has been unique in its *longue durée*, and its complex intermingling of cultures and communities. Nor was it ever *simply* colonial, and the other normalization models that now dominate Irish history writing – the British archipelago, *Ancien Régime* Europe, modernization and state formation – are all valid to some extent, and have greatly enriched our understanding of our past. In many respects Ireland does not fit the normal pattern of colonialism. Liam Kennedy had no difficulty in demonstrating the inappropriateness of the Third-World model to post-Union Ireland, for example. His main indicators were 'economic structure, living conditions and quality of life'.

A rather different pattern emerges if the focus is cultural formation, including language change. This has been the main concern of literary scholars, and Kennedy is properly severe on the often crude application of post-colonial theory to Ireland, combined with ignorance of historical context. However, the best writing on colonialism since the Second World War has seen it as a complex and contradictory process rather than one of 'simple dichotomy between colonist and colonised', as Kennedy characterizes it.[32] The critical fact about the Union in this regard is that it provided a new and dynamic framework for a colonial relationship already 600 years old, and reshaped it significantly, in particular by a massive acceleration and deepening of the process of acculturation, or, in the language of recent post-colonial writing, cultural hybridization, which had been a feature of the Irish experience even from the early Norman period. This has long been a major focus of my own research, particularly as reflected in the Irish novel between the

Union and the Famine, and, using historical more than literary or theoretical perspectives (but attempting to combine all three), I've been led to conclusions similar to those of recent post-colonial studies, including a rejection of nationalist models of explanation.[33] This rejection is what really makes a revisionist for Brendan Bradshaw, and poses a dilemma for literary and cultural critics who attack revisionism yet claim to apply post-colonial theory to Ireland.

Such has been my background, training and experience, insofar as I can reconstruct it and relate it to the kind of history I write and teach. Doubtless it omits aspects that are important, even to that narrow brief, being based mainly on all too-fallible memory, and conditioned inescapably, if largely unconsciously, by current concerns. It omits of course many of the most intense and personal experiences of my life – relationships, children, bereavements, literature, music, nature – though these indubitably shaped my view of the past as profoundly as those I've emphasized. Certainly it is true that changes and upheavals in my personal life – the breakup of my first marriage as well as the deaths of my parents – have forced me to reassess everything. The fact that my second wife, Clare O'Halloran, is now a colleague, a product also of UCD and Cambridge, and a historian of Modern Ireland, has clearly influenced how I now construct the narrative of my life, having teased it out incrementally with her over the years before I ever had any thought of writing it down.

PART II

Understanding 1798:
Historiography, Commemoration

Think now
History has many cunning passages, contrived corridors
And issues, deceives with whispering ambitions,
Guides us by vanities.

T.S. ELIOT, 'Gerontion'

CHAPTER 6

Histories of 1798: From Musgrave to Cullen

History is a dialogue between past and present, but it also involves, necessarily, arguments between its interpreters. This is particularly true of the histories of events and periods that still carry a powerful political charge, as the 1798 Rebellion does. It was largely a sense of unease at the kinds of interpretation most prominent prior to and during the bicentenary that led me to expand on my original research. Those interpretations in turn made it clear that they were reacting against earlier interpretations, which highlighted sectarian grievances, for example, or the importance of state terror and rumour, rather than the role of the United Irishmen in the outbreak and course of the Wexford Rebellion.

From the beginning, representations of the Wexford Rebellion have been shaped by political concerns. First into the field, and still the most important of the early histories, Sir Richard Musgrave's *Memoirs of the Different Rebellions in Ireland, from the Arrival of the English: also, a particular detail of that which broke out the 23rd May, 1798, with the history of the conspiracy which preceded it* (1801) was an ultra-Protestant account that minimized the role of the Orange Order and of official violence (and distorted that of the United Irishmen) in order to underline its main argument: that the Rebellion was simply yet another massacre of Protestants by Catholics, further proof of 'the sanguinary and intolerant principles of popery'.

A Waterford landlord and long-serving member of parliament for Lismore in the Devonshire interest, Musgrave had been a hardline magistrate against the Rightboy movement, which he considered a French-backed Catholic conspiracy, and was a prominent polemicist for Protestant Ascendancy. His history of 1798 was in part an argument against Catholic Emancipation, which had been promised as part of the Union settlement. In researching his *Memoirs* he was given remarkable access to official documents, and conducted an exhaustive series of interviews. As a result Musgrave's is a massive documentary history containing transcripts of documents now lost, and today is recognized as a major source on the Rebellion, enhanced by a recent scholarly edition with an elaborate index.[1] Musgrave is also now considered an astute commentator, behind his tedious eruptions of anti-Catholic polemic. For a long time the loyalist accounts he used, including those of depositions and courts-martial, were discounted as *simply* sectarian, treated as if Musgrave had actually written rather than cited them. The process of according these accounts their true value has only begun.

Notoriously, Musgrave's ultra-Ascendancy politics led him to link 1798 to the 1641 rising, with its potent Protestant myth of mass-extermination by Catholics, but he was far from being alone in connecting 1798 to 'the different rebellions in Ireland from the arrival of the English'. The events of 1798 were seen as a further response to the experience of colonialism in the accounts of prominent rebel leaders like Thomas Cloney and Miles Byrne, and in the anti-settler, anti-Protestant sentiments of Irish Jacobite verse and of ballads in English;[2] it is the perspective of novels featuring the Rebellion by Protestant writers like Maria Edgeworth and Charles Robert Maturin;[3] it is a perspective shared by Thomas Moore's *Captain Rock*,[4] and by Amhlaoibh Ó Súilleabháin's tales of magical realism.[5] Leaving aside Musgrave's anti-Catholic polemic, this was the dominant contemporary viewpoint.

Edward Hay published the main Catholic rebuttal of Musgrave in his *History of the Insurrection of the County of Wexford* (1803). He began by defending his own prominent role in Wexford politics throughout the 1790s in terms of his family's loss of their lands during the Cromwellian confiscations, and his subsequent awareness of his 'civil degradation as a Catholic'. Hay was typical of the new generation of wealthy, continentally educated and radicalized Catholics, and he may well have become 'a United Irishman in the civilian sense'.[6] His anxiety to distance himself from the rebel leadership may have led him to minimize the role of the United Irishmen; he certainly played down the role of Catholic sectarianism. Instead he portrayed the Rebellion as a spontaneous outbreak by an infuriated peasantry, goaded beyond endurance by injustice and the brutality of crown forces.

While far from being the whole story, this interpretation is valuable because it focuses attention on the role of the widespread popular terror, rippling southward from the Wicklow border, fuelled by rumour of Orange atrocities, and which had a parallel in the 'great fear' that characterized key phases of the spread of the French Revolution. Hay's main value is as an eyewitness to key aspects of the Rebellion, especially in the vicinity of Wexford town, and as an early questioner of other witnesses. On New Ross and Scullabogue his narrative is vague and second-hand for the most part, but interesting for Hay's trenchant criticism of the army's conduct after the battle, and for his attempt to minimize the scale of Scullabogue and to blame it on lower-class criminals and cowards. It is the account that would most likely have best represented the views of my ancestor John Rice, had he lived.

Thomas Cloney's *Personal Narrative* (1832) is indispensable on the battle of New Ross, in which he played a major role on the rebel side. He too was concerned to deny that he had been a United Irishman, as he did at his court-martial (the proceedings are published as an appendix) over thirty years earlier, but, leaving aside the fact that no proof to the contrary was produced then or has emerged since, this anxiety distorts one aspect of his account only. Its value lies mainly in the way it frames his experience within that of his local community and charts the course of the Rebellion in human as much as military terms. He portrays his leadership role as one forced on him by his neighbours, towards whom he is sympathetic but patronizing. His criticism of their ferocity and lack of control reflects the views of the wealthy middleman class to which he belonged, and which formed a core element of the rebel leadership. Even in its special pleading, his account is so dense with anecdote and incident as to constitute an important contribution especially to the social history of the Rebellion. With its core argument that the '98 Rebellion was above all a consequence of misgovernment, it can also be read as a contribution to the O'Connellite campaign for Repeal of the Union.

The Memoirs of Miles Byrne, Chef de Bataillon in the service of France, edited by his wife (1863) has recently been invested with great authority[7] as the first account to claim a significant role for the United Irishmen in the Wexford Rebellion. Dictated to his wife more than sixty years after the events they claimed to describe, these memoirs are full of retrospective judgments on strategy and tactics that owe everything to hindsight, and can reflect little of the actual experiences of the idealistic teenager who fought with Father Murphy's 'gallant little Irish army'. As Tom Bartlett has pointed out, these memoirs were also shaped by Byrne's immersion in French military culture throughout his adult life, and this included a strong 'distaste for insurgency', so that Byrne 'constantly stressed the military discipline and good order maintained by the Irish rebels, in effect denying that they were insurgents'.[8] On the other hand he doesn't show that they were United Irishmen either. In the first part of his account Byrne certainly emphasized his recruitment into 'the United Irish', and claimed that the organization was widespread in his area, but in his description of the actual Rebellion it was rarely mentioned. His hero, Father John Murphy, was never linked by him to the United Irishmen but described as 'a worthy simple, pious man', driven to Rebellion by the activities of the yeomanry. While clear that nothing could be further from their views than a 'religious war', Byrne repeatedly defended the priest-leaders as 'chiefs to lead us to victory', and he also portrayed the Rebellion as a matter of self-defence against a 'war of extermination' by 'cruel Orangemen'. He summarized his argument best himself:

> that the Irish people were not making a religious struggle but were carrying on a just war of self-defence against the most unheard of tyranny.

There is much evidence in Byrne, as we will see, that the campaign lacked any clear direction and organization. He complained, 'we were often at a loss to know from whom the orders came'; there was no command structure, a lack of basic provision like field-hospitals, and no supply of even rudimentary uniforms or badges. As in Cloney, such organization as existed was described in terms of local loyalties and the leadership of 'sons of gentlemen farmers'.[9]

A major source on the United Irishmen and '98 is Richard Robert Madden's seven-volume *The United Irishmen, their Lives and Times* (1842-60). Medically trained and widely travelled, Madden held a post with the Loan Board in Dublin for thirty years. While he also published travel books and literary studies, his main focus was on the Rebellion of 1798, the year of his birth. But Madden did not write a narrative or synoptic history of the Rebellion, and his somewhat chaotic mass of documentary evidence included far more examples of the anxiety of United Irishmen to distance themselves from the Rebellion than it did of their involvement, particularly in Wexford, on which he had little. That little tended to support earlier Catholic and rebel accounts.

> It has been stated by Hay, Cloney and Teeling, and truly stated by them, that there is no systematic concert between the rising of the people in the county Wexford and the plan of general insurrection formed in Dublin[10]

In a later edition he declared, 'The rebellion in Wexford was caused by the savage cruelties wantonly and barbarically committed on the people by the armed Orangemen'; and he quoted Hay approvingly, 'that it was no more than a tumultary and momentary exertion of popular resistance to a state of things found or considered insupportable ...'[11] He also echoed Hay on Scullabogue, and quoted a letter from Cloney, to him in 1843 on that Massacre. His interviews with survivors and relatives, including eyewitnesses of the mass burials after the battle of New Ross, are particularly valuable.[12]

Madden's second edition was influenced by Brother Luke Cullen, the Carmelite who was the first systematic collector of folklore about 1798, beginning a generation afterwards and focusing mainly on his native Wicklow, though with some related north Wexford material.[13] His main concern (like Madden's, indeed) was to collect atrocity stories from Catholics, and he was at pains regularly to refute Musgrave's Protestant equivalents. He linked the 'breakout of the insurrection in the County of Wexford' to 'the rancorous spirit that lay smouldering within the breast of a set of Cromwellian descendants of a portion of that county'. The Orangemen under Hawtry White, who kept out of the battle of Oulart, 'were the descendants of Cromwellian soldiers, and had been formed in the same terrible mould'. The savagery of the yeomanry after the battle of Arklow he ascribed to the fact that 'they knew that they held the land of the Catholics, and if the latter should succeed they would be likely to take possession of their own again'. He never dealt with the United Irishmen explicitly but shared with Byrne the emphasis on Father Murphy as 'our principal leader'.[14]

Thus, in his best-selling *A Popular History of the Insurrection of 1798* (Dublin 1870), the Reverend P.F. Kavanagh was simply endorsing the view, dominant in Wexford since the early ballads, that the Rebellion had been conducted by priests leading an ill-treated and infuriated peasantry.[15] In a period dominated by the revival of republican nationalism in the Fenian movement and its condemnation by the Catholic Church, this Wexford Franciscan had also every reason to minimize the role of the United Irishmen (not least in relation to the involvement of both his grandfathers). Apart from some folklore there was little new in Kavanagh, which was, essentially, a development of Hay's Catholic perspective, suiting perfectly an era of widespread clerical involvement in popular constitutional politics. Its influence (which can be exaggerated) was evident in the nature of the centenary celebrations, which were dominated by the clericalist Irish Parliamentary Party, with Kavanagh playing a prominent role. His 'Faith and Fatherhood' account found brilliant and enduring expression in Oliver Sheppard's powerful statue in the Square in Enniscorthy. Its dominant figure is that of 'brave Father Murphy', protecting and inspiring the rebel figure, a sturdy countryman, carrying both a sword and rosary beads.[16]

A more complex account had already appeared in W.E.H Lecky's monumental *A History of Ireland in the Eighteenth Century* (5 vols, London 1892).

Despite his own unionism, Lecky was highly critical of the role of the government in the outbreak of the Rebellion, and particularly of the barbarity of the ill-disciplined yeomanry and militia. But Lecky's account was not, as has been suggested, simply a reprise of 'the liberal Protestant line of post-1798 historiography', best exemplified by the Reverend James Gordon's *History of the Rebellion* (1803).[17] Lecky used many sources unavailable to Gordon, including Byrne's *Memoirs*, and with what Tom Bartlett has called his 'typical even-handedness' he gave due weight to contemporary accounts from across the political spectrum where he felt they were persuasive.[18] Gordon began his account with a lengthy history of the United Irishmen but concluded that their role was not crucial in Wexford, 'which had been but very recently and but partially organised'.[19]

Lecky felt that both Gordon and Hay underestimated the scale of United Irish organization, and that Byrne's account was more 'consistent with the progress that had been made in arming the population'. His reservations were explicit only in a footnote, which pointed to the failure of the United Irishmen to provide much military training or 'to appoint their commanders or to form them into regiments'. He also found little evidence for the spread of United Irish ideas to the poor. His 'own opinion' was that there was 'little positive political disloyalty' but 'much turbulence and anarchy among the peasantry'. The causes for this he finds in Cloney, his source for the motivation of the 'rabble of half-starved peasants' who fought under Father Murphy at the crucial battle of Oulart, and who appeared to Lecky as 'men who were assuredly perfectly indifferent to the political objects of the United Irishmen, but who were driven into rebellion by fear of Orange massacres, or by exasperation at military severities'. Lecky had emphasized the anger expressed in Byrne about ancestral lands stolen by 'English invaders', and this was also the theme of the contemporary document that he quoted most extensively, Henry Alexander's letter to Pelham on 3rd June 1798. This cited the colonial land settlements as 'the governing fact of Irish politics' in the second half of the eighteenth century, a perspective that struck a particular chord with Lecky, an absentee landlord whose *History* was, in terms of contemporary politics, a response to the campaign for Home Rule and land reform.[20]

Remarkably, seventy-seven years were to elapse before the appearance of the next general history of the Rebellion, Thomas Pakenham's *The Year of Liberty* (1969). Before that Charles Dickson's *The Wexford Rising in 1798* (1955) was the first devoted to events in that county since Hay. Dickson was an enthusiastic amateur, a Unitarian doctor, who had already written a life of the

Wicklow rebel Michael Dwyer. The reissue of his *Wexford Rising* in 1997 reminded us that this is still a valuable work, partly because, like Musgrave, Dickson included extensive quotes from contemporary documents throughout the text and in a series of appendices, to support what he proclaimed to be 'a balanced retelling of this painful and tragic but proud story... told here without a trace of bias, sectarian or otherwise'. He also used 'local knowledge', and his account of the battle of New Ross acknowledged a debt to the brothers Gerard and Patrick Donovan, and especially to the latter's 1948 account, 'A Commentary of the Commemoration'.

While dated now in its understanding of contexts especially, and often simplistic in its analysis, Dickson's work is interesting in its attempt to confront some of the basic historiographical issues, including the role of the United Irishmen. He concluded that those of the 'key leaders' who were United Irishmen were constitutionalists, that 'the clerical leaders' were swept along by sympathy for their parishioners, and that the 'rank and file' were 'on the whole in the succession of the Defenders', which makes their 'fanaticism ... more intelligible than it would have been had their inspiration derived solely from the principles of the United Irishmen'. On the other hand he seemed to reject the emphasis on the colonial land settlement, quoting the 1792 'Declaration of the Catholics of Ireland', which not only abjured the claim that it was lawful to kill heretics but also renounced 'all interest in and title to all forfeited lands, resulting from any Rights or supposed Rights, of our ancestors'. Yet the perceived need for such reassurance could equally be said to bear out Henry Alexander's contention about 'the governing fact of Irish politics'.[21]

Pakenham's *The Year of Liberty*, for long the most comprehensive and authoritative account, has been controversial from the beginning. In the preface to the work that has largely replaced it, Daniel Gahan recalled his 'shattering' disappointment on reading it as a seventeen-year-old and categorized it in remarkably extreme terms as 'a reborn version of the old loyalist interpretation ... best exemplified by the work of Sir Richard Musgrave'.[22] Colm Tóibín has recalled angry scenes at the book's launch in Wexford town, and agreed with Gahan's emphasis on 'the tone and use of language' about the rebels as the source of this anger.[23] Ten years older than Gahan and already embarked on my MA, I found Pakenham's book an exhilarating read, and in recommending it to my mother I was not being altogether mischievous. I felt that she would enjoy its harsh judgment on the conduct of the ultra-loyalists, and of the militia who had killed her ancestor. Despite this even-handedness, tone and language remain a problem, and the text is decidedly dated, not only in what now seem politically incorrect ways of describing the rural poor but more fundamentally in terms of modern research on popular culture and politicization. Yet the problem can also be traced, ironically, to Pakenham's determination to show the human cost of the Rebellion, and to compensate for the shortage of sources that are sympathetic to the rebels. As he was to show even more clearly in his later history of the Boer war, Pakenham has a particular interest in the chaotic and brutal nature of warfare, especially when waged against civilians, and his account of 1798 remains unique and indispensable for its attempt to communicate the human mess and suffering involved, as well as the aspects of communal culture, even carnival, that were also present. Its influence can be seen in Seamus Heaney's moving 'Requiem for the Croppies' published the same year, with its evocation of 'a people hardly marching – on the hike', a people's army in which 'the priest lay behind ditches with the tramp'.[24]

Pakenham is also at odds with recent interpretations in that he gave due weight to the evidence for powerful agrarian and sectarian currents running through the Wexford Rebellion, and his account lacked any trace of the usual nationalist pieties. His uncompromising opening sentence, while incontrovertible historically, contrasts starkly with the celebratory nature of the bicentenary: 'The rebellion of 1798 is the most violent and tragic event in Irish history between the Jacobite wars and the Great Famine.' Pakenham, like Dickson and Lecky, recognized the importance of the United Irishmen, especially in north Wexford, while concluding (as did contemporaries) that they were 'relatively inactive' in the centre and south of the county. The oddest aspect of Pakenham's work was his decision to describe the Scullabogue atrocity out of sequence, before turning to the battle of Ross. This loaded the narrative against the rebels, and went too far in counteracting the traditional excuse that news of army actions in the town (which he called 'a wild story') led to the massacre. On the other hand it may be seen as an extreme dramatization of the fact that every reading of 1798 is lit by the lurid flames of Scullabogue.[25]

My undergraduate classmate and fellow townsman Tom Powell criticized *The Year of Liberty* as 'essentially yet another account of the battles of 1798' in his remarkable MA thesis of 1970, which gave a new prominence to social and economic factors and had a more sympathetic understanding of popular culture. Though it remains unpublished, apart from an important 1976 article in *Studia Hibernica*, Powell's thesis has been very influential, particularly for Louis Cullen and the earlier work of Kevin Whelan, and it remains possibly the best analysis of the background to the Wexford Rebellion.[26]

Informed by recent work on the French peasantry and counter-revolution, Powell's thesis began with a pioneering study of County Wexford politics in the 1790s, followed by a still unsurpassed account of 'the riot of 1793', but its most important and original contribution lay in highlighting the crisis in the malt trade, which affected every social class and most areas of the county, and was, he argued, 'the marginal factor which made the difference' to the outbreak occurring in Wexford, and not, for example, in Kilkenny or Tipperary.[27] Powell concluded with what is still the only extensive study of the role of rumour, and what he called 'the great massacre fear', again using the French comparison. As part of this he dealt sympathetically with the evidence for United Irish organization in the county, and considered it in relation to agrarian secret societies and to the growth in Orangeism. In short, in its multiple and comparative approaches, its stress on complexity and its exemplary use of sources, Powell's study rehearsed the range of issues that a bicentenary, reflecting modern research, might have been expected to explore but, alas, did not.

This is all the more remarkable given the intensity and nature of research on County Wexford in the intervening decades, led by Louis Cullen, our most influential interpreter of the eighteenth century since Lecky, and also a native of New Ross. His early studies of Anglo-Irish trade (1968) and the Irish economy (1976) broke with the nationalist tradition of ascribing social and economic change mainly to political causes.[28] Equally radical was his application of some of the insights and techniques of the *Annales* school to eighteenth-century Ireland in his 1981 volume *The Emergence of Modern Ireland*, which transformed our understanding of diet and class in particular.[29] In his ever-more intense focus on Wexford, Cullen has shown the destabilizing effects of population movements on religious lines following the radical transformation of land ownership in the county by seventeenth- and early eighteenth-century colonization. This was to make north Wexford, in particular, the most evenly and abrasively divided part of Ireland, after south Armagh, by the last decade of the century.

What made Wexford's sectarian divisions noteworthy was that they occurred at all social levels, and that they transformed the politics of the county. Here an important new dynamic came from the younger generation of the Catholic élite, gentry, middlemen, merchants and professionals, many of them radicalized by time spent in France. Part of the movement countrywide that was making the Catholic question *the* radical issue in politics, they challenged local Ascendancy hegemony, and thereby intensified ultra-Protestant fears, not least by an alliance with liberal Protestants, including the early society of United Irishmen. Cullen's stress on Catholic politicization and radicalization was all the more persuasive by its location in a network of family and social connections clustered in certain areas. All of Cullen's work is marked by a keen awareness of local variations. [30]

The colonial nature of Wexford's economy and society, and of the distinctive and intense politics that developed there consequently, were also made clear in Daniel Gahan's early paper on the estate systems of the county. This differentiated the smaller Old English estates based on the old manorial system in the south and east of the country from the larger New English estates of the north and west, although overall, 'close on 90% of the land of Wexford was confiscated in the Cromwellian and Williamite settlements'.[31] This paper appeared in the landmark volume *Wexford: History and Society* (1987), which Kevin Whelan edited with Willy Nolan. Another contributor, the historical geographer T. Jones-Hughes, not only emphasized Wexford's particularly intense experience of colonization but linked this to 'the areas most prominently associated with the 1798 uprising', particularly the barony of Bantry, which, as we'll see, he identified as part of 'a powerful, stable Gaelic heartland', under intense pressure by the 1790s from the new modernizing estate system. This pressure was most keenly felt in the north of the country, and Jones-Hughes argued that 'the systematic pillaging of these great houses in the 1798 insurrection was a reflection of how the presence of the New English was resented in North Wexford'.[32] He also sketched the development of a new modernizing Catholicism in the county, and this was to be a particular focus of the early work of his former student, Kevin Whelan.

In his outstanding contribution to Jones-Hughes' 1988 *Festschrift*, which he also co-edited, Whelan mapped 'the regional impact of Irish Catholicism', superimposing on one another a series of maps covering, *inter alia*, the survival of parish records and the spread of hurling, which combined to give original and exciting multi-layered perspectives.[33] This work established historical geography as a major new force in Irish historiography and helped to establish Whelan as the most distinctive, and to my mind the most important, of a talented new generation of Irish historians. In the previous year, 1987, he had used a similar layered approach in outlining 'the religious factor in the 1798 rebellion'. This was traced partly in a series of still indispensable maps, for example, of Protestants killed and Catholic chapels burned, both clustered in the northern parts of the county. Looking particularly at the targeting of relatively recent Protestant newcomers such as 'the colony of Palatines', he found 'a purely sectarian motive ... evident in many of the killings by the rebels'. An excellent survey of the origins and spread of 'the great fear' in early 1798 led him to call the outbreak of rebellion a 'spectacular jacquerie', and show how it featured 'reprisals and paying off old scores'. Some of these related to Whiteboyism in the 1770s; others reflected an 'ancestral burden', 'this racial sense of opposition to the seventeenth-century settlers'.34

All of this exciting new research seemed to point to a radical reinterpretation of 1798, which would integrate social, economic, cultural and political factors and stress variations at local level. It seemed bound to feature the effects of colonization, changing patterns in landholding and settlement, sectarian rivalry on a range of social levels, and politicization, especially among better-off Catholics. The official bicentenary, however, inspired by a number of historians, was to focus attention exclusively on a single cause – United Irish leadership – and to marginalize all other interpretations.

Its historiographical justification was a seminal article by Louis Cullen, also in the 1987 *Wexford* volume. This hypothesised a significant United Irish presence in Wexford prior to the Rebellion, contrary to received opinion and to the accounts of the United Irish leaders themselves. Cullen had no new documentary evidence (nor has any come to light since) but he threw doubt on the contemporary accounts, particularly those of Hay and Cloney, and argued persuasively that they concealed the presence of a United Irish organization in order to minimize the nature of their own involvement in the Rebellion. Critical to Cullen's case was a list found in the house of Matthew Keogh, the rebel governor of Wexford town, which was important in the prosecution case against him that led to his execution. It was published by Musgrave as 'a list of leaders among the rebels', and Cullen used it, together with scattered references to the military ranks of rebel leaders and his unrivalled knowledge of kinship groups and radical politics, to project an organization of six or seven United Irish 'regiments' in Wexford and to link their distribution to the outbreak and early course of the Rebellion.

It was a *tour de force*, offering new understanding of hitherto puzzling aspects of the outbreak, but it was also presented scrupulously as a hypothesis and its limited basis in the contemporary documents was exposed fully.35 All of its elements remain open to question, and the evidence for the United Irish role is still tantalizingly fragmentary. This is reflected in Cullen's revisiting of the argument in his contribution to *The Mighty Wave* (1996), where he is again on firmer ground in deconstructing different phases in the interpretation of 1798 than in arguing for the late but crucial United Irish organization of west

Wexford. He makes it clear that even the basic facts about the presumed leaders, Kelly and Cloney, remain speculative, so that he can do no more than 'think that the conclusion may be inescapable that Kelly and Cloney were the leaders of the Bantry formation'. Indeed, his original article had relied heavily on the negative argument that nothing except the existence of an efficient United Irish organization could explain 'the well-defined pattern in which the units and their leaders emerged within the [first] three days'.[36]

In an important critique of the evidence and analysis put forward by Cullen, Tom Powell examined the case of Kelly and Cloney in detail to show what he felt to be unwarranted speculation about their putative role as United Irish 'colonels'. More fundamentally he pointed to problems with the list found in Keogh's house, which 'has many internal contradictions and is consequently of questionable provenance'. Why are five of the twenty-two names from outside the county? Why is the well-known Anthony Perry rendered oddly as 'John'? Why does the list include one priest against whom there is no other evidence, and another who died six months before the Rebellion? Why was neither priest on Bishop Caulfield's list of rebel priests, which Whelan saw as authoritative? Powell had no answers but felt it is at least equally likely that this was 'a fabricated "hit-list"', presumably planted on Keogh. On the other hand Powell gave reasons for accepting the truth of Anthony Perry's forced confession, rejected by Cullen, which gave details on the organization in his area but stated that it was incomplete in other areas.[37]

Perhaps the most important thing to say about Cullen's United Irish argument is that it should be read in conjunction with his earlier and uncontested work on land settlement, sectarian conflict and politicization, and not be considered (as it seems to have been in the bicentenary year) as obliterating that work. Louis Cullen, above all Irish historians, should not be claimed as the champion of any single-cause explanation for an enormously complex and controversial phenomenon. There is unlikely ever to be satisfactory documentary proof to support the idea of a significant United Irish organization in Wexford; on the other hand, the absence of such proof is not in itself a conclusive argument against it. It should, however, make us cautious about claiming too much for the Cullen thesis. Before looking at how it has taken some historians, and the official commemoration, into very deep and muddy water, recent research on the United Irishmen is worth noticing.

A persuasive new approach to the question of the role of the United Irishmen had been outlined as early as 1982 by Marianne Elliott, in her brilliant study *Partners in Revolution: The United Irishmen and France*. This assigned a key role to the Catholic secret society, the Defenders, in the politicization of the poor, and argued that 'all the signs are that they were republicans before the United Irishmen, and that it was their peculiarly Catholic interpretation of French promises and United Irish ideals which was espoused by the ordinary people'. Her analysis of how the modern revolutionary ideology of the bourgeois United Irishmen resonated in and through the indigenous Jacobite and agrarian traditions still offers the best model for Wexford, even though evidence for Defenderism as such in the county is patchy. Likewise, she showed how the French belief that Ireland 'might become England's Vendée' was taken up, not only by Tone but also by United Irishmen on the ground, who played 'upon traditional Catholic aspirations "to plant the true religion that was lost since the Reformation" or to bring about "a general division of the land" among them'. And when the French finally came, after the Wexford Rebellion had long subsided, it was precisely this traditionalism in the Irish who joined them that most struck and appalled them.[38]

Nancy Curtin's major work, *The United Irishmen: Popular Politics in Ulster and Dublin 1791-1998* (1994), provided a comprehensive analysis of the shifting engagement of the movement with local issues and popular culture. While she did not feature Wexford significantly, her findings clearly have implications for our understanding of the key issue of politicization in that county. She too pointed to the problem of limited sources, so that the picture 'must be filtered through the lens of magistrates, office holders and informers'.

Curtin's ability to use such sources imaginatively, and to combine them with the patchy internal evidence, is one of the strengths of this exceptional book. At the heart of her analysis – and of United Irish difficulties – was the attempted alliance between these 'petty bourgeois revolutionaries', 'deeply immersed in British radical Whig culture', and the dynamic but essentially sectarian Catholic secret society, the Defenders, who 'sought a reversal of the conquest'. That alliance, together with the paralysis induced by reliance on French intervention, contributed, in her view, to a once formidable organization becoming not only ineffectual but compromised. The problem inherent in trying to organize 'a mass-based conspiracy' was particularly well drawn. Early United Irish successes, she demonstrated, were spectacular: 'never again did an underground republican movement enjoy as massive a following or as formidable or extensive an organisation as the United Irishmen'. This strength was draining away, however, even before the Rebellion, under the combined pressures of state repression, economic expansion and sectarian polarization, and in the end sectarianism proved more powerful than republican virtue.

Sadly, the United Irishmen themselves contributed significantly to the sectarian surge, as Cullen and Whelan had already shown in the case of Wexford. Curtin concluded 'that the United Irishmen themselves were largely responsible, through their emotional propaganda for turning peasant fears into vengeful paranoia, for exacerbating sectarian tensions'.[39]

Before examining the fresh interpretations of the Wexford Rebellion that appeared just before or during the bicentenary year of 1998, it may be useful to take account of the crucial earlier role played by the local Commemoration Committee, established just after Cullen's article on United Irish organization appeared. In particular, contributions that historians other than Cullen made to its emphatic new interpretation of the Rebellion are worthy of note.

CHAPTER 7

Commemoration: Comóradh '98

There are interesting points of comparison between 1898 and 1998, most significantly in the politicization of the commemorations by competing strains of nationalism, and the ways they were manipulated to reflect contemporary concerns. Another common feature was that enthusiasm was greatest in Wexford, where commemorations were planned long before national committees were formed.[1]

A group of Wexford men in Dublin formed the '98 Club as early as 1879, while Comóradh '98 had been formulating its strategy since 1988. For that reason, as much as for its importance in the Rebellion, Wexford dominated both commemorations, and was to a remarkable degree taken over by them. Comóradh '98 (the commemoration of 1798, commonly referred to as Comóradh) was the initiative of local politicians and was representative not only of the various local authorities in the county but also of the nine ancient baronies that featured so prominently in 1798. From the beginning it was guaranteed ten years' funding by Enniscorthy District Council and Wexford County Council, and was driven over the course of the decade as a major development programme by successive county managers.

Comóradh's first significant venture was to organize an event for the bicentenary of the French Revolution in 1989, with an estimated 30,000 people attending a ceremony at Vinegar Hill. Here an elaborately worded memorial was unveiled, celebrating the 1798 Rebellion in terms of French republicanism. The following year, Comóradh became a limited company and produced a development plan, including the creation of an elaborate '98 Trail, connecting all the battle sites throughout the county, and of a permanent 1798 heritage centre in Enniscorthy. Three years later plans for this centre were given a boost by the commitment of government and European Union funding, and the purchase of the old Christian Brothers monastery. In 1995 Bernard Browne was appointed as full-time development officer to Comóradh and a separate fund-raising arm, Friends of Comóradh '98, was established.[2]

Given this level of sustained organization, planning and funding, it is not surprising that there was intense interest in the bicentenary among local communities in Wexford, in contrast to other centres of Rebellion. Part-funded by Comóradh, the number of new memorials erected in the county exceeded a hundred, most of them reflecting local pride (and sometimes interesting local differences); they were unveiled at ceremonies made particularly colourful by the attendance of one or more groups dressed as pikemen. These sprang up everywhere, featuring in documentaries and local pageants; some had clear political agendas (the pike in one hand ...) but most had none, though their particular combination of fancy dress and war-games could have an oddly menacing effect, especially given the gruesome character of the originals of the pikes now carried in fun. The marshalling and featuring of local groups was also evident in the big set-pieces organized by Comóradh '98, such as Vinegar Hill Day. An impressive series of parish histories and commemorative booklets were produced. Indeed, the most positive feature of Comóradh was the impetus it gave to the study of local history and the focus this provided for local pride and identity. The interaction between this enthusiasm of many ordinary people and the political and ideological agendas clustered around the wider Comóradh enterprise was complex, but could be seen, for example, at the elaborate openings, by national and local politicians, not only of the various memorials but of more ambitious acts of commemoration, such as the heritage centre in the reconstituted eighteenth-century farmhouse where Father Murphy lived at Boolavogue, the restored Evoy's forge near my birthplace at Carrigbyrne, or the extraordinary, architect-designed Tulach an tSolais (mound of light) at Oulart Hill, which celebrates the first significant skirmish of the Rebellion in terms of the Enlightenment.

The new heritage centres (the main one being the national 1798 Visitor Centre, Enniscorthy) also symbolize one of the main differences between centenary and bicentenary: commemoration is now a business as well as a political opportunity. This reinforced the drive to commemorate an acceptable, that is largely non-violent, version of the Rebellion, reducing it to the anodyne of 'heritage', pre-packaged, simplistic and politically correct, fit for mass consumption. The commodification of the pike offers a telling example of the dulling of sensibility involved in history as heritage. In the shop attached to the National 1798 Visitor Centre I found pins and brooches, pike pens, replica pike heads (metal and plastic), bronzes of pikemen and the endless reproduction of the stylized version that is the logo of Comóradh '98. Thus fetishized, the true meaning of the pike, whether as instrument of death and torture, or symbol of the resistance and bravery of ordinary people, is lost. This is but one example of how political and commercial interests have conspired with misplaced local enthusiasm to transform *comóradh* (commemoration) imperceptibly into *ceiliúradh* (celebration). This tendency was also evident in aspects of how the Famine was remembered in recent years, but its clear inappropriateness, given the impossibility of obscuring the human tragedy involved, gave it little scope in that context. Little inhibition has been apparent in Wexford, bearing out Louis Cullen's wry prediction that the commemoration would 'tend to simplify things', being 'a strange, communal, tribal activity rather like an All-Ireland, or a Rugby International'.3

The sporting analogy has proven all too apt, as was signalled on the cover of *Wexford '98: Calendar of Events*, issued by Comóradh '98. This featured modern hurling heroes as the central figures, with Father Murphy and the pikemen relegated to a supporting role, and was tastefully produced in the purple and gold colours of the county's GAA teams. Inside the cover the County Manager extended 'fáilte to all visitors to the county', and the Hon. Secretary of Comóradh '98 urged, 'come and join us for this great year'. The organization's first newsletter listed 'ten good reasons for commemorating 1798', one of them being 'that it will benefit our country touristwise'. The third newsletter announced excitedly, 'It's official! The 1998 Tour de France will start in Ireland', and include Enniscorthy as 'a stage to commemorate the 1798 Rebellion', describing this as 'a unique achievement for Comóradh '98. This belated arrival of the French, two hundred years later than expected, and with an army of 'over one thousand media' rather than soldiers, generated immense public enthusiasm, although it would be difficult to contend that it did any more to promote a better understanding of 1798 than it did to communicate the French passion for a sport that, for most spectators, was a momentary, multi-coloured blur.

Hurling is a different and altogether more serious matter, and here the confusion Louis Cullen feared was taken to extremes that upset many people. *The Wexford Echo*, to take a striking example of a widespread phenomenon, carried a full-page photomontage in colour on the eve of the Leinster semi-final against Offaly, superimposing a line of marching pikemen on a picture of Wexford hurlers in a pre-match parade. Over it was the quotation, 'We are the boys of Wexford, who fought with heart and hand.'4 While there is a tradition of '98 songs being part of the incidental colour at hurling matches, this went further, graphically *equating* hurling with fighting, trivializing the Rebellion even more than it inflated the importance of the game, and encouraged to do both by the bland celebratory nature of the official bicentenary. So ubiquitous was the comparison that the *Irish Times* report on Offaly's victory was headed, 'Dooley quells spirit of '98', while the first paragraph contrasted the 'massacre' of 30,000 in the Rebellion with the stunned amazement of 46,078 spectators in Croke Park at Offaly's last-minute goal.[5] After a lifetime of enthusiastic support, I was not sorry that Wexford made such a rapid exit from the All-Ireland Championships in 1998. At least we would be spared further orgies of this particular brand of 'patriotism'.

My interest in Comóradh '98, however, lies mainly in its energetic promotion of a particular historical interpretation of the Rebellion. This became clear almost at once in the elaborate text on the 1989 Vinegar Hill memorial, which featured a version of Louis Cullen's hypothesis about the United Irish direction of the Rebellion published only two years earlier. Apart from politicians and local government officials, the official Comóradh group was composed mainly of local historians, and most notably Nicholas Furlong, Kevin Whelan and Brian Cleary. Furlong, well-known journalist and writer, author later of a well-received life of Father John Murphy, was the most prominent locally. Whelan, then working in the National Library, and Cleary, a translator in Dáil Éireann, were Dublin based but were regular attenders at meetings and had a particular influence on the Comóradh presentation of the Rebellion.

The role of the historians was formalized in 1994 with the establishment of a Historians and Librarians Advisory Committee by Comóradh, chaired by Furlong.[6] It included Bernard Browne, who had published a good short history of Old Ross. Librarians Celestine Murphy and Jarleth Glynn represented the County Library service, which ran an excellent educational programme in connection with the bicentenary, producing a schools information pack, for example, which encouraged a much wider range of interest and interpretation than the official line.[7] Murphy, herself a fine historian, also edited the highly regarded *Journal of the Wexford Historical Society*, which gave a forum to different points of view, including mine.

However, Comóradh '98 itself had a very definite and narrow historical focus, encapsulated brilliantly in the brief text that accompanied its pike logo, 'The United Irish Revolution'. The influence of Cullen's article is again clear, but that use of 'revolution' instead of the hitherto ubiquitous 'rebellion' claimed a yet more radical character for the outbreak. I could not discover

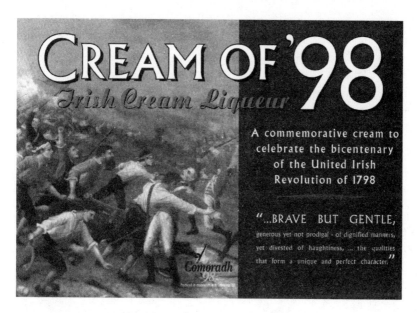

The Heritage Industry.

when the phrase was adopted or how it emerged: possibly its first use was by Kevin Whelan, in a 1993 article, though this referred to the Rebellion as a whole.[8] (The Comóradh '98 papers, under the control of the county manager's office were not made available to me, and I have had to rely on Comóradh publications, and the uncatalogued collection of bicentenary documents and ephemera in the County Library.) This radical interpretation was reinforced by novel claims that the rebels had established a 'Republic of Wexford' run by a democratically elected 'Senate' – the 'reconvening' of which became a major bicentenary project. One of the first tasks of the Historians and Librarians Advisory Committee was to consider the wording for the official notepaper of the Friends of Comóradh '98 in December 1994. The agreed text included the following: 'In 1798 armed revolution erupted and the nation's first Republic was established at Wexford with a Directory or Council of four Catholics and four Protestants and a Senate of five hundred leading citizens.'[9]

Whence came the hitherto unnoticed 'Republic' and 'Senate'? The first modern claim of a 'Wexford Republic' of which I'm aware was in an unexpected and unexplained postscript by Whelan to his 1989 paper on 'Politicisation in County Wexford', but this made no mention of a 'Senate'.[10] It next featured as a similar postscript to Brian Cleary's 1993 article on the 1792 campaign for a Catholic franchise.[11] I first became aware of claims for a Senate

The Wexford Echo, *11 June 1998*.

when I spoke at a seminar organized by Comóradh '98 in Wexford in February
1996. A programme note made the startling claim that I now know was
endorsed by the Historians and Librarians Committee: 'The nation's first
Republic was established at Wexford with a Council of four Protestants and
four Catholics and a Senate of 500 leading citizens.' Brian Cleary outlined the
shadowy and to me unconvincing case for this in his paper to the seminar on
'The Wexford Republic'. This was not published, but mine appeared later that
year in the *Journal of the Wexford Historical Society* and it included a demonstration that the claims being made for the Republic and Senate had no basis in

the historical record.[12] The only contemporary use of the term 'republic' was by Musgrave, who used it a number of times pejoratively, in passing and without a capital 'r', as part of his attempt to associate the rebels with the excesses of Republican France.[13] The organization of Wexford town by what Madden called 'the rebel council', had, as mentioned earlier, echoes of revolutionary Paris,[14] but the documents emanating from 'the Council for directing the affairs of the people of the County Wexford', fascinating and important as they are, never used the term 'Republic' or made the claim even indirectly. Its use by Musgrave was lent some colour by the clear influence of French ideology and revolutionary language on the rebel leadership, obvious in phrases like, 'we the people', 'citizens' and 'the natural rights and liberties of Ireland'. The open issuing of proclamations, not only using such language but ordering the administration of United Irish oaths, over the names of Bagenal Harvey as president and Nicholas Grey as secretary of 'the Council', shows how uninhibited they felt in expressing their political opinions, and that nothing would have stopped them declaring or invoking a 'Republic' had they wished.[15] The claim by Kevin Whelan, also in 1996, that in fact they did so and that 'the short-lived Wexford Republic ... administered the county during the rebel occupation', goes far beyond any acceptable reading of the evidence.[16] But then the claim was basically political rather than historical.

In an article commissioned by the *Irish Times* and published on 6 January 1998 I repeated the blunt assertion that like the 'Wexford Republic', the claim that it operated under a democratic Senate, had 'no credible historical basis'. On 8 April, the *Irish Times* published a letter from Wexford historian, Richard Roche, who cited Rev. George Taylor, a Methodist Minister, who wrote the first history of the 1798 revolution in 1800:

> No sooner had the rebels entered the town but they immediately began to organise the state. A Grand National Committee was set up, and a Committee of Five Hundred and a Council of Elders, and the premises of Mr. Cullimore was commandeered and was known in the Senate house.

Elsewhere in the text Taylor refers also to 'the rebel senate'. I replied, in a letter published on the 20th:

> It is more than three months since I first stated in the *Irish Times* (January 6th) that the so-called Wexford Senate 'has no credible historical basis'. I have been intrigued, although not altogether surprised, at the lack of a response to such a blunt challenge to this core feature of 'Comóradh '98' – until Mr Richard Roche's intervention (April 8th).

His letter nicely explains both the silence and my lack of surprise, with its tacit admission that the only contemporary reference to a 'Senate' is in George Taylor's account (1800). Mr Roche carefully describes this as 'the first history of the 1798 revolution', as if this gives it a particular authority. He equally carefully omits to mention that this is an ultra-loyalist, ultra-Protestant account, deeply hostile to the rebels.

Immediately following Mr Roche's selective quote, Taylor goes on: 'Matthew Keogh was appointed Governor and all the Protestants around the county, who had not escaped when the army retreated, were arrested and thrown into gaol. The priests and friars were busily employed in baptising the Protestant women and such men as were admitted into the rebel ranks.'

The full sentence which includes Mr Roche's other selective quote ('the rebel senate') goes: 'No sooner had the rebel senate sat than they were determined on the destruction of such as did not favour their cause.' I doubt if Mr Roche accepts this as acceptable evidence of the true nature of what he believes to be a 'United Irish revolution'; or, indeed, if he would cite Taylor as an authority on anything else.

The lack of any corroborating evidence from any source, and especially of any document among the many that survive from the rebel leadership that even mentions a 'Senate', makes it obvious that Taylor was adding the spectre of revolutionary France to that of a 1641-style sectarian massacre in his demonization of the rebels.[17]

I pointed to the irony involved in the fact that the 'ultra-loyalist smears' of Taylor and Musgrave 'should have been seized on in this bicentenary year to promote a new ultra-nationalist interpretation of the rebellion in Wexford'. Four days later, I ended a further letter to the same paper:

The onus is on those historians who continue to mislead the public in relation to those matters [including 'Republic' and 'Senate'] to either put up or shut up. Let us see some genuine, convincing evidence ....[18]

No such evidence has been forthcoming, despite Roche's promise of a 'definitive article' by Brian Cleary.[19] Instead he published an unreferenced Thomas Davis lecture on 'Wexford in 1798: a Republic before its time'. In it, though without any reference to my criticisms, he conceded in effect that he had no evidence:

Given Taylor's references to the Senate House and also to 'the rebel Senate' elsewhere in his text, and because the term succinctly conveys the revolutionary dimension to what was taking place there, the name 'Senate' is used in this article to describe those meetings where the leading citizens were brought together in numbers to legitimise decisions of the Republic …

However, he also accepted that 'There was no formal proclamation of the Republic'; instead, 'it was recourse to the people (i.e. in the Senate), for authority that made it a Republic as distinct from a mere military government'.[20] In other words Senate and Republic were *his* preferred terms (as, for other reasons, they were Musgrave's and Taylor's) for what the documentary evidence (which he cited fully) called by very different names! No wonder his last paragraph begins, 'The Wexford Republic remains a tantalizing image'.

How did this remarkable concoction become a major feature of Comóradh '98, despite the fact that the lack of evidence for it was known to local historians? I don't know the answer, apart from its undeniable attractiveness and its support for the idea of 'The United Irish Revolution'. Another reason may have been the endorsement of both terms by Kevin Whelan, first in his 1996 essay in *The Mighty Wave* and even more emphatically in *The Fellowship of Freedom* two years later,[21] discussed as 'commemorationist history' in the next chapter. This will also deal with the connection between the Comóradh '98 version of the Rebellion, the national commemoration orchestrated by government, and the Peace Process in Northern Ireland, which was in train throughout this period. Clearly the Comóradh '98 version was strongly nationalist, and it seems a fair speculation that the historians most prominently associated with Comóradh could be characterized in the same way. However, only Kevin Whelan (as seen below) has given us some sense of the political motivation behind his writings on 1798,[22] and the politics of the other historians can only remain in the realm of speculation.

A very practical reason for the adoption of the 'Senate' by Comóradh '98 was explained by Richard Roche in May 1996 in an article detailing their elaborate and expensive plans. 'The main fundraising vehicle will be a reconvened Wexford Senate, whose 500 members will contribute £2000 each for the honour of belonging to this historic body.'[23] The elaborate and widely circulated 'Invitation to membership' listed (ex) Taoisigh John Bruton and Albert Reynolds, the iconic figure of John Hume and the newspaper magnate Tony O'Reilly, as patrons, and announced:

> The grand convention of the Wexford Senate on Sunday 31 May 1998 will be the highlight of the Bicentenary Year when the President of Ireland will call an International Wexford Senate of 500 to order.

Yet this was notably absent from the events featured at the launch of the government's Commemoration Programme (though the Taoiseach did trace the government's 'political lineage back to 1798, when the first republics in Wexford and Connaught were declared').[24] When the rather reduced 'Senate' of 350 'reconvened' on 31 May, the President was also notably absent although she was in the vicinity, having opened the Father Murphy Centre the evening before. She did, however, 'mingle with the honorary senators at a tea party at Johnstown Castle'.[25] These odd goings on may reflect a sense that the 'Senate' had become an embarrassment. When Brian Cleary, chair of the sub-committee organizing it, tried to turn it into 'a private limited company ... to protect the liability of his committee members', he caused a serious rift in Comóradh '98.[26] The commercial aspect of the enterprise may also have seemed increasingly at odds with the idealism of 'The United Irish Revolution'. While Cleary claimed in the elaborate invitation to potential senators that 'the Wexford Republic re-emerges from oblivion as a profound symbol for pluralism and democracy', a circular from the Friends of Comóradh '98 stated, 'we want to make the Senate as effective a proposition as possible. From the corporate point of view it must be seen as a good way for a company to promote itself ...'[27] Thus elements of farce and commercialism knocked the shine off the Senate before it met for the first – and presumably last – time, despite hopes that it might become 'a permanent forum for the greater Irish family ... a focal point for the Irish across the world'.[28]

Given the relentless promotion of 'the United Irish Revolution' by Comóradh '98, it is remarkable that so few of the 130 or more local memorials erected in County Wexford during the bicentenary echo this view of the Rebellion. In the photographic record of all 1798 memorials, published by the Carrigbyrne Pike Group, only about 20 per cent describe the rebels as United Irish, while 4 per cent mention the 'republic'. The great majority record only a person or event, without ascribing motivation (about 8 per cent incorporate 'liberty, equality and fraternity' in the inscription), many using the same inclusive formula. The memorial at The Leap, site of a notorious sectarian atrocity in my father's home parish, is typical: 'In memory of and with respect for all the people of this locality who died in the insurrection of 1798. Suaimhneas síoraí go raibh acu' (May they have everlasting peace). Clearly most people, even among the minority of enthusiasts who organized such memorials, preferred to focus on the human, tragic dimensions of the Rebellion. And not one of the monuments from earlier commemorations, which are also shown in this fascinating and often touching record, mentions the United Irishmen.[29]

The contrast between these modest memorials and The National 1798 Visitor Centre, in Enniscorthy, the jewel in the crown of Comóradh '98, is stark. This presentation of the Rebellion as 'The United Irish Revolution' was designed professionally to a brief prepared mainly by Nicholas Furlong and others of the Historians and Librarians Committee. Opening the £2.6 million development, on the anniversary of the battle of New Ross, the Taoiseach, Mr Ahern, said:

> When all the bicentennial celebrations are over, this centre will stand as a reminder, as teacher and motivator, to inspire many more people to study and understand the important principles of republicanism and their changing implications for each succeeding generation.[30]

At least he was clear about what the government had paid its money for; the question as to how well it would help people 'to study and understand' the actual Rebellion was what interested this taxpayer. That the centre would have a clear polemical function had been signalled over a year earlier by Furlong, who predicted that it would 'remove unnecessary baggage, like sectarian division'.[31] This was borne out by the advance publicity brochure, which gave the historical outline of what was to be presented by the 'dramatic, interactive multi-media experience'. This made no mention of sectarianism (or even of Catholics or Protestants), or of economic crisis, or the conflict over land, or of any of the many deaths (except, of course, Wolfe Tone's). Instead, it seemed that the Rebellion was a product of 'The Age of Enlightenment', and was fought against 'counter-revolutionary reaction'. 'Wexford in 1798' was a matter solely of 'the scale and success [sic] of the United Irishmen's Wexford Rebellion'.

Not surprisingly, I had rather low expectations when I joined those trooping across the 'bridge to democracy'. However, its inscribed planks, linking 1798 in Wexford to key dates in the struggle against tyranny, from ancient Athens to revolutionary France, promised a more imaginative approach. Its silent endorsement of Oliver Cromwell as a champion of liberty, under the legend, 'London – 1649' even hinted at an unexpected revisionism. The exhibition itself sustained this laudable attempt at an international perspective, although its focus was narrowly on the United Irish theme, and not, for example, on popular insurgency.

Immersion in the 'experience' was rapid and total, as an impressive array of user-friendly technology bombarded the visitor with a great deal of historical interpretation (the 'storyline' was attributed by the *Irish Times* to historian Tommy Graham).[32] To begin with, this is rather difficult and abstract, with sections on pre-revolutionary Europe, Enlightenment-inspired revolution, and the debate between Burke and Paine. It was a relief to turn the corner and see the legend, 'Meanwhile in Wexford ...' This began promisingly, with interesting maps showing 'who owned Ireland' and 'who owned Wexford', and the text included Fitzgibbon's famous quote describing the Ascendancy class as 'an English colony', with 'confiscation their common title'. Unfortunately this was not connected to the Rebellion, nor was there anything else on the socio-economic background.

The Rebellion was introduced, instead, as 'the struggle between revolutionaries and counter-revolutionaries'. The course of the Rebellion was described in traditional terms, as a series of military engagements, but these were said to be directed by 'The Wexford Republic' under its democratic 'Senate', as well as reflecting the 'United Irish Military structure'. Opposed to the rebels were 'Loyalists ... made up for the most part of landlords and magistrates, many of whom also served in the military'. New Ross was described as a defeat for 'The United Irish Army', and the account of the battle featured the 'fact' that 'about 70 wounded rebels died when their temporary hospital was burned down by militia' (a highly contentious claim, analysed below). The non-combatants, men, women and children, mainly poor Protestants, burnt to death at Scullabogue, were reduced, unforgivably, to '100 loyalists ... Brutally murdered'. There was an attempt to give a sense of how combat might have appeared to rank and file rebels in a 3-D simulation of the battle of Vinegar Hill, which the visitor viewed through a forest of real (or, at least, realistic) pikes. I have to admit I didn't sit through the entire fourteen minutes of its mournful music and noisy sentimentality.

I wished I had lingered a little when confronted in the next area by a large 'political genealogy', depicting 'the legacy of 1798'. I wondered had the Taoiseach paused here to ponder whether this was quite what he meant by promoting the study of republicanism and its 'changing implications'. Doubtless he approved of Fianna Fáil being depicted in a direct line of descent from the United Irishmen (and perhaps of his political opponents, including Sinn Féin, being given the same accolade); he may even have nodded (although one hoped not) at the claim that all shades of Ulster unionist opinion were 'counter-revolutionaries'. But he almost certainly blanched, as I did, at the section depicting the line of revolutionary descent from the 1798 Rebellion itself. Following the traditional litany of 1803, 1848, 1867 and 1916 came not only the Provisional IRA, but the Continuity Army Council. (In the aftermath of the horrific bombing by the Real IRA in Omagh in August, the Taoiseach said of the bombers: 'They believe that they have some kind of mandate from some period in history that gives them some right to do this. Of course they have not.')[33] The same kind of nervousness about the complex legacy of republican violence was clear in the attempts of Comóradh '98 to distance itself from the Sinn Féin mass rally, addressed also across a sea of pikes by Gerry Adams.

It was with some relief that I entered the last section, where, the handout promised, 'beyond the play area for our younger visitors, four different interpretations of 1798 are compared and contrasted'. The visitor was told that 'while this exhibition is an attempt to present a balanced account of 1798, it is itself an interpretation. Future interpretations of 1798 are inevitable.' It is to be hoped that they will be treated more seriously than those travestied in the accounts given here on the giant portraits of four historians that dominated the room. Musgrave was mocked for his eccentricities in a quotation by Jonah Barrington, Miles Byrne was praised by Kevin Whelan and Thomas Bartlett, and Father Kavanagh simply dismissed in a couple of Whelan quotes.

Then one encountered the familiar, smiling countenance of Louis Cullen, the glowing colour of the photograph eclipsing the monochrome of the others. Here, clearly, was the icon and authority for the 'balanced account' we had experienced and, beyond that, for the whole Comóradh enterprise. Described correctly as a 'ground-breaking historian', his massive contribution to our understanding of the complex background to the Rebellion was reduced to the single but critical claim that 'he re-established the fact that the United Irishmen played a central role both in the planning and the conduct of the rebellion'. It should be a pleasure to see Wexford's finest historian so honoured in his native county, but it was difficult to escape the feeling that this was less *hommage* than exploitation.

Heading for badly needed coffee, I passed a number of plaques. One acknowledged EU support; another claimed that the 'vision of the United Irishmen' was 'central to the concept of modern European Union'. Yet another incorrectly ascribed the authorship of 'Maidin Luain Chinchíse' to Micheál Óg Ó Longáin, in the only reference to the Irish language throughout. At the next table in the coffee shop (which listed the membership of the modern 'Wexford Senate' over the counter) two elderly American women agreed on their impression of the 'experience'. 'Isn't it just terrible how the poor Irish are always being tortured and killed by the English?' There was little in this expensive exhibition to make the visitor query such views.

The new, officially approved interpretation of 1798 is reflected in very complex ways in the National 1798 Visitor Centre. The relationship between it and the politics of commemoration came more simply and sharply into focus in deciding the memorial for Scullabogue. The proposal to erect a 'suit-able, dignified and appropriate memorial'[34] seemed imaginative, a welcome response to the plea by the local historian Sean Cloney that it was time 'to face that horror'.[35] But the text initially proposed hardly supported Kevin Whelan's view that 'it shows a maturing of the proper consciousness in Wexford, ack-nowledging the Protestant population who were largely the victims of Sculla-bogue. You can't sweep these things under the carpet.'[36]

In the text first proposed by the Historians and Librarians Committee, the victims were described merely as 'prisoners' (by implication, prisoners of war) and seemed almost incidental to the real purpose of the proposed memorial, which was to reassure the public that 'the remorse of the United Irish at this outrage, a tragic departure from the ideals of their Republic, is shared by the people of Ireland'.[37] The implication was clear: the *real* trauma of Scullabogue was that experienced by the United Irishmen.

After some public protest and, it seems, private representation from Church leaders, very limited concessions were made; the inscription on the stone erected that summer read 'men, women and children' instead of 'prisoners', and it omitted reference to the 'Republic', but the 'remorse' and 'ideals' of the United Irishmen were still the main emphasis. This modest stone, hidden away in a quiet corner of the little Church of Ireland churchyard at Old Ross, well off the beaten track, sums up what upset me most deeply about the official bicentenary. It represented a lost opportunity, the triumph of a political agenda over the need and duty to remember. It is, fundamentally, a lie that echoes insidiously through the surrounding countryside, perpetuating the sectarianism it refuses to acknowledge.

We are told that the local Church of Ireland vestry approved the inscrip-tion but, as local Protestants who have spoken or written to me made clear, they felt they had no choice, in the interests of good relations with their Catholic neighbours. In a year when the Truth and Reconciliation Commis-sion in South Africa showed the value of confronting the still-recent horrors perpetrated by all sides in the conflict over apartheid, we proved incapable of acknowledging even the basic facts about a 200-year-old tragedy.

While the modern 'senators' who assembled on 31 May 1998 had their names inscribed in the National 1798 Visitor Centre, the victims of Sculla-bogue were not accorded even that simple dignity. Most of their names are known, unlike those of the vast majority of victims of the Rebellion. Better to have listed their names under even the simplest text, than to have robbed their deaths of much of their meaning. Nothing illustrates more the failure of

Comóradh '98 to educate its own community about its past, helped by the failure of a politicized historiography to meet basic obligations to sources and to honesty.

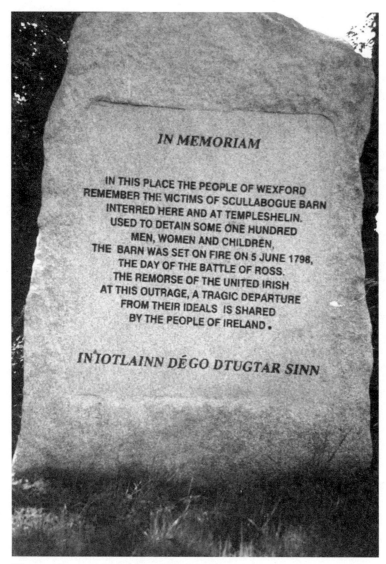

The significance of Scullabogue for Comóradh '98.

CHAPTER 8

Commemorationist History?

Roy Foster categorized some accounts, published around the time of the bicentenary, and that painted an entirely positive picture, playing down the role of sectarianism, for example, as 'commemorationist history'.[1] The term caused some offence,[2] but it is valid to consider the relationship of some of the history written during this period to the interpretation promoted by the official commemoration. This is not to imply bad faith. Historians, as we have seen, shaped the commemoration, and it would be remarkable if they were not also shaped to some degree by it, particularly given the possibilities opened up by Cullen's hypothesis. Certainly, historians were very conscious of the official line.

Daniel Gahan's impressively researched and well-sustained 1995 narrative history, *The People's Rising: Wexford 1798*, was clear about 'the fragments of evidence we have' on the United Irish contribution, but ventured that 'the state of the organisation' in Wexford on the eve of the Rebellion 'was probably similar to that in other southern counties'. It silently endorsed Cullen's hypothesis, printing a list of rebel 'Colonels' and 'Captains', but stated that 'the rebel leaders avoided any temptation to create a county-wide government, or to declare a "Republic of Wexford"' – a clear rebuttal of the Comóradh '98 claim.[3] His contribution in the following year to *The Mighty Wave* on 'the military planning' allowed him to stand back from the detail, and he was again circumspect about the United Irish organization and its role. While 'there were signs of planning and coordination' in the area where the Rebellion began, its progress was characterized more by confusion and disagreement. His tentative conclusion echoed Cullen's basic position: 'the strategic options that the rebels chose and the battle tactics they adopted are consistent with a movement inspired, not by those on the margins of society, but by those at its centre'.[4]

However, in his later and wider survey, *Rebellion! Ireland in 1798* (1997), Gahan took a more emphatic line, claiming the existence of a 'strong United Irishmen organisation' throughout central Wexford and referring to 'the rudimentary system of emergency government' in Wexford town as 'the capital of a sort of "Wexford Republic"'. As this publication lacked any reference to sources, we don't know what led the author to such a significant (if still tentative) change of mind. *Rebellion!* is described on its cover as 'the authorised book of the National 1798 Visitor Centre, Enniscorthy'.[5]

Like virtually all accounts (and many contemporary ballads), *The People's Rising* was shaped by fitting the narrative to the over-neat grid of a military campaign, a tradition which also foregrounded its heroic aspects. Throughout his writings on 1798 Gahan has also been commendably frank about the death and misery caused by the Rebellion. However, his dramatically new account of the Scullabogue massacre helped those who sought to reduce its sectarian character by claiming that it was a direct response to a similar massacre of a similar number of helpless people by the army. Gahan claimed that the shooting and burning to death of up to 150 non-combatants, including women and children, was probably preceded by and directly related to 'the worst atrocity to be committed in the war so far', the deliberate burning to death of seventy wounded rebels in a 'makeshift hospital' in New Ross.[6] He had no new sources for this hitherto unnoticed atrocity, only a reinterpretation of the much used accounts by Alexander and Cloney, both of whom described the burning to death of a number of rebels in a large house during the battle, but didn't mention a hospital. After I had published a detailed critique, showing that the sources cited simply don't support Gahan's interpretation,[7] he wrote an important account for *History Ireland*, silently amending the detail and omitting any reference to a hospital, but otherwise making the same claim about the deliberate killing of 'about seventy wounded rebels'.[8]

While the format used by *History Ireland* (no footnotes and only basic references) doesn't allow for the normal conventions of scholarly rebuttal or debate, the same is not true of the excellent local history journal *The Past*, where Gahan subsequently published a more detailed account, backed by 118 references. None of them mentioned my article, or the clear statements I made about the lack of any evidence for a hospital in the *Irish Times*.[9] The linkage of the Scullabogue atrocity to that of a prior, similar one in Ross was, instead, elaborated and refined, as part of a detailed, and in many respects useful, article, which silently acknowledged the force of some of the points I raised; it was now only 'possible' that some of the rebels burned in the four-storey house were 'wounded and helpless', while it appeared 'logical' that, as Alexander claimed, others were using the house to fire on the troops. But in different, wholly speculative ways, his original claim was not only repeated, but reinforced.[10] As noted earlier, it became part of the authorized story of the Rebellion presented by the National 1798 Visitor Centre.

The detail of my disagreements with Gahan will emerge in my account of Scullabogue. My concern is to illustrate the tendency of recent writing on 1798 in Wexford to both reflect and reinforce the political agenda of Comóradh '98.

A more significant and influential crossover between scholarly writing and the politics of commemoration seems to arise in the more recent contributions of Kevin Whelan, whose initial version of 1798 had emphasized its sectarian and colonial roots. Since 1990 his main emphasis has been on 'politicisation' as 'a central causal feature' of 1798,[11] and this has contributed significantly to what Jim Smyth has called the 'broad consensus ... stressing widespread politicisation' in recent research.[12]

Whelan's 1990 study of 'Politicisation in County Wexford and the Origins of the 1798 Rebellion' retained elements of his early approach. The United Irish threat, he wrote, came from their 'superimposition and fusion of political, economic and sectarian issues', while the new Catholic assertiveness was linked to the 'ancestral forces' of Jacobitism, triggering 'atavistic responses'. In general, he concluded, 'we should not be too quick to see the 1798 rebellion in isolation from its long gestation in the late eighteenth century'.

The 'politicisation' analysed here related mainly to the middle classes and gentry, and, again following Cullen, Whelan emphasized the sectarianized county politics of the 1790s, the collapse of the middleman system and 'the breakdown of the moral economy'. The key group, for him, as for Cullen, were the radicalized younger generation of middle-class Catholics, with their close links to France, to liberal Protestants and to one another. But, while stressing the role of 'a highly conscious political leadership' in the outbreak of rebellion, Whelan did not stress their membership of the United Irishmen. This article ended with what then had seemed merely incongruous, but in retrospect seems highly significant: the unsubstantiated claim that the rebel experiment in governing Wexford town had amounted to a 'Wexford Republic'.[13]

The paper preceding this in the conference volume *Ireland and the French Revolution*, by an odd coincidence, was by myself and also flagged politicization. Its focus was on the contemporary ballads of the Wexford Rebellion as reflecting the partial assimilation of modern revolutionary ideology to 'traditional political concerns', mainly religious and agrarian, which had their origins in 'the profoundly colonial nature of Irish society'. It tried to relate this to the growth of literacy, the spread of bilingualism and the popular radicalism of the Defenders, drawing, like Whelan, on Cullen's work, and on Smyth and Bartlett on Defenderism.

I contrasted these sectarian street ballads with the unconvincing bourgeois versions used by the United Irishmen in their attempts to politicize the poor, and argued that the ballads were 'important if crude reflections of the cultural climate in which the Rebellion operated, and as such suggest certain limits to the direction of current research'. I cited Cullen's work on the United Irishmen and Whelan's on the role of the Catholic middle class.

By a further coincidence I too ended with some reflections on the rebel rule of Wexford town, which I felt 'had some of the features of the more radical sections of Paris in the early months of the revolution'. However, I concluded, 'In Wexford the ideology of the Vendée [i.e. the area of Catholic counter-revolution in rural France] was to triumph and not that of the Paris commune, and the politicization of the Catholic masses was to have a strong sectarian orientation during the next critical half-century.'[14] It is easy to imagine how eagerly the ballads would have been cited during 1998 if, rather than supporting this conclusion, they reflected the assimilation of United Irish ideology. Instead, subsequent accounts of 1798 are silent about them, and have ignored their implications.

Whelan's second 1990 article on this theme, 'Catholics, Politicisation and the 1798 Rebellion', also highlighted pre-1798 sectarianism. Its main significance, however, was in broadening the debate to include the politics of the poor. Crucial in politicizing the poor, Whelan argued, was the alliance between the United Irishmen and 'the educated Whiteboyism of the Defenders':

> [This] represented an enduring political instinct in *le menu peuple* of the Irish countryside. Inherited traditions of the great upheavals of the seventeenth century, a polemical literature in Gaelic forced underground into oral transmission, a profoundly unequal society, split in easily visible ethnic and sectarian lines, rapid commercialisation associated with proto-industrialism, an impressive array of training grounds in the more purely agrarian secret societies – all combined to increase politicisation in the Irish Catholic poor in the 1790s.

This exciting multi-dimensional approach promised a new understanding of 1798 in Wexford, the crucial question being how the United Irishmen tried to connect with the various elements mentioned, including the Gaelic. Here,

Whelan merely noted that 'As Orange attitudes spread south in early 1798, the United Irishmen irresponsibly decided to utilise Catholic fears of its influence as a recruiting device.'[15]

Whelan's discussion of the Defenders anticipated some of the findings of Jim Smyth's important 1992 study, *The Men of No Property*. Smyth had already broadened the terms of the politicization debate in his contribution to *Ireland and the French Revolution*. Like Whelan, he argued that 'the politicisation of the common people, however uneven or inchoate, is a central fact of the decade'. He too stressed that in Defenderism, 'the rights of man and "levelling principles" fused with old Catholic resentments rooted in seventeenth-century dispossession'. He stressed above all that the main factor was 'collective experience':

> The politicisation process was an active one. The lower classes, as it were, learned their politics by doing; by engaging in the great agitations and campaigns and by bearing the brunt of the conflicts of the decade.

These conflicts increasingly were 'along lines of sectarian divisions'. Smyth concluded: 'The French connection and the Presbyterian origins and secular republicanism of the United Irish élite notwithstanding, the assessment of Dublin Castle and its spies after 1795 was substantially correct: Catholic grievance and seditious activity were inseparable.'[16]

Thus, the 'broad consensus' about politicization in 1990 appeared to be that its core dynamic was the interaction between new imported revolutionary ideology and the traditional agrarian and sectarian grievances that had their origins in seventeenth-century colonialism. Why did that consensus change so radically?

One obvious factor was the boost given to United Irish studies by the 1991 bicentenary of the foundation of the movement, following hard upon the bicentenary of the French Revolution. A two-stage academic conference, the first in Belfast, the second in Dublin, attracted financial assistance from (among others) the Irish government's Cultural Relations Committee, and was clearly conscious of the continuing political drive towards a resolution of the Northern Ireland conflict. The conference saw itself as 'replicating the almost simultaneous foundation of the United Irish societies in these cities'. This quote is from the preface to the conference volume that followed in 1993: *The United Irishmen: Republicanism, Radicalism and Rebellion*. The editors (David Dickson, Dáire Keogh and Kevin Whelan) also pointed towards 'the bicentenary of the insurrection itself', not least in terms of 'signposts' offered by the new work on the United Irishmen.

Whelan's contribution, on 'The United Irishmen, the Enlightenment and Popular Culture', was the most original as well as the most significant in the volume, marking an important progression in his argument about politicization. He began with contrasting portraits of the United Irishmen and the Defenders. The former, as 'bearers of the European Enlightenment', were bent on 'repudiating the past and specifically the Irish past'. Because their faith was in 'law as the sole vector of historical change', they concentrated on changing the system and 'felt there was no need to recast the people'. Yet, in order to spread the message of the Enlightenment, they had to try to 'politicise' popular culture, and not to 'valorise it'. This is what the Defenders did, having 'no wish to repudiate history, but rather to re-immerse themselves in it', and in particular the 'potent sense of dispossession'. Showing how 'Defenderism articulated a different world view to that of the United Irishmen', Whelan accentuated the contrast by excluding the Defenders' distinctive connections with revolutionary France, for example. Defenders were 'particularists not universalists, emotionalists not rationalists, exclusive not inclusive, realists not Utopians'. Most of all, of course, Defenderism represented 'the democratisation of the political culture of Catholics'. After this brief initial sketch, Defenderism virtually disappeared from the analysis, except for a brief mention of 'the merger of the two organisations 1795-1796', leading to 'the Jacobinising of the secret societies'.[17] How and to what extent this occurred should be at the heart of any analysis of the United Irishmen and politicization, and Whelan's inability to deal with it meaningfully here reflected both a general problem of evidence, and a particular problem of interpretation.

Instead of analysing 'the merger' he focused almost exclusively on the remarkable propaganda barrage mounted by the United Irishmen, aimed at both the 'literate populace' (newspapers, pamphlets, handbills) and the illiterate (ballads, prophecies, catechisms). Much of the oral propaganda, he found, was aimed at 'the evangelical and dissenting traditions', while what we know of the United Irish exploitation of lower-class social groups and sporting occasions was concentrated on the underworld of Dublin artisans.

Much of this was new and exciting, and I agreed wholeheartedly with the (implied) criticism of my paper on the Wexford and United Irish ballads, that 'historians have paid more attention to text than to context in assessing the impact of these performance genres'. Thanks to Whelan's characteristically flamboyant and erudite survey, we now know considerably more about contexts, but it was striking how far Whelan had gone to the opposite extreme by ignoring the 'texts' of popular culture, such as ballads and folklore. He wrote confidently of 'the successful penetration of popular culture by the United Irishmen', but the evidence he used was almost entirely from United Irish or official sources, and both had vested interests in exaggerating the phenomenon.[18] One unnecessary limit Whelan set himself came from his conviction that United Irish propaganda failed to penetrate Irish-speaking areas. As we'll see, Gaelic sources reflect such penetration, as do ballads in English and the records of courts-martial, but they also reveal, not surprisingly, that the new ideology was adapted to traditional perspectives, offering a new language for old ambitions. Whelan himself had always emphasized this in the past, but in his new analysis of how 'the republic' was brought to 'the village'[19] he gave far too little attention to the interpenetration of these very different worlds; he had too much on the production and dissemination of propaganda, and virtually nothing on its reception.

That this problem arose more from commitment to a particular interpretation rather than from difficulties with sources was suggested by Whelan's new treatment of Catholic sectarianism, which he had previously identified as a crucial factor in politicization. Here, while it was clearly a key component of Defenderism, it did not contaminate the United Irishmen, who were carefully insulated from it. Gone were the former strictures on their irresponsible exploitation of the issue in their drive to recruit Catholic members; now their only role was to strive 'to stem the spread of sectarianism'. Instead, sectarianism was exploited only by the state and was transformed from being a staple of popular culture to being solely a matter of 'counter-revolutionary sentiment'. In the end, Whelan criticized the United Irishmen not for failing to bridge the sectarian divide but for failing to recognize 'that there could be a genuinely popular counter-revolutionary impetus of this type'. Without explanation, and by sleight of hand, the issue of Catholic sectarianism had disappeared (presumably subsumed in Defenderism) and only Protestant sectarianism remained, though it was now 'counter-revolutionary sentiment', and aimed, presumably, at revolutionaries rather than at Catholics.[20]

It is difficult to avoid the conclusion that the revolutionary potential of Catholic sectarianism, as identified by Bartlett and Smyth, as well as by Whelan himself, had to be ignored lest it distract from what has already become for Whelan (and was soon to be adopted by Comóradh '98) 'the United Irish revolution', the resonant phrase with which this fascinating paper ended.

This approach was accentuated further in *The Tree of Liberty* (1996), Whelan's important collection of essays offered specifically as a contribution to the bicentenary of 1798, although the actual Rebellion was not dealt with in any of them. The 1993 paper just analysed was reproduced substantially, with the original title as a subheading, but there was some additional material, and one striking omission: the profile of Defenderism was gone, transferred to the opening essay in the book, 'An Underground Gentry? Catholic middlemen in eighteenth-century Ireland'. As a result, the United Irishmen were distanced even more emphatically from contamination by the traditional political culture that Defenderism represented.

The analysis of politicization was now split, effectively, into two discrete parts, with no effort made to view the phenomenon as a whole. The essay on Catholic middlemen dealt primarily with traditional culture, especially as it 'refocused from residually Jacobite to incipiently Jacobin forms', not least through this dynamic class inheriting the claims of the dispossessed Gaelic élites (to whom some were indeed connected) to be the true owners of forfeited estates.

The pervasiveness of this view and the extent of Ascendancy obsession with it was documented. Whelan used evidence from Gaelic poetry which led him to conclude that 'Irish Jacobitism ... provided indigenous ideological ingredients for the subversion of landed title, well in advance of the imported radical recipe from France.' He went on to repeat an argument he made years before, that 'the crucial custodians of tradition', or of what Corkery had called 'The Hidden Ireland', 'were the comfortable Catholic, big-farm class (a Norman-Gaelic hybrid) of South Leinster and East Munster, who provided stability and continuity'. They also provided popular leadership in the Wexford Rebellion, and as an example of 'the way in which new radicalism grafted into older stocks of resentment', he cited Miles Byrne on the participation of 'those who had been deprived of their property in land at the time of the Reformation and under Cromwell and above all, under William III, merely because they were Catholics'.

In this context Whelan's 1993 discussion of Defenderism made a new appearance. Here he made the significant addition to the claim that 'the Defenders signalled the democratisation of the political culture of Catholics': the phrase, 'the transition from Jacobite to Jacobin'. Whelan then dealt with Defenderism in the context of South Ulster only, but he'd signalled the importance of the Jacobite tradition also in Wexford. Yet in the chapter on 'The United Irishmen, the Enlightenment and Popular Culture' that followed, the focus was solely on United Irish 'Enlightenment propaganda', with virtually no reference to its interaction with traditional popular culture as radicalized by Defenderism, and, most emphatically, with no reference to sectarianism.[21]

This was dealt with in a separate chapter in *The Tree of Liberty*, which expanded on the argument put forward in the last paragraph of the 1993 paper, that sectarianism was important only as an element of the state's 'counter-revolutionary strategy'. The chapter title, 'United and Disunited Irishmen', seemed to promise an opening up of the discussion, but its limits were immediately set by the subheading, 'the State and Sectarianism in the 1790s'. 'Irishmen', it appears, were only 'disunited' because the state exploited 'atavistic feelings'; Catholic sectarianism was not significant until the despised Daniel O'Connell made it so decades later, and the Protestant variety was aimed not so much at Catholics as at the United Irish 'revolution'.

Read in the light of the previous chapter this argument is puzzling; in the much stronger light of modern research as a whole, it is bizarre. Once again, the only relationship of the United Irishmen to sectarianism was as naïve victims. He pointed to their attempts 'to smooth sectarian tensions in Armagh', but had not a word about their activities 'in exploiting and exacerbating sectarian tension' in Wexford, as he described them in his seminal 1987 article, which is omitted from the extensive list of Whelan's publications in the bibliography of *The Tree of Liberty*.[22] He scorned as 'fashionable' the argument developed by Elliott and Curtin that the United Irishmen were fundamentally compromised by the Defender alliance, while avoiding any engagement with the detailed evidence they used. He was right to point to the comparative neglect of 'popular loyalism' but wrong to imply that this was the only important dynamic in the politics of Irish sectarianism in the 1790s. His grudging, coded conclusion that the Rebellion did, indeed, degenerate into a bitterly sectarian conflict, begged the question why, having 'misjudged the depth of popular anti-revolutionary sentiment ... the United Irish revolution turned out not to be a painless coup, but a rancorous struggle, in which the lines of demarcation all too easily split along confessional cleavages'.[23]

No answers were to be found in Whelan's contribution to *The Mighty Wave: The 1798 Rebellion in Wexford*, also published in 1996. This reiterated the main argument of *The Tree of Liberty*, and was particularly concerned to deny any sectarian dimension to the Rebellion; but it also completed the process of redefining the question of politicization. Having sought to insulate the United Irishmen from contamination by popular culture, and especially sectarianism, he now sought (as they had done) to distance them from the violence of 1798. Anxious 'to ensure that history does not tragically repeat itself in the 1990s', he urged us to 'relinquish our obsession ... with pikes and deaths, murder, mayhem and martyrdom. We should instead stress the living principles of democracy and pluralism which the United Irish formulated.'

Some readers will have been reminded, irresistibly, of Whelan's former criticism of the United Irishmen for wishing 'to indulge in collective amnesia in order to stress the enabling rather than the disabling forces in Irish history'. Sympathetic imagination as well as amnesia was required to follow his analysis of the Rebellion in Wexford, especially the remarkable claim that 'Not just militarily but politically the United Irishmen in Wexford achieved a striking success in the short-lived Wexford Republic which administered the county during the rebel occupation.'[24] This ringing endorsement of one of the more contentious claims of Comóradh '98 made no mention of Gahan's denial that a 'Republic' had been declared, much less operated, and was supported only by reference to Whelan's own article in *Ireland and the French Revolution* ten years earlier.[25] *Its* only reference was to Edward Hay, who, while he gave an interesting insider's account of the 'committee' that tried to keep order and regulate the food supply during the rebel occupation of Wexford town, never mentioned a 'Republic'. Nor did he mention the 'Senate', that other phantom of Comóradh '98, which Whelan also unproblematically declared a fact in his contribution to *The Mighty Wave*.[26] No documentary evidence was cited, for the very good reason that none exists.

The effect of this repeated narrowing of perspective has been to make the Rebellion abstract rather than concrete, a matter of ideology rather than of killing, of idealism rather than of intolerance; to make it, in effect, how the United Irishmen, at their most romantic, envisaged it. It is a long way from the complex analyses of sectarianism and politicization with which Kevin Whelan began, and it seems strange that he, of all people, would be the main advocate of a one-dimensional analysis of 1798.

By now his enormous influence on the official commemoration was obvious, not least in the way that his writings echoed in the speeches of politicians. Thus, Síle de Valera, opening the 1798 exhibition in the National Museum in Dublin, laid down some of the guidelines for the bicentenary:

> Firstly, we must continue never to entertain a sectarian version of 1798. Secondly, we must stress the modernity of the United Irish project, its forward-looking, democratic dimension.[27]

Kevin Whelan curated that important exhibition for the National Museum and the National Library, and wrote the book that accompanied it, *Fellowship of Freedom: The United Irishmen and 1798*. As noted earlier, Whelan had already endorsed the claim about the 'Senate', without offering any credible source, but there had since been repeated public challenges to produce evidence. And so the claims made again in this official publication for the 'Wexford Republic', 'the most remarkable achievement of the rebellion', and the presentation, without comment, of an elaborate plan of this 'Republic's' structure, including the 'Senate', could only be read as both deliberate and provocative. (The plan carried in one corner the appropriate warning: 'Copyright Brian Cleary', though, yet again, no source was given.)[28]

This continued endorsement, without comment or citation, of such a major controversial claim raises serious questions, particularly in what is *the* official exhibition, carrying the prestige and authority of both National Library and National Museum, as well as of his own name, for the tens of thousands of people, many of them schoolchildren, visiting the exhibition and the many others buying the book. The 'Republic' and 'Senate' will now be, for most of them, as 'true' as the factual accounts of the various battles. It is hard to avoid the conclusion that we have here a case of what Butterfield proposed ironically, and Bradshaw pondered speculatively, 'purposeful unhistoricity'.

'Fellowship of Freedom' was, in many respects, an important and exciting exhibition, especially in revealing the under-utilized resources in visual materials of both institutions, and in the use of some excellent maps and charts. But it was also dominated by the voice of the text, colourful, often insightful but more often partisan and polemical. The author described himself humorously in the acknowledgments as 'a croppy boy', and this was unabashedly 'croppy' history masquerading as a text, 'guided by the visual archive, which illuminates historical and contemporary connections'.[29]

Instead the visual material mainly offered pegs on which to hang another opinion, in contrast to the more conventional and more scholarly Ulster Museum exhibition, 'Up in Arms'. This was less concerned to frame its material in one over-arching thesis, but rather drew on a number of experts to provide exemplary, and in some instances exceptional, commentary on individual items. Its monumental catalogue, compiled and edited by W.A. Maguire,[30] is an important source book as well as a model of balanced, dispassionate presentation, acutely aware of contemporary sensitivities but not ruled by them. A bleaker and more realistic view of the Rebellion comes through in contrast to the upbeat romanticism and sermonizing of 'Fellowship of Freedom'. It is a view that challenged visitors to confront the prejudices of their own communities, but did so by providing solid information and allowing them to think for themselves. It appealed successfully to people from different traditions, as Kathy Sheridan showed in her account of a visit with a mixed group from a small community, led by a Presbyterian minister and a Catholic priest.[31]

'Fellowship of Freedom', on the other hand, was content to preach to the converted, as well as being sometimes economical with the truth. This was further evident in an old, spurious claim, used here as an example 'of the extent to which United Irish principles activated the rebel army'. Whelan claimed that 'throughout the rising there were no attacks on women, children or political neutrals (like Quakers)'. This was followed by a careful account of the massacre at Scullabogue, in which those 'brutally burned in a barn' were described only as 'loyalists' and 'prisoners'. These weasel words masked the deaths of twenty-one women and children, and at least two Quakers (documented by Whelan himself in 1986).[32] Nothing could illustrate better the systematic distortion of what actually happened in 1798, in the interest of what was believed to be politically expedient.

The preface of *Fellowship of Freedom* actually claimed that its aim was 'a retrieving of memory that has been deliberately suppressed'.[33] The notion, here as elsewhere in Whelan's recent work, that the memory that has been suppressed is that of the 'Republic' and the dominant role of the United Irishmen, lacks all credibility, even on the level of common sense, but more so in the light of the clear historical record of what *really* traumatized individuals and communities in 1798. Whelan was quoted as saying at the start of the bicentenary:

> As Nietzche said, 'history is what hurts', and sometimes things hurt so much that they can't have articulation. It takes a long, long time for them to work through ... You can't restore the past, but you can restore memory and that's what the whole process of commemoration is about.[34]

Instead, the process of this commemoration has been about suppressing memory, both generally, as Whelan urged two years earlier, that of 'deaths, murder, mayhem',[35] and more specifically, as we've just seen, that of the less noble but all too human and profoundly traumatic aspects of a major rebel atrocity. Whelan's concern in this further example of 'purposeful unhistoricity' was, rather, to assert that 'This sickening event occurred against the instructions of the United Irish leadership' (a claim that is open to doubt, as we will see).[36]

Kevin Whelan was also named by government minister, Seamus Brennan, as 'the consultant historian to the National Commemoration', that is to 'the Government's 1798 Commemoration Committee' which Brennan chaired.[37] The proceedings, and even the composition of this committee, which had an initial budget of £250,000, and funded many national and local projects and events, are shrouded in secrecy.

A series of requests made by me to ever more senior civil servants in the department of the Taoiseach (the host department) to be allowed to consult the committee's files were refused, on the grounds that the Freedom of Information Act only came into effect during 1998. Yet I had not requested access under the Act but on the basis that I was a *bona fide* researcher, and that full access had been granted previously to a PhD student of Tom Bartlett's. Clearly there were sensitivities concerning the area of interest that I had specified, that is the role of historians in the committee's work, and I was not to be trusted. Only after I had pointed out that I would have to speculate publicly on the reasons for their refusal was I given the text of the key 'mission statement', agreed by the committee in April 1997, not in its original form but as part of briefing documents prepared for a Dáil question to the Taoiseach in December 1998, and which thus 'postdate the coming into operation of the Freedom of Information Act'.[38]

Why I wanted, particularly, to have official confirmation of this text, already known to historians,[39] will become clear shortly. This remarkable secretiveness may indicate that future historians will find it worthwhile to examine the workings of the national 1798 Commemoration Committee (and of the Famine Commemoration Committee, with which it seems to have overlapped, and even shared a budget for a while). I have had to rely on the public record of Dáil and Senate statements and debates.

There were a number of Dáil questions on the commemoration from mid-1996 but only two significant Oireachtas debates, one in the Dáil on 3 July 1998, and the other in the Senate on 9 December. During the latter, Minister Brennan paid thanks to his committee but named only two of them, Whelan and the secretary, Alice Kearney, who appears to have had a full-time role as she also 'headed the commemoration office in the Department of the Taoiseach' (in response to initial, informal inquiries I was told that the committee was made up mainly of civil servants from a number of government departments, and this may account in part for the secrecy). In responding, former chair of the committee, Avril Doyle (who had represented Wexford in the Dáil), also thanked 'the historians from all over the island, particularly Kevin Whelan, Tom Bartlett, Nicky Furlong and Daíre Keogh for their help'.

Brennan claimed that the input of the historians was crucial. First, he stated, 'we set out to avoid what we had identified as a flaw in the commemorations of 1898, 1938 and 1948. That is, the excessive emphasis on the Catholic Nationalist version of the rebellion which saw 1798 only a crusade for faith and fatherland'. This summarizes Kevin Whelan's view in *The Tree of Liberty*, but the minister went on to explain that this version was rejected less as bad history than because 'Invariably that partisan approach alienated many others, including the descendants of the Ulster United Irishmen, who had been so much to the forefront in the 1790s.' In seeking a more acceptable version, 'My Committee sought to take advantage of the fresh interpretations of 1798 which have been offered in recent years, notably by Louis Cullen, Marianne Elliott, Tom Bartlett, Daíre Keogh, Kevin Whelan and Nicholas Furlong.'

Brennan summarized 'this new interpretation' (note the singular) thus:

> It emphasises that what happened in Ulster was of a piece with what happened in Leinster, restores Belfast and the Presbyterian United Irishmen to the centre of the picture, presents the United Irish movement as democratic, pluralist and forward-looking and carefully exposes the propaganda which has infected so much of the received wisdom on 1798. Yet, we did not seek to suppress or to occlude the less positive features of the 1798 rebellion which was a bloody affair and was marked, regrettably, by atrocities on all sides.

However, as Avril Doyle made clear in her reply, there had been a conscious decision to minimize these 'less positive features'. 'Throughout 1998 efforts were made to relinquish our obsession with the military aspects of 1798, including pikes and deaths, murder, mayhem and martyrdom.' Instead, 'we stressed the living principles of democracy and pluralism which the United Irishmen so notably formulated. Too much emphasis on the gory details of the campaign can only distract us from the enduring legacy of the rebellion – the political vision and moral choices which impelled men and women into the field in 1798. It is that political vision we need to reclaim and remember.'[40]

This decision, in effect, to distort the historical record for political ends quoted directly from the guidelines proposed two years earlier by the government's 'consultant historian' for making the bicentenary 'open, inclusive and dynamic':

> Firstly, we must discard the now discredited sectarian version of 1798 ... Secondly, we must stress the modernity of the United Irish project ... and abandon the outdated agrarian or peasant interpretation. Thirdly, we must emphasise the essential unity of the 1798 insurrection; what happened in Wexford was of a piece with what happened in Antrim and Down ... we must relinquish our obsession with the military aspects ... We should, instead, stress the living principles of democracy and pluralism which the United Irishmen formulated. The gory details ... can only distract us from the enduring legacy of '98 ... And we need also ... to constantly adhere

to the international perspectives of the United Irishmen ... And, in particular, we must be generous in our acknowledgement of the Ulster dimension and especially of the enormous contribution of the Presbyterian tradition, with its enlightened emphasis on justice, equality and liberty. [41]

The echoes of this text in the 'Mission Statement on 1798', issued on 10 April 1997 by the '1798 Commemoration Committee' to diplomats, politicians and key civil servants, are unmistakable, and appear to bear out Seamus Brennan's contention that, 'rather than the government presenting an agenda to the historians, the historians presented an agenda to the government'.[42]

(1) To commemorate the ideals of the United Irishmen and the 'Fellowship of Freedom' that inspired them in 1798.

(2) The recognition of the 1798 Rebellion as a forward looking, popular movement aspiring to unity; acknowledging that what happened in Dublin and Wexford was part of what happened in Antrim and Down.

(3) Attention should shift from the military aspects of 1798 and be directed towards the principles of democracy and pluralism which the United Irishmen advocated.

(4) A focus on the international perspective of the United Irishmen and the enduring links which 1798 forged with America, France and Australia.

(5) To acknowledge the Ulster dimension and particularly the contribution of the Presbyterian tradition, with its emphasis on justice, equality and civil liberty.

(6) To focus attention on the ideals of the leaders of 1798 which still live in Irish history.[43]

Kevin Whelan thus wrote the script for the official bicentenary, and his phrases and formulations reverberated throughout the year in the speeches of politicians of all parties, but particularly those of Seamus Brennan and Avril Doyle. Setting the agenda through his writings, his influence over the official commemoration at local and national level, and his dominance of the media, he was a more powerful moulder of the bicentenary than the much-derided Father Kavanagh was – or could have been – of the centenary.[44] And sadly, this sometimes brilliant and often engaging historian, who had previously mapped so clearly the complex background to the Rebellion in Wexford, proved just as reductionist and simplistic in his approach – and, it would appear, from a similarly misplaced idealism. His motivation was stated clearly in the remarkable preface to *The Tree of Liberty*. His aim was to make the 1790s 'available in a fresh way, opening a generous space which has been artificially constricted'. The 'enduring relevance' of that decade was 'the still unattained prospect of a non-sectarian, democratic and inclusive politics ... That project remains uncompleted; understanding the reason for its momentous defeat in the 1790s can help in ensuring that history does not repeat itself in the 1990s.'[45] In echoing Whelan's words so strongly, politicians were not simply exploiting scholarly work for their own ends, but reflecting a shared approach to the contemporary Irish scene.

From the mid-1990s that scene had been dominated by the Northern Ireland 'peace process', the slow, often tortuous negotiations conducted by the British and Irish governments with political parties and rival paramilitaries to end decades of violence. It reached a culmination of sorts in the Good Friday Agreement early in the year of the 1798 bicentenary. On the face of it, commemorating the Rebellion, with its catalogue of state terror, sectarian conflict and competing atrocity, had little appeal, but other aspects chimed better with the peace process, especially the involvement of many Ulster Presbyterians, including Orangemen, in the United Irish organization. Capitalizing on this, the Irish government, through its Commemoration Committee, promoted a brazen but highly appealing and successful rewriting of history, focussing the bicentenary not on what actually happened in 1798 but on the admirable and helpful ideals of the United Irishmen.

This approach had been suggested to the government by Comóradh '98, as early as 1994. In a submission urging the Taoiseach to launch a national commemoration effort, the Wexford group pointed out that the centenary had been 'the prelude to a national resurgence'. The 'United Irish dream' was proposed as the basis for 'a commemoration fitting for the 1990s in which peace and reconciliation would be motivating forces, drawing in the descendants of the northern Presbyterians as well as southern Catholics and Protestants alike'. To clinch their argument they quoted a statement by Albert Reynolds in support of the Downing Street declaration (one of the landmarks of the peace process) in which he 'invoked the name and vision of the United Irishman in his efforts to persuade Sinn Féin and the IRA to give peace a chance'.[46]

Speaking to the Dáil in July 1998, the Taoiseach, Bertie Ahern was clear that the connection remained crucial:

> By an extraordinary conjunction of circumstances, part of the background to the bicentenary this year has been the negotiation and achievement of the first ever comprehensive peace settlement on this island ... I believe

that something of the spirit of the United Irish has entered into the making and implementation of the British–Irish Agreement.[47]

The exclusive focus of the official bicentenary on 'the spirit of the United Irishmen', at the expense of the 'less positive features' of the Rebellion was systematically developed by successive governments as a contribution to the peace process. As Éamon Ó Cuív, the only politician to reject this consensus publicly, put it: 'We are reinventing the Uprising for our own purposes. We want it to support the present process of peace and reconciliation.'[48]

Avril Doyle's first report to the Dáil in November 1996 emphasized the contacts being made with northern groups, especially the Orange Order.[49] In March 1997 she reported on a meeting with Brian Kenneway, Convenor of the Grand Orange Lodge Education Committee: 'I pointed out that it is the intention of the Government's 1798 Commemoration Committee to devise an inclusive commemoration programme which will reiterate the 1798 ideals of democracy, and religious and civil liberties for all.'[50]

In November 1997 the Taoiseach told Sinn Féin TD, Caoimhghin Ó Caoláin, that, 'the programme will focus attention on the ideals of the leaders of 1798 and will acknowledge the Ulster dimension, and particularly the contribution of the Presbyterian tradition, with its emphasis on justice, equality and civil liberty'.[51]

What was being excluded was admitted a month later when the Taoiseach replied to concerns expressed by Proinsias de Rossa 'that the events being commemorated are all violent', especially 'given the violence of the past twenty-seven years in Northern Ireland, which purported to be based on the history of 1798, 1848, 1916 and so on'. In characteristically opaque mode, Mr Ahern opined, 'Things have changed a little when one looks at the leaders of the 1798 rebellion. They are different to those we tend to associate with more recent events.' (A year later Minister Brennan was 'very pleased that there was no knee-jerk association between the Pike and the Armalite, which would have sullied the ideas of the United Irishmen, and their ideals'.) But it was true, the Taoiseach told Mr de Rossa, that 'Offence may be caused by the determination of some people to commemorate events in a more realistic manner.' [52]

The intent and effect of making the United Irishmen the sole focus of the commemoration was to make the Rebellion in Wexford primarily a matter of ideology and idealism, and to package it as not only entirely modern and progressive, but (hardest of all) a model for the peace process in Northern Ireland, in which the hopes of so many were invested. As Kevin Whelan told *The Irish Times* (24 March 1998):

This year's commemorations are evidence of a genuine appreciation of what 1798 was all about. The United Irishmen were trying to negotiate a political structure here and with Britain, capable of representing Irish people in all their inherited complexities and allegiances. The peace process today is trying to do the same thing.

Because 1798 was 'all about' negotiation and representation, the idealism of the United Irishmen had to be segregated clearly from what might appear as some of its unfortunate consequences. During the commemoration of the Great Famine in 1997 'revisionist' historians were berated for paying insufficient attention to the trauma of the Famine's million victims. It is hard to resist the conclusion that the call to ignore the dead of the 1798 (and to stress instead 'the living principles of democracy and pluralism') arose from the fact that those dead were inconvenient politically because they raised the unwelcome question of the responsibility of Irish republicans, while the dead of the Famine brought the responsibility of the British government into focus.

The issue of the responsibility of the United Irishmen for the predictable slaughter that their idealism precipitated was little discussed. Instead there was a convoluted attempt to have it both ways. Thus, it was asserted, the United Irishmen planned and controlled the Wexford Rebellion, yet bore no responsibility for its endemic sectarian killing, for example. As Thomas Bartlett riposted when Donal Ó Móráin had the bad taste to raise the issue of Scullabogue in the *Irish Times*, such activities 'do not at all impugn the United Irish message or subvert the United Irish project'.[53] The government, likewise, sought to distance itself from Scullabogue, approving the text for the memorial but informing Comóradh '98, that 'there would be no delegate from the Department at the ceremony and no ministerial involvement'.[54]

Thus the bicentenary was not only tailored to the peace process, it mirrored it in its attempt to reduce intractable political realities, like sectarian division and its associated violence, to aspirational linguistic formulae. Words have never mattered more in our politics, nor has the tendency in nationalism to re-invent itself ever been given freer rein. The United Irishmen offered soothing consensual words, the precedent of a link between Dublin and Belfast, and between Catholic and Protestant.

'Given the evolving peace process,' the Taoiseach told the Dáil during the bicentenary, 'it was inevitable that the vision of the 1790s could serve as an inspiration for the 1990s. The United Irishmen belong to every political tradition in Ireland and their example can help us to think imaginatively and dynamically about our current situation.'[55]

Their example, however, can also serve as a warning about the limits of idealism, and the violence of the 1790s is at least as relevant today as its vision. The role of the historian should be to inform rather than to inspire, to be true to the sources that survive, to tell what actually happened rather than to cloud them over with dreams of what did not. State commemoration may stimulate historical inquiry but it should not determine it.

PART III

5 June 1798

We cannot revive old factions
We cannot restore old policies
Or follow an antique drum.
These men and those who opposed them
And those whom they opposed
Accept the constitution of silence
And are folded in a single party.

T.S. ELIOT, 'Little Gidding'

CHAPTER 9

Sources

I n the nationalist version of 1798, reflected in the centenary ballads I learned in childhood, 'the gold sun of freedom grew darkened at Ross'. I remember a particular frisson whenever we sang this verse from 'Kelly, the Boy from Killanne', combining pride that our town was mentioned with sorrow at its unfortunate significance. Modern historians have endorsed the ballad's view of the battle for the town as a major turning-point in the Wexford Rebellion. As the first serious reversal in what had appeared up to then an almost effortless and seemingly irresistible campaign, it was a devastating blow to rebel morale and the rebel leadership. The sheer scale and horror of the killing was a factor in this and gives the battle a still wider significance. With perhaps as many as 1500 people killed in one day in a warren of narrow streets and lanes, it registers even on the European map of catastrophic events from the Age of Revolution.

The local trauma is most evident, ironically, in its virtual disappearance from memory, at least in such folklore as has been collected or published, and in the striking lack of awareness by most of the town's modern inhabitants that its peaceful streets witnessed such carnage. Previous commemorations have contributed to this amnesia. Foran's statue of the pikeman in the town centre, commissioned at the centenary, does not depict the battle itself or represent death, but rather a moment of rebel nobility before the battle, with the lowered pike bearing the soon-to-be-dishonoured flag of truce.

In the morning of that same day, beside the major rebel camp at Carrigbyrne eight miles away, the massacre of up to 150 men, women and children at Scullabogue barn was also felt at the time to mark a turning-point in the Rebellion, with the exploitation of its strongly sectarian nature contributing to the collapse of the outbreak in the north, effectively ending dreams of Protestants and Catholics as 'United Irishmen'.

Modern accounts, while claiming an impact on the Presbyterians of County Down, have also highlighted the internal divisions that had already fatally weakened the northern Rebellion.[1] Locally, Scullabogue's basic character of neighbour targeting and killing neighbour, largely on sectarian lines, has normally been denied and continues to be so; even more than in the case of New Ross, this is a trauma still unresolved. In the aftermath of battle and massacre, the old-style United Irishman Bagenal Harvey was replaced as rebel Commander-in-Chief by Father Philip Roche, lamenting, according to a local informant of Musgrave's, 'that the war unexpectedly turned out to be purely religious'.[2] All of this highlights the importance of 5 June in querying the official bicentennial interpretation of the Wexford Rebellion.

The battle of New Ross and the massacre at Scullabogue do not, of course, represent the Rebellion in all its aspects; the character of the outbreak varied, in important respects, from area to area. But a detailed study of that bloody day can yield new insights into the key and related issues of rebel motivation and United Irish leadership. It can also give a sense of how the Rebellion appeared to ordinary people caught up in an abnormal situation, and can thus rescue it and them from interpretations that concentrate on the gentry and bourgeois United Irish leadership and the role of the rebel priests.

Despite the scale and significance of both battle and massacre, the surviving documentary evidence, especially for the former, is disappointingly scant. The handful of short dispatches from the military (the basis in turn of newspaper reports) offer a clue, perhaps, to the paucity of the record. The battle seems to have resembled a tornado, an elemental force of stunning ferocity, which struck with little warning and departed as suddenly, leaving a trail of devastation, no clear memory, and a sense of bewildered disbelief. This is also reflected in different ways in the two main narrative accounts of the battle, one by a participant and leading rebel, the other by a somewhat eccentric loyalist eyewitness.

Thomas Cloney's *A personal narrative of those transactions in the county of Wexford, in which the author was engaged during the awful period of 1798* was published thirty-four years after the fact, in 1832. As Cloney was the only surviving leader of the rebel forces who attacked New Ross, his account of the battle is invaluable, and often vivid, but it is also strangely patchy and incomplete.

More immediate, colourful and comprehensive is the account by James Alexander, a liberal loyalist onlooker, written in the aftermath of the battle and published in Dublin in 1800. *Some account of the first apparent symptoms of the late rebellion in the County of Kildare and in the adjoining King's County, with a succinct narrative of some of the most remarkable passages in the rise and progress of the rebellion in the County of Wexford, especially in the vicinity of Ross; and a minute detail of the battle fought in and near that town on the 5th of June 1798, in a letter to Wentworth Alexander Esq., of the Monastereven Cavalry* was dedicated to the commander of the garrison, General Johnson, but Alexander was also openly critical of the excesses of the army and of conflicts between militia and yeomanry; he had a real if limited sympathy for peasant grievances, and connected with that, it seems, he had some fluency in Irish. An ex-soldier who had seen service in the American colonies, he was now a teacher (writing his Account during snatched moments in the classroom, 'amidst the prattle and noise of little innocents');3 he was also, possibly, a Quaker, to judge by some incidental remarks and by his wearing black clothes, which proved critical on the day of the battle, sometimes endangering his life, sometimes saving it.

His account is self-consciously literary, striving for effect, but it is also knowledgable in military terms, and separates out what he claims he saw from what he learned later from extensive interviews with some of the garrison's heroes and with captured rebels. Most remarkable is its slightly zany quality, capturing and matching the black humour and elements of carnivalesque that characterized some of the actors on both sides in this theatre of death. Alexander had also published an article in *Walker's Hibernian Magazine* as early as November 1798,4 based on interviews with rebels coming into New Ross, seeking amnesty, two weeks after the battle.

This rebel testimony is mediated through a conventional liberal Protestant politics, which saw improving resident landlordism as the key to social justice and stability. The greatest challenge facing the historian is how to avoid some similar reductionism. The fact that rebel perspectives survive largely in the official record is a particular difficulty, but studies of peasant insurgency worldwide show the rich potential of such sources. In Ireland recent work by Tom Bartlett, for example, demonstrates that court-martial records, despite their obvious biases and limitations, can offer unique insights into the minds of the poor, whether witnesses or accused.5 In keeping with the cataclysmic nature of the battle of New Ross, there are few court-martial records; most of those killed in the aftermath, whether rebels or townspeople, were tried, if at all, by 'drumhead' court-martial and executed immediately, with no record kept.

On the other hand the series of courts-martial arising from the Scullabogue massacre make it one of the best-documented incidents of the Rebellion in Wexford. Ordinary rebels also emerge as complex figures, sometimes even as sympathetic ones, in the depositions of 'suffering loyalists' seeking compensation after the Rebellion, and in the diaries or later accounts of loyalist prisoners.

The main official archive is in two related collections, the 'Rebellion Papers' and the 'State of the Country Papers', and, as Deirdre Lindsay points out, it 'requires cautious use'.[6] Consisting mostly of the letters of Dublin Castle correspondents and informants, the archive reflects best the mutual reinforcement of fear and paranoia by Castle officials and elements of the embattled Ascendancy. Its collection, organization and survival resulted from a particular combination of circumstances in the 1790s and again in the 1890s, when the crude listings, still in use a hundred years later, were made. It has major gaps, which have distorted earlier accounts. In particular, Louis Cullen has argued convincingly that its lack of evidence for United-Irish activity in Wexford is far from conclusive.[7] The failure to develop a modern catalogue for this archive prior to the bicentenary greatly inhibited 1798 studies, particularly at local level; it also raised further questions about the priorities of the national Commemoration Committee. The main value of this official archive for my study proved to be its records of courts-martial.

Over thirty years ago Thomas Pakenham felt that, being forced to rely on such second-hand, tainted sources to depict rebel perspectives, it was 'impossible to avoid giving offence'.[8] This proved to be all too true, and his colourful *The Year of Liberty* (1969) was perceived by some as depicting the rebels as 'an unruly mob, cowardly but cruel, and motivated above all, by religious hatred'.[9] This reflects the traditional nationalist expectation, articulated by Fennell (and quoted earlier), that history writing will represent 'the nation' as 'always, in some sense, right minded and right-acting'.[10] Such expectation is undoubtedly still a factor in making some historians resistant to listening to rebel 'voices', even when mediated through more sympathetic, traditional forms such as contemporary ballads in English, folklore (almost entirely in English) and, above all, political poetry in Irish.

More significant reasons for this deafness, however, are a limited view of what constitutes proper evidence, and an inability to decipher Irish-speaking voices that is cultural as well as scholarly in origin. These sources reflect the penetration of traditional perspectives by the ideas of contemporary radicalism and revolution, but this new politicization of the poor cannot be understood if entirely divorced from an understanding of the still-vibrant traditional political culture.

The most interesting contemporary reflection on the battle of New Ross is a poem in Irish, 'Bualadh Ros Mhic Thriún', collected by Seán Ó Doinn for the Protestant antiquarian John George Augustus Prim in the 1830s. Apologizing for the delay in sending 'the four verses relative to the bloody engagement at Ross in '98', Ó Doinn explained that 'delays are often unavoidable in rescuing from oblivion all that can be gleaned from the native tongue of Ireland in its declining days'.[11] The loss of so much Gaelic material is one reason why we have so little evidence regarding the motivation and outlook of the rebel rank and file in 1798, compared with the extensive documentation on the official side and *its* preoccupation with the French-inspired radicalism of the bourgeois leadership of the United Irishmen. It is a loss hardly noticed by historians, who have all assumed that the rebels in Wexford were English-speaking. It was an assumption I shared when I began this research, despite my awareness of the Ó Doinn poem and my long-standing interest in the politics of the Gaelic poetic tradition.

As the realization dawned that the countrymen who carried out the rebel attack on New Ross, 'all brave men of the Barony of Bantry', were strongly Irish-speaking, exciting new possibilities of understanding their motivation and their traditional political culture opened up. The significant body of evidence that supports this view of rebel culture as strongly Gaelic will be explored later, but it includes the diary of a bishop's parish visitations in the 1750s, various travellers' accounts up to the 1830s, surveys carried out by proselytizing societies in the decades after the Union, and the mapping of Gaelic surnames. An account by my own grandfather should have alerted me to this key factor long ago. All of this evidence led me, however belatedly, to pay more attention to a feature of Alexander's *Account*, which it is easy to glide over as just another example of local colour. He reported and translated speech in Irish in conversation with country people before and after the battle, and during the battle itself he recorded rebel speech several times in Irish, as will appear later. He also recorded them speaking English, and this bilingualism, while it helps to render the Gaelic dimension virtually invisible, also offers a key to the ways in which traditional attitudes were open to radical new ideas in this period of modernization and revolution.

Once it is accepted that the rebels were still connected to a traditional Gaelic culture, they can be understood in new ways and their insurgency in 1798 can be connected more clearly to the long history of colonial conflict in the area. It may be objected that the nature and extent of the survival of the Gaelic tradition in the barony of Bantry cannot now be accurately measured, and this is true. But, however shadowy to us, it is a reasonable inference that this tradition was still meaningful to those connected with it linguistically, and that an attempt to reconstitute it from such contemporary sources as survive is worthwhile. To fail to do so would be to accept that this particular and highly distinctive 'subaltern voice' has indeed been silenced forever, and to echo the consensus among Gaelic scholars that (in literary terms) it is not worth recovering.

In this view, which echoes a nationalist paradigm, the Gaelic literature of this period is seen as a crude and static folk culture, lacking in continuity with the 'great tradition' that, according to the canon, ended with Ó Rathaille. But, as new research on the Jacobite poetry of the earlier eighteenth century has shown, an alternative view is possible, reflecting the contemporary relevance and dynamism of the Gaelic tradition, which can be extended into the 1790s and beyond. The lack of other Gaelic material from the New Ross area that comments on 1798 is understandable, given the difficulties encountered by Ó Doinn a century and a half ago, but there are still ways into this culture and its revolutionary potential in the 1790s, the most revealing and remarkable being a sequence of 1798 poems (including one on Wexford) by the Cork poet and scribe Micheál Óg Ó Longáin, which are analysed below. Sophist-icated urban radical as he was, and steeped in the Gaelic literary tradition, Ó Longáin clearly cannot be taken *simpliciter* as a spokesman for illiterate coun-trymen from the Bantry barony. But he does indicate the revolutionary poten-tial of the tradition to which they were also connected, however tenuously, and which was echoed in the contemporary local ballads in English.

Like Ó Longáin's poems also, the verses collected by Ó Doinn reflect a world view that combines, with no apparent sense of incongruity, the local and the cosmopolitan, the traditional and the modern. The unknown poet welcomes Napoleon's defeat of the Austrians '*mar do chualas insa news dá léamh*' (as I heard read in the newspaper), a vivid image of the common combination of bilin-gualism and illiteracy, the poet keeping abreast of events in Europe through the public reading aloud of a newspaper account. He makes no direct connection between the French victory and the rebel defeat at Ross, other than to note that as he 'heard it read' on 5 June, the battle was raging in the town. Indeed, far from seeing it in terms of contemporary European revolution, he describes the battle in the language of earlier religious and colonial conflicts.[12] The Jacobite dimen-sions of the verses collected by Ó Doinn are also examined below.

This seemingly archaic tradition (predicting the return of the long-defunct Stuarts, who'd restore the old Gaelic élite and the Catholic religion) dominated poetry in Irish throughout this period, and allows some insight into how the modernization of traditional perspectives operated, how Jacobitism took on elements of Jacobinism, however briefly, and how Alexander could record rebels in New Ross speaking Irish in a traditional vein, and yet, one speaking in English before his execution, declaring 'I die fighting for my country.'[13]

The importance of the Jacobite tradition in understanding peasant insurgency does not end with 1798, and its continued prominence in popular songs in Irish (*amhráin na ndaoine*) for another half-century would also seem to endorse the value of Ó Longáin in our attempt to reconstitute the world view of the Bantry rebels.

These *amhráin*, many composed by illiterate poets like Raftery and Máire Bhuí Ní Laoghaire, represented almost by definition the views of the local rural community on which the poet was often dependent, and they survived in song tradition down to modern times only because of their powerful resonance in the popular mind. In them the language, imagery and aspirations of the old Gaelic élites are transformed into vehicles for communal anger at landlords, agents, magistrates, tithe collectors, proselytizers, apostates and 'peelers'.

By contrast, the language of modern European revolution, which makes a brief but important appearance in Ó Longáin's verse, is conspicuous by its absence in these songs.[14] Politicization of the rural poor in the 1790s, whether by Defenders or United Irishmen, while undoubtedly an important factor, was simply another (and, it seems, transitory) layer added to older, more atavistic and visceral concerns, arising from a still recent (in the case of Wexford very recent) traumatic experience of dispossession and colonization.

Modern work on such politicization often accuses older scholars of patronizing the poor by assuming that they had no politics. It seems equally patronizing, however, to assume that the only way the poor could be politicized was by the absorption of élite ideologies from France. These could certainly give new means of articulating popular grievances against injustice, but their power to do so depended on their perceived relevance to older indigenous ideologies, which were equally 'political' and valid to those who held them. Thus, it is wrong to dismiss sectarianism, for example, as simply a divisive counter-revolutionary tactic, and as if it was a new element in 1798. The colonial land, religious and political settlements of the seventeenth century were deeply sectarian, and the Gaelic/Catholic response to them inescapably so also, as is reflected in the contemporary poetry.

As in Northern Ireland to the present day, sectarianism can become a shorthand for basic conflicts over political and economic power at all social levels. It constitutes as real a political ideology, in that sense, as the principles the United Irishmen took from revolutionary America or France. We may find such a political culture regrettable, but we should recognize it as an important reality. Sectarianism in the 1790s articulated a coherent political position on both sides, as did Catholic tenants clinging to the dreams of repossessing lost lands. The demand for restoration can be as powerful a vehicle for change as the clamour for revolution, indeed it often fuels it. Breandán Ó Buachalla has shown that while Jacobite *aisling* (vision) poetry had its basis in a deeply conservative, royalist ideology of 'return, renewal, restoration', it also 'carried a powerful millennial message of individual and communal liberation' with which all social classes could identify. It was 'potentially and eventually a radical rhetoric'.[15]

Thus, while Whelan considers the Irish language to have been a barrier to United Irish attempts to politicize the poor,[16] it is possible to see it instead as a vehicle of politicization in a world that was undergoing a fundamental linguistic revolution, whose trauma was disguised if not lessened by a complex web of bilingualism. Most Gaelic poets of the 1790s could write in both languages, and many used English models as well as English words and phrases in their texts. They were, among other things, the interpreters of the ever-more obtrusive outside world to the poor.

The Jacobite poetry and songs of the late eighteenth and early nineteenth centuries show the ways in which that interpretation blended traditional political perspectives – sectarian, agrarian, millenarian – with those of contemporary revolution, and ultimately of mass democracy. Millenarian beliefs involving the recovery of a lost Eden were at least as potent as the revolutionary pretence to be creating the world anew by inaugurating the Year I, as the rebel committee in Wexford town dated some of their documents. The rural community, from which the rank-and-file rebels overwhelmingly came, had, and retained, its own traditional politics, and the tatters of Gaelic materials that survive are indispensable to understanding it.

There are also major problems about understanding the experience of that largely forgotten group, the townspeople. Naturally, there are extensive sources for some of the Protestant families who dominated the politics and trade of New Ross, particularly the Tottenhams, although few that I can discover regarding the Rebellion. The Minute Book of the exclusively Protestant Corporation doesn't mention 'the late rebellion' until November 1799, when payment was authorized for 'a nightguard of Yeomen' who protected the inhabitants 'during and immediately previous' to it.[17] In these records the Catholic inhabitants, although probably a majority, are invisible.

John Rice's gravestone,
St Stephen's Cemetery.

A large if unquantifiable number of those killed in the aftermath of the battle by rampaging government troops were undoubtedly local Catholics, like my ancestor John Rice, yet they have not left even that most rudimentary proof of their existence: gravestones. Extensive research in the local graveyards produced only two that we can connect to the battle. One is that of John Rice in St Stephen's, which simply records the date, 5 June 1798.[18] The other, in St Mary's, is more explicit. It marks the grave of a member of a prominent Protestant family, Francis Robinson, aged twenty-two, 'late of the Ross Yeomanry who was killed in an engagement with the rebels at Ross on 5th June, 1798'. The contrast between the two neatly encapsulates the power dynamic in the town at that time. The Catholic especially if, like Rice, in trade and therefore at the mercy of the Corporation, had to be discreet; the Protestant was able to honour a life given in service to his community. If the family story is true, the same could be claimed of Rice's death, yet even the recording of the date of the battle on his gravestone by his son, years later, could be and possibly was read as a bold political act. The uniqueness of his tombstone also reflects the likelihood that most of the local dead, buried as we know in mass anonymous graves, were poor Catholics.

Even for a relatively prosperous businessman like Rice, we have no other records, beyond the family story and possibly the recording of the baptisms of some of his children and the death of his wife in the parish registers. (There were a number of families called Rice in the town.) He almost certainly leased his main property from a Tottenham (it is still occupied by a member of the family, and still leased from the Tottenham estate), but no trace of this survives in the estate papers or in the Registry of Deeds in Dublin. This is not surprising. Catholic leases often went unrecorded, especially if short-term or sub-lettings. Thus a small-town 'rising' Catholic, like John Rice, left virtually no trace in the historical record, and would have left even less but for the manner of his death.

We can only speculate about his life, and especially about his politics, from what we know of his class, and from his wealthier cousin downstream, who was almost certainly his main customer and possibly his banker. But the case of Edmund Rice only illustrates the extent of the problem. Despite exhaustive research involved in the process of his proposed (now virtually guaranteed) canonization, basic facts about his life in the 1790s, including even his wife's name, cannot be documented. What is clear is that, like most wealthy Catholics, he was ostensibly loyalist in 1798, and as a major army supplier had unusual freedom of movement, even at the height of the Rebellion.[19]

As for United Irish penetration of New Ross, there is no evidence of this in the scant records of the movement, and while disloyalty at least can be inferred from the discovery of pikes in the houses of a handful of poor Catholics, huddled under the medieval walls, the court-martial records of the trials of local people after the battle never raise United Irish membership. A recent attempt[20] to describe everyone known to have died in the town at the hands of Crown forces as United Irishmen, including John Rice, has no basis in anything other than the political correctness (or wishful thinking) of the official bicentennial.

CHAPTER 10

Background: Old Quarrels and New Politics

T he town of New Ross owes its life, its character and its importance to
the broad, beautiful and dangerous tidal river Barrow, or, more accurately, to the complex confluence of Barrow, Nore and Suir, one of the
great river systems of Europe. As a deep-water inland port twenty miles from
the open sea, halfway between the key sea ports of Waterford and Wexford,
and entrepot of the rich hinterland of the Norman stronghold of Kilkenny, it
was for more than a century the main port of the Norman colony until its
rival Waterford gained the upper hand politically, pushing it into a long, slow
decline. In the late sixteenth century, noting its 'sudden decaie', Richard
Stanihurst quoted an 'ancient prophecy current in the time of Henry VIII':

Rosse was, Dublin is and Drogheda shall be The best of the three.[1]

Its Gaelic name, Ros Mhic Threoin (as I learned it) or Ros Mhic Thriúin
(as it is officially designated now), combines the still recognizable topography
of a wooded promontory ('Ros') over a bend in the river, with the name that
one legend ascribes to the son of a Viking prince, another to 'the courtier of
Tara referred to in St Patrick's life'. Thus, the wooded promontory of the son
of Treon. No trace of a Viking settlement remains, nor of the early Celtic
monastery of St Abban, also said to have been located there.[2]

In its modern, documented phase, the town is rather an early Norman
foundation, said to have been started in 1190, and recognized as 'Nova Villa
Pontis Whilhelm Marscalli', or the new town of the bridge of William Marshall, by King John during his visit there in 1210. It thus has claim to be 'the
first city fortified or otherwise built by English hands on Irish soil'. Later
called 'Rossponte', it was also known early on as 'New Ross' to distinguish it
from the earlier manorial settlement in the countryside, six miles away, at 'Old'

Ross. Its location had immense strategic as well as commercial importance for its founder, William, Earl Marshall, who had come into possession of most of Leinster through his marriage to Isabella, daughter of the first Norman leader, Strongbow, and Aoife, the daughter of his local ally, Diarmaid Mac Murchadha, Gaelic ruler of the province. Its importance was both underlined and enhanced by the construction of a bridge – a difficult and costly enterprise – creating a land link to what is now Kilkenny and Waterford, and strengthening the colony in this key march or border area.

According to legend, King John was present at a hunt when Marshall's hound brought down a stag on the new bridge; this image became the Marshall's seal (and, indeed, for a time during the early years of Henry III, the royal seal of England), and later the coat of arms of the Corporation of New Ross, and ultimately of the Urban District Council. Today versions of it decorate both the plinth of the monument to the 1798 rebels, and the Tholsel, opposite, centre of the Protestant Ascendancy, to which the rebel figure offers symbolic defiance. It is a reminder that the town was then surrounded by forest, the home not only of game but of the hostile Gaelic clans, most notably McMurroughs and Kavanaghs. Not long after its foundation and 'contrary to the border statutes then in force forbidding the levying of blackmail, permission was conceded to the citizens of New Ross to pay the Clan Kavanagh ten marks yearly in consideration of which the latter undertook to protect the town from the aggressive attacks of other neighbouring clans'.[3]

The initial prosperity and importance of the town can be measured by the number and scale of its thirteenth-century religious foundations. A very fine Early English parish church (originally called Christ Church, then St Mary's) had an associated religious house, possibly Augustinian. The Franciscans were established in Priory Street by 1250 (succeeding the Crutched Friars), and the Dominicans were established across the bridge shortly afterwards. According to legend still current, the Crutched Friars were driven out violently by the townspeople, leaving behind their curse that the river would claim three victims a year from the town. The Friars certainly evoked a papal censure, which the local bishop was still trying to revoke, unsuccessfully, in the 1630s, and which may have never been lifted formally. But of more immediate concern to the inhabitants by the mid-thirteenth century was the need to defend the town and its trade against attack, and this led to the building of an elaborate structure of walls, towers and gates in 1265.

Apart from the river (down to which the walls came, and which completed the town's defensive perimeter), nothing was to mark the town's history and culture as much as its walled character. It was a remarkably ambitious enterprise, which long remained out of proportion to the actual size of the town (even today, there remain greenfield areas within the original circumference). Spanning a full league (c. 4.5km), and thus longer than the walls of Waterford, Kilkenny or Drogheda, they were said by Stanihurst to have been 'in circuit equate to London walls', with 'three gorgeous gates'.4 Their planning and execution entirely by the townspeople was celebrated in a long poem in Norman French by Friar Michael of Kildare, which is concerned mainly to detail the unique communal effort involved, with different groups, by occupation, offering their labour free on successive days of each week, beginning with the vintners on Mondays, and ending, remarkably, with 'the ladies' on Sundays. The poem also includes an apologia for the vast undertaking:

> When it is complete there will be no need to have a watch. They can sleep soundly – no one should blame them for wanting to enclose their town: when the town is securely closed and the wall encircles it completely, not an Irishman in Ireland will be so bold as to dare attack it.5

Avril Thomas has commented that, while the wall's 'sheer size' must have reflected optimism and economic success, the poem suggests a sense of unease, probably that potential traders would be put off by their obligation to contribute to its maintenance.6

Within a century of the wall being completed, the town proved to be still vulnerable to attack by 'Irish enemies'. A letter patent of Richard II in 1381 accepted 'that the same town is so seated on the borders near our Irish enemies and rebels, that the greater part of the walls and towers ... lie prostrated to the ground, and the county adjacent for four miles in circumference waste and destroyed by the same enemies'. In the following decade the *Annals of the Four Masters* record: 'An army was led by Arthur Mac Muragh, King of Leinster, against the English, and he burned Ros mic Triuin, with its homes and castles and carried away from it gold, silver and hostages.' Nine years later, in 1403, Henry IV allowed the 'Sovereign and Community' of Ross to pay a black rent to Mac Muragh, and to trade with the Irish, 'as their town is situated on the Marches and on all sides encompassed by Irish enemies'.

Throughout these early centuries Ross fought a war on two fronts, the other being a trade war with Waterford, fought through Parliament and the court but also erupting at times into armed conflict. In 1518, for example, an inquiry was established into the attack by named Waterford citizens, who 'with many Spaniards, Frenchmen, Bretons and Irish came riotously with a fleet of boats and ships' and attacked Ross 'in piratical and warlike fashion'. The town's sad economic decline, from 'oon of the best townes in this land' to 'utterly dead and wasted', was ascribed by the Council of Ireland to 'the contynuall war and adnoyance of the Kavanagh's and the contentions betwixt them and Waterford'. Thus, despite the famous walls, the towns continued to suffer, in Stanihurst's graphic phrase, from 'a crue of naughtie and prolling neighbours', and in particular 'the greedie snatching of the Irish enemies'.7

This brief outline of the *longue durée* of a colonial enclave beset by Gaelic enemies is not just the kind of perspective that might occur to a modern historian of the 1798 Rebellion, anxious to establish certain patterns. In the first imaginative treatment of 1798 in Gaelic prose, Amhlaoibh Ó Súilleabháin, living in nearby Callan, wrote in 1826 the story of 'Tóruigheacht Chailmfhir Mhic Mearcuraidh'. This remarkable mixture of traditional *Fiannaíocht* romance and contemporary Gothic portrays the battle of New Ross as one of Gaelic lords, successors to the Fianna, leading 'Clanna Gaodhal' in another attempt to break English chains ('Slabhra na Sasanach').8 Fourteen years earlier, in a very different attempt to develop a 'Gaelic' Gothic, Charles Maturin also depicted the 1798 Rebellion as led by Gaelic warriors in 'ancient Irish dress'. His 1812 novel *The Milesian Chief* was also remarkable for its sympathetic portrayal of the doomed romantic hero of the Rebellion, especially given Maturin's position as a clergyman of the Established Church, proud of his role (as he claimed) in the defence of Dublin against the threat of rebel attack.9

The relationship between New Ross and its 'Irish enemies' had never been simply a matter of armed conflict. There were regular complaints about the presence of native Irish in the town and occasional attempts to expel them. On the other hand the Duke of Ormond, in 1538, condemned the unprovoked killing of 'Cahir Mac Artes Standarthe berrer and 3 more of the said Cahir's men, being at peace', during a religious festival, by a group of 'Englishmen prepensidly'. This relationship was further complicated by the Reformation, as many prominent families in the town continued to share a common religion with the Irish outside the walls. In 1606 'the Sovereign and Burgesses' were bound over to answer charges in Star Chamber of disrupting official religious services, and it was also alleged that 'the greatest part of the townsmen be obstinate recusants' (i.e., refusing to attend services in the Protestant state church). In 1641, following the powerful lead of Richard Butler, Lord Mountgarrett, the town declared for the Confederation, and Butler's kinsmen, the Duke of Ormond, laid siege unsuccessfully to what had now become, improbably, a stronghold of 'rebels' and 'the Irish', according to

Ormond's chaplain. The depositions later made by Protestants seeking compensation include complaints against the 'rebels in Ross', spurred on by 'Romish Priests', utilizing standard atrocity stories of violence to Protestant corpses as 'heritiques' and the killing of young children 'by running them through with their pykes'.

Cromwell had better luck than Ormond, and the town surrendered after a warning bombardment (leaving 'three bullets' in Aldgate or Bewley Gate) and Cromwell's assurances of 'the reality of my intentions to save blood and preserve the place from ruine' (to be echoed by Bagenal Harvey in 1798). He was relieved to take 'this place of good strength' so easily. However, during the 1650s the area outside the walls seemed to remain at the mercy of the Irish (now 'Tories or outlaws'), with various Kavanaghs still to the fore. Attempts were made to get Englishmen to settle in the town, and the collector of customs and excise was censured because he 'hath married an Irishwoman contrary to ye declaration'.[10]

Under the Act of Settlement and Explanation (1666) virtually the whole town became the property of the Earl of Anglesey, but its Corporation continued to be dominated by Catholic or quasi-Catholic families, Dormers, Butlers, Colcloughs and others, and some of their elaborately decorated tombs can still be seen in St Mary's. They featured in the celebration of the receipt of a new Royal Charter in 1687. The account of the elaborate public ceremony involved includes the only use of the Irish language in the Corporation records. As representatives of the army paid their respects to the Corporation, they were 'saluted by sixty young women, well dressed, and dancing with their pipes before them, saying in Irish, 'De vahe Waister Meare agus vat boune gurev Rey Shames,' which Hore renders as 'Sé do bheatha a Mhaighistir Meara agus fada buan go raibh Righ Seamus' – (Your health, master Mayor, and may King James be long secure). Two years later a foreign visitor to the town attacked the inhabitants for their superstitious popery and their treatment of 'ye poore Englishe'.[11]

This blurring of the distinction between the colonial town and its 'Irish enemies' ended with the Williamite Settlement and the subsequent Protestant monopoly of the Corporation. Two new families established an early and remarkably long-lasting dominance. The medieval position of Sovereign, to which the Corporation elected one of its members annually, was held by either a Tottenham or a Leigh (or shared by both) virtually every year between 1725 and 1834. They filled the borough's two seats (also elected by the Corporation) in the Irish Parliament from 1727 to the Act of Union, and in the United Kingdom Parliament one or other frequently represented the town (now reduced to one seat) down to 1868, when Lieutenant-Colonel Charles George Tottenham was replaced by Mr Patrick MacMahon, the first Catholic to represent the town for nearly two hundred years. By the 1790s the Tottenhams provided the leadership of the 'Protestant Ascendancy' faction in the whole county, in the person of the Earl of Ely, who controlled or was powerful in nine of the county's sixteen borough seats. His uncle Charles Tottenham by then effectively 'owned the town of Ross'.[12]

The basis of the family's hard-line politics was laid in the early eighteenth century, when the sense of siege from hostile native forces recurred. A 1730 memorial to the Lords Justices in Dublin, sent by the Sovereign, Charles Tottenham, on behalf of the Burgesses, Freemen and 'the Protestant inhabitants of the town', petitioned for the repair of the barracks and the retention of the garrison on the grounds that 'the inhabitants of the said towne and the country adjoining being for the greater part most violent Papists, part of the Army's being quartered therein is a great security of the Protestant Interest of that part of the Kingdom'. Pointing out that the town was 'frequently invested with riots', the petition argued that without troops they would be 'exposed to the fury and outrage of a disaffected riotous population with whom they are surrounded'. This new sense of siege was clearly heightened by the fear of the Catholic population in the town itself.

In 1758 the Sovereign (again a Charles Tottenham) petitioned the Lord Lieutenant to be allowed to use the troops, 'now quartered in the said town' against 'a very numerous, furious and outrageous mob' who had tried to prevent the export of corn through the port, and had been reinforced by armed country people from across the river in Kilkenny. Even in a petition to Parliament in 1786, asking for the removal of restrictions on the importation of tobacco through the port, the Sovereign (jointly Charles Tottenham and Robert Leigh) felt it appropriate to remind Parliament of the town's series of Royal Charters, 'in consideration of the zeal of the inhabitants in sheltering the English from the depredations of the native Irish'.[13] It seems likely that the attack on the town in 1798 was seen by the Sovereign (again, Charles Tottenham) in similar terms.

By then the Tottenhams and their allies had considerably more at stake than in 1730. The *Dublin Magazine* described New Ross in 1764 as 'a beautiful sea-port of extensive trade, one of the sweetest situated places in Ireland ... it is vastly improved within these ten years through the means of Mr. Tottenham, Surveyor-General of the Province of Leinster, who caused a spacious Sessions House, Market House, a fine vaulted Assembly Room and a Charter School, after the most rural pretty taste ... to be built'.[14] The Market House became the chief municipal building and was eventually called the Tholsel, from the 'toll-stall', where market tolls had been collected since the thirteenth century, and where the Market Cross had stood until destroyed by the Cromwellians. Beside it was the Bridewell, or gaol, and attached to it the Guardhouse. The Tholsel and Guardhouse were together called 'the Main Guard' during the 1798 battle, and proved to be the rock on which the rebel attack broke. There was a rich symbolism to that. The inscription over the doorway at the Tholsel reads, 'The first stone was laid July ye first, the Anniversary of the glorious Battle of the Boyne.' The inscription on the keystone of the arch reads 'Libertate Asserta Vicit Veritas' (With liberty declared, truth has conquered). The building thus made a political statement, as well as serving a variety of civic and commercial functions, and by the 1790s that statement was being articulated by the Tottenham faction in terms of 'Protestant Ascendancy': the idea that the retention of the Protestant political monopoly was fundamental to the survival of the constitution and of civil and religious liberties. While that mindset was a response to recent relaxation in the 'Penal Code' against Catholics, it also reflected old insecurities.

However, the Tholsel also bespoke some revival in the town's fortunes and considerable optimism about its future. Designed by English architect Knox, who had designed the Horseguards in London a few years earlier, it has a well-proportioned classical elegance, with the fine clocktower and cupola its most arresting features. Until the mid-nineteenth century its ground floor was an open space, enclosed by railings that filled the arches; there 'the last representatives of the ancient Guilds of the town plied at their respective crafts'.[15] Arthur Young's brief visit to the town nearly thirty years after the Tholsel was built suggests that it was still sunk in its old torpor. While 'ships sailing up to the town ... enliven the scene not a little', its trade was 'languid and trifling. There are only four or five brigs and sloops that belong to the place.'

Young was more intent on making a political point (that 'those noble harbours on the coast of Ireland are only melancholy capabilities of commerce') than investigating the reality, and the town in fact enjoyed a new modest prosperity through its share of the Newfoundland and provisions trade that was transforming more dramatically the fortunes of Waterford.[16] It continued to be hampered by restrictions on imports but its coastal trade was significant, for example in the lucrative Dublin malt market trade during the 1790s.[17] When Samuel Elmes, a comfortably-off Protestant farmer at Old Ross, wrote to his

nephew in London in March 1798 urging him to settle in the town, he could
cite 'different men in Ross that began upon a very small property that is now
thriving very fast'.[18] One of his friends was the merchant Thomas Keogh,
responsible, according to Alexander, for adding to the 'lofty stores lately erected on the ballast quay' further buildings near the new bridge.[19]

The lack of a bridge since the mid-seventeenth century had long been
seen as an obstacle to development, and the magnificent toll bridge, built in
1796 at a cost of £11,000 by a company incorporated by Act of Parliament
and headed by Tottenham, was a striking vote of confidence in the town's
future. It 'will be a beautiful object from the Quay', Tottenham had promised
his daughter. Built of oak, '510 feet long, 40 feet broad, with a causeway of 150
feet and a portcullis 27 feet wide to admit vessels, it rested on 24 sets of piers'.
It too was to play a crucial role in the battle for the town in 1798.[20]

Official and commercial New Ross centred on the old network of streets
and quays on the level ground beside the river. Here the private houses were
high and slated, and some were grand, none more so than Tottenham's town
house, built on the site of the original Augustinian Friary. Here too were a
number of older timber-frame houses, some serving as shops, reached by a
wooden staircase, which reminded one English visitor in 1779 of Chester.[21]
But the bulk of the population within the old walls lived on the streets rising
steeply from the Tholsel, or the warren of lanes connecting them. Halfway up
the slope slated houses gave way to thatch, some of the poorest dwellings
being huddled against the walls.

Near the top of Main (now Mary) Street the great medieval church of St
Mary's was a partial ruin, though still in use. To one side and lower down the
hillside a large military barracks offered vital security, as we have seen, to the
Protestant Freemen, diminishing the fear of engulfment by the sea of poverty
on the slopes above them. The picturesque situation of the town, well caught
in the 1797 etching by George Holmes, thus gave a false sense of harmony and
tranquillity. Its landscaped, cultivated environs reminded Reverend James Hall
of 'Bedfordshire and the well-cultivated counties of England'.[22] But viewing
the town from across the river, and setting the scene for the battle of 5 June
1798 in his remarkable 1828 novel *The Croppy*, Michael Banim, Catholic post-
master of Kilkenny city, described it thus:

> From the opposite bank of the river, when the distance is sufficient to
> obscure the frequent features of want and ruin in the poorer dwellings,
> and whence are prominently visible some better structures, the Church
> and a mass of romantic ruins, mingling with and ennobling the cabins on

New Ross in 1796, *drawn by G. Holmes, engraved by J. Walker, London 1801.*

the hillside, all relieved by height and slope, meadow and plantation, and having for foreground below, the quay, and a few taper-masted vessels at its side – a whole picture is presented, which the lovers of landscape would pronounce to be as peculiar as it is pleasing.[23]

The slope added to the daily toil of the inhabitants, being so steep, according to Lewis, 'as to render the communication between the upper and lower parts extremely inconvenient'.[24] However, as loyalist James Alexander noted after the battle, the same precipitous fall of ground made the town vulnerable to attack, and the original rebel impetus owed much to this topography.[25]

By the late eighteen century there was also a significant and growing population outside the walls, especially in the 'Irishtown', a broad street on the brow of the hill, whose name recalls the attempted exclusion since the town's foundation of its 'Irish enemies', relaxed gradually on commercial grounds. When Alexander described entering it through the Fair Gate he was clear that

New Ross *by W.H. Bartlett, in G.N. Wright,* Ireland Illustrated from Original Drawings *(London 1832).*

it involved 'turning our backs to Ross'.[26] The renaming of that gate (originally Bishop's Gate) reflected the transfer of the market to the open area beyond it from the town centre earlier in the century, and the erection there of a new market cross to replace that destroyed in 1649 by 'The Iconoclasts', as Hore calls them.[27] The Irishtown thus became a symbolic centre of the old religion as well as a market area and 'new' town. The housing was mixed, some prosperous slated houses in the 'lower' Irishtown, and again in the prosperous mill village of the Maudlins just beyond it; 'All the rest of the broad street, or Irishtown consists of low cabins'.[28]

Twenty years after the battle John Bernard Trotter found that 'the market here is very good and plentiful. The country people come in great numbers to it, and are in general well dressed and respectable, speak Irish, and are almost universally Catholic.' The only distinctive group of poor townspeople noted by Trotter were the boatmen on 'the limestone and sand boats', who were 'large, muscular and well formed'; 'their loud conversation in Irish and vehement gestures as they passed made a novel and animated scene'.[29] Some local fishermen, as we'll see, were later suspected of carrying messages from the rebels in the town to those assembled across the river, but the ordinary people make frustratingly few appearances in contemporary accounts or the records of the courts-martial. Some, clearly, were disaffected and joined the rebels, but this does not appear to have been widespread or significant.

Nor should we equate Catholics entirely with poverty or ignorance, any more than with disaffection. In the 1950s Maureen Wall charted the rise and consolidation of a Catholic middle class, which became organized and politicized initially against trade restrictions imposed by Protestant corporations, including that at New Ross.[30] More recently Kevin Whelan has argued for a vibrant modernizing Catholicism centred in the belt of rich farmland stretching from south Wexford across to Limerick.[31] His important outline of 'the Catholic community in eighteenth-century county Wexford' focused on Catholic middlemen as 'an underground aristocracy with an alternative culture', and pointed to the growth in the towns of Catholic organizations (confraternities, sodalities, charitable societies), which were also centres of political mobilization. What had begun as a politics of deference was radicalized during the 1790s, though most prosperous Catholics remained conservative and conformist, and kept a low profile at local as well as national level.[32] Thus we know little of the better-off New Ross Catholics who would have been the backbone of the Sodality of the Christian Doctrine, founded in 1798.[33] Their growing confidence and prosperity was to become apparent immediately after the Rebellion in the building of a fine new parish church opposite Tottenham's townhouse in 1808, and of a new, much enlarged Augustinian college the following year. Eight years later a Carmelite convent was founded with a school attached. More surprisingly, the Augustinians leased the site of their new college from Charles Tottenham, in gratitude, it was said, for the fact that a New Ross Augustinian had helped him to escape from a French prison in 1792. Also in 1809 the Houghton Fever Hospital and Dispensary was founded, run by a board of twelve Catholics and twelve Protestants, including the rector and parish priest.[34]

Among the better-off Catholics of the town was my ancestor John Rice, and the little we know of him comes mainly from family tradition. He was born in Callan in 1756. His extended family featured long-established and prosperous farmers and businessmen. His cousin, Edmund, born six years later, joined his uncle's provisioning business in Waterford, which was focused on the Newfoundland trade and received a great boost with the outbreak of the war against France in 1792. New Ross, with its close ties to Waterford and its prosperous hinterland, was an obvious location for a branch of the Rice provisioning business, and it was likely that this was what brought John Rice there; it's not known when. New Ross was also linked to Callan through the Augustinians, long established in each town. Edmund's brother John joined the order in New Ross in 1792 before moving on to Rome, and Edmund continued to pay his expenses through the New Ross house, and may have been a regular visitor; we know that he travelled a great deal through the region on behalf of the family business.[35] Thus it is likely that John Rice's pig-buying and bacon-curing business in New Ross was closely associated with his cousin's enterprise, and shared in the lucrative provisioning of the army and navy in the 1790s. Edmund Rice, it seems, had a military pass, and was able to continue his business trips even at the height of the Rebellion.[36] We can also speculate that while John Rice grew up in a Gaelic-speaking environment in Callan, by the 1790s he was part of a Catholic revival that focused on religious and charitable organizations, rather than the political arena. Through his wife, Mary Doyle, he was connected to another successful Catholic family, the best-known member of which was to be her nephew, James, the future Bishop of Kildare and Loughlin – 'JKL' – who was born in the Irishtown in 1786, and was delivered by his half-brother, a successful doctor in the town.[37] As a Catholic businessman in a town dominated by an ultra-Protestant Corporation, Rice had every reason for prudence. In his case this was all the greater in that the landlord from whom he leased the two-storey house and the out-buildings which housed his bacon-curing business was almost certainly Charles Tottenham, from whom he may also have leased an office on the Quay, and some land near the town.[38]

'BRAVE MEN OF THE BARONY OF BANTRY': THE BACKGROUND OF THE REBELS WHO ATTACKED NEW ROSS

When James Alexander walked close to the rebel camp at Corbet Hill on the evening before the battle, relying on his clerical-style clothes and knowledge of Irish as protective cover, he met a group of drunken 'peasants', armed with pikes, who spoke to him comically in both English and Irish.[39] This may appear a cliché, familiar from stock 'stage-Irish' characters and soon to be elaborated on in novels by Maria Edgeworth and others, but Alexander, while sometimes patronizing, was an astute and not unsympathetic observer of the rebels, and made remarkable efforts to describe and understand them. He captured two crucial features here: the rebels who attacked New Ross were, for the most part, poor countrymen and were bilingual, or more accurately, perhaps, between two languages. Such usage of the term 'peasant' was general, and was often descriptive rather than pejorative, but it had no precise meaning, and could embrace relatively prosperous farmers as well as more marginal tenants and the rural poor, depending upon the background of the user. For Thomas Cloney, the only rebel leader at the battle to leave an account, his followers were 'country peasants', 'armed countrymen', as distinct from the 'respectable farmers', like himself, who led them.[40] The pattern of peasant insurgency in Ireland over the four previous decades had featured variations of this alliance between wealthy farmers and their socially inferior neighbours.

These 'bold peasantry of our respective neighbourhoods' were 'all brave men of the Barony of Bantry', to quote Cloney again.[41] Bantry was a large barony, covering the area roughly between New Ross and Enniscorthy to the north-east, and bounded by the Barrow and Slaney rivers. For centuries, as ntoed, it had been frontier territory in terms of Norman settlement, its Gaelic inhabitants, led by the dominant Kavanagh sept, regularly attacking the walled colonial town from the thirteenth century. The trauma and dislocation of more recent colonial settlement, and the management, occupation and use of land that followed, had added significantly to feelings of alienation and resentment throughout rural society.

The seventeenth-century colonial revolution, as we've seen, was radical in Wexford, amounting to an almost total transfer in land-ownership.[42] Little wonder, to quote Kevin Whelan's *The Tree of Liberty*, that 'Catholic middlemen families were obsessed, almost to the point of neurosis, with ancestry, family background and the Cromwellian rupture'.[43] Ten years earlier Whelan had written of the 'ethnic anguish' of Miles Byrne, and 'this racial sense of opposition to the seventeenth-century settlers' in Cloney; and in mapping out the sectarian dimensions of the 1798 Rebellion he showed the continued significance of the southern boundary of the 1620 plantation.[44] But such feelings extended below the level of the descendants of former Gaelic proprietors, now middlemen, and had become part of the sense of grievance of the less well off in relation to tithes, rents or changes in custom. To quote Whelan again, 'at all levels of Wexford Catholic society we find memories of this Cromwellian original sin'.[45] In a similar vein, Lecky's interpretation of 1798 placed great stress on what a correspondent of Chief Secretary Henry Pelham called 'the long and gradually ripened vengeance' that 'the lower Catholics' cherish against those who, in Lecky's words 'invaded their temples, murdered their forefathers and appropriated their estates'.

This letter from a magistrate on 3 June 1798 argued:

As long as the property of the country exists; as long as the recollection of the British Law of Gavilkind exists, and Irish names remain, so long will the lower Irish hope to gain what they think, whether justly or unjustly, their hereditary property. I have talked to many of their prisoners, and their only motive assigned for rising was to *make Ireland their own again*.[46]

As well as the Spenserian emphasis on 'Irish names', there is an echo here, albeit unconscious, of recurring themes in Irish Jacobite poetry. This had a particular resonance in the Bantry barony, which even after seventeenth-century colonization retained a strong Gaelic identity. Using the distribution of family names and the survival of 'unconsolidated' landholdings, the historical geographer Tom Jones-Hughes identified it as part of 'a powerful stable Gaelic heartland' into the early nineteenth century. 'Unconsolidated' farms involved 'scattered parcels of land in open fields', sometimes linked to clusters of farmsteads 'by a mesh of trackways'. This remnant of older forms of communal landownership was particularly prominent around Courtnacuddy and Killanne. In contrast to the south-east of the county where the small, fragmented Anglo-Norman estate system still survived, and to the north, dominated by the new, larger commercial estates and denser Protestant settlement, Bantry contained strong traditional elements intermingled with some new large modernizing estates, whose landlords, such as the Carews of Castleboro, were often more liberal in politics than their northern counterparts.[47] This was one reason why, as Cloney put it, 'Although the majority of the landed proprietors in my neighbourhood were Cromwellian settlers, the Protestant and Catholic middlemen of that quarter entertained kind feelings towards each other': however, the Catholic couldn't forget 'the political slavery under which he laboured'.[48]

The area had its own focus of sectarian animosity, even before the introduction of Orangeism in the year prior to the Rebellion. The settlement of German Palatine families in the Ram estate at Old Ross in 1709 caused resentment,[49] which was given a new impetus when this 'colony with the strange-sounding names' became stranger still by embracing Methodism in the mid-eighteenth century.[50] As late as the 1760s there was further Protestant settlement, with Robert Leigh of Rosegarland replacing Catholic with Protestant tenants around Newbawn, 'for electoral purposes'.[51] Added to the tension between an unusually deep-seated traditionalism and rapid modernization, these developments made the area a centre of Whiteboy disturbances in the 1760s and 1770s, with Palatine families like the Hornicks, and new Protestant tenants like the Cottons, being particular targets, as they were to be again in 1798 when the Old Ross colony was devastated and centres of new Protestant settlement were heavily targeted.[52]

One crucial arena for what Jones-Hughes called 'the battle between traditionalism and modernisation' was the Catholic Church. The radical reorganization of the rural parish structure extended the breach with tradition to the use of new names, and the building of chapels on new sites, particularly in 'the Gaelic heartland'. Thus, Courtnacuddy (part of the newly created parish of Davidstown) is an example of the new 'chapel villages',[53] one reason, perhaps, why it was attacked in the Orange backlash after the Rebellion. Davidstown incorporated the old parishes of Templescoby and Rossdroit; the latter area was to be notorious for sectarian violence in 1798.

The new, modernizing Catholicism, so well delineated by Kevin Whelan, with its revitalized structures, its drive for conformity and church building, its lay confraternities, sodalities and charitable societies, may have centred on towns like Wexford and New Ross, but its influence was also being felt prior to the Rebellion in the countryside.[54] It was to take several decades into the new century before clerical reform and control were fully established, and traditional practices largely abandoned, but the process was well advanced among better-off farmers, even in traditional areas like Bantry, and this class was already providing many of the new reforming clergy. The priests who took prominent roles in the Rebellion in this area, notably Philip Roche of Poulpeasty and Mogue Kearns of Rathnure, were marginal men, at odds with the Church authorities, in part because scandalously immersed in the lifestyles of their congregations. Their appeal to rank-and-file rebels owed even more to traditional belief in the miraculous powers of the clergy, a manifestation of the superstition targeted by the reform movement.[55] The opposition of the bishop and the vast majority of the clergy to the Rebellion reflected a political tradition of pragmatic loyalism as well as the new Catholicism, but it alienated them from many traditional Catholics in the short-term. Thus James Doyle, the parish priest of Davidstown, who called for decisive military action against the rebels, had to admit: 'I have lost my influence with the people.' He was one of the priests cited by the bishop as having been treated with contempt by the insurgents.[56]

The new clergy were also important agents of a different and less visible revolution, the uneven but accelerating replacement of Irish by English in this period. The nature of the historical record and the complex bilingualism through which this radical cultural change was mediated, and perhaps rendered less traumatic, have made it difficult to trace. In the absence of any detailed study of the process there is also a tendency to exaggerate the pace and finality of this language shift, particularly in ostensibly 'English' areas, like Wexford, and to ignore the indicators of a marked local variation.[57] The evidence for significant daily use of Irish in Bantry into the 1820s is patchy but compelling. Bishop Sweetman's 1753 'Visitation Book', while mainly concerned with the state of the clergy, especially their vestments and chalices, also recorded when sermons were delivered in Irish, in itself an indication, perhaps, that this was a declining practice. It was one, however, of which the bishop approved, and he found it mainly in Bantry. 'One of ye best, if not ye best Irish sermon I ever heard', was given by Reverend Michael O'Brien of Bree. The Reverend Martin Edmond of Killanne not only gave a sermon in Irish to his own flock but repeated it for congregations in Rathgarogue and New Ross. That this was due to his being a noted preacher rather than to a lack of proficiency on the part of his colleagues seems clear from the fact that the parish priest of New Ross preached a sermon in Irish in a nearby rural parish.[58] There is little direct evidence for the use of Irish in the area over the next half-century, but a number of witnesses testified to its continued strength in the decades after the Rebellion while also stressing the spread of bilingualism. Thus an English visitor, John Trotter, noted in 1819:

> The Irish language is spoken most generally in the County of Wexford … Is it not surprising that in the very part where the English first settled this language should to this hour remain and flourish?

He noted that 'the country people' conducted their business at fairs in the towns through Irish, but in his attempts to engage 'peasants and farmers' in conversation he found no difficulty 'as most of them spoke English as well as Irish'.[59] Five years earlier William Shaw Mason noted rather smugly about the Adamstown area, 'the Irish language, which was generally spoken, is getting rapidly out of use, and the civilisation of the county is rapidly supplying its place'. However, the Reverend James Gordon in nearby Killegney added a significant caveat to such assessments: 'The language among the peasants, except the Protestants, in their discourse with one another, is mostly Irish, but they all speak English. The only man who could not speak English died a few years ago.'[60] More impressive than such anecdotal evidence is the fascinating 1814 survey by Christopher Anderson, a Scottish advocate of the use of Irish by Protestant evangelists. He noted that in Killegney, people 'usually converse' in Irish, while English is 'spoken by a minority'. In Adamstown, while Irish is 'spoken by many', English is 'generally understood'. He also argued that even if most people can now speak English, it is not 'expressive of the thoughts, the opinions, the feelings of the man'. 'Language', he concludes, 'still remains a thing of choice, or a matter of taste.'[61] All of this underlines the significance of James Alexander's repeated testimony that the rebels at Ross spoke both languages but that their instinctive language in times of danger was Irish.

In his undated manuscript account of 'Traditions in Courtnacuddy', my grandfather Thomas Dunne supported the folklore that Donnchadh Ruadh MacConmara spent some time in the parish, claiming: 'I have heard an old man, John Brien, repeat some of the famous Munster poets extempore verses on local subjects.'[62] He dated these to the decade 1740-50, part of which the poet may have spent as an itinerant teacher in the Sliabh gCua district of east Waterford, so it is not impossible, though unlikely, that he wandered as far as the similar Blackstairs region of west Wexford. This sense of an oral tradition in Irish is significant, and the fact that little of it survives from eighteenth-century Wexford should not prevent us from considering its potential for illuminating popular culture at the time of the Rebellion. Particularly important to the political aspects of this culture is Jacobite verse, notably the *aislingí*, or vision poems, none of which survives from this area, to my knowledge. The only contemporary Wexford poet identified by De Vál, Séamus Ó Murchú, lived in the Shelbourne barony, south of New Ross, and was active in manuscript production. He wrote religious verse and elegies, but no Jacobite poetry that survives.[63] This is not unusual; his better-known Mayo contemporary, Riocard Bairéad, was politically active, possibly even a United Irishman, but left no political verse.[64]

As argued earlier, Jacobite poetry came to articulate popular grievances, particularly against the new landlords and the Protestant clergy. This was largely because its focus continued to be on the dismantling of the colonial settlement, particularly the land settlement, widely regarded as lacking legitimacy. Ó Buachalla has argued that its powerful sense of Gaelic and Catholic identity constituted an 'Irish Nationalist rhetoric'. The recurring elements that he identified can certainly be regarded as articulating a proto-nationalism, which conditioned the reception of modern Enlightenment and Romantic ideas of 'the nation' at a popular level during the period of European revolution. These elements he listed as 'the providential mode of thought, the racial and religious exclusiveness, the geographical integrity of the island, the indescribable purgatory of the Irish'. The radical potential of this poetry increased with the widespread peasant insurgency of 'Whiteboyism' under a variety of names, from the 1760s; and resided particularly in what Ó Buachalla has called its 'potent millennial message of personal and communal liberation'. Increasingly the consoling prophecies of providential deliverance focused on land and religion, as for example:

> Luther's followers will altogether be destroyed as the saints foretell and authors think; the poor Irish who were vanquished by acts of law will be free and established in their ancestral lands.[65]

In *Aisling Ghéar*, Ó Buachalla showed how Gaelic sources substantiated official fears that the use of Jacobite airs, for example, or the wearing of Jacobite white at Whiteboy events reflected widespread expectation of French help in support of a popular uprising against grievances like enclosure or tithes. He cited examples of popular songs in which the Whiteboys anticipated the coming of the Pretender, or in which the latter is actually called 'Mo Bhuachaill Bán' (My White Boy).[66]

The Jacobite poetry written by Micheál Óg Ó Longáin in 1797-9 will be analysed below as a rare example of the interaction of this traditional radicalism with the new language of the United Irishmen, and thus as a possible key to understanding the motivation of Irish-speaking peasant 'insurgents' in the Wexford Rebellion. An early *aisling* of his, written in macaronic form, may serve to illustrate another aspect of the Jacobite view of the agrarian secret societies that were such a feature of the barony of Bantry. Dated 'an tam tháinig na Buachaillí Bána, 1785' (the time the Whiteboys came, 1785), it refers, in fact, to the anti-tithe 'Rightboy' movement that convulsed Cork at that time, and marked important advances in the scale and co-ordination of peasant protest. Although Rightboys targeted Catholic priests' dues as well as Protestant tithes, Ó Longáin's poem invokes traditional Jacobite sectarianism, the apparition promising that when Charles Stuart comes, 'Beidh báire is céad ar Sasanaigh is fanatics dá gcrádh gan cabhair / Is gearr go mbeidh Rex in Albain, is Aifreann dá rá gach am'. Ó Longáin's own version runs, '"Tis then we'll banish Protestants, in Scotland I'll have my seat / Long live the Roman Catholics to flourish well bright and fair' – a loose translation, which equates 'Sasanaigh is fanatics' (English and fanatics) with 'Protestants', for example.[67]

The tradition in Jacobite poetry of seeing local events in terms of the age-old struggle between Gael and Gall may have made easier such assimilation of modern revolutionary ideology to traditional Jacobite forms as occurred in the 1790s. One of the best-known Whiteboy poems, 'Béil Átha Ragad' (Ballyraggett), deals with the major 1775 affray in Kilkenny that followed the attack by a large armed group of Whiteboys on the house of the Catholic landlord, Robert Butler, prominent in the 'Anti-Whiteboy League' begun by the local parish priest. Yet the poem describes the 'buachaillí bána' as fighting for 'clanna bocht cráite Gael' (the poor persecuted Irish) against 'na Gallaibh' (the foreigners).[68]

The strength of this traditional peasant insurgency culture in Bantry, in the years immediately prior to any United Irish organization of the area, can be seen most dramatically in the large-scale 1793 outbreak, often called 'the first rebellion'. This 'formidable rising' featured 'rebels' armed with pikes marching on the towns of Enniscorthy and Wexford, after rapid and widespread mobilization. It was sparked by an ultra-Protestant magistrate taking two men prisoner for administering oaths at Davidstown chapel. A large crowd marched to Enniscorthy to demand their release, but the magistrate's response was to arrest sixteen others and to lodge two of them in Wexford gaol. Within two days a crowd of several hundred countrymen (including, it was said, some Protestants) armed with pikes, scythes, and some firelocks threatened to burn the town if the prisoners weren't released. Troops opened fire after a confused fracas, during which their officer, Major Valloten, and the rebel leader John Moore were both killed. At least nine and possibly as many as twenty-five of what Wexford Corporation later called 'a dangerous and riotous mob' were killed by the troops and six more were subsequently executed.[69]

A contemporary ballad described the killings in religious terms: 'when Romans were slaughtered in Wexford the month of July'. However, the verse ended with criticism of 'the clergy', whose 'allegiance is now for the Crown'.[70] The text of the tombstone erected by Moore's parents, at Carnagh near New Ross, was more circumspect, calling on 'each Christian' to pray for 'that noble boy' who was 'killed by the army'. But it also included a subtle endorsement of whatever organized form of peasant insurgency mobilized the rebels, noting that he 'on his oath that day in truth did die'. The fact that both this memorial and the obelisk erected to Major Valloten were attacked in 1798 shows how 'the first rebellion' continued to be a live issue during the second.

What motivated it? George Taylor, a local loyalist, later blamed Defenderism, but there is no evidence and little likelihood that the Defenders were in the area at such an early date.[71] The explanation offered by local clergyman George Handcock, that it was a riot against conscription into the militia, may have more substance, and would help to account for the anti-clerical sentiment of the ballad, as priests were targeted in Wexford for co-operating with this unpopular measure. Tom Powell pointed out that anti-militia disturbances had peaked in the area two months previously, although the resentment involved continued to be important. He opted instead for Edward Hay's explanation of 1793 as a resurgence of traditional Whiteboyism, visible for the first time since 1779, due mainly to a depression in the local agricultural economy. Powell linked the outbreak particularly to changes in the local tithe farming system, long a focus of Whiteboy concern. The oath taken in Davidstown (and presumably by Moore), according to an informant of the magistrates, was 'to cut down their own clergy to a certain rate of parish dues, not to take tithe from tithe proctors, nor pay more than six pence per acre for tillage' – a classic 'Rightboy' formulation. Powell pointed out that Moore was an assistant to the local tithe proctor George Giles, and speculated that he may have been one of those who lost out in a restructuring of tithe-letting.[73]

The emphasis on tithes also featured in the account given to the French visitor de Latocnaye when he visited Wexford shortly afterwards, and he commented that the suppression of 'this revolt' of 'the Whiteboys' prevented a much greater outbreak, akin to the French Revolution.[74] Clearly there was no question of that in the 1793 episode, which was part of a traditional pattern of local outbreaks, though on an unusually large scale.

POLITICIZATION IN THE LATER 1790S

A number of new factors forced 'the second rebellion' five years later into an entirely new pattern. These included a far deeper economic crisis as the key trade in malted barley collapsed, a more virulent and volatile sectarianism with the spread of the Orange Order (and the widespread 'great fear' of impending massacres arising from this), and a complex process of politicization, including the creation of a new insurgency network by the United Irishmen, at least at leadership level. There are few traces of the group that could offer a vital key to the transition from 1793 to 1798, the Defenders. Lecky linked them to the 'obscure disturbances' of 1793,[75] but according to Whelan this 'shadowy organisation' was unlikely to have penetrated the county until 1797. If its existence could be proven, even then, however, he believed it 'would help explain the bitter sectarian tinge which coloured many of the rebels activities in the rebellion'.[76] What Cullen has called 'the problem of understanding the Defenders, and their aim and spread'[77] is unlikely ever to be resolved satisfactorily because of the patchy nature of the evidence. Whelan offered one interesting clue to a possible Defender influence in Bantry in the year prior to the Rebellion, with the return of Father Mogue Kearns to Killanne after his expulsion from the Meath diocese for Defender activity. The priest reported by Musgrave to have said Mass for the rebels prior to the battle of Ross was the same Father Kearns who 'wore a broad cross belt and a dragoon's sable under his vestments'.[78]

Whelan also speculated that Defender influence could account for the belief in millenarian prophecy articulated by the Wexford rebels, although this was also a feature of the older Jacobite tradition. Indeed, one of the examples of this that he cited referred to King James having rested on a local hillside, and the rebels believing that 'the Irish would again muster on that hill, strong and victorious'.[79] This was from the testimony of Jane Barber, one of a number by loyalist women who spoke about their experiences of 1798. In these accounts the rebels are often portrayed sympathetically, and the opinions of servants and tenants highlighted.[80] They also tended to bring millenarian expectation to the practical level of reversing the role of masters and servants. Thus, the rebel who arrested Jane Adams's father declared 'that our Saviour's prophecy was now fulfilling, when he said, "the first shall be last and the last shall be first"; that *we* had been *first* long enough'.[81]

The turning of the world upside down was also anticipated in religious terms. Elizabeth Richards spoke to 'a strange looking old man' who told her that the Rebellion had been forecast twenty-five years earlier 'by a stranger who came to his father's home'. She learned later that he had been reluctant to tell her 'that part of the prophecy was that the Roman Catholic cause would be victorious'.[82] Even if Defenderism was not significant in the Bantry barony, it was 'a genuinely popular ideology spontaneously generated from "below" in response to the crisis of the 1790s', according to Smyth, and what he called its 'loose, fluid cluster of ideas which tapped into the sources of lower-class Catholic solidarity' illustrated how the Jacobite tradition could be adapted to a form of popular radicalism, and blend with ideas assimilated from revolutionary France.[83] The most obvious example of this was the transformation of traditional expectations of help from the Continent. As Bartlett put it:

> When the French Revolution burst upon a startled world, the Gaelic mind, essentially the outlook of the lower orders, found no difficulty in assimilating French developments into the by now time-honoured themes of deliverance from abroad, besting the Saxon and destroying the Protestants.

Defenderism resembled Jacobitism most clearly, perhaps, in its antipathy to the colonial settlement of the seventeenth century. 'It was', to quote Bartlett again, 'anti-Protestant, anti-English, anti-settler in a way that the earlier [agrarian] movements were not.' This perspective is crucial in any assessment of the extent to which the rural poor were politicized by French revolutionary ideology in the 1790s. This was not a simple process of assimilation, as if the peasant mind was blank, a *tabula rasa*. It was a matter, rather, of fitting whatever filtered through of the new ideas to existing concerns and perspectives, as

United Irish attempts to propagandize the poor recognized. Bartlett has also pointed out that it was the fusion of the new revolutionary impulse with the old Gaelic tradition of deliverance that created 'a revolutionary dynamic' in Defenderism.[84] Similarly Breandán Ó Buachalla has connected the Jacobite motif of 'saoirse' with the revolutionary slogan of 'Liberty'.[85] And more powerful than any revolutionary concept may have been the *example* of successful popular revolt, the realization of the millenarian dream of a world turned upside down that the news from France principally communicated.

The process of politicization also had a strong local impetus during the turbulent 1790s, during which the sectarian character of County Wexford politics generated unusual public excitement. The liberal challenge to the powerful ultra-Ascendancy faction, led by Ely and Ogle, owed much of its strength to Catholic support, not only from the old gentry leadership, but also from the newly radicalized Catholic middle class, including many better-off farmers. For example, the signatories of the 1792 address in support of the new and more assertive leadership of the Catholic Committee in Dublin included the father of Thomas Cloney, as well as others from the barony that were prominent in 1798, like Thomas Devereux of the Leap and Robert Carty of Birchgrove.

Some of the next generation voiced a more revolutionary radicalism, as can be seen in the letter written by Thomas Devereux's son Walter to his brother in New York on the eve of the outbreak in Wexford. Walter was also planning to 'leave this land of tirany' soon, 'if the times are not settled'. Clearly he anticipated some form of resistance from 'the majesty of the people'; Irishmen wanted to 'be free'. Among 'our respectable and honest countrymen in the gaols of the Kingdom' he instanced Arthur O'Connor and Oliver Bond, and he seemed to identify with 'the short haired people … called Cropps', which may indicate United Irish membership, or at least influence. It seems that both Walter and his father fought in what his mother later called 'the Wicket Rebellion'.[86]

Politicization extended further down the social scale with the extension of the franchise to Catholic forty-shilling freeholders in 1793, some of whom doubtless did interpret this reform, as Westmoreland believed, to mean 'an end to rents, tithes and taxes'. Likewise, organized resistance to the Militia Act in the same year involved many ordinary people in active opposition to government policy.[87] All of this renders more believable the claim by Edward Hay to have collected 22,000 signatures in County Wexford in support of a petition against the recall of Fitzwilliam in 1795.[88] Even before it took the form of a rampaging Orangeism in 1797, the extremism of the dominant Ascendancy group in Wexford had done much to radicalize Catholic opinion. Thus, for example, their blocking of an attempt by the leading liberal Carew, to include Catholics in his Volunteer corps clearly antagonized Thomas Cloney, who had hoped to join it. He later described it as 'a convincing proof of the fatal policy that drove Wexford into Insurrection'.[89]

While it is impossible to gauge the impact of this highly sectarianized politics on the rural poor, it may be seen as part of the pattern identified by Donnolly and Clarke in the introduction to their seminal collection, *Irish Peasants: Violence and Political Unrest 1780–1914* (1983). 'It is no accident that the greatest peasant movements in Irish history – the Defender movement of the 1790s, the Tithe War of the 1830s and the Land War of 1879-1882 – all occurred at times when the Catholic or nationalist challenge to the Protestant Ascendancy was at a high point.'[90] The Wexford Rebellion involved the greatest and most sustained peasant mobilization and insurgency of the eighteenth century in Ireland. What distinguished it was not only its scale, and the ability of the rebels to fight major battles against trained soldiers, but also that its leadership included priests, Protestant landlords, members of old Catholic gentry families and wealthy farmers. Their role raises large, complex questions about social relationships and politicization, but the attention of historians has focused almost exclusively on claims that they were United Irishmen, carrying out a concerted plan and motivated by a single revolutionary ideology.

These claims remain speculative and unverifiable because, despite the intense focus of the bicentenary on them, no new evidence has been found to support them. The situation in the barony of Bantry illustrates the difficulty particularly well. In Cullen's hypothesis this area was organized late but was then built up rapidly by Cloney and Kelly. The very lateness of the process meant that it went undetected by the authorities and so the two Bantry 'Regiments' were able to play a key role in the fighting.[91] Fundamental to the credibility of this scenario is the evidence for Cloney and Kelly being United Irish 'Colonels'.[92] John Kelly remains a remarkably shadowy figure, apart from his brief if crucial role in the battle of Ross. Indeed, one of the few discoveries made during the bicentenary was that his father was a prominent member of the Church of Ireland (it has always been assumed that Kelly was Catholic) – if the evidence relates to the right 'John Kelly'.[93] The same caveat applies to the only document connecting Kelly to the United Irishmen, a letter from the local magistrate Caesar Colclough to Dublin Castle in June 1797. This told of Colclough's attempt, which he believed successful, to persuade, 'the son of a man of respectability in this neighbourhood' whose 'name is Kelly' to identify the one local man he had admitted swearing into the United Irishmen, and to cease his activities. His ability to do this came from government intelligence that Kelly himself had been 'sworn' earlier in Dublin, and which Kelly, it seems, admitted. Even assuming that this is 'Kelly the Boy from Killanne', 'there is nothing here to support the contention that he had the position of Colonel in the United Irish organisation', as Powell points out.94 What is likely is that the man involved felt so compromised in the eyes of the authorities that he had little option but to join the Rebellion when it began.

There is even less evidence to connect Cloney to the United Irishmen. The magistrate who received information on him, Reverend Thomas Handcock, later claimed he had proof of his 'treason' (which was not specified), but it wasn't enough to arrest him. Indeed, Handcock's account is mainly concerned with his attempts to quieten Cloney's agitation arising from rumours of Orange atrocities.95 It had been alleged that Cloney had been seen with William Putnam McCabe at an inn, and much has been made recently of McCabe's role as a United Irish organizer in Wexford. However, R.R. Madden's judgment (based on McCabe's own account) that this role 'was not successful' must stand, in the absence of any new evidence to the contrary.96 And even if Cloney did meet him, this is hardly proof that he was a United Irishman, much less the 'Colonel' of a 'Regiment'.

It is, of course, possible and even likely that Kelly and Cloney were United Irishmen; nor is the absence of solid evidence conclusive proof that there was not widespread United Irish recruitment in the area prior to the Rebellion. Some magistrates and priests were certainly concerned that this was happening. Handcock warned Dublin Castle about the distribution of seditious literature in his parish and of attempts to recruit members of the Clare militia stationed in Enniscorthy into the United Irishmen.97 Father Shallow, parish priest of Adamstown, in defending himself against charges of being implicated in the Scullabogue massacre, claimed to have combated 'the doctrines and tenets of the United Irishmen' from the time that he supposed them to be 'making strides in my parish or neighbourhood', on the basis that they came from 'French atheistical revolutionary principles'.98 However, this sort of retrospective, vague and politically expedient account adds little to our understanding of the process or scale of recruitment. And even if we assume that recruitment was extensive, what would that have meant? Are we to believe that these farmers and their followers, as well as organizing with remarkable speed and so secretly as to leave no trace, also underwent such intensive indoctrination that their traditional political culture had been replaced in a few months by the United Irish version of Liberty, Equality, Fraternity? Or, is it not more likely that this was absorbed into earlier traditions and concerns, as was indicated in the letter written from near New Ross in late April 1798 by the Protestant farmer Samuel Elmes? While able to reassure his nephew that 'we are very easy in this part of the county from those men who call themselves United Irishmen', 'in some remote parts of the county they still commit depredations, houghing cattle etc'.[99] A similar suggestion of continuity with older forms of peasant insurgency can be found in folklore, gathered in Rathnure, about 'a man named O'Brien who was found by the military swearing in two Whiteboys before 1798' in Davidstown.[100]

Thus, whatever United Irish recruitment took place almost certainly exploited existing sectarian/agrarian grievances, which in the months before the Rebellion became immeasurably heightened and were focused on what Whelan has called, 'a great fear in the spring of 1798 ... a fear of bloody sectarian massacre', which was played on 'by manipulators on both sides'.[101] The importance of the rumours of imminent massacre that swept through the Wexford countryside in these months can hardly be exaggerated, with Protestants and Catholics each living in such fear of attack that they abandoned their houses at night and slept in the open.[102]

On the Catholic side these fears came to focus on a new phenomenon in the county, which rapidly became a graphic colourful shorthand for ancient animosities and present nightmares: the Orange Order. According to Whelan there were only three lodges in Wexford in May 1798, all in the northern part of the county and associated with ultra-Protestant magistrates, like Hunter Gowan, and the reign of terror operated by some yeomanry corps. The association between Orangeism and counter-insurgency terror was strengthened by the arrival of the North Cork Militia in Enniscorthy, some of whom 'publicly wore the Orange insignia and thereby became a living, walking embodiment of every Catholic nightmare'.[103] For some local Protestants, like the Letts of Rathsilla, on the other hand, the Order probably offered reassurance as well as a means of demonstrating their loyalism. And so they rode in full Orange regalia to a lodge meeting in Enniscorthy, which 'made them more obnoxious than many others of their name and religion to the ferocious and bloodthirsty papists'.[104]

While the actual organization of the Orange Order in Wexford may have been small-scale and confined to one area, it became a potent symbol of the official reign of terror throughout the county, and was seen as part of a continuum of sectarian animosity operating since the seventeenth century. It thus became a powerful recruiting agent for insurgency, and the exploitation of the Orange scare by the United Irishmen in the area of its greatest strength is evidenced in the account by Miles Byrne.[105] The increasing use of flogging, half-hanging and the pitchcap by yeomanry and militia was associated with Orangeism in the public mind and was grist to the rumour mill. As Hay put it, 'Great as the apprehensions from Orangemen had been before among the people, they were now multiplied tenfold, and aggravated terror led them in numbers to be sworn United Irishmen, in order to counteract the supposed plan of their rumoured exterminators', who were believed sworn 'to wade ankle deep in their blood.'[106] In other words, many of those who did swear the United Irish oath almost certainly did so out of fear or revenge rather than ideological conviction. Thus Miles Byrne claimed that he was 'forced' to take part in the Rebellion by the brutality of the army: 'I say "forced" because it was impossible to remain neuter.'[107] As Cloney put it, 'Where was the alternative for me [as] a Catholic ... and under the ban of a furious Orange ascendancy, and their rapacious satellite, a bloodthirsty Yeomanry and a brutal magistracy.' He also regarded the atrocities committed by the military and moving ever nearer to his own area as an attack on his class. The killing in the ball-alley in Carnew was of 'twenty-six farmers' by drunken Orangemen; the burning of the chapel at Boolavogue was accompanied by the destruction of 'about twenty farmers' houses'. Likewise the initial skirmish with a small cavalry troop at the Harrow involved 'some of the farmers and their men', who had decided to take a stand.[108] The Rebellion, in his account, began as a series of small-scale local reactions to draconian measures by the military. How, then, did it become so formidable, so quickly?

CHAPTER 11

Rebellion: The Background to the Battle of New Ross

In Cloney's account, the crucial and remarkable victory of 'the people' over about a hundred North Cork Militia at Oulart on 27 May was led by a 'quiet, inoffensive' curate, Father Murphy, angered at the brutal treatment of his parishioners.[1] According to Byrne, Murphy 'encamped on this hill for the purpose of giving an opportunity to the unfortunate people who were hiding to come and join him', and the battle resulted in 'the glorious victory obtained by the people over their cruel tyrants'. In these accounts there is no sense of United Irish planning or organization; all decisions were made, seemingly instinctively (and in Byrne's view, often foolishly), by Father John. As he prepared to move on to attack Enniscorthy, the nearest large town, he was joined by 'all the fine brave young men of the most respectable class of farmers in the neighbourhood', who 'agreed to obey and comply with Father John's instructions ... Thus he became general in chief.'[2] One of the participants at Oulart, Peter Foley, gave Brother Luke Cullen an even more prosaic account of the battle between 'the royal troops and the people'. While Father Murphy was 'our principal leader' he was 'of little use to us'. Effectively there was 'no commander', only a common determination 'to stick together'.[3] As described below, this was also the nature of the rebel attack on New Ross.

The victory at Oulart, the first by the rebels against a considerable force in the open field, was the biggest single factor in spreading the revolt, and suggests an alternative to Cullen's view that only a significant United Irish organization could explain such rapid and widescale mobilization as occurred. According to a recent account, it 'electrified the country, tempting many to join, who might otherwise have hung back', and this is even more true of the capture on 28 May of Enniscorthy with minimal opposition.[4] What began as scattered local insurgency had unexpectedly and fortuitously gained in strength and momentum, and the importance of this was exemplified by the rallying of Cloney and his neighbours to the rebel side only at this point.

Drawing on the work of Charles Tilly, Tom Powell argued thirty years ago that the revolt in the Vendée, with its rapid, large-scale mobilization largely in response to state oppression, provided a parallel for the Wexford insurgency.[5] The comparison had also struck contemporaries: the United Irish leader William McNeven told a House of Commons committee, 'we never meant to make our country a La Vendée or the seat of *Chouannerie*' (i.e. the guerrillas in Brittany).[6]

More recent research on peasant insurgency in France strengthens the parallels with Wexford in 1798. As Jones's survey of this research put it, 'Nobody would today dispute the notion that the peasantry waged their own revolution, which imperfectly coincided with that of the bourgeois.' He identified 'peasant mobilisations' with a 'clear sense of direction' in eight principal areas, some connected with the 'Great Fear' of August–September 1789, most sparked off by economic grievances. Common to all local studies, Jones argued, is the fact that 'the impetus for the insurrection came from within the local community'. This was demonstrated above all in the Vendée, where 'the first rumbles of discontent' (mainly against conscription) on 3 March led to 'a counter-revolutionary army' of 10,000 able to attack a large town on the 14th,[7] described by Donald Sutherland as 'really a vast pilgrimage of entire communities under the nominative command of quarrelling officers'. The peasantry were the driving force of that revolt, motivated by their deep-seated concerns about land tenure and tithes.[8] Similarly, Clay Ramsey's work on the peasant revolts sparked off by the Great Fear focused on 'the shared mentality of its participants' and located 'the striking social cohesion' involved in the practical concerns of rural life, in this case 'consensual notions about the production, sale and distribution of the food supply'.[9] In Sutherland's analysis of the revolt of the Chouans, the leadership of large farmers was crucial in attracting widespread peasant support.[10]

While Ireland lacks the extensive local archives that have transformed scholarly understanding of revolutionary France, there is clear, if patchy evidence for similar patterns in the barony of Bantry in 1798.

In Cloney's account, the attack on Enniscorthy was by 'Insurgents led by Mr. Thomas Synott [his uncle by marriage], Mr. John Rossiter and other respectable farmers', but during these early days Cloney remained at home as rumours of Orange massacres swept through the countryside and all believed themselves 'involved in one common ruin'. People came together 'for mutual protection and advice', and 'several nights were spent under the shelter of ditches, the homes being deserted by night, and the furniture of every kind removed, from an apprehension of their being consumed'. It was only on 28 May, when the news of the taking of Enniscorthy reached Moneyhore and the surrounding areas, that groups of young men began to congregate in large numbers, and to drift towards the rebel camp on Vinegar Hill. Cloney used the excuse, common to all rebel leaders who survived, that he acted under pressure, in his case from 'a large body of men' who besieged his father's house; he was also motivated by fear of state repression, when he 'joined the people'. The sense of special pleading was reinforced by his insistence that 'I proceeded as a Volunteer among many others, to Enniscorthy, without authority or command. I belonged to no society under the United Irish organisation.' He may well have played a more proactive role than he admitted in the meetings 'for mutual protection and advice',[11] but the case for United Irish direction of events at this point remains weak, especially given that the initial focus of many Bantry rebels (possibly including Cloney and his neighbours) was against local Protestants, and on ancient quarrels.

In Cloney's guarded language, after the fall of Enniscorthy 'some excesses were now committed which were, on reflection, deeply to be regretted'.[12] Whelan was less guarded in his 1987 article: 'In its initial phase, the campaign became one of reprisals and paying off old scores.' His mapping of the burning of Protestant houses showed significant concentration around Davidstown and Old Ross, which he explained by noting that 'a fierce animosity to newcomers fired the campaign against the Palatines in Old Ross and their kinsmen in Killanne'. Of the latter, the rebels singled out the family of George Hornick, who had led the local Defence League against the Whiteboys in 1775 and killed three of them in repulsing an attack on his house. He was, according to Whelan, 'the first target of Fr. Philip Roche in 1798'; as he was piked to death, George Hornick was asked, 'Do you remember 9th *July* 1775 now?'[13]

In the anonymous manuscript account Whelan cited, however, the fate of George Hornick seems to have been rather different. Together with other Protestant families, he had taken shelter in the fortified house of the Reverend John Richards of Grange, where 'Priest Roche at the head of a gang of rebels came ... to demand him, and that all the rest should be spared.' But the attack failed, and Hornick and the others escaped to the comparative safety of New Ross.[14] This was also the account given by George Taylor in 1810,[15] and by Musgrave, who attributed to the rebels at Scullabogue, who were about to kill George's brother Philip (who had fought beside him in 1775), the query 'whether he remembered the Whiteboys on the 9th June 1775'.[16] What is clear is that the Hornicks were targeted because of their earlier opposition to Whiteboyism, a very specific example of the continuity between earlier peasant insurgency and 1798.

A year after the Rebellion, Robert Carty of Birchgrove, a prominent local rebel leader with a background similar to Cloney's, was found not guilty of the murder of George Hornick's son (also George). He gave evidence of his success in protecting 'afflicted and defenceless loyalists' against 'the almost ungovernable fury of the multitude', pointing out that 'no sanguinary religious bigotry has been attributed to me'.[17] The fate of Hornick's other son, Robert, illustrates the nature of the forces from which Carthy sought to distance himself. Left for dead on Vinegar Hill in the first wave of systematic killing of unpopular local Protestants, he managed to escape (rushing down the hill past a group of women prisoners, including Jane Barber, who described him as 'a naked man ... [with] dark streams of blood running down his sides'[18]). He made his way six miles across country, though badly wounded, only to find his family fled and the house burned. 'He then hoped to meet some humanity among his neighbours, but there was no such thing to meet with', and he was killed at the infamous gravel pit 'in the bloody parish of Rossdroit'.[19]

This anonymous account drew a contrast with the treatment of Protestants in adjoining parishes in Bantry, as did that of the Reverend James Gordon, grateful for the fact that 'the Protestants of Killegney' (where he became rector after the Rebellion) had been exempt 'from the general slaughter'. This he attributed to 'temporising conformity with the Romish worship', with the connivance of an enlightened parish priest (whereas the Protestants of Killanne were saved from being burned to death in their church only by the arrival of the military). The Killegney Protestants still lived in fear, and to illustrate this, and 'the difference between the superior and inferior classes of Romanists', Gordon told how 'Captain' Gornaghan, 'a labouring peasant', threatened the then rector and his family, forcing them to 'the Romish chapel' and, with a 'Fanatic mob', threatened to put them to death, 'declaring that no religion, except that alone which God permitted, must any longer be professed'. They were saved by Jeremiah Fitzhenry, a brother-in-law of the prominent United Irishman John Colclough, and 'the rest of the Romanists', who 'would not consent to it'. Gordon added that the fact that Gornaghan had not been 'molested' since the Rebellion was 'a strong proof of the moderation of the Protestants of this parish'.[20]

The complexity of Catholic–Protestant relations in this deeply divided area is illustrated further by the 'boisterous interference' of the Reverend Philip Roche on behalf of two Protestant brothers named Robinson, whose Catholic tenants interceded for them.[21] Likewise, at the trial of Thomas Cloney, several local Protestants swore that they and others taken up in the initial mustering of the rebels at the Leap had not been prisoners, but volunteers; also that Kelly, not Cloney, was in command and was instrumental in saving some Protestants from being taken to the Vinegar Hill camp. This hint that some local Protestant farmers joined the rebels (though one 'volunteer', James Wiseman, swore that he had been ordered to join by Kelly, and later obliged to stay) may relate to the likelihood that Kelly was a Protestant. Another witness for Cloney, John Stilman, a shoemaker and a former yeoman, claimed to have fought with the Enniscorthy garrison before being forced to join the rebels. However, Richard Newton King, Esq., claimed that 'In the year 1793, when there was an Insurrection in this county', Stilman was among 'the rebels', and had refused to give information to the authorities. He added, 'I believe he was sworn a United Irishman at that time.'[22] This anachronistic linkage of the 1793 outbreak to the then entirely constitutionalist United Irishmen finds an echo in the anonymous testimony, cited earlier, which gave an odd though perhaps not unusual account of what being a United Irishman meant in 1798. It quoted a rebel telling how he knocked down and beat the brains out of a Protestant, although he respected Protestants and 'lived and got his bread' by them, because, 'not having taken the United Irishman's oath he feared that they would kill himself, and thought he could not take a better step to save his own life … as he saw that their design was to kill all the Protestants'.[23]

We are dependent on such disconnected glimpses in trying to understand how the Rebellion was initially perceived and operated in the Bantry countryside. At a popular level, it seems clear that strong sectarian feelings were uppermost, sometimes connected with conflict over land. Yet, as in 1793, some local Protestants may have joined the Rebellion, and others were protected, including some landlords. Those targeted particularly were the Palatines, still poorly assimilated to local patterns of accommodation, as well as ultra-Protestant activists like the Croshee brothers, three of whom were murdered at the 'gravel pit near Davidstown'. The attempt to implicate Cloney in this killing was half-hearted,[24] but the trial of John Bryan for the killing of Nathaniel Croshee gives further glimpses into communal attitudes.

The chief witness against him was Bridget Francis, a young serving girl of 'Nurse Redmond's', but even the defence witnesses testified that he was a rebel 'captain', one claiming that 'men of property' were often so called, another that he had heard him issue a command only once, when 'protecting a poor woman that the rebels wanted to ill-use'. According to Francis, Redmond's son told his mother that he had seen the Croshees hiding in a boghole and she in turn informed Bryan through Francis. The killing, by her account, was a communal affair, reminiscent of some ritual Whiteboy punishments. 'There was a great many with guns, pikes and pitchforks' at the murder, and Redmond's son (who was her own age, about fourteen) 'asked leave for me to go to see the Croshees killed. I got leave and went.' A defence witness indicated that the reasons the Croshees were targeted was that some of the older Croshees were yeomen (those killed were described as mere 'boys'). A prosecution witness described the surviving brother as 'a Loyalist and violent in consequence of his suffering in the rebellion', that is, 'eager to apprehend rebels, for which reason he has many enemies among the rebels and their favourers'. Evidence was given that he broke furniture in the house of the accused after the bodies were found.[25] Clearly, they were neighbours and well known to one another.

Throughout the Wexford countryside, and away from the set-piece battles and affrays, the Rebellion conformed to such familiar patterns of agrarian and sectarian conflict. Much, almost certainly most of this violence was by the forces of the state, both militia and local yeomanry units, whose campaigns of murder often had their origins also in local disputes. None of this state violence appears in the official record. No yeoman was ever prosecuted for murder, just as only 'suffering loyalists' were eligible for compensation. Under various flags, banners and uniforms (and none), a great deal of the killing in the Wexford Rebellion was of and by neighbours. This was a striking feature of the best-documented rebel atrocities, at Vinegar Hill and Scullabogue, and it was reflected in the bewildered, if sometimes naïve, response of local Protestants. Thus, Samuel Elmes Jr wrote to his father, back safely on his farm at Old Ross, on 21 June 1798: 'Who could have thought the people we so long nurtured with every kindness, would be the instrument to massacre us, 'tis a dreadful thought.'[26] Barbara Lett ended her account with her response to the sight of the heads of executed rebels stuck on spikes in Wexford town after its recapture: 'the human heart was turned to stone at that time'. Her prayer was, 'May we never more fall into the hands of neighbours, who are more barbarous than a foreign enemy.'[27]

Cloney was understandably concerned to distance himself from such communal violence and to present his participation in terms of an honourable military campaign. He was appalled at the indiscipline and summary executions that marked the rebel camp he joined at Vinegar Hill, and pessimistic about anyone's ability 'to subdue the disorderly passions of an enraged multitude', or to give direction to 'the people', who were 'divided into parties and cabals'. In his account, this chaotic scene was transformed by the arrival of two prominent United Irishmen, John Henry Colclough and Edward Fitzgerald of Newpark, released from gaol by the Wexford garrison in order that they might plead with the rebels to disperse and who, failing in this, took control. When they arrived:

> All now was disorder and confusion, and a few hours was likely to end this local Insurrection, which never had been matured by previous organisation, or settled plans, but had its origins in the great principle of self preservation.[28]

In other words, it is implied, contrary to Cloney's underlying argument (and paradoxically, more clearly than anywhere in Byrne's account of the campaign), that disorganized local insurgency was transformed into a more formidable movement by these United Irish leaders. But the reality may have been different. Gahan believes that both of them, but especially Fitzgerald, made strenuous efforts to persuade the rebels to go home. His view that this stance was 'an extraordinary one for a prominent United Irishman' is clearly based on the assumption that the Rebellion to this point was following a concerted United Irish plan. Colclough was sent back to Wexford town to announce failure, while Fitzgerald was made a virtual prisoner by the rebels, 'and treated practically as a traitor'.[29]

Reflecting this confusion, perhaps, it is not clear in Cloney's account who, if anyone, was now in command, and how the decision to march on Wexford was made. Following the logic of the United Irish explanation, Gahan has Kelly and Cloney immediately joining 'the leadership circle' on their arrival at Vinegar Hill on 29 May,[30] but Cloney described this as happening the following day, when the rebels massed at the Three Rocks for the attack on Wexford town. Finding Edward Roche, John Hay and Edward Fitzgerald 'disinclined to assume authority' (a view Byrne endorsed), he was put forward by 'some of my neighbours', and in turn Cloney proposed John Kelly, Robert Carty and Michael Furlong.[31] There was still very little sign of military organization at the Three Rocks, with newcomers finding their neighbours by 'calling each other aloud by the names of their different Baronies' (the basis also for musterings in the north of the county days later, in Byrne's account). The successful ambush of a detachment of Meath Militia and Royal Artillery, en route to reinforce the Wexford garrison, was led by Cloney, Kelly and Furlong and owed more to 'irresistible impetuosity than military skill' according to Cloney.[32] What Gahan has called the 'headlong charge with bayonet and pike down the hill',[33] ensuring victory for the Bantrymen in this, their first, and very brief, engagement, was to be repeated a week later in the remarkable early breakthrough that began the largest and bloodiest battle of the Rebellion, at New Ross.

The evidence from those early days, therefore, points to a priest- and farmer-led peasant insurgency in the Bantry barony, fuelled by rumoured and real atrocities and sustained and spread by an initial series of victories, culminating in the unopposed taking of Wexford town. This view is reinforced by a reading of Byrne's account of those days, and of the second phase of the campaign in the north of the county in which he participated. Indeed he was critical, above all, of its enduring insurgency features.

His first major engagement, the attack on Newtownbarry on 1 June, was a disaster, the first significant setback for the rebels, and was characteristically blamed by Byrne on the failure of their leader, Father Mogue Kearns, to take his teenage subaltern's advice on military tactics. As in his earlier account of Oulart, we are presented with an undisciplined 'little army' of peasants, led by a priest and a farmer. Byrne was critical of the failure over the days following to adopt rudimentary uniforms or badges, even by 'the chiefs and officers that were known in the United system' (a rare reference by this point of the narrative, and one that appears to recognize them as a distinct and probably minority element). Such organization as existed was based on standard-bearers calling men to the colours by calling 'the names of the baronies, towns or parishes'. The banner of his own Monaseed corps featured 'harps and green emblems, put on by handsome young ladies', but for a Volunteer Corps of 1782. It had been taken from Lord Mountnorris's residence at Camolin Park. Such military experience as existed was provided by former yeomen, and throughout his account of the rest of the campaign Byrne complains of the lack of a clear command structure, so that 'we were often at a loss to know from whom the orders came'. His frustrations at the manifestations of an undisciplined insurgency were evident also, for example, in his criticisms of the 'useless retaliation' of house burning, and his emphasis on 'how much we stood in need of discipline and some kind of control, to prevent our young men scampering throughout the county without an object in view'. He described the march in Arklow as more like one 'to some great place of amusement than to the battlefield'.[34] Throughout the Rebellion there is a clear pattern of individuals and groups leaving the campaign and melting back into their community, sometimes rejoining later. All ranks had the tendency to return home for a night or more whenever possible. For example, after the capture of Wexford town Colclough and Fitzgerald went home, as did Cloney, who also slept at his father's home before and after the battle of Ross.[35]

In the taking and organization of Wexford town the tension between insurgency and United Irish-directed Rebellion was also evident. Bagenal Harvey, a prisoner of the military, the best known old-style United Irishman in the county and soon to become, briefly, rebel Commander-in-Chief, refused the request of Wexford's mayor and assorted magistrates that he go to the rebel camp at the Three Rocks to urge respect for lives and property when the town was taken. He refused on the basis that the rebels were not from his part of the county and that he had no influence with them. Instead he wrote a note that pleaded, with little apparent confidence: 'If you pretend to Christian charity, do not commit massacre, or harm the property of the inhabitants, and spare your prisoners' lives.'[36] Likewise the ill-defined group of rebels from the area to the north who actually took the town (and whose leadership remains obscure) swept aside a similar plea by another prominent United Irishman, Edward Fitzgerald.

The rebels launched a widescale hunt for loyalists, with sporadic killing and more systematic imprisonment, 'so that on the 31st of May the gaol of Wexford became absolutely crowded'. Among the prisoners was the magistrate Edward Turner of Newfort, taken while Bagenal Harvey's dinner guest. The pleadings of Harvey, Hay and Fitzgerald were useless when 'a great mob of country people' demanded that he be surrendered to them.[37] The fate of the loyalist prisoners, eventually crowded into overflow accommodation in the Market House, was to remain the key test of who controlled the main rebel stronghold. The chief focus and concern of what Gahan called the 'governing committee' of prominent citizens[38] (only one of whom was a United Irishman, according to Hay)[39] was the control of 'the mob', and its proclamations continued to stress Harvey's initial appeal to spare property and lives.

Like the rebel camp at Vinegar Hill, this experiment in rebel government is one of the best documented episodes of the Rebellion, and it is unfortunate that the bicentenary stress on the phantom republican 'Senate' seems to have obscured the need for a detailed study of the operation of this committee and the nature of its relationship with the more populist and sectarian element, led by the notorious Captain Thomas Dixon, which eventually swept its fragile authority aside and carried out the mass execution of loyalist prisoners in the dying hours of rebel control.[40] What seems most relevant here is the continuation of a pattern begun after the taking of Enniscorthy, when large numbers of loyalist prisoners were crowded into inadequate accommodation, many clearly victims of vendettas by individual rebels, and up to 400 of them killed systematically over the twenty-three days the camp at Vinegar Hill survived.[41] Here and in Wexford town there were sustained attempts at forced conversions to Catholicism and the rebel leadership, such as it was, proved ultimately to have little control over its followers.[42] This pattern forms an important and too often ignored background to the Scullabogue massacre.

In Thomas Cloney's account of the initial rebel occupation of Wexford town, mob violence threatened even rebel leaders like himself if they intervened to save Protestant lives. Cloney was anxious to stress that he was active in that regard, successfully protecting 'my early guardian', Valentine Gill, by confirming his terrified claim, 'I am a Roman Catholic and an United Irishman.'[43]

But the rebel armies were almost immediately on the move again, leaving Wexford on the 31st determined to complete rebel control of the county by taking the remaining key towns of Gorey, Newtownbarry and New Ross. The northern contingent moved rapidly under Edward Roche; the Bantrymen and those from the southern baronies took a strangely leisurely pace in their march westward towards New Ross, under the new Commander-in-Chief, Bagenal Harvey, and Father Philip Roche. Cloney, and apparently Kelly, went home, rejoining Harvey two days later at Carrigbyrne.

Harvey was in some respects an obvious choice as leader. A Protestant landlord with strong liberal credentials, he had been a prominent local United Irishman from the constitutional phase of that organization, and his gaoling had made him a popular hero. As Louis Cullen has pointed out, there is no evidence that he held any military rank in the revolutionary United Irishmen.[44] He was certainly a reluctant, and for much of the time, a frightened leader, his 'weak frame and delicate constitution', making his precarious position even more intolerable.[45] Musgrave's story that he initially planned, with the help of his gaoler, Gladwin, to flee Wexford with the garrison, may not be true but it is certainly believable (and entirely understandable). When first approached by the town authorities to intercede with the besieging rebels he was found hiding up the chimney of his cell, and he remained throughout a rather pathetic, ineffectual, though ultimately a more dignified figure.[46] His lack of authority was evident from the beginning in his failure to protect Turner, and was to be a major factor in the defeat at New Ross.

This image of a man compelled to lead a popular insurgency with which he had little sympathy and over which he had even less control is mirrored in that of the other leading United Irish figure who marched with him to New Ross. John Henry Colclough, a Catholic doctor and old-style radical, had already demonstrated his ambivalence to the Rebellion when sent by the Wexford garrison to talk to the Enniscorthy rebels. He had then gone home and after several days determined to return voluntarily to gaol, having 'probably ... turned his back on the rebellion', according to Gahan.[47] On his way there, he was met by the retreating garrison and used as a hostage before being released, entering the town only the following day and finding himself a 'Colonel' in the rebel army. He was to lead – or possibly to follow – his men from the battlefield at Ross in the very early stages.

Had Bagenal Harvey moved quickly and decisively to attack New Ross, which was poorly defended until 3 June, it is likely that this strategic town would have fallen as easily as Enniscorthy did, and possible that the Rebellion would then have spread into south Kilkenny and east Waterford. Instead, he delayed for four crucial days, first at Taghmon, then at the hill of Carrigbyrne, eight miles from the town, which became one of the largest rebel camps of the campaign. We can only speculate about the reasons for such slow progress. Gahan pointed to a more general rebel 'paralysis' during these days, right across the county, a dramatic and sudden loss of momentum and initiative. His hypothesis was that this was caused by the first serious rebel reverses, particularly at Newtownbarry, by the start of a major government counter-offensive under Lake, and above all by the news of the utter failure of the Rebellion in Dublin on the 2nd. In addition, Harvey had to wait for reinforcements, as many of the expected rebel contingents from the southern baronies were slow to arrive and many of the Bantrymen, already several days in the field, had gone home and stayed away for several days more.[48] This points to the most likely explanation for both Harvey's inaction and the general paralysis – that there was no clear command structure or sense of direction, and poor organization and little discipline on the ground. The momentum that had carried this large-scale peasant insurgency to such remarkable and unexpected success could not be maintained indefinitely. The rebels were not soldiers who regarded themselves as under military orders, but country people, anxious about their families and needing to rest, eat and recover from their wounds. Little military skill had been required in the pell-mell of events from Oulart to the taking of Wexford town. Now, however, they needed to operate strategically and to organize on a number of fronts, at the very time when the state's counter-offensive was finally lumbering into action. Gahan accuses Harvey of 'complacency',[49] but it seems more likely that he was apprehensive, indecisive and in despair at the chaotic nature of the rebel 'army', which he was experiencing for the first time.

Harvey's delay and the chaotic nature of camp life provided both opportunity and context for the gathering up of Protestant prisoners from the surrounding countryside, as had been done from the beginning at the rebels' permanent camp at Vinegar Hill. In the four days prior to the battle of New Ross up to 150 prisoners were taken and lodged in the house, barn and other outbuildings of Mr King at Scullabogue beside the rebel camp. Most of them came from what Gahan called the 'conspicuous settler enclaves', which were the products of recent 'Protestant colonisation' at Foulks Mills, Fethard and Tintern to the south and south-west, and Adamstown to the north-east. Twenty-nine came from the little village of Tintern. Most of those taken were probably tenant farmers of modest means; on the Colclough estate at Tintern, for example, Protestants held sixty out of seventy-one tenancies, but their holdings were, on average, half the size of those held by Catholics.[50] Others, as Whelan has pointed out, 'were typical of the poor Protestant population of a small landlord-induced village – a shoemaker, a slater, two weavers, a mason, a butcher, a labourer'.[51] The most remarkable feature of the sweep was the inclusion of at least thirteen women and eight children. Only men were imprisoned at the other rebel camps, or in Wexford town, so far as we know. Furthermore, 'at least fifty of the prisoners, and perhaps many more, were related to at least one other prisoner, suggesting that the rebels tended to identify entire families rather than just individuals as their enemies'.[52] This, in turn, reflected the existence in the area around the camp of a number of fiercely resented, easily identifiable and highly vulnerable communities whose landlords and other leading figures had fled to the shelter of the towns, or were with yeomanry units at Duncannon fort.

Popular resentment against these communities had an economic as much as a cultural basis, and this was reflected in the fact that those who captured the prisoners were not only their neighbours, but their rivals in the highly sectarianized local economy. The rebel leader at Tintern was John Houghran, a stone mason; Catherine Power described those who had taken her husband Pat, also a mason, as 'John Flaherty of Tintern, tailor, Michael Regan and Pat Hogan, labourers of Saltmills'. Joshua Colfer, 'servant of Mr. Clarke, a Maltster', was in charge at Fethard, and his first target was William Jordan, servant to the Reverend John Kennedy. The farmer Patrick Dobbyn of Oldcourt,

Adamstown and his three sons were taken by their neighbours Thomas Kavanagh and William Power. Likewise, Richard Grandy was taken near his farm at Kilbride by a group of neighbours, nine of whom he named.53 Houghran and Colfer both claimed to be acting under the orders of Michael Devereux, a prosperous farmer-middleman from Battlestown, between the camp and the town, and he certainly directed a number of the Fethard and Tintern raids. It may be that his motives were more strategic (one court-martial witness believed that the idea was 'to get man for man from the prisoner ship at Duncannon')54 and that his reliance on Houghran and Colfer for local knowledge resulted in the particular socio-economic profile of the prisoners taken. Inescapably, that profile also had a powerful sectarian dimension, reflecting what had been fundamental in the establishment of these new enclaves. All those accused of taking prisoners were Catholics; the overwhelming majority of those taken were Protestants.

At least nine Catholics are known to have died at Scullabogue, and this was seized on from the beginning to deny any sectarian intent. One of the defence witnesses at Colfer's trial, Richard Power, claimed that there were fifteen Catholics, but of the four he named, three appear to have been Protestants, and the fourth was not recorded.55 Recently, in the most detailed analysis of the atrocity to date, Daniel Gahan also argued for fifteen Catholics on the basis that 'unless there is evidence that an individual was Protestant', they were Catholic. However, it seems incongruous that his list of Catholics killed includes Carlisle, Fanner and Reel, for example, especially given the importance he assigns to names in his presumption that three of the killers at Scullabogue – Mills, Ellard and Turner – were Protestant.56

Whatever the number of Catholics involved, too much should not be read into their presence among the victims at Scullabogue, given that those we know a little about were clearly included because of their Protestant connections. Mainly they were servants, like Patrick Prendergast and Patrick Shee, or grander retainers like Thomas McDonnell, steward to the ultra-Protestant landlord Leigh. William and Mary Ryan, with their daughters Eleanor and Elizabeth, were included, it seems, because another daughter was a mistress to a soldier at Duncannon. Sean Cloney and Kevin Whelan claim that among the Catholics killed were wives and children of the notorious North Cork Militia, but there seems to be no direct evidence for this.57 The conclusion that Richard Power was brought to under cross-examination seems inescapable today. Having initially argued that the presence of Catholics was significant, he was asked, 'Do you believe it was for being Protestants they were burned at

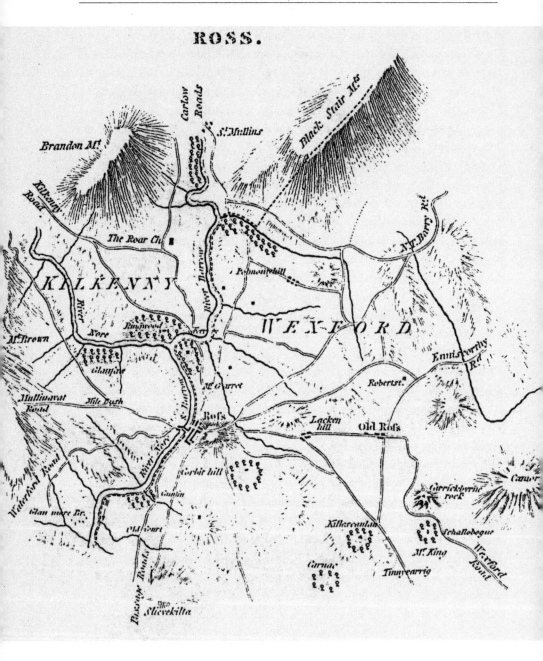

ROSS.

Musgrave's map of the area around New Ross.

Scullabogue?' Answer, 'It showed very plain that it was for that.'[58]

Gahan argues that the taking of prisoners was 'anti-loyalist' rather than anti-Protestant, and implies that the targeting of 'loyalists' (i.e. government supporters) underlined the planned, United Irish-led nature of the operation.[59] However, neither the term 'loyalist' nor the implication behind it features in any of the court-martial defences of those accused of taking or killing the prisoners and, indeed, in its contemporary use it seems to have been a matter of Protestant self-definition solely. In any case, it is hard to see how it applied to lowly tenants and artisans, not to mention women and children. Whelan, likewise, claims that 'a very clear distinction was observed between loyalists (politically active Protestants who had joined the Yeomanry or the Orange Order) and neutrals (like the Quakers or liberal Protestants …)'.[60] Yet there is no evidence that any Scullabogue prisoner was either a yeoman or Orangeman, while at least two were Quakers, Samuel and John Jones. The notion of Quaker immunity is hardly borne out by the account written by Dinah Goff of Horetown House, two miles from Scullabogue. This prosperous, popular Quaker family was regularly threatened and believed they owed their survival to the intervention of the local priest and their ability to feed large numbers of rebels. One of them told Mrs Goff that 'when this business is over, the Quakers are all to be driven into Connaught, where the land is about two pence an acre, and you will have to till *that* and live on it as you can'. Another declared that Goff's sons would have been killed, if present, 'and then the estate would be theirs'.[61]

All contemporary accounts support the view that Protestants were targeted as such. At Houghran's trial, for example, this was agreed by both prosecution and defence witnesses. Sarah Smith, detailing how her husband was taken, said the prisoner 'gave orders that he and all the Protestants they could find that day should be sent to Scullabogue'. The chief defence witness, Patrick Murphy, made the same point three times in a short statement, claiming that the prisoner 'slept at my house about a mile from Tintern the night before the Protestants were taken, on that day he left my house about ten in the morning, in the evening he told me that he had been met by a party going to take up the Protestants, who forced him to go along with them. Prisoner told me the Protestants were taken prisoner to the camp and expressed "great sorrow at it".'[62] Yet Colfer also found much support for his contention that he did not have 'a wish to murder all the Protestants', and according to some witnesses his anger was directed specifically at Orangemen, although the two he named, Kennedy and Clarke, had already left the village.[63] Hatred of Orangemen was also cited in relation to some of those tried for the killings at Scullabogue,[64] and while there is no evidence of an active Orange presence in the area, rumours of massacres spreading out from the north of the county where there was significant Orange provocation had almost certainly given this new manifestation of the traditional enemy a feared folkloric presence.

The complex nature of Catholic–Protestant relations in the targeted communities and some further insight into the motivation and outlook of rank-and-file rebels can be found in the detail of the fullest of the court-martial accounts, that of Joshua Colfer, not only prominent in the taking of prisoners in Fethard, but also virtual ruler of the village during the brief period of rebel control. Colfer, who was illiterate, had worked for William Clarke, a Protestant maltster and brewer, and a member of the local yeomanry corps, now safely ensconced at Duncannon Fort. Evidence was given that Colfer 'brewed beer at Mr. Clarke's brewery and sent it to the rebel camp at Carrigbyrne'. One witness claimed that he was 'ordered to do so by Devereux', which gave some support to Colfer's standard defence that he was 'forced into rebellion'. So did the evidence of defence witnesses, which portrayed him as the virtual defender of the village against the demands of Devereux, anxious, for example, to protect the family of another yeoman, James Agar. (Indeed, the evidence of this trial seems to suggest that the kin of better-off Protestant yeomen were protected: it was the poor Protestants who were taken.) Colfer's relationship with his master's family is particularly interesting. A sense of easy familiarity, even of a kind of friendship, comes through the resentment expressed in the evidence of the eldest boy, Philip Clarke, then thirteen:

> Witness says he was one day whistling the tune of the Protestant Boys – prisoner and another was casting bullets – prisoner said something against the Protestants – he did not threaten witness, who is a Protestant – prisoner told witness that that was the time to be christened as the priest was in town and prisoner told a Catholic boy who was there that he should get a book and teach witness and his brothers the catechism – witness was not baptised by the priest, but the prisoner thought he was – witness was one day in the brewhouse when the prisoner and others were talking about Orangemen – prisoner said there was not one like him in the county who was not sworn.

These vignettes give a fascinating sense of the Rebellion in a domestic setting – the boy provocatively whistling a loyalist tune as the rebels, led by his father's servant, make bullets and abuse Protestants, then defending his father against the charge of Orangeism, with Colfer articulating the common belief that all wealthy Protestants were part of this active conspiracy against Catholics. Philip resented even more, however, the fact that Colfer not only held meetings of local rebels in Clarke's house but 'appeared to be the owner and master of the house'. This ties in with the evidence of another witness who claimed that Colfer tried to get him to kill *his* master, on the basis that all Orangemen 'ought to be killed'.[65] The motif of servants thinking themselves 'the masters now' recurs, as we have seen, in Protestant accounts, reflecting a widespread sense on both sides that the Rebellion presaged a social revolution, a world turned upside down.

Asked by Colfer, 'Do you believe you, your brothers and sisters were in some measure protected by the prisoner?' Philip Clarke answered, 'He used to tell me sometimes that there should be no fear of me.' Clarke also agreed that all the Protestants remaining in Fethard were 'in [Colfer's] power' had he chosen to harm them, and that there were no murders of Protestants in Fethard itself. Philip also told the court, however, that the Protestants who remained 'were saved by being supposed Catholics'; the same emphasis on forced conversions appears here as in Vinegar Hill and Wexford town. In Fethard it became a life-saving fiction, thanks to the local priest, Father James Doyle, who encouraged the widespread pretence of conversion while privately reassuring Protestants. A defence witness and neighbour of Colfer's, William Hardis, first denied that he had been pressured to conform, though his wife had pretended to do so. He then gave this graphic account:

> The priest called us all Protestants together into a room and lighted a candle for fear of the bad people, and kept us about an hour and told us that there were a great many bad people about the place, that they might soon be out of it, and the place be quiet again.

The same witness, in claiming that to save himself he was forced to go even further and join the rebels for a period, said that the Rebellion was presented to him entirely in sectarian terms:

> I was sworn by Patrick Murphy to be true to the Catholic war. Question: What was meant by the Catholic war? Answer: I suppose it was to hurt us the Protestants. Question: Do you believe your being so sworn protected you? Answer: I believe Murphy swore me that I might be protected. I do not think he meant to hurt me … Question: Do you believe that the Protestants who remained in Fethard were saved by its being supposed they were baptised and going to Mass? Answer: I believe it was in some measure. Question: Do you believe the prisoner [i.e. Colfer] badly inclined against the Protestants? Answer: He was as bad as the rest.

He even added that Colfer too was 'concerned in the Catholic war'. This devastating charge came at the end of a lengthy cross-examination of a witness who began by *defending* the prisoner.[66] The tending of Fethard Protestants to paint Colfer's sectarianism as less extreme than that of the unnamed power he answered to – presumably Devereux – is interesting and suggests the ability of mixed communities to find accommodation in a sectarian society, so long as the normal routines of life were maintained. In Scullabogue barn, by contract, Protestants were literally lumped together in an undifferentiated mass.

The evidence at the trial of John Houghran, 'who seemed to have the chief command at Tintern', has many similarities to that given about Colfer. There was the same emphasis on searching for Protestants, as in the revealing remark by Sarah Smith that, after her husband was taken (later followed by her brother, sister and niece), the rebels 'then went to search for another Protestant family'. There was the same pattern of forced conversions: Houghran advised Sarah Smith 'to go and have herself christened and told her they must all be of one religion, for it was that they were fighting for'. On the other hand Joseph Kelly, who claimed he was forced to join the rebels to save his life, said 'that before he was permitted to join he was advised to take the United oath', which Houghran administered.

No one connected Colfer with the United Irishmen. Nor was Colfer accused of the kind of petty tyrannies that Houghran was charged with, such as threatening the widows of men killed at Scullabogue that 'he would collect us all together and send us after our husbands', or refusing food to a woman who hadn't converted. Yet the Protestants John Porter and Thomas Ryan, who claimed they were forced to join the rebels 'and made to stand guard at Tintern', failed to give clear evidence against Houghran. In answer to the question, 'Did you ever hear that the prisoner ordered Smith to Scullabogue?' Ryan said disingenuously, 'I never heard it from anyone I could depend on. I heard it from women and children who said they were by.' Richard Synott went further and claimed that Houghran had refused Devereux's orders 'to collect all the Protestants and keep them until he should call for them', on the grounds that 'it was a thing too bad for him to do'. Questioned by the court, 'What did the prisoner think was to be done to the Protestants when he said it was too bad a thing for him?' Synnott said he didn't know, and the prisoner interjected, 'I thought they were to be brought up to camp.'[67]

Colfer's trial hinged on whether he knew that the prisoners he sent to Scullabogue would be killed. Several witnesses claimed he did not. James Murphy, for example, while he 'heard prisoner talking of Orangemen and he said they ought all to be killed', did not believe Colfer knew 'what was to be done to the prisoners at Scullabogue', and he never heard of him being at the camp. Philip Clarke, however, believed Colfer knew the barn would be burned and was frequently at the camp, as most of the Fethard rebels were, besides which 'there were expresses daily' from the camp. It was the lengths that Colfer went to in order to prevent the Clarkes being sent to Scullabogue that told most against him. The main defence witness, Richard Power, had to concede as much.

> Q: Do you believe the prisoner thought any harm of sending Protestants to Scullabogue?
> A: I don't think he did.
> Q: Why then did he get the children of Mr. Clarke baptised to prevent them being sent to Scullabogue?
> A: I don't know what to think of it.

The court seemed to echo this, for while it found Colfer guilty of sending Protestants to Scullabogue and of conspiracy to murder them, and declared he should therefore suffer death, it concluded that 'there are certain circumstances which induce the court to recommend that the prisoner, Joshua Colfer, should be transported for life to Botany Bay'. Perhaps his protection of the Protestants remaining at Fethard, and especially the Clarkes, was decisive, or perhaps the court accepted his final statement that 'I was never instrumental in or privy to the death of an individual.'[68]

The fact that the killers were a different group, with no clear connection to those who took the prisoners, must also have told in Colfer's favour. We cannot know the extent of his knowledge, but it seems clear that, like Houghran, he was deeply uneasy. This unease was shared by the Catholic priest for the parish in which the camp was situated, Father John Shallow, who was asked by Elizabeth Dobbyn of Adamstown to intercede on behalf of her husband and three sons. According to her deposition, he replied, 'That he would not go near the rebel camp; that if he did, he would be in as much danger as said Patrick Dobbyn and sons.' And, because he 'shuddered and seemed to be shocked' on hearing how many of her family were at risk, she guessed they would be put to death, and that the priest 'knew what would happen'.[69]

Shallow's own account, published as part of Bishop Caulfield's reply to Musgrave, confirmed that he had, indeed, a sense of foreboding. He claimed he went to the camp, 'spoke to her husband in prison, solicited and petitioned a committee (as I supposed) then sitting in said house [King's] in his and his

sons favour in as humble and pathetic a manner as I could, and was absolutely refused, nay ordered out of the apartment by one of "the members"'. While
he failed to free the Dobbyns, he claimed to have rescued 'a female child of
about eleven years of age, who clung to me at Scullabogue on the second of
June aforesaid and whom I do verily believe I brought out unperceived by
almost the entire guard'.[70] The implication that at least one guard turned a
blind eye may also suggest similar concern at the likely fate of the prisoners.

The inhuman conditions in which they were kept must have confirmed,
to both the prisoners themselves and their guards, a sense of their doom.
Elizabeth Dobbyn said she first saw her family 'confined in a dirty pigyard',
but when she returned later to the camp, they had been 'removed into the
barn, which was full of prisoners, crowded as close as they could stand'.[71] The
barn, which measured only 34 feet by 15, was packed with at least 113 people,
including all the women and children, the Catholics and the poorer Protestants. A few more important Protestants, like Richard Grandy, were lodged in
greater comfort in 'Mr. King's house', where they were interviewed by Harvey
among others. There is no evidence that the bulk of the prisoners were ever
questioned, or that Harvey took any interest in those imprisoned in the barn,
apart possibly from intervening to save Philip Clarke and his mother who,
according to Musgrave, had in fact been brought to Scullabogue in spite of
Colfer's efforts. If it is true, as Musgrave claims, that Harvey 'discharged them,
gave them a pass to return, and desired that no more women or children
should be taken prisoners', it seems likely that this was because he was aware
of their social standing.[72] It also implies that he knew about the other women
and children in the barn, but was unwilling or unable to help them. The overcrowding Elizabeth Dobbyn reported was already severe on 3 June (Shallow
corrects this to the 2nd). Add to this the very warm weather, and conditions
inside the barn by the 5th can only be imagined.

According to Dobbyn,

> a woman who was a prisoner called for a draught of water and one of the
> rebel guards asked them if they would drink salt water and said,
> 'Damnation to you, ye Orange dogs, down with your prayers.' And a rebel
> woman said, 'Do they want water? Give them poison.'[73]

It is easy to dismiss this as the sectarian hyperbole common in loyalist
depositions, but there's no evidence that the prisoners were any better treated,
and the atmosphere described seems credible in the light of the evidence we
have of feelings in the local community generally. The overcrowding, the ill-
treatment and the enveloping of the prisoners in the hysteria of the Orange

menace all involved a dehumanization that made mass killing not only possible but likely. All that was needed was an intensification of fear and paranoia, and a spark to light the tinder. This was provided by news of the devastating reversal at New Ross on 5 June.

Thomas Cloney's *Narrative* makes no mention of the gathering of prisoners at Scullabogue, but does recount the burning of the Protestant chapel at Old Ross on 2 June, with which he was charged at his court-martial a year later. More than three decades on, Cloney was still arguing the case for the defence. He described how, having finally rejoined Harvey on that day, he was asked to lead a party against some local yeomen 'assassins' who were killing defenceless people between Carrigbyrne and the town. He agreed only after 'two different gentlemen' refused, 'in disregard of military discipline'. The chapel was burned during this pursuit 'by some stragglers who followed us from our camp', and while he believed this was wrong, it was understandable, given the effects of government atrocities on 'uneducated men' who, if treated properly, would have continued in their true character as 'the light-hearted peasantry of Ireland'.

While it suited Cloney to continue to characterize the Rebellion as an 'insurrection' lacking 'any settled plans or organisation', there is little evidence to the contrary, and this general sense of indiscipline amounting almost to chaos was an important aspect of the atmosphere that had already spawned a series of atrocities and would soon result in the horror at Scullabogue.74 But Cloney's account of the Old Ross burning is disingenuous, to say the least. Given the dislike of the Palatine settlement, it is not surprising that this chapel should be the only Protestant one burned during the Rebellion, just as virtually all the Palatine houses had been. Pointing this out, Whelan argues that Cloney was 'involved', his cousin being 'the only propertied Catholic' in the area.75 Hay took Cloney's side, but noted that his efforts to get more information on the incident failed.76 Clearly the local community had closed ranks, especially after Scullabogue. The burning of the Old Ross chapel adds to the sense of an intensely sectarian and polarized atmosphere in the area around the camp in the days leading up to the battle.

The Old Ross Palatines had fled already to the safety of the town, and the destruction of their property may reflect rebel frustration that they, unlike the Tintern and Fethard Protestants, had escaped. One of them, Thomas Elmes, wrote from New Ross on 3 June:

Thursday we had intelligence of their approaching Old Ross, when all the Protestant inhabitants in one hour fled to Ross, where we are at present protected by the goodness of Charles Tottenham, Esq., who generously gave several new houses, the best in town, to Old Ross people … They (I mean the rebels) have burnt all our houses and property in Old Ross, so that we shall be in great distress, if we survive.

Charles Tottenham, the town's Sovereign and leading property owner, had more than humanitarian interest in the refugees. Thomas Elmes quickly found himself 'a Yeoman of the Ross Horse Guards', and 'so much harried that you'll excuse the scrole I send you. There is alarms this moment, farewell.'[77] By then the garrison had been reinforced significantly, but when the Elmes and their neighbours poured into the town on 31 May the situation had been desperate indeed.

The town's only defence was a small corps of local yeomanry, under Tottenham, which numbered less than 150. Desperately hoping for reinforcements from Waterford or Kilkenny, all he could to do was dig trenches at the high ground of the Irishtown and at the Three Bullet Gate where the rebel attack seemed likely to be concentrated. The medieval town walls were some help, but they were in a dilapidated state, and some of the old gates had been widened. The topography of New Ross, 'so overhung with eminences, some gradual, some very steep', meant that few towns in Ireland 'are more easy of attack'. This was the view of James Alexander, who, despite being a veteran of the American war, had refused to join the yeomanry on the basis of his commitment to his pupils. Tottenham was not amused, dismissing education as 'but a secondary consideration; the defence of property is a primary one' and declaring the refusal of an ex-soldier 'on such an emergency' was 'a disgraceful circumstance'. His cavalier treatment of Alexander during the battle and his foisting on him of the unpleasant task of getting rid of the corpses after it may be traced to this contretemps. Other potential defenders were busy fleeing the town weighed down with their possessions and many who stayed, like Tottenham, sent their families to Waterford and from there to Wales for safety.[78]

The poor of the town had little choice but to stay, even when a proclamation was issued on the eve of the battle that all not in uniform were to leave. Many of them were considered by the authorities to be disaffected, and thus real or potential rebels, but little evidence survives of rebel activity among townspeople before or even during the battle, in contrast to Enniscorthy. When Alexander had arrived months earlier he noted that the same 'emblems of disaffection among pretended reformers' that had appeared in his previous place of residence, Monasterevin, Co. Kildare, could be seen on the streets of Ross. There were 'men of a certain description … wearing green silk handkerchiefs about their necks, green waistcoats, green strings to their watches and so forth'. Yet a search for weapons on St Patrick's Day 1798 had produced little to worry the authorities and Ross, to outward appearances at least, seemed peaceful:

> very peaceable and very quiet, making some allowance for the natural effects of just and terrible apprehension, which soon nearly died away. Then a cloud of sullen tranquillity seemed to brood over the whole face of the town, without any very observable interval of that hilarity which I think is very congenial to the inhabitants.[79]

Indeed, that same month, Samuel Elmes could urge his nephew in London to return and set up business in Ross, not only because the town was thriving but because 'we are growing easier here about a French Invasion, our countrymen here are better united'.[80] The authorities were less optimistic and offered rewards for information about those 'meeting for the purpose of administering of unlawful oaths'. Alexander's 'cloud of sullen tranquillity' seems more apposite (and had the benefit of hindsight), and this must have been darkened further by the regular passage of carloads of rebel prisoners through the town in the early months of 1798, on their way to prison in Duncannon Fort or to being press-ganged into the fleet. These were probably victims of the brutal government campaign to force the surrender of weapons and in early 1798 that campaign also began to operate in the environs of the town, to Alexander's dismay. He heard of the burning of the houses of suspected rebels in the countryside nearby (though not in the town itself, where proclamations had been posted demanding the surrender 'of all firearms and offensive weapons' under threat of house-burning and free quarters), with Tottenham's ally, the magistrate Standish Lowcay, especially active. He heard of the 'flogging and strangulation' of suspected persons 'in the barrack yard' and was particularly upset at witnessing the torturing of a hermit from Camlin Wood and a rural hedgeschool master (who answered the magistrate in Irish), both of whom were later proved innocent and compensated. While Alexander believed that no good came from such cruelty, he consoled himself in retrospect 'that the severities in general served to accelerate the rebellion and thereby very considerably to weaken its progress'.[81]

Donovan speculated that the 'up-street' population – the mainly Catholic poor, living in the lanes of the upper part of the town and in the Irishtown – were rebel sympathizers, and this is likely; nor is the lack of any evidence for it surprising.[82] To quote Miles Power's successful defence against a charge of murdering a prisoner at Vinegar Hill: 'where nothing but confusion, terror and irregularity prevailed, a man in my obscure situation in life could have been particularly noticed only by my neighbours and intimate acquaintances'.[83] Some poor Catholics came under such particular notice, as we will see, when accused of inciting the rebels to kill their Protestant neighbours, but none were charged with participation in the Rebellion; any who did so probably died as anonymously as they had lived. All we have otherwise is the story, almost certainly apocryphal, of Lord Mountjoy being shot by a baker's boy firing from an upstairs window during the battle.[84]

It may be that Tottenham and his allies had such a powerful grip on the town as to make open disaffection unlikely. But nothing could prevent the contagion of rumour, the great stimulant of Rebellion. When Alexander arrived in 1797 he heard 'confused talk about Orangemen' and fear among the people of being burnt out of their homes by this terrifying, unseen force. (There was no Orange lodge in the town, so far as is known.) This fear was obviously intensified by the rumours of massacres in the north of the county as the Rebellion broke out, and was given a local impetus by the activities of the yeomanry in the vicinity of the town, and further by the influx of the Palatines. These were disliked by 'the poor inhabitants of the town' as 'swaddling thieves' according to Alexander – a reference to their prominence both as Methodists ('swaddlers') and as successful, tough-minded businessmen and farmers. Given their ostentatious Protestantism, it is understandable they were also believed 'all Orangemen' and charged with having been 'the occasions of this rebellion'. They gave some support to this view by their fiery conduct in a part-time militia, called 'Glory-men' by Alexander from the paper worn on their hats, proclaiming 'Death or Glory'. They were disarmed on the eve of the battle on the grounds that their lack of a uniform would be a danger to them, but Alexander implied that their fanaticism and lack of discipline were considered a liability.[85] George Hornick, veteran of the campaign against Whiteboyism, was disgusted, having arrived in the town with 'my own seven stand of arms and a two barrelled gun of Mr. Richards'. Had he been allowed to use them he 'would have done service to the town and honour to my name'.[86] The garrison also was not immune from the general rumour-fed panic and hysteria of the days before the battle, with a report of 'horrid carnage' by the rebels at Borris, for example, proving to have originated from the accidental discharge of a dragoon's pistol.[87]

The sense of New Ross being under siege in the days before the battle was given a cultural and historical dimension in Alexander's account of the two trips he took through the surrounding countryside. On 1 June he went to Waterford on behalf of his principal, Mr Carr, whose daughter was attending the new Quaker school at Newtown. On the way he met 'a gentleman' who 'seemed, by his conversation, to be no enemy to "the United"', as he called them. Then he was stopped by a menacing crowd of country people near Glenmore, the area from which the Wexford rebels expected help from their Kilkenny brethren in the attack on the town. Alexander was allowed to go on after he spoke to them in Irish, 'in a grave *broguenier* tone'. He was surprised to get 'a look of veneration' as well as the reply, "'Go dieu to slann muistir,' i.e., 'God speed you sir,'" but then realized that as well as 'hearing my bog notes and language', they had mistaken him for a priest because of his black clothes.

On the 4th he took a much greater risk by walking to Corbet Hill, a mile from the town, where the rebels were already gathered in force, ready for their belated attack. Once again he was on a mission for someone else, this time the prominent Quaker merchant Cullimore, checking on the safety of his family who lived at the foot of the hill. He was stopped by 'a small party of peasants', who turned out to be 'rebels armed with pikes' and who 'all appeared dead drunk'. Two of them interrogated him, 'one in English and the other in Irish; but both in such unintelligible jargon as would on any other occasion provoke laughter'. When he assumed an air of authority and challenged them, they also imagined he was a priest and dispersed. Meeting a militia man on his way back to the town, Alexander warned him of the danger and had a stone thrown at him for his pains. He noted that the man had a 'green bough' in his hat; in his account of the battle, the largely Catholic militia often appear as covert or suspected rebels. Before leaving the area of Corbet Hill Alexander had looked through a hedge at the rebel camp and was 'convinced that *the great body of the people* were the rebel army'.[88] Thus, the threat to the town came, as it had for centuries, from Irish-speaking country people, whether the potential rebels at Glenmore or those already in arms at Corbet Hill, and they appeared to Alexander, as Pakenham was to describe them, 'a whole countryside in motion', or, in Seamus Heaney's words, 'a people hardly marching – on the hike'.[89]

On the day that Alexander went to Waterford, generals Johnson and Eustace had at last been ordered to march from there to reinforce the Ross garrison. They arrived in the town on the 3rd, with Alexander and Miss Carr attaching themselves to the mile-long column on the final miles of their journey from Waterford.[90] General Henry Johnson, who now took command of the garrison, was an Irish Protestant, a career soldier who had served with no particular distinction in the American war and more recently in the unglamorous area of army recruitment; now in a time of extreme danger he was to be given an unexpected chance for glory and a belated reputation. He commanded a mixed force of (mainly Catholic) militia from the Donegal, Clare and Meath regiments, some Dragoons and Midlothian Fencibles, the town's Yeoman Cavalry and, crucially, some artillery. The garrison were given a further boost on the 4th with the arrival of a contingent of Dublin Militia under Lord Mountjoy, the former Luke Gardiner, an early champion of Catholic relief in the Irish Parliament.

The vulnerable yeoman garrison of 150 men, all that Tottenham had to defend the town the day Harvey stopped unexpectedly at Carrigbyrne, was now swollen to over 2000 mixed troops; the odds no longer favoured the rebels. Not that too much could be claimed for the greater professionalism of the army. Yeomen near Wexford had refused to obey orders given by Lt Colonel Maxwell some days earlier. The militia, as Sir John Moore was to find two weeks later, were 'extremely undisciplined' and 'except that they are clothed with more uniformity, they are as ignorant and as much a rabble as those who have hitherto opposed us. Our army is better armed and provided with ammunition; that of the rebels has the advantage of zeal and ardour.'[91] The class prejudice is obvious (the militia, like the rebels, coming over-whelmingly from the rural poor) but the military judgment reflected recent experience, including that of the battle of Ross.

The atmosphere in the town had also changed significantly on the eve of battle, with an assertive military presence further darkening the townspeople's 'cloud of sullen tranquillity'. As Alexander described it:

> Ross was now a strong garrison and as such exhibited a very unusual appearance. The streets perpetually resounded with the martial drum, the ear-piercing fife, or the shrill twanging or warbling notes of the hoarse trumpet or bugle. But all did not seem to awaken people from a gloomy, dark, horrible lethargy, which seemed more or less to pervade the countenances of almost all but the military themselves.

There were complaints about abuses of the billeting systems, and at the soldiers' boisterous behaviour and obscene language as they crowded the narrow, hot streets, covering everything in a thick dust. The town was not only stiflingly hot, and pungent with the odour of horses and men, it was also short of water, its wells dry and barely a trickle in the town's conduit. This was to have an important bearing on the outcome of the battle. The tension in the town is well captured in Alexander's account of how, on his return from Waterford, 'dressed in black, booted and covered in dust', he was again taken as a priest but this time as a rebel spy by 'an active magistrate, then in the Ross Cavalry' (and later identified as Tottenham's main local ally, Standish Lowcay). Though Alexander's true identity was quickly established, he was followed home by a group of soldiers who might have killed him but for the intervention of a group of Antrim Militia to whom he had given a lift on the journey from Waterford.[92] Throughout his account Alexander believed himself as much in danger from elements in the garrison as from the rebels, whether ultra-loyalist yeomen or trigger-happy militia, hostile to anyone not in uniform. And even at the height of battle, he depicted the local Protestant yeomanry and the mainly Catholic militia as profoundly, and sometimes fatally, at odds.

CHAPTER 12

5 June 1798: The Battle

While contemporaries agreed that the battle of New Ross was 'doubtless the most bloody battle of the Croppy War', and probably the most decisive, they also recognized the difficulty of giving a clear account of the events of that day.[1] Madden argued that it was one of the few actions in the Rebellion properly called a 'battle', but this may give a misleading sense of coherence.[2] All contemporary accounts agree on the chaotic nature of the fighting and the difficulty of establishing a clear sense even of its main phases. For military observers, like Surgeon Jordan Roche, the day presented 'such a scene of confusion' as 'perhaps never happened before in any country. Cavalry, infantry – men, women and children, like a torrent running towards the bridge; and pikemen and musketeers shouting after them.'[3] An artillery man, witness to some of the worst slaughter, used the same simile to describe the human tide in its pell-mell descent from the upper to the lower town. 'The rebels pouring in like a flood, artillery was called for and human blood began to flow down the street. Though hundreds were blown to pieces by our grapeshot, yet thousands behind them, being intoxicated from drinking during the night and void of fear, rushed upon us.'[4]

This was not a single flood pouring in relentlessly on the garrison, but something more intermittent, and following a number of channels over a remarkable twelve hours. The only rebel account summed it up best. 'All was disorder and confusion', wrote Cloney. 'There was no reconnoitring, no changes of position, or great military skill displayed on either side, but two confused masses of men struggling alternatively to drive the other back by force alone.'[5]

The warren of narrow, curving, often steep streets meant that no one had an overview of the battle, and that it followed a pattern of ever-shifting, intense and lethal localized engagements, following the ebb and flow of attack, resistance and counter-attack. Although writing over thirty years later, with a number of accounts available to him, Cloney did not attempt a full account, but was content to describe only his own experience. While Alexander was careful to distinguish 'what I saw from what I heard', he made strenuous attempts to pull together accounts he had from a large number of the garrison as well as from captured rebels. Yet he too could not manage a coherent narrative, and apologized for the way it became 'so expanded with observation and anecdotes, entangled with retrograde accounts and allusions, broken with apologies and knotted with anticipations'. Its broken nature may best be seen as mirroring a bewildering day. But Alexander, Shandean in his self-awareness and readiness to engage humorously with the reader, found consolation in a reflection that may also sustain the modern (or, even, postmodern) historian: 'All history is only a series of anecdotes recorded in a dignified style and illustrated by comments.' He hoped some day to draw it all together 'in a style that may merit the name of *History*'.[6] His avoidance of that style, of course, is what makes his 'succinct narrative' such a remarkable and revealing book.

Leaving the prisoners at Scullabogue under the control of John Murphy's Rosegarland Corps, the large rebel force under the nominal command of Bagenal Harvey moved at last on 4 June from Carrigbyrne to Corbet Hill, which commanded the eastern approaches to the town a mile away. Here, according to Cloney, the leaders planned the attack at 'a Council of War', but spent more time feasting and drinking 'Mr. Murphy's good wines' at nearby Talbot Hall.[7] Their followers, 30,000 according to Musgrave, but probably at most 10-15,000 strong, were also 'very drunk' according to Alexander's observations, and by all accounts they were very noisy, continuing throughout the night 'wanting to fire their cannons', while 'from huzzas they changed to hideous yells, which to my ear were awfully expressive of their infernal designs'.[8] They needed to summon what courage they could, having no experience of fighting beyond a few skirmishes. Their Commander-in-Chief could do little to prepare them, being no soldier, and having little stomach for the business. New Ross was his first and last engagement. He clearly hoped that the town might fall bloodlessly, given the rebels' overwhelming numbers and their victorious progress to date, and had he attacked on the 2nd this might well have happened.

The letter carried by his emissary before the attack reflects this optimism and is remarkable for its admission of his inability to control his followers.

Sir,

As a friend to humanity, I request you will surrender the town of Ross to the Wexford forces, now assembled against that town; your resistance will but provoke rapine and plunder, to the ruin of the most innocent. Flushed with victory, the Wexford forces, so innumerable and irresistible, will not be controlled, if they meet with resistance. To prevent, therefore, the total ruin of all property in the town, I urge you to a speedy surrender, which you will be forced to in a few hours, with loss and bloodshed, as you are surrounded on all sides. Your answer is required in four hours. Mr. Furlong carries this letter, and will bring the answer.

The letter was dated 'Half past three o'clock morning, June 5th, 1798', implying that Harvey would not attack until seven thirty, and this proposed long interval gives weight to Harvey's later claim that his emissary Furlong also 'had private instructions to propose a reconciliation' to Tottenham. Indeed, it seems clear that the ultimatum of 5 June was addressed to the Sovereign of Ross, who Harvey knew might be influenced by the appeal to protect property.[9] Clearly he did not know that General Johnson was in command of the garrison and he may have had a poor understanding of the extent to which the town's defences had been strengthened. It is hard to imagine what he envisaged as 'reconciliation'.

Harvey's battle-plan was understandably sketchy, but it was not without merit. It involved a three-pronged attack, two aimed at the major gates at the top of the town and closest to Corbet Hill (Three Bullet Gate and Market Gate), and the third at the eastern or Priory Gate at river level. The three simultaneous attacks were to converge on the town's defensive nerve-centre, the Main Guard at the Tholsel, and beyond it, the vital bridge over the Barrow, at the far side of which there may have been expectation of reinforcement from south Kilkenny rebels. Much of Harvey's plan was anticipated by Johnson, who placed his main strength, the Clare and Dublin Militias, at the Market Gate and Three Bullet Gate respectively, while the yeomen cavalry were drawn up on the Quay, keeping them out of the way of the rebels' long lethal pikes, so effective against horsemen, and in reserve as a final defence against capture of the bridge. (It also kept them out of the way of the militia men who had already shown their antipathy towards them.) Crucially, Johnson had also strengthened the Main Guard with two swivel guns, which commanded the main lines of the likely rebel approach, along South Street from Priory Gate and down Mary Street from the Three Bullet Gate and Market Gate.

Johnson was, doubtless, confident of the ability of trained troops to beat an undisciplined insurgent force, however numerous. If so, his confidence was to be tested severely, even though the rebel superiority in numbers was not nearly as great as the garrison initially believed, and many of their accounts were later to claim. Observing the first wave from the barracks, Surgeon Roche 'supposed that there were 3000 rebels in the town', and Cloney gave the same figure. The effective strength of the garrison was probably less than half that number, although Alexander ended his account rather oddly with the claim by local yeoman hero Michael McCormick, his main military informant, 'that not more than six hundred soldiers fought on the day of the battle'.[10] If that is true, both the rebels and the garrison fought at about one-third of their nominal strength. McCormick's remarks seem to have been aimed at elements in the garrison who, according to Alexander, had been provocative and tyrannical before the battle, but had kept out of harm's way during it.[11]

In marked contrast to the energetic Johnson, Harvey took no part in the battle, seems not to have directed the rebel action, and proved incapable of sending in reinforcements when asked and when they might have consolidated the initial rebel success. But he did at least stay until the end, moving to the Three Bullet Gate after it was taken, and remaining there, a sad and isolated figure. This was more than could be said of the other prominent United Irishman involved, John Henry Colclough of Ballyteige, whose 'batallion' was to attack the Market Gate but instead, for reasons never explained, 'deserted', to use Dickson's blunt language, and took no part. His men, 'encouraged to consult their own safety as he did', spread 'tidings of a total defeat' across south Wexford.[12] That left the two notional Bantry 'batallions', led by the young farmers Thomas Cloney and John Kelly, to attack the Three Bullet Gate, and a detachment from Forth and Bargy led by a man named Boxwell assigned to Priory Gate.[13]

According to Cloney, the two Bantry 'batallions' involved in the attack numbered 500 each.[14] Hay claimed that many of the original Bantry fighters 'abandoned their stations'.[15] It is also likely that there were groups of rebels from other localities not known to us. Kelly was wounded in the very early stages and took no further part in the action. Boxwell is a shadowy figure and is likely to be the 'John Boxwell, of Sarshill, a Protestant gentleman' who, according to Cloney 'was killed early in the day'. Cloney, by his own account, was active in the first phase, but came downtown where the main action was only when most of the garrison had fled and then only briefly. He was also to

*Edward Foran's statue of
Michael Furlong and his
flag of truce.*

the fore in two aborted sorties, including a belated and half-hearted attempt
to break through to the Irishtown, for which he could muster only a handful
of volunteers.[16] In other words, the most sustained passages of rebel action
appear to have been *without* leadership in the conventional military sense, and
to justify Lieutenant William Crawford's repeated admiring references to them
as 'insurgents'.[17] In Hay's words, those who carried the fight throughout that
long bloody day 'did so from individual courage and intrepidity'.[18]

Virtually all eyewitnesses agreed that the battle lasted approximately
twelve hours, starting around 4 a.m.[19] The outline of events is also reasonably
clear, though the main phases and their timing cannot be established with certainty. The rebels broke through the Three Bullet Gate with unexpected ease
and swept down the hilly streets, taking three-quarters of the town in four or
five hours, but failing to dislodge the artillery post at the Main Guard, to break
through to the Quay, or to launch a successful attack on the Irishtown. The
majority of the garrison (led, or possibly followed, by Johnson) retreated across
the bridge and abandoned the town for a period. When the rebels failed to

consolidate their gains by sending in reinforcements or securing the bridge or launching co-ordinated attacks on the isolated garrison outposts at the Main Guard and the Irishtown, Johnson rallied his men, returned and drove the rebels back, recapturing much of the town.

A number of effective rebel counter-attacks kept the issue in doubt until mid-afternoon. Captain Bloomfield, in charge of the artillery at the heavily pressed mid-town post near St Mary's churchyard, believed the rebels 'were in possession of the town three times, and were as often repulsed with great slaughter'. The first phase is the best documented, and we also have reasonably clear accounts of the defence of the Main Guard; the rest dwindles into Alexander's 'string of anecdotes', the most significant of them focused on rebel efforts to capture or use artillery pieces, or to take strategic locations, or on the burning of houses by both sides. The timing and sequence of most of these episodes cannot be fixed with any certainty, but two constants remain: the twelve-hour duration in intense heat, and the horrific rebel death toll of at least a thousand, the grisly piles of corpses greatest where their main lines of attack met concentrated artillery fire at the Three Bullet Gate, Neville Street, Mary Street and South Street.[20] This crucial battle offers a distillation of the whole campaign in military terms – initial success by massed rebels against trained troops at close quarters and in confined spaces broken against well-positioned and directed artillery and by firing from fortified buildings; re-markable determination and courage ground down by superior fire-power.

The prelude, the shooting on sight of 'one Furlong, a rebel delegate … With a flag of truce, and proposals for surrendering the town and garrison', became emblematic of the rebel sense of loss and betrayal and of the epic sav-agery of the battle that followed.[21] Matthew Furlong, a young farmer from Templescoby, a neighbour of Cloney's, had volunteered for this dangerous mission after Harvey's other aides-de-camp (called 'gentlemen' derisively by Cloney) had refused.[22] Their reluctance was understandable, given the ten-dency of the garrison outposts to fire at the slightest provocation after a night of tense apprehension. Major Vesey recorded that 'early in the night, a man ran in from their post to acquaint us that it was their intention to attack us and that they were resolved to conquer or die'.[23] The uncertain first light of dawn made it less likely that 'a young man in black' would be recognized as an emis-sary, even had there been an inclination to treat him as such.

While his shooting almost certainly happened out of sight of the massed rebel forces, word of it spread quickly and, according to Cloney, 'rendered the people so furious that they became unmanageable', abandoning the plan of

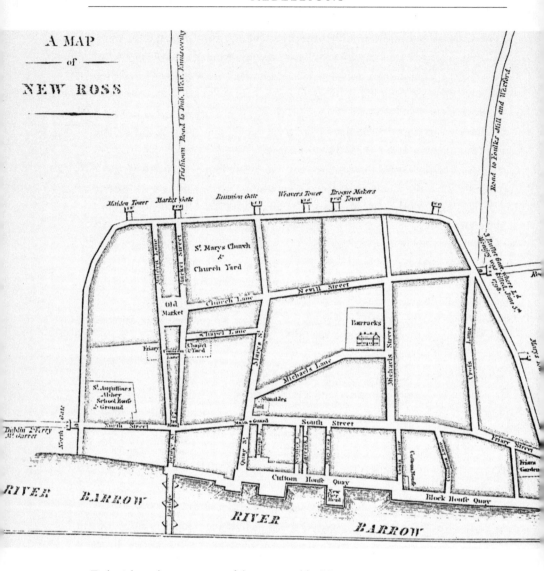

Early eighteenth-century map of the town used by Musgrave.

their leaders and, in Maxwell's words, 'rushed by a sudden impulse, in a mighty but disordered torrent along one road on the Three Bullet Gate, instead of making a combined movement on the open town'.[24] This description fits the common image of the rebels as an undisciplined mob, ruled by emotion, but the response to the killing of Furlong had a very specific cause and one that was fundamental to the Rebellion as a whole. It came from his family, friends and neighbours among the Bantrymen, led by Cloney and Kelly, who were already poised for an attack on the Three Bullet Gate. The attack, in other words, established the pattern that was to sustain the rebel action through this arduous day, the ties of neighbourhood and kinship.

'A person who was forced to attend them in their march' on New Ross informed Musgrave that the rebels 'moved by parishes and baronies, each having a particular standard'; this accords with the evidence of Cloney and Byrne, as we have seen. Musgrave's informant added 'that in their way they stopped at a chapel, where Mass was said at the head of each column, by priests who sprinkled an abundance of holy water on them'. This finds an echo in the folklore of my family, which records the rebels receiving Communion in Ballymacar, beside Corbet Hill, at a house then occupied by the parish priest of Cushinstown and later by my grandfather. However, Musgrave's depiction of the start of the battle (echoed in Maxwell) is entirely fictitious. As 'not less than thirty thousand rebels approached the town', he describes the scene thus:

> A great number of priests, with their vestments on, and crucifixes in their hands, by moving through the ranks, and animating them by their harangues, kindled a degree of enthusiastic ardour in them, which nothing but fanaticism could inspire.[25]

No eyewitness account, not even that by the ultra-loyalist George Hornick, supports this claim and, indeed, New Ross was the only major action of the Rebellion that did *not* feature a priest-leader. Some were to blame the rebel defeat on this fact and to use it to justify the replacement of Harvey by Father Philip Roche in the aftermath.[26] (There is no record of Roche taking part in the battle.) Instead, the attack was led by Kelly, with Cloney in support, and using the traditional 'rude stratagem of driving cattle against the ranks of the enemy', as they had done successfully at Enniscorthy. The trenches dug across the approaches to the Gate and deadly fire from the garrison meant that this tactic did not succeed completely, though all agree that it had some success.[27] Overwhelming pressure from Kelly's pikemen gradually forced the defenders back through the gate, while Cloney assisted in cutting down a detachment of dragoons sent by Johnson to retrieve the situation. Rebel success in this early breakthrough was due to the weight of numbers, the efficiency of the pike at close quarters and the remarkable bravery and persistence of the insurgents.

Major Vesey of the Dublin Militia claimed that the rebel leaders 'force the country people into the front when they attack, make them drunk and push them forward'. Lieutenant Colonel Robert Crawford, the most gifted of the garrison's career soldiers, was more admiring. He wrote to General Lake how 'the insurgents yesterday attacked this place in great force and with great vigour. They behaved in a manner that one could not have expected of them – in their first attack they seemed quite regardless of fire.' He told General Craddock that he had abandoned his earlier 'contemptible … opinion' because 'I never saw troops attack with more enthusiasm and bravery.'[28] Cloney made the same point years later in more pejorative terms, when he pointed to the remarkable achievement of the taking of the Three Bullet Gate 'by an undisciplined, badly armed, and ungovernable body of country peasants'.[29]

Another feature of the initial rebel breakthrough was to have a major influence on the nature and course of the battle (and to make any clear view of it even more difficult): the burning of houses. This was done initially by the rebels, who fired the easily ignited thatched houses of the poor that clustered along the walls and lined the lanes of the upper town. The scale of this house-burning, adding considerably to the heat and confusion, was remarkable. Alexander counted a total of 286 burnt houses (perhaps a quarter of all the houses in the town) and showed how they marked the main lines of rebel advance from the upper to the lower town. The use of the same tactic by the garrison later in the battle was to result in one of the most gruesome episodes of a horror-filled day. It is in this initial phase also that we have the only reference to townspeople joining with the rebels. Alexander wrote:

> As soon as the insurgents began to enter the town, and in this fiery manner to proclaim their approach, several of the inhabitants from about the town-wall, whose houses had on the *last Patrick's day* been searched in vain for pikes, now appeared with pikes ready mounted, and joined the rebel army in the conflagration and the battle.

This implies that the numbers involved were not significant, and only one is named in a footnote designed to show 'that those villains had (further than conquest) diabolical designs at heart against Ross of a piece with those afterwards perpetrated by them at Wexford bridge, Vinegar Hill, Enniscorthy and Scullabogue'. This was 'a weaver by the name of Crea' who lived 'by the town wall' and who 'ran with his pike into the house of a loyalist just opposite to him, and with whom he had been upon habits of intimacy'. He encouraged 'a throng of rebels' to kill his neighbour 'as a Protestant', but was foiled by a Catholic woman who swore that the intended victim was a Catholic. [30]

While it appears that no Ross man was tried as a rebel, several local women were court-martialled for encouraging them. The attempted murder of a man named Dowsley was said to have been incited by Catherine Whelan, 'a Romanist, his neighbour and as he thought his friend', who, the court was told, 'clapped her hands with joy on seeing the rebels enter the town, and welcomed the boys (as she called them) to Ross and said, "They should kill Dowsley as he was a Protestant."' He was saved by another Catholic neighbour, Mary Foley, who whispered the appropriate Catholic responses in his ear so that he could survive the rebel 'catechism'.[31]

A similar story emerged at the trial of Anstice Lynch, which also gives a vivid picture of the more domestic nature of the early fighting inside the town wall before the major rebel assaults downtown. The similarities to what happened earlier in Tintern and Fethard are striking. Lynch was accused of inciting the killing of John McDaniel, an old soldier and 'a cripple' from wounds received in the American war. He testified that his house was 'between the Three Bullet Gate and the Fair Gate', and that he had opened his door to 'the King's Troops', so that 'they might retreat back and forwards'. When they were forced down the hill, 'the Rebels came into my house and asked my wife why she had not set the house on fire. I was standing in the floor, and as the Rebels came in, I said God bless us, and one of the party said he would not touch me being a cripple, but that they must burn the house.' Going in search of his son, McDaniel went into the prisoner's house and 'she turned me out and called to the rebel who had told me he would not hurt me ... saying that I was an old soldier, an Orangeman (meaning a Protestant) and a bitter enemy to the rebels and desired him to kill me'. While 'this rebel whose name is unknown to me' tried to do so, she 'continued at the door encouraging' him and 'clapping him on the back'.[32] While the battle was dominated, as we will see, by intense street fighting largely between men from the surrounding countryside and militia men (many of them Catholics) from Clare, Donegal and Dublin, with the town's inhabitants cowering in what remained of their houses, it seems likely that some of the townspeople, Catholic and Protestant, also took the opportunity to target their neighbours.

When Kelly and his men broke through the Three Bullet Gate they precipitated the remarkable 'torrent running towards the bridge', bringing the battle with bewildering speed into the very centre of the town by Cross Lane and Michael Street, the approaches least well defended once that crucial gate had so unexpectedly fallen. Indeed, the large barracks half-way down Michael Street was undefended and almost empty of troops. The usual criticism, first voiced by Cloney, that Kelly exceeded his orders and by his precipitate action (or failure to restrain his troops) jeopardized the whole rebel attack, presupposes a level of rebel leadership that was clearly lacking. It seems more meaningful to see Kelly's charge, linked with the more cautious advance through Priory Gate, as giving the initial impetus and confidence that resulted in the taking of much of the town. Would Kelly have capitalized better on this initial advantage had he not been wounded in the rather half-hearted attack on the barracks? Clearly he was a charismatic figure; 'his men were greatly attached to him and would have followed him through any danger' according to Cloney.[33] However, there seems no reason to agree with Byrne's inflated claim that he had the military talent 'to have become the Hoche of Ireland', and his subsequent reputation owes more to the centenary ballads than to his impact on the Rebellion, in which he played no further part.[34] The barracks at this point contained only a few dragoons and Surgeon Roche, who 'did not perceive it was attacked', and while the rebels got some of its store of weapons they seem not to have used it as a command post even though, as Roche pointed out, it 'commands a view of a great part of the town'.[35] But that exhilarating downhill charge at the head of his neighbours made Kelly the epitome of 'insurgency', and this may account for the fact that after his execution in Wexford weeks later, he had the grisly honour of having his head stuck on a spike over the courthouse alongside those of the socially more prominent leaders, like Harvey and Grogan. Barbara Newton Lett, who witnessed this, may have been closer than Byrne to Kelly's true greatness and significance in her description of him as 'an humble person named Kelly from Killanne'.[36]

A good example of the confusion surrounding key events, even in this initial and comparatively well-documented phrase, can be seen in the different accounts of the killing of Lord Mountjoy, commander of the Dublin Militia and the most notable casualty of the day. Cloney believed he was killed by 'a rash hand' in retaliation for the death of Furlong.[37] Johnson's terse report that he 'fell early'[38] is echoed by Mountjoy's second-in-command, Major Vesey, though he stated that 'he was wounded and taken prisoner early'. However, in Vesey's account of the battle overall, this happened in the aftermath of Johnson's counter-attack (around midday), and his mangled body was found only in the final onslaught by the garrison.[39] This is the most authoritative report, but it is likely that many other stories circulated. A manuscript account by a field officer described how 'Mountjoy was riding a little way ahead of his regiment when he was shot from a window by a Baker's boy.' Forty years later, when 'inquiring into matters connected with the battle', this officer found the assassin living 'unmolested' in the town.[40] This draws attention to a feature of the battle that recurs in several reports – firing from houses – but the shooting by a baker's boy appears in no other account.

The battle for New Ross had two focal points apart from the Three Bullet Gate. In the upper part of the town, artillery posts at the corner of St Mary's

churchyard and down Church Lane at the Old Market (or Bullawn) confronted the rebel advances along Neville Street (which becomes Brogue Lane near
Mary Street), as well as giving added protection to the Clare Militia stationed
in the Irishtown and guarding the most direct route to the bridge. Downtown
at the Main Guard a small detachment of the Donegal Militia with two ship's
swivel guns commanded South Street (and hence, rebel approaches through
Priory Street, Cross Lane and Michael Street) and also the lower part of Mary
Street, which the rebels gained for periods, not only after fierce fighting at St
Mary's churchyard and the lanes nearby, but also infiltrating through Barrack,
or 'Bake-house' Lane ('Michaels Lane' in Musgrave's map).

The Main Guard, occupying part of the town's civic and historic centre,
the Tholsel, proved to be the key to the battle, the rock on which repeated
rebel attacks broke ('not one of their column escaped death' in the first attack
down South Street, according to Major Vesey). While the rebels had some
muskets, they were hampered in their use by lack of shot and poor-quality
powder, nor were they able to make significant use of the few artillery pieces
they began with or briefly captured except for a howitzer, operated for a while
'by one Boxwell, formerly of the Royal Irish Artillery', according to Alexander.
While there was much fighting at close quarters, the action was dominated by
repeated attacks on artillery positions by rebels armed mainly with pikes, and
this also accounts for the exceptionally high death toll, particularly through
the use of chain shot in the narrow, crowded streets. Piles of corpses provided
a gruesome map to the main centres of action. When Alexander finally left his
house 'to see the town and the slain' he 'saw the streets literally strewed with
dead carcasses':

> The greatest slaughter was in the Main Street [i.e. Mary Street] especially
> near the Churchyard. The piece of cannon planted on an eminence just
> above the Church-lane did very much the greatest execution of any other.
> Next to the Main Street the greatest slaughter was round the Town-wall
> where the battle raged. Next, the Chapel-lane, 'twas horrible'. Next,
> Brogue-maker's-Lane, Michael-Street and Cross-Lane; in all of which
> lanes the number of slain on the same length of ground was pretty equal;
> with this exception, that in Brogue-maker's-Lane, many were burned to
> ashes, of which we could have no knowledge or conjecture.[41]

The pattern was set from the beginning, when a cannon near the town
wall was taken for a while by rebels 'who ran up to the very muzzle of it, and
made its attendants to retreat'. According to Alexander, this fact led Major
Vesey to exclaim:

Had those rebels been properly trained and seasoned, and were they to fight in a loyal cause, how valuable to their country would they be! The devil in hell, and all his troops of fallen angels (provided they were mortal) could not withstand them. I shall think more of Irish courage than ever I did in my life.

Alexander also gave a graphic account of the near-capture of the Church Lane cannon:

Drop numbers of them did, but still the rest pressed on! Nay large numbers of them got into the burned cabins, within ten yards of the cannon, trampling on the glowing embers, and loosening stones from the tumbling walls with their pikes; flung them in such heavy showers, and with such amazing force and judgement on the soldiers at the cannon, that they were just beginning to give way, when their courage was re-animated by the approach of 'the gentleman with the brazen helmet'.[42]

This was local yeoman Michael McCormick, the hero of Alexander's account, of whom more anon. Just beyond that fierce action, Captain Bloomfield commanded the cannon in the Old Market, and gave a similar account:

They appeared as insensible of danger, as if there really had not been the least, they were so desperate as to march up to the face of my guns several times, 'tho I was supported by strong detachments of Infantry.[43]

The best known of these stories, recounted in the main anti-rebel accounts, those by Taylor, Musgrave and Maxwell, and depicted most memorably in Cruikshank's cartoon, is that of the so-called 'wig-cannon'. Musgrave's account captures the role of the story in depicting the rebels as crazed savages:

One rebel, emboldened by fanaticism and drunkenness, advanced before his comrades, seized a gun, crammed his hat and wig into it, and cried out, 'Come on boys, her mouth is stopped.' At that instant the gunner laid the match to the gun and blew the unfortunate savage to atoms. This fact has been verified by the affidavit of a person who saw it from a window.[44]

This version still has currency, even with some modern historians,[45] despite the existence of Alexander's account. His source would appear to have been one of his military informants, and he can only locate the incident 'somewhere in the body of the town'. But the detail is technical, graphic and convincing.

[The rebels] rushed on the piece, and though numbers of them fell by the musquetry, and others by the sword, they pressed on, repulse after repulse, until one of them caught away the worm. [Footnoted, 'i.e. a pole with an iron screw on one side, for the purpose of drawing the charge'.] The piece now being discharged, an old rebel took off his wig, and clapping it upon his pike, rammed it into the cannon, exclaiming, 'Huzza! the town is our own'. And so it was – just then; its worm being gone, the gun becomes useless, in as much as the men were obliged to spike it and break the carriage. Nonetheless, the rebels thought to make use of it ... This cannon, for a long time after the battle lay on the bridge and was called 'the wig cannon'.[46]

While Bloomfield held out in the Old Market, the rebels held the area around the churchyard on several occasions, and burned the thatched houses of the surrounding lanes. One slated house, belonging to a Protestant publican named Sabourin, on the corner of Brogue Lane and Mary Street, proved 'too large to be easily burned without losing considerable time', and the soldiers interrupted the rebel attempt to set it on fire (and also attacked 'poor Mrs. Sabourin', according to Alexander, from 'the circumstances of the insurgents being found there' – just one of several stories of innocent townspeople, even well-known loyalists, being terrorized by the military). Possibly about the same time, the rebels occupied perhaps the tallest house in the upper part of the town, higher up Mary Street on the churchyard side. Certainly it was prominent enough to be observable from the Quay, where Alexander was trying to follow this phase of the battle from the comparative safety of his own house, sometime after half-past ten.

> Looking towards the Main Street, once more, I beheld a slated house of about four stories high, towards the upper end of that street, just set on fire. And the flames increased rapidly amid horrid shrieks, which were soon drowned by the increasing noise of musquetry pretty near and of cannon at some distance.

In the second part of his narrative, moving from what he saw to what he heard, Alexander gave what was, presumably, Michael McCormick's account of this horrifying occurrence.

> A slated house, about four stories high, in the Main Street, near the top, and on the Church-yard side was occupied on every floor by rebels, who fired out of the windows on the King's troops. Mr. McCormick, being informed of this, got under it, and with the very able and active assistance of Mr. Roger Unsworth, trumpeter of the Ross Calvary, set it on fire and burned seventy five almost to ashes. They were not, every one, burned alive. Two or three of them, attempting to take shelter in an oven back-

George Cruikshank's version of The Wig Cannon, *from W.H. Maxwell's* History of the Irish Rebellion in 1798 *(1844).*

wards were shot and so burned. One rebel, a brave fellow! escaped through the flames. While he was making off, Mr. McCormick ordered Mr. Nowlan, quarter-master of the 5th Regiment of Dragoons, to shoot him; which he immediately attempted to do, but missed fire, and the rebel got completely off unhurt, except by a slight scorching.47

Several features of this account are noteworthy, particularly the naming of those responsible, and the justification that the house was being used to fire on the troops, including, presumably, those operating and guarding the cannon in the churchyard lower down the street. Alexander's account of this incident is the only one we have and, not surprisingly, is the only source cited for the following very different account in Daniel Gahan's 1995 narrative, *The People's Rising*, which turned the four-storey building into a 'makeshift hospital' and made its burning part of Johnson's counter-attack after his temporary retreat across the bridge.

Because the soldiers gained control of the northern sector with such speed, several rebel units suddenly found themselves cut off from their comrades. Among them were the seventy or so men in the makeshift hospital, and these now became the victims of the worst atrocity to be committed in the war so far. As soon as it was discovered what the building was being used for, a detachment of soldiers surrounded it. Then somebody, perhaps several men at the urging of an officer, perhaps a lone individual, set a fire on the ground floor. The building was dry inside, and flames spread quickly to the upper floors. When they realised what was happening, the helpless men inside began to scream so loudly that they could be heard all over the town. The soldiers in the street below watched unmoved as the entire building became an inferno and as the shrieks inside gradually died away. One man somehow managed to escape and ran through the smoke and confusion back towards the rebel lines. Everyone else inside died.[48]

Those involved are not named but their motivation is clear; they set the fire because they *knew* 'what the building was being used for', that is, the care of the wounded, and they watched the deaths of these helpless men 'unmoved'.[49]

None of this can reasonably be inferred from Alexander's account. In an endnote Gahan admits that 'Alexander describes this post as a rebel stronghold, held by men firing from its windows … But in other sources it is described as a hospital … which is a more plausible one.' The only 'other source' cited, Cloney's *Narrative*, p. 44, merely said of the atrocity at Scullabogue that 'it was excited and promoted by the cowardly ruffians who ran away from the Ross battle, and conveyed the intelligence (which was too true) that several wounded men had been burned in a house in Ross by the Military' – no mention of a 'hospital', or seventy-five victims, and no identification of the house.

Cloney's anxiety, like Gahan's, was to balance the atrocity at Scullabogue with a similar atrocity earlier at New Ross. This was manifest again after Cloney's account of the killings on Wexford Bridge, when 'in justice to the insurgents' he recounted how they had learned such behaviour from 'magistrates, military and Yeomanry', instancing the burning of the 'insurgent hospital of Enniscorthy' and 'the Insurgent depot of wounded men' in New Ross. Finally, in the list of government atrocities with which he concluded his *Narrative*, Cloney equated the killings at Scullabogue and Vinegar Hill with that of 'more than 150 sick and wounded insurgents' in 'the house' in New Ross and 'the hospital' in Enniscorthy. He went on to cite Hay as his authority for the statement that seventy-eight 'wounded men' were 'burned by the military at New Ross'.[50] However, Hay, following Alexander, simply says that '75 persons were burned to ashes'; if he had had any information that they were 'wounded men' he would undoubtedly have emphasized this, given the degree to which his history of the Rebellion is focused on recounting government atrocities.[51] These were widespread and appalling before, during and after the battle of Ross, and without doubt largely created the climate of fear, hatred and bloodlust that produced similar atrocities by the insurgents, whether small-scale, routine and lost to history, or the large-scale lurid dramas of Scullabogue, Vinegar Hill and Wexford Bridge. But for some modern nationalist historians that is not enough; an exact parallel seems necessary.

Alexander's account had its own biases and limitations, as has my own attempt to make sense of it and of the other surviving slight and patchy evidence for the events of 5 June 1798. One of Alexander's great virtues was his clear acknowledgment of his sources, which were largely military. Above all, he claimed 'the account is justified by the gallant McCormick',[52] who is also, indeed, its hero, as he is of other contemporary accounts of the battle. Taylor described him as 'Michael McCormick, an inhabitant of New Ross and formerly a Quartermaster of the 5th Dragoons', who was distinguished by his 'brazen helmet'.[53] A member of the local yeomanry corps, he was, according to Alexander, General Johnson's principal aide-de-camp during the battle. One reason why Alexander's account of the burning of the four-storey house rings true is that he was unlikely to have identified his hero so clearly with anything that could be represented as an atrocity. As we will see, he was not adverse to reporting genuine atrocities – even by local yeomen – as such.

Alexander described General Johnson as 'the hero of the fifth of June' for his personal bravery and for 'animating his troops'. Indeed Alexander acknowledged that the stress laid by all on the courage of the rebels served to highlight 'the merit of this courageous, skilful and intrepid commander'. A year after the battle, Alexander sent him a gift of a ruby ring, with a letter which he published in his *Narrative*, thanking him not only for his services to 'this kingdom at large' but more particularly for saving Alexander's life on the eve of the battle when he was in coloured clothes, and thus in danger of being shot by 'a justly enraged soldiery'. Yet, reading a little below the surface of Alexander's text a very different picture emerges, that of an ill-disciplined garrison deeply divided between militia and yeomanry. Likewise, Alexander's defence of Johnson and the Dublin Militia for the retreat across the bridge is weak and unconvincing, especially the claim that it was 'an absence of but a few minutes, though it may appear longer through my account'. His odd, ostensibly naïve remark about the ruby ring he sent his 'hero' (that it was one 'which I obtained in the West Indies last war considerably cheap') may have in fact a more ironic resonance, and one more in harmony with this very knowing, often tongue-in-cheek text. In this reading the far more convincing portrayal of McCormick as the *real* hero takes on a different and more political meaning; it appears as a critique not simply of Johnson, but of the garrison as a whole, militia and yeomanry alike, with particular exceptions. These included Edward Devereux as well as McCormick among the local yeomen; Major Vesey of the Dublin Militia; and some members of the Donegal Militia, particularly those who held the crucial artillery post at the Main Guard throughout the day.54 This critique of the garrison, sustained largely by inference, was clearly McCormick's as well as Alexander's. Their friendship, and shared judgment may have had a basis in the fact that each had previous military experience, but also in strong religious convictions, different in kind but both unorthodox: neither was a member of the town's Anglican establishment. McCormick was a Methodist; Alexander probably a Quaker.55

Alexander gives this characteristic description of McCormick in battle:

> Mr. McCormick was flying from street to street, from post to post, rallying or urging on the King's troops, splitting the skull of a croppy now and then, en passant! Fighting at one post, he would roar like a lion at a parcel of fugitives to join. It was done! My Donegal man, as I call him, showed me a dead rebel, whose skull Mr. McCormick absolutely cut in two!

McCormick's zeal was in pointed contrast to many in the garrison, who refused to follow his lead. One moment rallying the soldiers under siege at the churchyard cannon from stone-throwing rebels ('For shame soldiers … do no give way to their *beggars-bullets!*'), the next he was 'haranguing' the troops who had fled across the bridge, 'to return to their duty, and offering *fifty guineas* to any *fifty* men who would accompany him to a charge, at which *he would give the lead*'. Earlier, his bravery was placed in mute contrast with the refusal of 'a certain officer commanding a cannon', to follow Johnson's orders to 'shift your position nearer to the Three Bullet Gate', and with another 'certain officer of horse' refusing an order 'to charge his troop at the Three Bullet Gate', and instead going 'capering over the bridge'.56

While thus exposing Johnson's lack of authority, and the cowardice of some of his officers, Alexander also emphasized repeatedly that there was a deep and often deadly division in the garrison between the mainly Catholic militia and the Protestant yeomanry. One of his main informants, his unnamed because unknown 'Donegal man', told him:

> 'The way to know a *croppy soldier* is, *by his hatred to a Yeoman*. Why, sir, there is a Yeoman now in the battle, worth forty brave soldiers. *The gentleman with the brass helmet* [Mr. McCormick] I assure you, sir, that some of our

troops fired at *him*'. I afterwards asked Mr. McCormick, *if this was true?* And he declared it was.

Mistaken yet again for a priest, this time by a group of militiamen, one of whom said enough 'to show he was a rebel'. Alexander reported him to the authorities, and 'the rebel soldier was since hanged'. The violent prejudice shown by some militia men to the local yeomanry also extended, according to Alexander, to the 'loyal refugees called Glory men' – that is, the Palatine Methodists, disarmed by Johnson before the battle:

> Mr. Edward Devereux of the Ross cavalry (of whom also the Dublin Regiment speaks highly) saw a soldier on the day of battle thrusting a large piece of white paper under the band of a dead rebel's hat, and not knowing that he was observed, the knave turned about, exclaiming, 'There's Death and Glory for you. See what rebels those Glory-men are.' One of the Yeomen (Francis Robinson) left his post and went into the battle. He was soon shot by a corporal, who was since hanged for disaffection.[57]

Robinson's gravestone in St Mary's churchyard, as mentioned earlier, is the only one in the town apart from that of John Rice in Catholic St Stephen's that bears the date 5 June 1798. It is ironic (especially as the inscription on Robinson's grave implies that he was killed by 'the rebels') that both were probably victims of the undisciplined militia, the former for being a loyalist, the latter as a suspected rebel.

The depiction of McCormick as the hero of the battle in Alexander's account is part of his attempt to present a more favourable picture of the Methodist 'Glory Men'. Prominent among the other local heroes of the day were Alexander's 'loyal friends' the Dowsleys, who had a large house near the bottom of Mary Street with a bow window, which gave him temporary shelter when caught in crossfire. 'From the windows just over my head they shot great numbers of [the rebels] in *Bake-House-Lane* where the villains stept in to prime and load.' They thus played an important part in the defence of the guns at the Main Guard, vulnerable to a sudden rebel assault from the lane. Alexander's comment, 'This brought to my mind the observation on disarming the Glory-Men,' suggests that the Dowsleys were also Methodists. After the battle, when he 'was appointed temporary Major to the unarmed loyalists' (his ironic description of the unpleasant role assigned to himself and other non-Ascendancy loyalists of clearing the streets of rebel corpses), his group of 'about seven hundred inhabitants' featured 'the *Glory Men*, most certainly loyal', and 'now ... a respectable part of our yeomanry'. But some of Alex-

"Ireland is a small but
insuppressible island
half an hour nearer
the sunset than Great
Britain"

Thomas Kettle

Appletree Press

General Henry Johnson, with a picture of New Ross in the background (engraved by Robert Dunkarton, after a painting by Robert Woodburn, 1801, courtesy National Library of Ireland).

ander's villains were also local loyalists. The summary killing of a wounded suspected rebel after the battle by 'one Christopher Gefford of the Ross Yeomen' was recounted with distaste:

> The face of the corpse had the evident mark of a foot from the left eye across the cheek. I did not enquire whether the man was kicked dead or alive, but went on my way.

Later, he claimed that 'a tyrannical Yeoman of whom I complained was imprisoned for some weeks', which seems rather surprising given his own relationship with Charles Tottenham, the yeoman commander, who as we have seen, had been angry at Alexander's refusal to join the Corps. Also, in the days prior to the battle, Alexander had been targeted as a spy by Tottenham's protégé, Standish Lowcay.[58]

The depiction of Tottenham during the battle is curious. His support role – he was kept in reserve on the Quay throughout – gave little scope for heroics, but some commendation of the town's Sovereign might have been expected. Instead he is depicted in at best an irresponsible, at worst a malign role in his treatment of Alexander. The ambiguity resides in the narrator's characteristic black humour in describing his own adventures. When he emerged from his house on the Quay it was after 8.30, and the battle had raged for four hours, but he imagined it still outside the town walls. 'Otherwise', as he put it, 'I should not have acted so madly.' Outside his door he met Tottenham, who joked with him, then 'requested that I would go and take a peep into the *Main Street* and see what news'. Spurred on by the jeers of some of Tottenham's men at his boast of being an old soldier, 'off I ran to the Main Street directly; though followed by peals of laughter' – the laughter being due to the knowledge that he was going unwittingly into danger. Having engaged in further raillery with some soldiers in the Main Guard, he advanced up Mary Street and suddenly found himself among the rebels who were advancing slowly towards the Main Guard, as the Ross Yeomanry clearly knew to be the case. When, after an hour and a half of hair-raising adventures, Alexander again gained the comparative safety of the Quay (being involved in further militia–yeoman conflict on the way), he again encountered the jocose Captain Tottenham, who began with the same ironic question as earlier, 'Well, what news?' Alexander's report how 'the King's troops are overturning the rebels like ninepins' ended with characteristic humour; the rebels after their 'great huzzas and firing' were 'now all as silent as Quakers'.

Oblique criticism of the callous way this 'Quaker' had been exposed to mortal danger was reflected in Alexander's final comment on the episode; 'a facetious gentleman requested me to *take another walk for news to the Three Bullet Gate*, where the battle raged. But I begged to be excused.' It is not surprising that Alexander's narrative did not criticize the powerful Sovereign directly, but the portrayal of Tottenham and his party throughout is a dark and even hostile one. Alexander's account of how he essentially had to force a public reconciliation with Standish Lowcay (now named as 'the loyal and zealous magistrate, who had on the 3rd June 1798, through a mistake, challenged me as a rebel before the Antrim Militia') on the first anniversary dinner for the battle, further illustrated his uneasy relationship with the dominant Ascendancy party.[59]

The first phase of the battle ended in stalemate, with the rebels capturing much of the town but becoming too exhausted and disorganized to sustain their attack against several key, well-defended points. While much of the garrison had fled across the river, they left a sufficient presence to prevent all access to the bridge and provide the basis for a counter-attack. While the initial rebel success was remarkable, particularly given the apparent leadership vacuum, it also had clear limits, failing to spread the conflict to the Irishtown through the Market Gate, or to overrun the post at the Old Market through Chapel and Church Lanes. Thus the most direct route to the bridge from the upper town (down High Hill from the Old Market and bypassing the Main Guard) was cut off. Also, and most surprisingly, they appear to have made little effort to penetrate to the Custom House Quay, where the local yeomanry cavalry remained on standby.

What most decisively ended the rebel advance, however, were the swivel guns at the Main Guard. Their use of grape and chain shot ('twenty-three successive discharges', according to one report) in the narrow streets created havoc in the rebel ranks. Alexander was an uncomfortable witness to their first experience of this devastating firepower. Advancing up Mary Street, he encountered an advance party of rebels cautiously descending, still hidden from the Main Guard by the curve of the street. After 'a dreadful pause', with 'neither rebels nor soldiers fully appearing to each other' (and Alexander taking cover between Dowsley's bow windows), there was a flurry of musket fire, Alexander noting that 'the rebels' balls flew … amazingly feeble. Hence it was evident that their powder was wretchedly inferior to that of our troops.' But, when 'the soldiers opened their cannon upon them' they 'blew numbers of them off their legs… the explosion was dreadful! Some of the grape knuckled the flag just by my foot, and rose to a great height.'[60] Despite further attempts at a frontal assault, and others to mass for a charge at Michael's (or Bakehouse) Lane, close to the guns but out of sight, the Main Guard battery proved invulnerable, helped by covering fire from the Dowsley house across from the Lane.

The fact that it took many more hours for this superior firepower to tell decisively said much about the courage and determination of the rebels, and the military incompetence or disorganization of the garrison. The battle's ebb and flow was echoed in the confused reports of the relays of soldiers calling at Alexander's house on the Quay for refreshments. 'One party … would inform us, *that the King's troops were gaining upon the enemy rapidly*, another would inform us of *the very reverse* … But about 12 o'clock they all came with the heavy tidings, *that the rebels were in possession of the upper part of the town.*'

It was only at this late stage, by Alexander's account, that the retreat of much of the garrison across the bridge occurred, lasting only a short time, as 'about one, my Donegal man and some others' told him that 'the rebels were now completely dislodged', with the return of the Dublin Militia.[61] But Jordan Roche, in the only eye-witness account of the garrison's retreat, seems to suggest that it began much earlier. Watching from the barracks, which 'commands a view of the greater part of the town', he 'saw plainly most of our little army retreat over the bridge to the county of Kilkenny and turn left towards Waterford. Between 6 and 7 it was supposed that there were 3,000 rebels in the town.'[62]

It is not clear that the two sentences refer to the same part of the morning, nor should too much be read into Cloney's remarkably terse account, which also seems to suggest that Johnson's retreat followed immediately on the initial rebel success. It was 'equally extraordinary' to Cloney that Johnson fled ('panic struck') and that the rebels failed to capitalize on his departure by taking the 'two weak points' of the Irishtown and Main Guard. His explanation was the chaotic nature of the battle, the fact that 'all was disorder and confusion',[63] and this is echoed in Roche's observation that 'the rebels were dispersed throughout the town in the greatest confusion looking for *one another*'.[64] These accounts can be reconciled with Alexander's, if the retreat is seen as gradual, occurring over the course of several hours, beginning with some of the Dublin Militia who were stationed near the Three Bullet Gate, and joined gradually by the large numbers of the garrison who, by McCormick's account, took no real part in the fighting. Johnson (and, in Alexander's account, McCormick) may have followed much later in an attempt to get his men to return when the rebel attack finally came to an exhausted halt, and they searched desperately for something to drink.

While Alexander's anxiety to minimize the nature and duration of the retreat raises suspicions about the timescale he offered, it fitted into his account of the battle overall and was supported by other incidental evidence. In particular, his clear eyewitness testimony that the *initial* rebel appearance in lower Mary Street came after 8.30 a.m. raises major doubts about Gahan's account which, taking up the hints in Cloney and Roche, has Johnson's counter-attack beginning at around this time. And, while he followed the events after 10 a.m. from his house as best he could, relying mainly on reports from individual soldiers, Alexander also offered persuasive evidence for the continued fighting in the upper Mary Street area and renewed attacks on the Main Guard.[65]

Whatever the timing of the retreat and return of the majority of the garrison, the limitations of the initial rebel success are not in dispute and these account for their failure to take the bridge and raise its 'excellent drawbridge ... on a principle the most simple and convenient that can well be conceived'.[66] This would have made a counter-attack (or reinforcements from

The Tholsel, New Ross: in 1798 the ground floor was an open arcade.

Waterford) impossible, and kept alive the possibility of later advancing into Kilkenny. But they never had access to the bridge. This fact may also help to explain why the Kilkenny rebels failed to join in the battle.

As noted, Alexander had seen evidence of rebel activity near Glenmore some days before, and on the 5th twenty-five soldiers of the Dublin Regiment under Captain Dillon were captured there as they fled the battle. The bodies of many of them were found next day by the Roscommon Militia under Colonel King, who had turned back at the same point when marching from Waterford to reinforce the Ross garrison on the day of the battle. Some of the fleeing garrison had told him that the town had already fallen when he was two miles outside Waterford, which he left at ten o'clock. However, he continued on to Glenmore:

... in a straight line, about two miles and a half from Ross; whence, with the assistance of a good glass, he saw smoke issuing from the town, but could not discern any troops in it; from which he concluded that his intelligence had been well founded. He, therefore, thought it prudent to retreat.

He had marched twelve miles, and his observation of the town can hardly have been earlier than 12.30, which would thus seem to support Alexander's account. Gaffney, the leader of the Glenmore rebels, 'a miller in very good circumstances', was captured by King and hanged next day at Ross according to Musgrave.[67] Alexander put his execution three weeks later, and referred to the Kilkenny rebels in his defence of 'the Ross infantry' who 'were foolishly censured by some for not quitting their station on the bridge, and going into the heat of the battle'. This would have jeopardized the security of the town, because 'a rebel captain of the name of Gafney ... had a force of 2,500 rebels waiting near Glenmore to enter the town by that way. He had perpetual intelligence from Ross.'[68]

The claim that there was regular communication between the town and the Kilkenny rebels is borne out by evidence given at the court-martial of Thomas Joyce, Pierce Ryan and Augustine Lee for the murder of Robert and Matthew Taylor, the toll-keeper for the bridge and his son. The murder was said to have occurred on the Kilkenny side of the river at around one o'clock on the 5 June, after the troops had re-crossed the bridge (further corroborating Alexander's timetable). This was the testimony of Catherine Everett, near whose house at Tinnerany the Taylors were killed. Also, 'My house was burned on that day by a party of United men, as I believe. They were in coloured clothes.' Under cross-examination, she said:

> The battle was this time going on in Ross. I have heard that messages were going back and forwards the whole day and that there were orders sent for a great party of men (who were gathered on the road ready to join the rebels in Ross) that they should not burn or murder any more. I was the last that left my house. I heard the rebels shout at the back of my house, but they kept as much out of my sight as they could lest I should know them.

Thus, they were locals, and the murder of the Taylors may have been just another example of 'neighbourly murder'. One witness claimed that Ryan jumped on the body of the old man, saying 'that it was long ago he ought to have been killed', and the toll-keeper, a local and menial representative of the Protestant Corporation, was probably disliked as such.[69] But it may also have reflected the frustration of Gaffney's men at their inability to cross the bridge, which was in effect guarded on both sides after the temporary retreat of most of the garrison.

The defence seemed to concede the case initially, arguing that there had been a general pardon for 'all homicides committed in the Rebellion during heat of blood while the battle raged'. The accused had been 'in the hearing of the dreadful roar of the cannon and din of arms'; they had been 'flushed and elated' with hopes of victory; and in any case the victims had fired on them first. However, Ryan and Lee also called alibi witnesses. The credibility of Joseph Keeffe, testifying on behalf of Ryan, was doubtless undermined by the fact that, 'this witness at first swore he could speak Irish only, but afterwards delivered his testimony very fluently in English'. Two witnesses appearing for Lee lived near him at 'Mountgarrett Lane' on the Ross side and a little upriver. John Martin, giving evidence, stated:

> I am sure my neighbours kept their houses, but I have heard and believe that many of the people of Ross ran away with their lives … I never heard that people were crossing and recrossing the river the whole day in cots.

'Cots' were (and still are) small flat-bottomed boats used for salmon fishing, then a thriving activity, and Mountgarrett, where there was also a ferry, was out of sight of the town and probably home to many of the fishermen. This specific denial of the use of cots tends to confirm Catherine Everett's story and to indicate the means by which people and information flowed over and back across the river, independent of the bridge. While Ryan and Joyce were found guilty and sentenced to death, Cornwallis agreed with the opening argument of the defence that the case was covered by the amnesty.[70]

Back in the stifling noonday heat of the town, exhausted by seven or eight hours of fighting, lungs filled with smoke from the burning houses and many of them weak from loss of blood, the rebels were desperate for rest and refreshment and unable to carry the fight any further after having taken most of the town. Their conduct during this lull in the battle was later blamed for their defeat, Hay first articulating the view of them 'sullying their bravery with drunkenness'. The late nineteenth-century ballad 'The Boys of Wexford' turned this into an excuse, reminiscent of the moralizing of late seventeenth-century Gaelic poetry, 'Twas drink that brought us down'.

Such judgments reveal the social and moral disdain with which the rebels were often regarded, even by their defenders. They are akin to the judgment of Musgrave that many of the rebels were from the start 'emboldened by fanaticism and drunkenness', or Captain Bloomfield's claim that 'their tenacity is attributed to intoxication'.[71] However, such charges need to be put in context.

Even before the battle the rebels were suffering from lack of sleep and probably hungry from a week or more of living on haphazard and inadequate field provisions, and some were weak from old wounds. When Alexander was finally able to leave his house he witnessed a terrible scene:

> Amongst the slain in the Main Street I saw bodies with frightful wounds of about one fortnight's standing, evidently distinguishable from those received on this day. It is almost incredible that men with such large deep wounds, could bear the fatigue, even of their march from Wexford or Enniscorthy.

Many more now bore fresh wounds and all were utterly fatigued by their remarkable exertions over a very long morning. There was little water in the town, and in any case, beer was part of their ordinary diet, while whiskey was used by all classes as a restorative, as it was during the battle by the garrison also. Alexander describes soldiers 'earnestly begging a little refreshment' at his door:

> The poor fellows' faces were discoloured with the powder; their mouths and teeth quite black, and their saliva as thick as gum water. They begged hard for a glass of spirits which was given then ... These men were soon succeeded by others, and so on till the battle was over; few of them delaying more than five minutes each time.[72]

The real scandal of this pause in the fighting was the failure of the rebel leadership to consolidate their gains by sending in reinforcements and outflanking the Main Guard, using the lanes leading to the Quay where the small reserve force, mainly composed of local yeomanry, could hardly have withstood a determined onslaught. Harvey appears to have had little contact with his men, and Cloney, the only surviving officer in the field, having cautiously ventured downtown, clearly despaired of the situation:

> After being some time in the town, and finding our men entering houses, to seek for liquor and refreshments, we found it prudent to retire to the Three Bullet Gate, lest the main body of the King's troops might return and take advantage of our confusion.[73]

He was thus in no position to describe Johnson's counter-attack, which was focused, naturally, in the very area he had left. What was remarkable was not that the leaderless rebels collapsed with exhaustion and took what drink they could find, but that within a brief time they were able to resume the fight and offer fierce resistance to the returning troops. In this, adrenalin must have been more important than alcohol, fuelled by a powerful will to survive, by intense loyalty to one another, and a burning sense of injustice.

In the romantic loyalist accounts of Johnson rallying his troops, he appealed to them initially and unsuccessfully as 'your General', and then as 'your countryman', which succeeded because 'the chord of national honour was touched'.74 Alexander's account, while it romanticized the general on a personal level, had him employ a more traditional military appeal. It also showed the initial leadership coming from Alexander's local hero:

> Coming to the bridge … he found his brave *McCormick*, haranguing a party of them to return to their duty and offering *fifty guineas* to any *fifty* men who would accompany him to a charge, at which *he would give the lead*. This offer was not regarded, but the very sight of their gallant *General* roused them. *His* word soon prevailed; but when he informed the Dublin Regiment that their brave Colonel was slain, and even mangled by rebel pikes, there was no bounds to *their* fury. They were determined to conquer and revenge, or die to a man, and well they fulfilled the former part of their resolution.75

The ironic note, faint but clear, gives an early indication of Alexander's disapproval of the conduct of the troops in the later stages of the battle and especially in its aftermath. But while they did ultimately 'conquer and revenge' they found it no easy task. The account of an artillery officer who took part shows how the conflict resumed where it had left off, at the battle's epicentre, the Main Guard, and how the same patterns were repeated:

> In retaking the town … shocking was it to see the dreadful carnage that was there; it continued for half an hour, obstinate but bloody: the thundering of cannon shook the town, the very windows were shivered to pieces with the dreadful concussion. I believe six hundred rebels lay dead in the Main Street; they would often come within a few yards of the guns.76

This account places the 'wig-cannon' episode in this phase, as does Alexander's. Indeed the latter's split narrative adds to the general sense of confusion about the sequence of events. The clearest apparent contradiction between his version of what he himself saw and what he pieced together from military sources concerns the burning of the four-storey house in Mary Street, which he 'witnessed' from his house around half-past ten, but described in detail (using McCormick's account) as part of the retaking of the town after one o'clock.77

The more it is looked at in detail, the clearer it becomes that a reliable narrative even of the main events cannot be constructed from the surviving evidence. The recapture of the town, as Patrick Donovan concluded fifty years ago, involved the main 'unrecorded battles' of the day, further proof for him of 'the absence of any tangible pattern in the fighting'.[78]

What is clear, however, is that rebel resistance continued to be fierce, and that the crucial difference between the sides continued to be the superior firepower of the garrison. According to one account, the rebels continued to fire their few muskets, even when they had 'no ball or buttons left', hoping that 'the noise will frighten the horses'. By contrast, 'some of the regulars fired *one hundred and twenty rounds per man!*' Cloney described how, having 'remained some time at the Gate', he attempted to join the resistance to Johnson's return at the Main Guard:

> We mustered as good a force as possible and entered the town again, by what is called the Brogue Maker's Lane [part of Neville Street], which leads down nearly on a line with the Church. To this spot we brought down one of the howitzers, taken at the Three Rocks, with which to fire on the Main Guard, but on going down some distance beyond the Church, we were so warmly fired on from the houses that we were obliged to retreat.[79]

Even when the rebels could bring their captured artillery pieces into play, they lacked the expertise to make effective use of them. The other howitzer was well directed briefly by the ex-artillery man, Boxwell. Wounded, he had himself tied to the cannon, 'but through his bungling assistants, he was killed and the piece taken'. This is Alexander's version, which makes Boxwell 'a martyr to rebellion'. A captured artillery man who was forced to operate a captured 12-pounder became 'a martyr to loyalty', being shot by the rebels for deliberately aiming too high.[80] Much more successful was Captain Bloomfield, now directing a mobile artillery unit:

> After the rebels had been beaten back twice, they assembled in the greatest force they could, to conquer or to die, when most luckily I burst twenty shells in their line which was ready formed, and dispersed them. They, however, continued to get together, 'tho not in so great force and entered the town again.[81]

And so it went on, with the rebels gradually worn down, their numbers, never very great, shrinking visibly, until Cloney 'proposed to General Harvey that we should send a kind of forlorn hope through some open fields called *beurheena slanaigh* to attack the Clare Militia, which throughout the day maintained their position … in the Irishtown … we could not muster above forty men for the purpose', and they were quickly forced to retreat under 'most galling fire'. His account of the battle then ends abruptly: 'Here the contest ended, after about thirteen hours almost constant fighting, with considerable loss to both sides.' Thus, for Cloney, the fighting ended at 5 p.m. (George Hornick put it at 4 p.m.), whereas Alexander was told it was safe to view the aftermath in the downtown area after 2.30. This is consistent, as the final phase of the battle was fought in the upper town, with the rebels gradually forced to retreat through the Three Bullet Gate that they had so unexpectedly breached in the early morning. There Cloney found a half dozen 'jolly old topers' of 'that class termed middleman' who had spent the day drinking a cask of port wine, 'with seeming indifference to the fate of Ireland, now in the balance'. As he prepared to mount his horse, 'in a very desponding state indeed, in company with my commander-in-chief', he was accosted by the 'famous Amazon whose name was Doyle', a neighbour from Castleboro, and often 'the gallant point of war' in his account. She now bullied him into persuading a number of reluctant, exhausted men to carry away with them their remaining howitzer, her 'dear little cannon'. As they moved off, Cloney 'rode slowly with Mr. Harvey. Indeed I was so overpowered with fatigue that I could not ride fast, and soon began to fall asleep on my horse. Mr. Harvey proceeded while my horse turned to the ditch to graze, and there, within half a mile of the town of Ross I remained asleep on my horse's back for more than an hour.' He was saved by the inability of the equally exhausted garrison to give pursuit. After a rest at the house of his Old Ross relatives, Cloney reached Carrigbyrne at nightfall and slept at a house at Ballyshannon.[82]

This account, plausible in itself, also allows him to make the unlikely claim that he heard of the massacre at Scullabogue only the next morning. But before examining that other terrible event of 5 June 1798, and its relationship to the battle, it is important to look briefly at what little further evidence there is for the culture and possible motivation of the rebels who showed such remarkable courage at New Ross, not least because it also offers a key to understanding those who carried out the massacre.

Alexander noted that many of the rebel corpses wore Catholic symbols, like scapulars, and he was impressed by the religious conviction of condemned rebels that he visited in the town gaol.[83] In his systematic questioning of former rebels coming to the town to avail of an amnesty a month later, he found that:

> They complained one and all of the misery of this country through the perpetual absence of the possessors of its greatest wealth; and they complained still more bitterly of their own particular sufferings through

griping and oppressive landlords. They also muttered something, which I cannot now well remember, concerning rackrents, and the connivance of nominal justice at all their sufferings, which they believed to proceed from no other reason than their being Roman Catholics.[84]

In part this fits well with what we know of the background of the Bantry rebels, but the emphasis on absenteeism seems more the voice of liberal Protestant critique rather than of peasant insurgency.

We can come closer to hearing the authentic rebel voice in Alexander's crucial evidence that those who attacked New Ross were bilingual, and in times of extreme danger instinctively Irish-speaking. The day before the battle he had been amused at the mixture of Irish and English spoken by a drunken group he spoke to near Corbet Hill, and in his first encounter with armed rebels during the battle his knowledge of Irish may have saved his life. Caught between rebel muskets and the guns of the Main Guard, and finding precarious shelter between the bow windows of Dowsley's house, he tried to take advantage of 'a dreadful pause':

> I popt out my head and asked the rebels *if I might pass through them*? But an old, strong, well-made man, in a very wretched trim lift up his clumsy withered claw and shook it at me, exclaiming 'Fon! Fon! Fon' [Wait! Wait! Wait!] I took his advice and kept close.

Shortly after this, 'my friend Mr. "Fon, Fon!"' was one of those blown 'off their legs' by the cannon. Later, running to regain the safety of his own house, Alexander had a second encounter with a rebel:

> Passing by the barrack lane, a rebel came out and levelled an old musket at me, but presently crossed himself [thinking Alexander a priest] and took aim at a soldier, in doing which, he was himself shot, by a Dublin Militiaman. As he fell, his piece went off, and he exclaimed, "*Scolt en Deoul*", "The Devil split you!" – his last words.[85]

These reminders of the Gaelic dimension of rebel culture fit what we know of the slow and uneven pace of language change in the barony of Bantry.

The four verses of 'Bualadh Ros Mhic Thriúin' ('The Defeat of New Ross'), collected by Seán Ó Doinn, were almost certainly fragments of a larger composition and are not altogether clear in their meaning or sequence.[86] While the unknown poet seemed to welcome the victories of Napoleon, 'mar do chualas insa *news* dá léamh' (as I heard read in the newspaper), he did not describe the battle of New Ross in terms of contemporary European revolution, but rather in the language of seventeenth-century religious and colonial conflict, the enemy being 'Clann *Luther*' who were 'go tinn dubhach i dtúis an lae' (sick and sad in the beginning of the day). The poem's explanation of their ultimate victory was also in the seventeenth-century tradition of ascribing what Dáibhí Ó Bruadair called 'An Longbhriseadh' ('The Shipwreck') of the Gaelic world to the sins of the Irish themselves. 'Is gur treascradh na fearaibh groí le dúil sa mbraon.' (And the fine men were overthrown from fondness for the drop, i.e., of alcohol.) The third verse seems out of sequence, the fourth being on the battle:

> Is dá mbeadh long agam faoina hancaire ina luí chois trá
> Do thriallfadh ina ndiaidh suíd 'on bhFrainc nó 'on Spáinn
> Ag cur tuairisc na mbuachaillí ba airde cáil,
> 'Bhíodh go tréan ar Chnoc Fíodh na gCaor nó ar shliabh le cáil …
> (If I had a boat lying at anchor beside the strand, that would follow after them to France or Spain, asking after the boys of highest renown that used to be strong on Vinegar Hill or on a hill with renown …)

Ó Doinn commented, 'It may be inferred from the third verse, that, when the lamp of hope had gone out, and the bitter end had come, that members of the United Irishmen fled to France and to Spain.'[87] But the text speaks only of 'the boys', and it is anachronistic to think of defeated rebels fleeing to Spain, which is, instead, a traditional Jacobite reference point. The likelihood that these verses are only a fragment would explain the absence of clearer indications of standard Jacobite motifs, championing the Stuart cause, whose return to the throne of Great Britain would, according to Gaelic poets from the early seventeenth century onward, lead to the restoration of the old native nobility and the Catholic religion. The Stuart cause was by now purely symbolic, but the traditional expectations of the old Gaelic élites concerning the dismantling of the colonial land and religious settlements had been taken over by the rural poor and 'Bonny Prince Charlie' had become an unlikely symbol of popular aspirations concerning rents, tithes and basic justice.

In Appendix A, the contemporary Gaelic verse of United Irishman Micheál Óg Ó Longáin is examined, particularly for what it reveals of the impact of United Irish thinking on traditional Jacobitism. The evidence of the oral song tradition, usually called 'amhráin na ndaoine' (the songs of the people), and composed often by illiterate poets for their own communities may be more relevant to our purpose. Their survival as a vibrant part of popular culture over succeeding generations obviously owed something to the music to which they were sung, but also points to the likelihood that their sentiments and concerns continued to be those of ordinary people. Serious collection and transcription of these songs did not begin until the end of the nineteenth century, making it impossible to date them accurately, but relatively few of those that survived appear to be contemporary with or to relate directly to 1798.[88]

An exception may be the earliest *aisling* attributed to the West Cork poet Máire Bhuí Ní Laoghaire, called 'Ar Leacain na Gréine' ('At Daybreak') and inspired by the sighting of the French fleet at Bantry Bay in 1796. Instead of the usual expression of hope or prophecy, the 'spéirbhean' (vision woman) can report at last the arrival of the French, claiming 'go bhfeaca sa an fleet I bh-Faoide' (that I saw the fleet at Whiddy), although 'tháinig scaipeadh ortha ón ngaoth, faraoir' (they were scattered by the wind, sadly).

Her message was still one of hope, though cast entirely in traditional terms. The ships will return, bearing 'gearthocaigh ghroidhe an Laoiseach / san Spáinneach dá réir' (the brave warriors of King Louis, and the Spaniards also), and the result of their victory will be 'Beidh talamh gan chíos, gan íoch / Gan cáin is gan phléidhe / Beidh cruithneach is im is saill / Ar an gclár againn féin' (We will have land without rent, tax or litigation. We will have corn, butter and salt on our tables).

Her songs also exemplify the continued and often vehement use of the anti-colonist, anti-Protestant language of seventeenth-century poetry, notably that of Dáibhí Ó Bruadair, with the enemy being described as 'búir' (boors), 'póirc' (pigs), 'tál so Chailbhin choimhthigheach' (these foreign descendants of Calvin), and their strange names are mocked by her: 'Barnet agus Beecher / Hedges agus Faoitigh' (Barnet and Beecher, Hedges and White).[89] There were clear echoes of these sentiments at Scullabogue.

CHAPTER 13

The Killings at Scullabogue

I've discovered no contemporary Irish-language material about the this massacre at Scullabogue, although there may be an echo of it in the popular song 'Sliabh na mBan', first anthologized by Seán Ó Dálaigh in 1860 but probably composed shortly after the Rebellion.

The third verse begins,

> 's é Ros do bhreoigh 's do chloígh go deo sinn,
> Mar ar fágadh mórchuid dínn sínte lag,
> Leanaí óga ina smól ann dóite
> Is an méid d'fhan beo dhíobh cois claí nó scairt
> (It was Ross that sickened and defeated us forever, where many of us
> were left stretched and exhausted, and young children burnt to cinders
> there and those who still lived in ditches or thickets.)[1]

There is no reference in contemporary sources to the burning of children in the town, and these lines may be read as a coded reference to Scullabogue, ascribing its most notorious feature to the army. Thus it can be seen as an early example of transferral or deflection of responsibility, similar to Edward Hay's graphic account of the burnt-out cabins in the town, 'so thronged that the corpses of the suffocated within them could not fall to the ground'. Aware of how this mimicked eyewitness accounts in Musgrave of Scullabogue barn after the fire, he immediately denied any connection, while emphasizing that the army was equally capable of 'dreadful enormity'.[2] A verse of the popular local ballad 'The Ballyshannon Lane' likewise tells how 'when the barn was all in flames' (there is no reference to its occupants), 'My aunt Kate stood at the gate / Herself and child were slain'.[3] This pattern is also to be found in the family story of John Rice, with which this book began, and to which it will soon return.

The lane in question is close to the site of the massacre, and an earlier verse of the ballad celebrated it as the place 'where the Hessian brutes, they bit the dust / And Cromwell's crew were slain'. The Hessians were foreign mercenaries who loom large in folklore and ballads about 1798, though their actual role in suppressing the Rebellion was small and late.

Sean Cloney links their demonization to popular dislike of the Palatines, and certainly they came to symbolize the combination of cruelty and abrasive foreignness long associated with the Cromwellians.[4] The ballad's reference to 'Cromwell's crew' evokes the language of Gaelic poetry from the time of Ó Bruadair, and of contemporary 'amhráin na ndaoine'. The overwhelmingly anti-settler, anti-Protestant nature of that tradition, with its dehumanization of the enemy and its emphasis on revenge, offers an important avenue through which to approach the mentality of those who took and those who killed the Scullabogue prisoners.[5]

More conventional sources offer little evidence in this regard. In contrast to the trials of Joshua Colfer and others accused of taking the prisoners initially, the courts-martial of those accused of carrying out the killings made little attempt to establish motivation. The focus was on the identity and role of those who participated, while the courts had little interest in reflecting the culture or concerns of the accused or of various witnesses. Indeed, court records helped to make the still-vibrant Gaelic element of that culture invisible, as is exemplified in the infamous rigged state trial of John Devereux for an implausible range of rebel activity, including involvement in Scullabogue. It featured a defence witness, John Cody, who placed the prisoner far from the battle of Ross yet seemed to report him as encouraging others to join the rebels there. In the transcript Cody's evidence is recorded as if given in English, and we would not know that it was, in fact, given in Irish by a poor man with little English if the prisoner had not pointed this out in explaining the discrepancy.[6]

The Scullabogue trials record evidence of standard anti-Orange sentiment uttered by some of the accused. Thus John Turpin claimed that Thomas Parle, in killing John Moran, called 'to the people to look at the Orange ribbon at the Orange dog's breast'.[7] This seems credible in the light of the evidence for the heightened sectarian atmosphere of the preceding days and the pervasive fear of Orangeism. Some of James Alexander's informants justified 'the burning of Orangemen' (including 'the hell-fire set' killed at Scullabogue) by their burning of the homes of suspected rebels and the general threat they posed.[8] Several of the witnesses quoted by Father Shallow in his defence claimed that the rebels had threatened to kill him as 'worse than any Orange-man', while William Johnson, an old piper, was allegedly put in the barn for playing (presumably at the demand of the yeomanry) the new Orange tune, 'Croppies Lie Down'.[9]

It also seems fair to speculate that the traditional and lethal mixture of sectarian animosity and agrarian grievances against the Palatines and other recent Protestant settlers strongly marked the Rosegarland rebels under the command of John Murphy of Loughnageer, who had been left in charge of the prisoners. They seem an odd choice for that role, given that they were one of the very few local units with actual fighting experience. Was it their own decision, reflecting a particular interest in some of the prisoners? We cannot know, but many of them were likely to have had experience or knowledge of the abrasive sectarianism of the nearby Leigh estate and this may explain the opinion of the prosecution witness Richard Sylvester that this particular corps 'seemed very willing to do the duty ordered them'.[10] Among the dead were Leigh's Catholic steward, Thomas McDonnell, and Francis Mark and his son Edward, Protestants who may have been tenants or servants on the estate.

The possible importance of a background of agrarian grievances is also highlighted in George Hornick's account of how the killers of his brother Philip at Scullabogue 'asked him did he remember the Whiteboys in the year 1775', when the brothers had beaten off an attack on their house.[11] Likewise the raiding party that targeted local Quakers, the Goffs, threatened that their sons 'should soon be killed, and then the estate would be theirs'.[12] Many rebels were likely to have shared the hopes of the Irish song, 'Sliabh na mBan', that victory would mean 'Gaeil bhocht arís 'na gceart' (the poor Irish restored to their rights), 'cloí ar mhéirligh' (renegades defeated), and in more concrete terms, ''s ní dhíolfam feoirling leo cíos nó sraith' (and we will not pay them a farthing in rent or in kind).[13]

Gahan has identified 'the hard core of the killers', but while this is helpful the communal dimensions of what happened should not be lost sight of.[14] There is a sense of an audience in some of the trial material. Thomas Parle, in the evidence quoted above, for example, appealed to 'the people' in killing Moran as an 'Orange dog'.[15] Among the camp-followers at Scullabogue (possibly a large group) were some women. Long after the Rebellion one of them, now a domestic servant, surprised her Protestant mistress by blurting out, 'It was I went for the lighted turf which set fire to the barn at Scullabogue.'[16] Of course she may have been seeking to shock or to draw attention to herself for some reason, but this anecdote, in indicating a sense of long-suppressed guilt, highlights a human aspect of this tragedy not normally visible. But communal solidarity was also sufficiently powerful to ensure that Harvey and the other rebel leaders would fail 'to discover the perpetrators of the horrid deed', and Sean Cloney speculates that they simply went home, melted back into the landscape.[17]

The sense of community involved also crossed the religious divide in important ways. One Protestant memoir ascribed the rescue of young Benjamin Lett and his sister from Scullabogue to 'two faithful neighbors of the Letts – Romanists – Thomas Murphy of Park and Brien of Ballymorris'.[18] The sense of it being a shared tragedy comes across in the remarkable testimony of 'F.R.', in a letter headed 'Ross, July 20th '98'. Referring to the 170 Protestants that he believed to have been the victims at Scullabogue, he wrote: 'About 20 of these sufferers I was personally acquainted with, some of them were my intimate friends. I pass within two miles of the melancholy spot every month and often converse with those who knew every particular relative to it, both loyalists and rebels.'[19] A sense of this wider community is also suggested by the very limited nature of the evidence volunteered by many prosecution witnesses in the various trials.

According to Richard Grandy and Robert Mills, who were present, the massacre began 'about nine o'clock' in the morning, and the anxiety of various accused to produce alibis for that time would suggest that this was generally accepted.[20] Most accounts agree that it was precipitated by rebels fleeing prematurely from the battle eight miles away in Ross, where in fact the tide didn't turn decisively against them until after midday (and where the infamous burning of the four-storey house did not happen until after 10.30). They were probably from the main body of Harvey's 'army', massed outside and above the town and not involved in the fighting. If so they would have had a very confused sense of what was going on out of sight below them in the narrow smoke-filled streets, where many rebels already lay dead in their attempts to advance from the Three Bullet Gate into upper Mary Street.

The slow and costly pace of the rebel advance (in contrast to the experiences in Enniscorthy and Wexford) may have caused a sense of crisis, leading some to flee towards Wexford town, passing Carrigbyrne camp on the way. Hay actually blamed such 'cowardly ruffians' for the massacre,[21] but according to Cloney they merely 'excited and promoted it',[22] and the court-martial accounts make it clear that it was carried out in a highly disciplined way by the guard commanded by John Murphy of Loughnageer.

Richard Sylvester, one of the prisoners who survived, spoke in a number of trials of a series of 'expresses' arriving at the camp, all ordering Murphy 'to destroy the prisoners', which implied orders from above, presumably from Harvey, who had left Murphy in charge.[23] But there is no supporting evidence for this and the nature of Harvey's response to the massacre scene tells against it. Robert Mills, one of the killers and the main prosecution witness in the trials, likewise talked of 'orders to burn the barn' and claimed that these were resisted ''till three men arrived and said that a certain priest had given orders that the prisoners should be put to death'.[24] John Ryan, a rebel who claimed he left the scene before the massacre, said that 'two men came on horse-back and said Fr. Murphy ordered the prisoners to be put to death'.[25] This Father Murphy was a curate from Taghmon, another marginal figure, suspended several years before by the bishop. The dramatic and suspect deposition account by Michael Askin claims that he met Murphy 'riding very fast' from Ross, who 'cried out, we are defeated, Bagenal Harvey has ruined us; I will go to Scullabogue and destroy every soul in it'.[26] Yet no witness actually placed him at Scullabogue, and it seems odd that he sent others to speak for him. John Murphy showed some loyalty to Harvey, sparing the life of Richard Grandy, for example, because he carried a pass from the rebel Commander-in-Chief. But the killing of the prisoners was almost certainly on his own initiative. There is no evidence that John Murphy killed anyone himself, and the question never arose in court, because he had been executed summarily in Wexford town on the collapse of the Rebellion. Writing to Madden in 1843, Thomas Cloney claimed that Murphy 'contended at the immediate risk of his life for the protection of the unfortunate victims, until he was completely overpowered'.[27] There was no hint of this in any contemporary account, or in his own *Narrative* of a decade earlier. Instead the evidence is clear that Murphy not only gave the orders but supervised their execution closely and forcibly.

As Gahan points out, the killings were not a matter of mob-frenzy, as stereotypically portrayed in Cruikshank's well-known illustration, but a military-style operation carried out by a small number of men, perhaps as few as seventeen. These were watched, and in various ways assisted, by a much larger group, but there was no real suggestion in any of the trials of the initiative being taken by the crowd. There was no hint of recourse to any kind of trial or appeal to legal forms that marked similar rebel executions on Vinegar Hill. The military aspect was most evident in the systematic shooting of up to thirty-seven of the prisoners held in the house on the lawn outside, in groups of four, who were first made to kneel, and many of whom were finished off with pikes.[28] There was a sense of theatre about these killings, as in Thomas

Parle's appeal to the audience in killing John Moran. Sylvester's evidence that 'some of them pulled off their clothes with zeal to begin the bloody deed' also suggests rebel bravado,[29] while the detail added by survivor Richard Grandy has the same effect: 'that the spearmen used to take pleasure in piercing the victims through, and with exultation licking their bloody spears'.[30]

It appears that the nearby barn, crammed with exhausted and distressed prisoners, was set on fire only after these killings were finished. The scene for several days already of remarkable cruelty and suffering, the barn must have loomed large in the minds of all once the 'orders' came. A sense of foreboding for some, of excited anticipation by others, that those inside were already doomed is evident in the accounts of those days by Elizabeth Dobbyn, Father Shallow and others.[31] Why else were they being treated in that appalling way? Some of the evidence of the trials suggest that the burning was not as carefully premeditated as the earlier killings. One witness described 'some of the people … looking for a faggot to set fire to the barn', although in another trial he described a group of seven or eight men with pikes systematically setting the fire by igniting the thatched roof.[32] Even if the burning was initially unplanned by Murphy, it seems clear that he supervised the brutal prevention of any prisoner escaping. Robert Mills was 'ordered by Captain Murphy to go to the barn door, where there was a guard placed to prevent the loyalists from getting out whilst the barn was on fire'.[33] In another trial he testified that 'he saw the prisoner at the door of the barn amongst the rebels with a pike in his hand which he held (as a soldier does his arms with charged bayonet) pointed towards the door'.

At the trial of Matthew Furlong he gave a similar clinical account of his own role:

> The roof was on fire, and the loyalists were trying to force open the door to effect their escape, but were prevented by the rebels, of whom the prisoner was one, and he made several stabs of his pike at those who endeavoured to get out, particularly a woman, and on striking her he bent his pike.[34]

Testifying against Phelim Fardy, whom he had known for twelve years, Richard Sylvester offered the most sensational detail, which was seized on by Musgrave and dramatized further by Cruikshank. He claims he 'saw a child … force itself almost out of the barn, when a rebel on perceiving the child instantly darted his pike into it, when it gave a shriek and expired'.[35] Whatever the truth of this incident – and it is no more far-fetched than Mills' account of stabbing the woman – it reflected the consciousness that there were children among those burned and suffocated to death.

Much of the evidence at the trials focused on the forge, which was 'in the same yard as the barn', and where one witness placed 'Ellard the smith … mending the pikes of the rebels that had been bent or broke by stabbing the people at the barn door'.[36] Mills testified that he himself 'had straightened his pike there', and there are other accounts of the malfunctioning of these crude, handmade weapons.[37] Romanticized now – a symbol of 'Comóradh '98' and staple commodity of the heritage industry – the pike was a notoriously inefficient weapon at close quarters, and the killing of prisoners was often a gruesomely slow and painful business. At the trial of Michael Murphy, accused not only of 'raising the thatch … for the admission of fire' but also with Matthew Furlong of having 'speared a man who was endeavouring to make his escape', it was further alleged 'that he and Furlong went afterwards to the forge, which was near, to sharpen his pike, and on being asked whether they were all dead, the prisoner replied, "I'll engage they are all settled".'[38] This accords with other accounts of bravado among some of those most active in the killing, but other rebels present may have shared the horror expressed by Patrick Furlong, who claimed to have run away before the killing began, telling a neighbour that 'there was a dreadful story at Scullabogue and that he was running from it'. Prophetically he told another rebel deserter, John Ryan, that what had happened 'would kill us all'. Ryan claimed emphatically, 'I knew nothing at all about the barn,' although Sylvester, who had hidden with him, pointed out that the barn was only a hundred yards away and was set on fire within minutes of his escape. Others in the rebel camp were less squeamish, according to the same witness, who claimed that after being brought back from the barn to the front of the house he saw 'the rebel women and men … stripping and rifling the bodies of the dead'.[39]

Perhaps less than two hours after the massacre began 126 persons that we know of had been killed in cold blood. Their names were first listed by Musgrave and Taylor; the most authoritative modern list has been compiled by Gahan, and is the basis of the listing here.[40] On the evidence of the original lists I have revised Gahan's calculation of Catholics killed from fifteen to eleven; and, so far as we know, all of them were imprisoned and killed because of their connections with local Protestants. Like the Protestants killed, they were ordinary civilians, with the exception of Thomas McDonnell, the Rosegarland steward. Three Catholics were among the twelve women killed; the nine victims classified as 'children' (at least five were teenage boys) were all Protestant, as was Thomas Parslow, described as 'almost an idiot'. The men we know about were tenant farmers, servants, labourers and artisans.

George Cruikshank's notorious drawing of the Scullabogue massacre, from W.H. Maxwell's History of the Irish Rebellion in 1798 *(1844).*

Apart from Sarah and William Daly, wife and son of a yeoman, none had any known connection with the military; they were only 'loyalists' in the general sense that this was used as a synonym for 'Protestant'. Nearly half of those killed were related to another victim and most died mainly because they belonged to recently established and deeply resented local Protestant settlements.[41]

Many were probably known to their killers, as they had been to their captors. But while the list has to be analysed and argued about in this way, it should also be allowed to speak for itself.

[254]

NAME	RESIDENCE	SEX	OCCUPATION	RELIGION (P — PROTESTANT C — CATHOLIC)
Basset, Walter	Tintern	M	–	P
Bell, Thomas	Tintern	M	–	P
Besley, David	Tintern	M	–	P
Box, Joshua	Tintern	M	Weaver	P
Box, James	Tintern	M	Child (12) son of Joshua	P
Boyce, George	Tintern	M	Butcher	P
Boyce, Samuel	Tintern	M	Shoemaker	P
Brophy, John	Curraghmore	M	–	P
Byron, Edward	Horetown	M		P
Canney, George	Tintern	M	Weaver	P
Carlisle, James	Tintern	M	Labourer	P
Chamley, John	Horetown	M	–	P
Cook, Robert	–	M	Butler to Rev. Hawkshaw	P
Cook, Mrs	–	F	Wife of Robert	P
Cottom, John	Adamstown	M	Farmer	P
Cottom, Samuel	Adamstown	M	Farmer	P
Cruin, David	Tintern	M	–	P
Cruise, George	Tintern	M	–	P
Crumpton, Samuel	–	M	–	P
Dalton, John	–	M	–	P
Daly, James	Enniscorthy	M	Child (14) son of Sarah	P
Daly, Sarah	Enniscorthy	F	Wife of yeoman	P
Daly, William	Enniscorthy	M	Child (17) son of Sarah	P
Davis, Richard	St John's	M	–	P
Dobbyn, Elizabeth	Oldcourt	F	Widow of James	P
Dobbyn, Henry		M	–	P
Dobbyn, James	Oldcourt	M	–	P
Dobbyn, Patrick	Oldcourt	M	Farmer (father of Rd Saml & Wm)	P
Dobbyn, Patrick		M	–	P
Dobbyn, Patrick		M	–	P
Dobbyn, Richard	Oldcourt	M	Child	P
Dobbyn, Samuel	Oldcourt	M	Child	P
Dobbyn, William	Oldcourt	M	Child	P
Duffield, James	Tintern	M	–	P
Duffield, John	Tintern	M	–	P
Eakins, John	Foulksmills	M	–	P
Eakins, Thomas	Foulksmills	M	Son of John	P
Eakins, Thomas	Tintern	M	–	P
Eakins, William	Slevoy	M	–	P

Edwards, [Mr]	Kildavin	M	–	P
Ellison, Allan	Killanne	M	–	P
English, John	St John's	M	–	P
Esmond, Thomas	–	M	–	P
Esmond, William	–	M	–	P
Fanner, William	T'shannon	M	–	P
Field, Owen	St John's	M	Weaver	P
Finley, Holland	Kilcormack	M	–	P
Giffard, Milward	–	M	Surveyor of Excise	P
Gray, William	–	M	Weaver	P
Gray, Andrew	–	M	Child (17) son of William	P
Hannard, Joshua	–	M	–	P
Hannard, Mary	–	F	–	P
Hornick, Philip	Killanne	M	Farmer	P
Hurley, Edward	–	M	–	P
Johnson, William	–	M	Piper	C
Jones, John	Abbeybraney	M	(Quaker)	P
Jones, Samuel	Abbeybraney	M	(Quaker)	P
Jordan, William	Foulksmills	M	–	P
Jordan, William	Fethard	M	Servant to rector of Fethard	P
Kelly, Thomas	Tintern	M	–	P
Lindsay, John	Clongeen	M	(aged 21)	P
Lindsay, William	Clongeen	M	Child (19) brother of John	P
Lewis, Richard	Tintern	M	–	P
McDonnell, Thos	Rosegarland	M	Steward to Mr Leigh	C
Miller, Robert	Tintern	M	–	P
Monk, Edward	Rosegarland	M	–	P
Monk, Francis	Rosegarland	M	Father of Edward	P
Moran, John	Clongeen	M	(aged 20)	P
Neal, –	Ballybrennan	M		P
Neil, Daniel	Camolin	M	–	C
Neil, William	Camolin	M	Tailor (father of Daniel)	C
Parslow, John	Oldcourt	M	–	P
Parslow, Thomas	Oldcourt	M	(father of John)	P
Pierson, John	Tintern	M	Shoemaker	P
Plunket, Francis	–	M	Farmer	P
Plunket, Ms	–	F	Wife (or sister) of Francis	
Powel, Mr	–	M	–	P
Power, James	–	M	–	P
Power, John	Tintern	M	–	P
Power, Joseph	Horetown	M	–	P
Power, Oliver	–	M	–	P

Power, Patrick	Tintern	M	Mason	P
Power, Thomas	Tintern	M	-	P
Power, James	Tintern	M	Child (15) son of Thomas	P
Prendergast, Patrick	-	M	Servant	C
Presley, Ann	Tintern	F	-	P
Presley, David	Tintern	M	-	P
Presley, Jane	Tintern	F	Sister of Ann	P
Pyne, William	-	M	-	P
Reason, Henry	-	M	(Quaker)	P
Reel, William	Tintern	M	-	P
Restwicke, Edward	-	M	-	P
Rillagh, Edward	-	M	-	P
Rooke, Henry	-	M	-	P
Ryan, William	-	M	-	C
Ryan, Mary	-	F	Wife of William	C
Ryan, Eleanor	-	F	Daughter of William	C
Ryan, Elizabeth	-	F	Daughter of William	C
Shee, John	Ballybrazil	M	-	C
Shee, Thomas	-	M	Servant	C
Simmons, Samuel	-	M	-	P
Slator, Mr	Smithfield	M	-	P
Sleater, Thomas	Wales	M	Cattle Buyer	P
Slye, Edward	-	M	-	P
Smith, George	Tintern	M	Slater	P
Stannard, Joseph	St John's	M	-	P
Stannard, Mary	St John's	F	Wife of Joseph	P
Thomas, Anne	-	F	-	P
Thornton, Edward	-	M	-	P
Trimble, John	-	M	-	P
Trimbly, James	St. John's	M	-	P
Turner, Samuel	Taghmon	M	Schoolmaster	P
Tweedy, James	Fethard	M	-	P
Tweedy, John	Tintern	M	-	P
Vaughan, Miles	Tintern	M	-	P
Wade, James	Coolstuff	M	Mason	P
Wade, James	Killanne	M	-	P
White, Hyacinth	Mulrankin	M	-	P
Whitney, John	Adamstown	M	-	P
Whitney, Thomas	Oldcourt	M	-	P
Whitty, Thomas	Rathsillagh	M	-	P
Wilcock, John	-	M	-	P
Williams, Margaret	-	F	-	P
Younge, Elizabeth	-	F	-	P

We know as much as we do about the victims mainly because of affadavits later sworn by relatives, claiming compensation as 'suffering loyalists'.[42] It is paradoxical that we know far less about those tried for their deaths, the court-martial records not being concerned to establish age, occupation, religion (or even place of residence in some instances), except in the case of the two Protestants accused of the killings, John Ellard the blacksmith and John Turner, son of a Taghmon yeoman. Both claimed to have been forced to participate by John Murphy, and while this was a standard plea of rebels before the courts, in both these cases it seems justified.[43] Gahan believes that the main state witness over most of the trials, Robert Mills, was also a Protestant, and while this seems likely, we know virtually nothing about him.[44] There is no record that he was brought to trial for his admitted part in the killings, nor of any deal he may have made with the authorities. All we have are the transcripts of his testimony, and these throw up some interesting insights and questions. He knew the prisoners well, Quigley and Sullivan for more than ten years, Mahony and Keeffe for five. At the trial of Patrick Furlong (known to Mills 'a long time') the accused claimed to have left the camp before the killing and to have confessed all he knew when obtaining a 'protection' from the military after the Rebellion collapsed. Mills, however, was emphatic that he 'was at the barn when prisoners were trying to escape', and he added:

> The day the prisoner got his protection I heard him in the streets of Taghmon say to one of his comrades that he had finally blindfolded Colonel Furlong ... The prisoner's brother and sister offered me a bribe not to prosecute and he this day in the dock told me his life was in my hands.[45]

The sense of social familiarity across the bitter sectarian divide of that time and place may seem surprising, but a similar picture of Fethard emerged during the Colfer trial. It is even possible that Mills' carefully pitched and nuanced testimony over the various trials echoed some widely shared sense of communal justice. His clear endorsement of the guilt of Daniel Sullivan, for example, may be related to his uncharacteristic volunteering of an opinion about a prisoner's moral state in his case: 'he did not seem sorry for what had passed'.[46] Likewise, testifying that Thomas and John Mahony were 'prodding with their pikes at those that were forcing their way out [of the barn]', he denied that they were acting under duress, even adding (despite his claim in relation to himself), 'I am sure any man that was at the barn door was a willing person in the business.' This blunt assertion may be related to his further testimony that John Mahony was a rebel activist: 'The Sunday before the barn was burnt I saw him making pikes at Mrs. Goff's forge.'47 By contrast, while he placed Michael Quigley at the scene, Mills was clear that he never saw him 'commit any act of violence'. (Another witness, William Shaw, a prisoner at Scullabogue until taken 'to serve the cannon' at Ross, testified that he heard Quigley 'explain his dislike to the business'.)48 Mills gave similar testimony about sixteen-year-old John Tobin, agreeing this time with the defence of duress: 'I do not think he could have gone away without being in danger of his life.'49

Those executed for killing the prisoners at Scullabogue were brothers Nicholas and Thomas Parle, and John and Thomas Mahony, Redmond Mitchell (or Miscelly), Matthew Furlong, John Keeffe, James Leary and Michael Murphy. Also executed were Patrick Furlong and Patrick Sullivan, although the evidence established only that they were present and carrying pikes. Quigley and Tobin were transported instead, partly at least due to Mills' evidence. Ellard and Turner were acquitted, their claims of duress accepted by the courts. Gahan speculates that the acquittal of these Protestants, and indeed the fact that most of the Scullabogue trials took place only in 1799, represented a closing of Protestant ranks.50 But the Catholics Quigley and Tobin were also dealt with relatively leniently, and the records of these courts-martial suggest a real and even impressive attempt to establish the facts. The contrast between them and the clearly rigged trial of Walter Devereux, executed in Cork, also in part for involvement in the Scullabogue killings, is striking.51

The guilt of John Murphy also seems beyond doubt, although his motivation must remain mysterious. If he was bowing reluctantly to 'orders', or to some kind of peer or community pressure, why did he make certain that the firing of the barn would have the direst consequences? We can never know, but his role raises a major question mark over attempts to distance the United Irishmen from the massacre.

Indeed, more generally, we will never know properly what caused or motivated these appalling happenings. Panic at the apparent defeat at New Ross may make it a particular manifestation of the 'great fear' of sectarian massacre and reprisal that had gripped all communities even in the days before the Rebellion began, and which remained a constant feature throughout. The killings occurred in a highly charged sectarian atmosphere, which almost certainly included a strong element of conflict over land, as it had in this area for decades. From the beginning the massacre has been explained in terms of revenge, and this was certainly a factor. However, there is no evidence that it was in revenge for any *particular* atrocity; there were enough real examples of army terror-tactics, including against civilians, to ensure that the Rebellion would feature such counter-atrocities. Edward Hay was told that some of 'the sanguinary ruffians concerned' had narrowly escaped the 'persecutions and tortures of every kind – whippings, strangulations and hanging without trials', said to have been used by the army in Ross in the preceding days.[52] This may have been a factor in the systematic dehumanization of the prisoners over a lengthy period, which made their ultimate destruction easier. The shorthand of 'Orange dogs' or 'heretic' must also have been significant in this process, as was the invisibility of the victims as individuals in the dark crowded barn. More tenuous, but perhaps decisive, may have been the group dynamic, better documented in many such atrocities in more modern times, which leads to the killing of helpless victims simply because such absolute power over others can generate an explosive and lethal combination of bloodlust and panic.

All contemporary accounts agree about Bagenal Harvey's 'horror' and 'anguish of mind' when he discovered the massacre on his return, dejected from the defeat at Ross. As Taylor described it:

> The murdered Protestants were to be seen in every attitude; they were so close that several were standing up against the walls, and many lying in heaps in each other arms, among the ashes of the timber of the house; while their bodies looked frightful, being burned to a cinder. He turned from the scene in horror, wrung his hands, and told those around him that 'as innocent people were burned there as ever were born, and that their conquests for liberty were at an end'. He then said privately to a friend, 'I see now my folly in embarking in this cause with these people; if they succeed, I shall be murdered by them – if they are defeated, I shall be hanged'.[53]

While this report was grist to Taylor's political mill, it was echoed in a letter which Harvey wrote three days later to his friend Francis Glascott, who had asked for his protection. Harvey was in despair, and could 'scarce protect myself'. He had got involved 'in the hopes of doing some good and preventing mischief'; but the shooting of Matthew Furlong before the battle 'has set the people mad with rage, and there is no restraining them ... God knows where this business will end; but end how it will, the good men of both parties will be inevitably ruined.'[54]

Musgrave, while also expressing some sympathy with the rebel leader as 'a man of honour and humanity', claimed that Harvey was 'filled with horror and shame at the massacre, having set it on foot'.[55] While not even Musgrave suggested that he actually ordered the killing, questions remain, as noted earlier, about his knowledge of the condition of the prisoners in the preceding days; his stress on their 'innocence' in Taylor's account underlines this aspect of his role.[56] His relationship with John Murphy is also a factor, not least in his decision to leave the Rosegarland Corps in charge. Cloney's claim that 'Mr. Harvey and every one of the leaders, and all persons who had influence, used every possible exertion to discover the perpetrators of the horrid deed … but in vain', lacks credibility.[57] Harvey did issue a proclamation, threatening all who failed to respect life and property with court-martial and death. It stressed several times the power of the 'commander-in-chief', but like all such proclamations it was evidence instead of helplessness, if not of hand-washing, and it was his last act in a role he had never filled with any conviction. He was replaced by Father Philip Roche, Harvey lamenting, according to an informant of Musgrave's, 'that the war unexpectedly turned out to be purely religious: that the priests had got absolute sway'.[58] According to the Taghmon yeoman William Fleming, a prisoner of the rebels, Roche then preached a sermon stating 'that they were fighting for their religion, their liberty and the rights of their ancestors, and that they must persevere', and 'extirpate' any Orangemen in their ranks.[59]

While this may be discounted as too neat a summary of the kind of 'evidence' sought by ultra-loyalist magistrates about rebel motivation, it is hardly out of character with what we know either of Roche, or of the feelings of the rebels in and about Scullabogue. It seems likely that many of them would have agreed with 'the strange looking old man' who told Elizabeth Richards on 17 June that the defeat at Ross was due to 'their being commanded by B.B. Harvey (a Protestant gentleman of good fortune), but now he said, "They have got one of the right sort at their head (Priest Roche), they'll take it with all pleasure."' He also claimed that the Rebellion had been prophesied twenty-five years earlier 'by a stranger who came to his father's house', and said 'that the Roman Catholic cause would be victorious'.[60]

Not alone did the rebel leaders fail to punish those responsible, but they were also very slow to remove the bodies of the victims. When William Fleming returned to Scullabogue on 7 June to look for the body of his friend Robert Cook, who had been burned in the barn with his wife, he reported:

> [I] could not distinguish one body from another, from the injuries the said bodies sustained from the fire. That some of said bodies were entirely consumed, that the heads and limbs of others were also consumed, but the bodies remained entire and very much discoloured. That the features of such persons as were not consumed were so black and so discoloured, that he could not distinguish one from the other. That the bowels of some of the said bodies lay exposed on the floor. That some of the said bodies lay

against the wall, as if in the act of praying. That a heap of the said bodies lay near the door of the said barn, to which they flocked, as informant verily believes, for the sake of fresh air, to prevent suffocation.

The flat, emotionless language and legal phraseology serve to heighten the horror of the scene. And while Fleming met a rebel who could make a joke, and express 'much seeming satisfaction', the trauma involved for the relatives and friends of the victims must have been mirrored on the rebel side.[61]

For whatever reason, the bodies were still undisturbed two days later when Elizabeth Dobbyn entered:

> [I] found the barn burnt and full of dead bodies, all in a standing posture, some with their limbs burnt off, and others with the bowels hanging out, and others with their faces and features disfigured with the fire. The deponent could not distinguish the body of her husband and sons from the dead.

According to her testimony, her sufferings did not end there. A few nights later her house at Oldcourt 'was entered by a great number of men armed with pikes, who said they came to search for Orangemen, having heard that deponent harboured them'. In mid-September another raiding party killed her neighbour Shepherd Parslow, who was staying at her home, presumably because his own had been burned; he had left the safety of New Ross to save his harvest. Herself and her mother were injured during the attack, and when Elizabeth asked 'if it was not a sin to use a poor Christian so cruelly? they replied she was no Christian'.[62]

Such depositions certainly suited the purposes of local ultra-loyalists, and the more complex agenda of Richard Musgrave, but the evidence also supports Elizabeth Dobbyn's testimony to a powerful sectarian dimension in the Scullabogue killings. This inevitably made the massacre the centrepiece of Musgrave's attempt to describe the Rebellion in terms of the powerful Protestant tradition about 1641, with its core image of a savage, un-trustworthy Catholic population, bent on their extermination. Not surprisingly he repeated the most sensational Scullabogue stories, and it has been claimed that he did so in ways that evoke Temple and Foxe's *Book of Martyrs*.[63] Yet even in detailing these stories his tone is remarkably restrained. For example, his account of the killing of the Quakers, John and Samuel Jones, has fewer of the standard images of Protestant 'martyrdom' than Dinah Goff's later account, which features torture and their heroic refusal to change their religion to save their lives.[64] Musgrave is content, for the most part, to summarize or quote the evidence of the depositions and the courts-martial, using their prosaic style in his own narrative and printing many of the key documents in his large appendices.

While Musgrave's own prejudices were and are easy to discount, it was this formidable array of evidence that made it both important – and difficult – to refute his account. Edward Hay's *History of the insurrection of 1798, giving an authentic account of the various battles fought between the insurgents and the King's army* – first published two years later in 1803 and the basic Catholic account – illustrates the problem. Crucially, Hay did not attempt to match Musgrave's documentary approach, though the evidence was open to a more critical and complex reading, but instead used a standard series of narrative devices, designed to deflect blame or palliate or reduce the horror.

Hay's treatment of Scullabogue was also shaped by his overall argument that the Rebellion was the product of a sectarian state and its collusion with Orange atrocities against Catholics, which led to a spontaneous popular uprising against intolerable oppression. And so, Scullabogue was a retaliation by 'the sanguinary ruffians involved ... for like deeds of desperate cruelty practised against themselves', and was precipitated by 'an infuriated multitude of men and women', seeking revenge for the cruelty of the army at New Ross. His only comment on the evidence of the trials was that it proved 'that the unbridled multitude are as precipitate as [they are] indiscriminate in their deeds of outrage'. While nothing 'can palliate, much less excuse such unnatural and detestable atrocity,' he felt 'it is but justice, however, to observe, that in this horrid transaction, no person of superior condition – none above the mere *canaille*, or lowest description of men – was at all concerned'. Another tactic of Hay's was to reduce the number burned from the 184 claimed by Musgrave to eighty. This was purely his own deduction from the size of the barn, but he felt 'surely it must prove grateful to every mind to be so agreeably undeceived respecting the fewer numbers of victims'. Finally, 'to counteract the reports of religious intolerance, it must be stated that fifteen or sixteen Catholics shared in the sorrowful catastrophe'. In sum, it had nothing to do with the 'brave men' of the rebel army, even less to do with their leaders and in any case the scale and sectarian nature of the atrocity had been much exaggerated.[65] This remains the standard nationalist response to Scullabogue.

Local folklore reflected a similar anxiety to transfer or deflect the blame. There are hundreds of stories about the Rebellion in the vast Irish Manuscripts Commission collection made in the 1930s, but only one that I can trace about Scullabogue. It was told by a local man, James Doyle of Carrigbyrne, then eighty-seven years old:

Me Aunt Nelly often told me all about the burnen of Scullabogue barn. She said they could hear the roars of the poor people in the barn and that they were so frightened they ran away to the moors. She said the people weren't burned it was smothered they were. The roof on the barn was set fire to and the poor people all fell on top a' wan another with fright as they were smothered – about ninety or so – 'twas no one from his place that put 'em into the barn – it was thought it was from Clongeen parish they were an' 'twas a fella named Jim Sinnott who gathered them up. Me Aunt Nelly said that the way they tested them to see if they were Protestants was if they couldn't say a Hail Mary. Then they were said to be Protestants. Many of them asked to be hanged – you know they were brought out an' shot any of them that were alive – and the tree that was to serve as the gallows was there till very lately.[66]

This story has a number of remarkable features, not least its echoing of the stories of sectarian intent and forced conversions in loyalist depositions. Its main function, however, is to insist ''twas no one from this place put 'em in the barn'. Another local version of this, articulated by my late uncle Michael Galway of nearby Misterin, had it 'that there was a barn there where Cromwell burned the Catholics'. This was said sincerely, as a well-known fact.[67]

CHAPTER 14

New Ross: The Aftermath of the Battle

My family's story about the death of John Rice can read as a counter-narrative to the Scullabogue atrocity. Here is a Catholic attempting to save women and children, who are killed by soldiers and not by rebels. But before reconsidering that story it is necessary to return to the town and to attempt to describe the aftermath of the battle. John Rice's death was only one of many as the military went on the rampage after the rebels finally abandoned New Ross. As Major Vesey of the Dublin Militia wrote to General Lake, 'the carnage was shocking, as no quarter was given, the soldiers were much too exasperated and could not be stopped'.[1] Colonel Crawford saw the militia as the main culprits, describing them as 'quite un-governable'.[2] Contemporary accounts generally echo the judgment of moderate loyalist James Gordon, writing of the Wexford Rebellion in general:

> I have reason to think more men than fell in battle were slain in cold blood. No quarter was given to persons taken prisoner as rebels with or without arms ... How many people fell in this manner, or were put to death unresisting in houses, fields and elsewhere, would be as difficult to state with accuracy as the number slain in battle.[3]

Two survivors told Madden years later 'that after the battle was entirely over as many were shot and suffocated in the burned cabins from four o'clock in the afternoon till night and were hanged the next day as were killed in the fight'.[4] Donovan cites 'a well-founded and general tradition' of systematic bayoneting of prisoners in Windmill Lane, remembered for many years afterwards by the townspeople, with 'the men raising their hats and the women crossing themselves as they passed by' the site.[5]

James Alexander, chosen by the commander of the garrison to organize the clean-up of the town and the disposal of the bodies, gave a characteristically ambivalent account. He praised Johnson for ordering the discharge of all weapons and an end to shooting, and for his crackdown on looting by 'some of the King's troops'. Admitting that some soldiers continued firing against orders, he went on, 'Whether any of the inhabitants were now shot, I believe none but soldiers can tell, for I could not perceive a single man in coloured clothes [i.e. not in uniform] but myself.' However, he in fact witnessed a number of shootings, and continued to fear for his own life, admitting that the soldiers 'thought no more of shooting any man in coloured clothes that day than of shooting a dog'.

He also made the point that many of the out-of-control militia were Catholics, like the two Dublin Militia, 'whom I actually brought to the Augustinian convent and introduced to the clergymen there'.[6] Doubtless it was also a Catholic militia man who warned Mary Whelan of Mountgarrett Lane to stay indoors as 'the soldiers were shooting all that were in coloured clothes'.[7] Alexander gave instances of other soldiers being targeted, as they had been during the battle, and doubtless some loyalists were among the victims as they were weeks later after the recapture of Enniscorthy. Barbara Newton Lett gave examples of this, and of an officer who 'could not be persuaded that a loyal man had escaped the fury of the enemy'.[8] Indeed Alexander's appointment, as he styled it mock-heroically, 'temporary Major of the Ross unarmed loyalists', was in part because Johnson was 'apprehensive lest any of the loyal or peaceably disposed inhabitants of the poorer sort should starve for want of provisions, or suffer death as rebels from the fury of the soldiery'.[9]

Alexander's most pressing task was to dispose of the hundreds of corpses that filled the streets downtown where 'the greatest slaughter' had occurred, and in the lanes and burnt-out thatched houses of the upper town. He had 700 men at his disposal, but 'the freemen', especially 'the more respectable', were not asked to do the work, and the remainder were divided into two 'garrison' (or working) parties, one to ensure a supply of food, the other, 'by much the greatest in number', to dispose of the dead. They included the much derided 'Glory-men', mainly Old Ross Palatines, who may have taken some grim satisfaction in their task. It took several days at least, while the surviving townspeople ventured out into the streets in search of food and drink as the heat wave continued, so that 'the stench was intolerable'.[10]

Fifteen years on the Reverend James Hall was told how, 'as hundreds of men lay dead in the streets of New Ross nearly two nights and days ... the women began to lay aside fear to walk among them undismayed'.[11] Alexander in his *Account* seems reluctant to describe how the bodies were disposed of, writing instead about his problems in organizing basic provisions (even for his own men), the comic efforts made by some of his 'officers' to write out passes, his continuing problems with the local yeomanry, and his conversations with rebels coming back into the town to seek amnesty. Only at the end of a 'supplementary postscript' does he tell us:

> A considerable number of dead carcasses, both of rebels and beasts, were thrown into the river, but the far greater part of them were buried at the town wall, and though several cart-loads of roach lime were thrown in upon them, such a noisome stench began to exhale from them in a few days, that we were apprehensive lest a plague should prove the consequence.[12]

Decades later, Madden was shown the site of the mass burial by 'two of the surviving witnesses of the Battle of Ross':

> ... their bodies were thrown into a hole on the side of a hill facing the town, immediately below the Carmelite Convent; the total number of the dead bodies of the rebels killed fighting, and of the people killed in cold blood by the troops after the fighting was over, which were thrown into the pit was 'six hundred odd'. I was informed by one of the persons who saw the bodies thrown in and had to draw one of the cars employed in carrying them to this place.[13]

This undignified anonymous mass burial, including so many countrymen from the surrounding area, 'hitherto a harmless, peaceable people', led one onlooker to hope that it might at least prevent others like them 'from being duped and prevailed upon to desert their families and cornfields, to be shot by disciplined men, against whom it was utterly impossible they could prevail'.[14]

Clearly more complex forces in their communal and personal experiences brought the rebels to their violent, tragic deaths, which were often heroic as well as pointless and predictable. It is impossible to calculate precisely the scale of the tragedy for their communities in terms of the numbers killed, but it is important to understand what is suggested by the evidence. Louis Cullen's radical reassessment of 'rebellion mortality' in Wexford in 1798 extrapolates backwards from the 1821 census, and especially marriage and birth rates, to reach the 'very tentative conclusion' that the figure overall should be about 5600, rather than the 20,000 still quoted by historians. As he points out, this much reduced figure is actually 'more disturbing' than the traditional 'mind-numbing and meaningless' one, amounting as it does to one in six males aged sixteen to sixty.[15]

He is dubious about Alexander's 'conjectured' figure for New Ross, of 2600–3000, but Alexander's more exact statement that 'of those 1010 were counted in the streets of Ross only' is likely to be a body count arrived at by his men.[16] (The figure of 3000 quickly became established in the town, quoted not only by military observers like Captain Bloomfield and Surgeon Roche, but also recorded in a note in Latin in the Mass-book at the Augustinian convent, translated as, 'today the rebel enemy was driven from the assault on the town with great slaughter estimated at 3000'.)[17] We also have accounts of the rebels removing some of their dead ('a very moderate number', according to Alexander's rebel informants, although Sir Edward Cooke was told, 'They had numerous wagons to carry off their wounded'), and we can assume that many, perhaps most, of the townspeople killed both during and after the battle were removed and buried by relatives (as John Rice was). In addition corpses were still being found in the fields around the town for weeks afterwards. Finally Alexander detailed the dead and missing among the garrison as 172.[18] The total death toll, therefore, is likely to have been as high as 1500, or over 1600 if the dead at Scullabogue are included. Donovan claimed that 'no such slaughter has occurred in Ireland since the battle of Aughrim'[19] (where over 7000 died), but compared to a traditional battle between trained armies on open ground, that of 5 June 1798, with its mass killing of poorly armed insurgents and defenceless locals in a half-dozen narrow streets, may appear far more shocking, almost impossible for us to comprehend.

Most of the dead of 5 June 1798 remain as anonymous as in their mass burial. Army dispatches named some officers killed, and others are mentioned by Alexander. Cloney named some neighbours but most rebel deaths were remembered only in family or neighbourhood stories. A few, relating to the north of the county, were collected by Luke Cullen in the half century after the Rebellion, but there was no systematic attempt to collect folklore around New Ross until the great schools project of the Irish Manuscripts Commission in the 1930s when only a handful of them survived. One, told by Martin Walsh of Dunmain, is remarkable as a seemingly straightforward historical narrative:

> When the Wexford insurgents were camped on Corbert [sic] hill on the 4th June, in the ranks of the Wexford men were two brothers Lacey's [of] Cushinstown Co. Wexford. They left their home to the youngest brother Jimmy, they gave instructions to him to look after the farm until their return. At 11 o'clock that night Jimmy informed his mother he could see the camp fires on Corbert [sic] hill. He told her he would like to go. His mother told him if he wished to go, to bring in the cows and leave them

in the house for the morning, and if he would see his eldest brother Tom to send him home to her. But when the battle took place in the morning at three o'clock the three brothers Lacey's took part in the battle. Tom Lacey and his brother Willy were killed at the Three Bullet Gate. Young Jimmy was killed in Wexford Street. The mother went next day with her pony and cart, taking a pattern of the clothes which they wore. So that she would know them, because the British soldiers had a habit of hacking the faces of the dead rebels. She found her three sons and brought them home to Carnagh graveyard and with the help of some friends and neighbours they were buried there. No stone or slab mark their graves and more is the pity.[20]

Why did these local farmers join the 'insurgents'? The only clue offered by this story is the impatience of the youngest at being left behind, and wanting to join his brothers in their big adventure. Many of the details give the story authenticity, as they fit what we know from contemporary sources. Thus the battle begins early in the morning; the deaths occur at places where we know the rebels suffered serious losses; the story of the mutilation of the faces of the rebel dead finds an echo in Alexander's account of the killing of a wounded rebel by the local yeoman Christopher Jefford.[21] The sense of the burials being both communal and clandestine is reinforced by the enduring sorrow at the lack of anything to 'mark their graves'.

In his analysis of 2500 graveyard inscriptions in the county, Brian Cantwell records 'very few' references to the Rebellion.[22] His speculation that this was due to political expediency seems borne out by the fact that of the two relating to 5 June 1798 found in New Ross, only that to the yeoman Francis Robinson actually mentions the battle, which local loyalists continued to commemorate on the anniversary for years afterwards. The other, to John Rice, simply records the date,[23] but that also resonated with significance, a private equivalent of the loyalist commemoration, and its meaning was preserved in a family story about his death. This was not collected until 1949, when Brother W.B. Cullen (later my novice master) interviewed my aunt Margaret (Maggie) Roe (née Rice) as part of his research on the family of Edmund Ignatius Rice.[24] Maggie's daughter, Bride Roe, gave this version of the story in a marginal note to her excellent Rice family tree, in 1984:

> He was executed by a group of English soldiers because he had sheltered some women and children in a loft behind his home during the battle of Ross. The hiding place was discovered and all were killed. Finally John Rice was dragged outside his front door and a Hessian officer drew a sword to cut off his head. However, John Rice caught the sword in his

teeth and would not let go. Then he was dragged down the street, and shot at the cross at the Irishtown.

There are some interesting differences in a letter by Jack Rice (Bride's uncle and mine) published by the *New Ross Standard* on 23 January 1976:

Being a lame man, but very strong, he was guarding a few hundred women and children who were hidden in a loft. The entrance from the street was through a high arched doorway up a long narrow paved yard (still to be seen). John Rice was challenged by one of the enemy who were 'mopping up' after the third retreat across the river Barrow. His only weapon, a stout cudgel, was knocked from his hand, the enemy swung at his head with his sword, but Rice clamped his teeth on the naked blade, and grasped the enemy around the throat, holding his grip until the man died. Rice was then killed.[25]

It is understandable that the oral transmission of family stories would involve variations. These may reflect the historical experiences of succeeding generations for example or, as here, the politics, personalities or gender of particular narrators. Thus the difference between 'executed by a group of English soldiers' and 'killed' by 'the enemy' may be explained by my Aunt Maggie's fervent nationalism (shared by her husband Eddie, a republican internee in the Curragh in the 1930s) and Uncle Jack's more amused view of politics. Likewise his exciting image of his namesake, with a sword clamped in his teeth while he had his enemy by the throat, may owe something to his fondness for stories of mobsters from his time in Chicago. The fact that each version has details lacking in the other probably reflects their common origin in a more elaborate account, elements of which got lost over time, but some of these particular details also connect the stories to the wider tradition about the battle. Thus, Bride's account of the Hessian echoes one of the most common motifs in the local folklore, while Jack's reference to repeated retreating by the garrison across the river is similar to the account given by Donovan.[26] Both also give present-day contexts for John Rice's death, Jack by pointing out that the house was unchanged, and Bride by locating it at the old market cross in the Irishtown. Of greater significance than such differences, however, are the core elements common to both versions: that John Rice, while a non-combatant, was remarkably brave and strong; that he was killed in attempting to protect women and children; that he was executed summarily by the military. The version that Maggie Roe gave to Brother Cullen supports Jack's account of Rice being shot after killing his assailant.[27] Two main questions need to be addressed. How do the various elements of the family stories relate to con-

temporary sources? And what can the story of John Rice add to our understanding of 5 June 1798?

The evidence for Rice being a non-combatant is indirect and circum-
stantial, much of it coming from the connection said to exist between his business and that of his cousin, Edmund, in Waterford. This business was well-
established and successful, based partly on the Catholic-dominated Newfoundland trade, partly on the more competitive provisioning of the British
navy. Having supported the 1792 declaration of the Catholic Committee,
Edmund's name was missing from the more radical (but still loyalist) Addresses
of 1793 and 1795. According to his later confidant Austin Dunphy, he was 'one
of the very few persons who, during the rebellion of 1798 was allowed to pass
unchallenged at all the military posts in Carrick-on-Suir, Waterford, Clonmel,
Tipperary and Limerick'.[28] There is a romantic family tradition that he helped
a connection by marriage, John Rice of Newlands, near Callan, to escape to
Newfoundland in 1798 after he fell foul of the authorities for some unknown
reason. But everything we know of him suggests that by then Edmund,
increasingly devout and close to the new Bishop of Waterford, Thomas
Hussey, would have supported the Hierarchy's condemnation of the
Rebellion. John Rice of New Ross had the added incentive to display at least
outward conformity in being not only a Catholic trader trying to build up a
business in a town dominated by an ultra-Protestant Corporation, but also the
tenant of its Sovereign, Charles Tottenham. It seems that his death did not
result in his family losing trading privileges or the occupancy of their house,
suggesting that, whatever view the authorities had of his death (assuming they
knew anything about it), it was not seen as that of a rebel.

It is somewhat surprising that Rice did not leave the town for the comparative safety of Waterford, as many of the better-off inhabitants did in the
days before the battle.[29] Did he stay to protect his property? Or did he feel
that a prominent Catholic was in little danger from the rebels? His house and
business in the Irishtown were in the prosperous part, farthest from the town
walls and past the key intersection with the road leading from the rebel camp
at Corbet Hill. Called by locals 'Boreen-a-slána' (probably 'Bóithrín na nEas-
lán', the road of the sick, from the nearby Maudlin Hospital), this had been a
vital approach route in Harvey's original plan of attack, in anticipation of
which the Clare Militia under Major Vandelour were stationed where it
entered the Irishtown. They had to deal with only one rebel assault, a brief
abortive affair according to Cloney, but a heroic defence against overwhelming odds according to one of Alexander's military informants.[30] In any case the

John Rice's house, Irishtown, still occupied by the family.

Clare Militia held this strategic position throughout the day. One result of this was that while many of the thatched cabins lower down were set on fire, the more substantial houses in the upper Irishtown were protected. Thus it is very likely that women and children from the lower part crowded there for safety and that Rice's substantial premises, set back from the street, would have attracted many of them.

But even here, residents and refugees alike must have had the same experience as Mary Whelan of nearby Mountgarrett Lane, who told a court-martial, 'I was also very much frightened when I was in my own home during the battle.'[31] In Donovan's account of events in the Irishtown, based heavily on what he knew of local tradition, women and children also feature:

> All day the soldiers were sniped at from a distance. To counter this they rounded up such women and children as they could find and locked them in a mud-built shed to be used as hostages, but in coming to shoot the first hostage they found that a hole had been bored through the back wall and that the hostages had vanished. The Clares found the Irishtown folk subtle antagonists in other ways.[32]

While in this story women and children are under threat of death by the military but have the initiative to escape, in Bride Roe's version of John Rice's death they are 'all killed'. There is no contemporary or folklore evidence for such an atrocity, just as there is none for the burning to death of children in the town as described in 'Sliabh na mBan'. This element of the story may be seen instead as a response, doubtless unconscious, to the atrocity at Scullabogue. In the tradition of denial or displacement discussed above, it features a Catholic heroically defending, rather than killing women and children, who are the victims instead of the army.

The possibility that John Rice was killed by a Hessian is more easily discounted. These German mercenaries, 'General Hompesch's Dragoon Riflemen, improperly called Hessians' as ex-soldier James Alexander described them, did not arrive in the town until the 19th.[33] But their fearsome reputation for cruelty and ruthlessness loomed so large in folklore about the Rebellion that they were retrospectively placed at virtually every major episode of the Rebellion in ballads and stories.[34] A story collected in many parts of the county featured a lone woman killing a Hessian with a mallet as he bent to light his pipe at her fire. In one version from Ballycullane, near New Ross, a widow whose son had died at the Three Bullet Gate exulted, 'I killed a Hessian for myself.'[35] One function of this semi-comic revenge story may have been to empower those who had been in reality defenceless victims of the violence of the time, just as John Rice's death was given meaning by his attempt to protect the helpless. Likewise the claim that he killed one of his assailants before being shot may be on a par with the stories about killing a Hessian. In this case the victim figure is not simply resourceful and powerful, but also a romantic hero with supernatural strength. This is suggested by the wonderful image that so captured my imagination as a child, of his grasping the sword with his teeth.

An intriguing and more prosaic alternative – put by me to my disbelieving mother many years ago – might be that he was killed by or at the behest of a business rival in the New Ross yeomanry corps. We know from Alexander that some of them were prominent in such killings.[36] Charges were later made, especially against Standish Lowcay, Tottenham's main ally and Alexander's enemy, who was said to have exploited the aftermath of the Rebellion to protect his own economic interests.[37] But it seems very unlikely that Rice could have been targeted in that way in the chaos and heat of the moment, and this is confirmed by the fact that his family were allowed to thrive in business subsequently. In fact we do not need to resort to such fanciful speculation. The likelihood is that he was killed by one or more of the Clare Militia, who had particular reasons for becoming (as Lieutenant Colonel Crawford described the militias generally) 'quite ungovernable'.[38] They had had a frustrating day, removed from the main action and the target of taunts (and even fire) by some of the yeomanry as well as the rebels. The fact that most of them were Catholics and countrymen like the rebels, and that some indeed were covert United Irishmen, may have made their conduct all the more extreme. But the killing of John Rice was not remarkable; it called for no special circumstances. The routine summary killing of any man found 'in coloured clothes', whether or not he offered resistance or was trying to protect others, is so well attested that we need seek no further explanation. The other details of the family story may reflect some degree of fact or simply an understandable desire to give meaning to what was otherwise a random, meaningless death, one of many such, as this bloody day drew to its anarchic close.

Like Scullabogue, it highlights a feature of the Rebellion which was overwhelming for contemporaries but has always been downplayed by histories or commemorations concerned mainly to celebrate it (as the family story does) in terms of heroism or idealism. John Rice was a classic victim of war, the innocent bystander in the wrong place at the wrong time, paying the ultimate price for the ideologies that led men into insurgency or counter-insurgency, whether the crude sectarianism of the time, old dreams of lost lands or the unthinking idealism of bourgeois revolutionaries. His name and his story are among the very few to survive the indiscriminate slaughter of that day because his son, also John, then eight years old and said to have been a witness, erected that significant gravestone in St Stephen's, and because he lived on until 1866 when his grandson (and my grandfather) was thirteen. He in his turn lived until 1945, when I was three. Those two unusually long lives, and my mother's, between them cover virtually the whole of the 200 years since John Rice was killed. Little wonder that his memory has stayed so fresh and that the shadows cast by 1798 have seemed so dark.

ENVOI

It now seems remarkable to me that the version of John Rice's story that I heard was not more overtly nationalistic, especially given the strong convictions of my mother and most of her generation, and that Aunt Maggie gave her version to Brother Cullen in the heightened atmosphere of 1949 just after the 150th anniversary of the Rebellion. My mother would have been as delighted as I was angered by John Rice's name being included in 'a record of the United Irish in Co. Wexford in 1798', published by the Wexford Branch of the National Graves Association.[1] As she said in response to my provocative undergraduate musings all those years ago, 'I know he died for Ireland.' My dislike of this kind of interpretation probably owes something to the normal reaction of each generation to the pieties of its parents', as well as to the training I was then undergoing in the hotbed of 'revisionism' at UCD. I may even, in another common pattern, be favouring my father's approach over my mother's, given his clear dislike of the intense nationalism of his own father, Thomas Dunne of Courtnacuddy, whose ballads about 1798, written in the 1870s, are so full of the patriotic fervour largely absent from the story of John Rice. And perhaps Thomas Dunne in turn was reacting against the support his family had traditionally given to their landlords, the Carews of Castleboro. According to my grandfather's manuscript history of the family, Arthur Dunne of Toumallogue got little thanks for his work on behalf of a Robert Carew in an election campaign in 1818. This account deals with 'the troubled time of ninety-eight' only in terms of its impact on relations with a distant branch of the family.[2]

A beguiling fantasy, bringing the history of the Dunnes and Rices together in the cauldron of Rebellion (rather than on a Fair Day in the Irishtown in the 1930s), would have John Rice actually killed for harbouring *rebels* (women and children being substituted to help the family survive the aftermath), among them the same Arthur Dunne of Toumallogue who escaped during the excitement surrounding the killing of Rice! While I offer this as a possible storyline for the film of this book, I'm afraid that it lacks historical credibility. True, just as John Rice has been recruited posthumously as a United Irishman, Arthur Dunne has been enlisted among the Bantry rebels at Ross in that excellent booklet, *Davidstown-Courtnacuddy Remembers 1798*, but as indicated earlier the evidence makes it extremely unlikely that Arthur Dunne joined his neighbour Thomas Cloney.[3] The absence of any hint of a family tradition that he did is also telling, especially given Thomas Dunne's fascination with both family history and the Rebellion, of which he approved wholeheartedly.

Is this silence perhaps an example of what Kevin Whelan has castigated as the repression of folk memory by 'clerical sanitising'?[4] The family's clerical connections may have called for some discretion but hardly for denial of any involvement. Father Kavanagh for example was proud to be 'the grandson of a "Rebel"', even if, as Cullen claims, he was coy about his grandfather's involvement with the United Irishmen.[5] The lack of such a pedigree may even help to account for the fervour of Thomas Dunne's ballads but more important was the romanticization of the Rebellion, initially by the Young Irelanders and later by the 'Faith and Fatherhood' interpretation of Father Kavanagh. The ballads also draw on local tradition and have faint echoes of both the street ballads popular at the time of the Rebellion, and of the older Gaelic tradition that he claimed was still alive in the district when he was young. While thus a palimpsest of successive accounts and interpretations, the different layers are not equally visible and the inflated rhetoric of romantic nationalism over-colours everything else, like a varnish too thickly applied.

I might well have ended up, like grandfather, a farmer more interested in history than husbandry, and he would have been well suited to the privileged, leisured life of the modern academic. As I sit with his journals open on my desk I am reminded again of how much our lives are shaped by happenstance as well as by the choices we make and the times we live through, and how my history writing, like his ballads, is the product of a particular experience and education, and coloured by a particular (if less easily described) politics.

Each generation produces a version of 1798 to suit its needs and circumstances. While my account of its most bloody day is based on detailed consideration of all available evidence, it remains just that, my account. It makes no claim to truth, only to being as true as possible to the evidence. It is my version, at this point in time, of these stories.

> ... and every attempt
> Is a wholly new start, and a different kind of failure
> Because one has only learnt to get the better of words
> For the thing one no longer has to say, or the way in which
> One is no longer disposed to say it. And so each venture
> Is a new beginning, a raid on the inarticulate
> With shabby equipment always deteriorating
> In the general mess of imprecision of feeling,
> Undisciplined squads of emotion. And what there is to conquer
> By strength and submission, has already been discovered
> Once or twice, or several times, by men whom one cannot hope
> To emulate – but there is no competition –
> There is only the fight to recover what has been lost
> And found and lost again and again: and now, under conditions
> That seem unpropitious. But perhaps neither gain nor loss.
> For us, there is only the trying. The rest is not our business.
>   T.S. ELIOT, 'EAST COKER'

Historians tend, no doubt romantically, to think that it is their business to write in order to shape the future, as well as to describe the past.

My son Oisín will be fifty-five in 2048, the same age as I was during the bicentenary. He has shown interest in this project, intrigued especially by a visit we made to John Rice's grave, since when he has made occasional efforts to grapple with the difficult concepts involved in the fact of an 'ancestor' who was shot 'hundreds of years ago'. For children the idea of a past that does not include them is hard to grasp, and so he was a little cast down to find that New Ross was not still the smoking ruin I had described. His passion at that time was the *Star Wars* trilogy, and his most prized possession a 'light-sabre' that glowed and made noises exactly like the one used by his hero, Luke Skywalker, in the films. Brandishing it one day he confided, 'You know, our great – whatever it is – grandfather would have been all right if he'd had one of these. Then he could have killed all the bad guys.' The reference is modern but the militaristic mindset is traditional and its appeal to a five-year-old understandable.

I hope that the dead of '98 are still remembered in 2048, but that by then they will have been freed at last from the tyranny of the living, no longer press-ganged into scenarios that fit the dominant nationalist agendas of the day, as happened in 1898, 1948, and in 1998.

APPENDIX A

The Gaelic Poetry of Micheál Óg Ó Longáin:
A Case-Study in Politicization

The best-known composition of Cork poet Micheál Óg Ó Longáin (1766–1837), 'Beir litir uainn do'n Mhumhain' ('Carry a letter from us to Munster'), is one of the few contemporary poems in Irish known to me that comments on the Wexford Rebellion.[1]

Ó Longáin was immersed in all aspects of the old élite Gaelic culture because of his main literary activity, which was the copying of Gaelic manuscripts. This highly specialized work rarely paid well and throughout his life he was a poor man, surviving by manual labour and as an itinerant teacher. However, though sunk in the direst poverty, 'im dhubhsclábhaí bheag bhocht' (as a menial labourer of the lowest kind), he continued to regard himself as a poet and scholar. Over three hundred of his own compositions survive, scattered among the thousands of pages of his scribal output. Even more remarkably, many of these poems were glossed by their author with contextual and other commentary. The manuscripts also contain many other references to his life and to his extensive network of friends and correspondents, mainly fellow-scribes and book and manuscript collectors. This circle of Gaelic intellectuals – hedge-school teachers, labourers, tenant farmers, gardeners (including Seán Ó Cinnéide in Enniscorthy), stonemasons, and some priests – has been mapped in remarkable detail by Breandán Ó Conchúir. As both he and Neil Buttimer have shown, Ó Longáin and his local circle were modern, mainly urban, radicals with a sophisticated understanding of both linguistic and cultural worlds and a keen interest in European affairs. They saw the need to develop new strategies to enable the Gaelic tradition to survive, and planned to publish contemporary work in Irish and even an Irish-language newspaper.[2] Their failure to do so either illustrates how far the linguistic revolution had gone already or how closely literary production was tied to wider market forces.

Instead, Ó Longáin's poems were written for his friends, neighbours and especially his fellow poets, and it is possible that some of these were involved with him in the United Irishmen. The evidence for Ó Longáin having been a member is inconclusive, but occasional hints in his writing may support the assertion of a government informer that he was one, and over the same period there is an otherwise unexplained gap in his scribal output.[3] On the other hand the activist he identified with most clearly, his cousin Tomás, appears to have been no more than a local Whiteboy or possibly Defender leader, and the colouring of traditional agrarian and sectarian grievances with the new vocabulary of revolutionary France could be equally well explained by such a connection.[4]

Regardless of his active political involvement, the key question about Ó Longáin's verse is the extent to which it fits the pattern that Bartlett discerned in Defender texts, in which 'the theme of deliverance, the central feature of Gaelic literature for over two hundred years, was fused with the very real prospect of French help, to form a revolutionary dynamic'.[5] If he was indeed a United Irishman, his writings in this period would appear to confirm that this new brand of radicalism made relatively little impact on the traditional perspectives that most profoundly shaped peasant insurgency.

These perspectives were articulated in an early *aisling*, written in macaronic form and dated 'an tam tháinig na Buachaillí Bána 1785' (the time when the Whiteboys came, 1785). The nineteen-year-old Ó Longáin was here referring to the anti-tithe Rightboy movement that convulsed Cork during that and the following two years. For a time it seemed to unite some local Protestant gentry figures with traditional Whiteboy protest, but the young poet's perspective was more traditional and sectarian, notably in the apparition's promise that when Charles Stuart comes, 'Beidh báire is céad ar Sasanaigh is fanatics dha gcrádh gan cabhair / Is gearr go mbedigh Rex in Albain is Aifreann dá rá gach am'. Ó Longáin himself translates this as, ' 'Tis then we'll banish Protestants, in Scotland I'll have me seat / Long live the Roman Catholics to flourish well, bright and fair.'[6] A series of more conventional *aislingí* followed, some of simple optimism, others laying particular emphasis on the sufferings of the sad remnants of the old learned classes (including himself reduced to 'seanabhróga' [old shoes]) and on the cultural consequences of colonialism: 'A gríocha dá líonadh le Ghallanósaibh / 'S gan puinn meas ar Ghaeilge ná sheanasceolta' (Their lands being filled with foreign ways / Without the slightest respect for the Irish language or for old stories).

In other early poems there were elements of the *aisling ghéar* (bitter vision) of Ó Rathaille's well-known dark, pessimistic versions, particularly in the 1795 poem 'Maidean drúchta ar startha ag scrúdadh' ('One dewy morning while I set to studying tales'). Lamenting the sad fate of the Irish, persecuted by 'Gallabh Dúra daordha an fhill' ('Rigid, oppressive, treacherous foreigners'), the poet got little consolation from the 'spéirbhean' (beautiful woman), but instead warnings against involvement in the affairs of this sad life: 'Tá baoghal mór 'na chionn / 'S gan ann go léir, mo léan, acht ceo nó cúr' (There is great danger involved / And nothing there, sadly, but fog or foam). Her final comment was, 'Is na fiafraigh díomsa puinn, ná fheadhar aon rud' (And don't ask me anything. I know nothing). In a more cheerful conventional *aisling* the following year there was a return to the promise of the Irish being in the ascendant and foreigners banished, but this was simply the tired old formula lacking any real conviction or contemporary context.[7] Like most of his poems to this point, it could have been written by any number of poets almost any time in the eighteenth century.

The language, especially of the introduction to what might be termed his first 'United Irish' poem, 'I dtairngreacht Naomh' (In the prophecy of saints) in 1797, seems therefore all the more fresh and exciting. He explains his reasons for writing it:

Do ghríosú bhfear nÉireann de gach aon chreideamh agus to háirithe clanna Gael fána bheith díleas dea-rúin deiscréideach i gcomhcheangal grá páirte cumainn agus lánmhuinterais agus i ngrá dearbhráithreacais le chéile, ionas go mb'fhusaide dhóibh an cluiche seo do bhreith, agus iad féin a shoaradh ón ndaorchuing sclábhaíochta féna bhfuilid le cian d'aimsir.

(To urge the men of Ireland of all religions, and especially the Gaelic Irish, to be loyal, well-intentioned and discreet in a covenant of mutual love and fellowship and association and of fraternal regard for each other, so that it may be easier for them to win this contest and free themselves from the oppressive slavery under which they have been for a long period.)

This rare echo of United Irish language in a contemporary Gaelic text certainly gave a new context for the traditional emphasis in the text on the liberation of 'Clanna Gael' (which had long signified both 'native Irish' and 'Catholic'). The fact that the introduction (as in all of these poems) was added later may help to account for the fact that the actual text of the poem contained only a faint echo of its sentiments, but instead had the same mixture of traditional Jacobitism and contemporary Whiteboyism noted previously in the case of the Máire Bhuí song. The invocation of a union of creeds and the principles of fraternity translated awkwardly into an appeal to 'Clanna Gael' to join with all other enemies of the 'Danair' ('Danes', i.e., foreigners), even if he be a 'Sagsannach … nó Quaker cruaidh' (an Englishman … or a severe Quaker). The enemy was described in terms which, while anachronistic, also reflected the new sectarianism: 'claon-shliocht Chailbhin bhréin' (the foul perverse descendants of Calvin). However, while victory over them would mean 'Gaeil I ngradam mhuar' (the native Irish in high esteem), and 'míle búr ag béicigh' (a thousand boors roaring), it would also meet contemporary concerns to abolish tithes and unjust taxation, and more fundamentally, 'an talamh go léir bheith saor go buan' (all of the land free forever). The poem ended with the classic Jacobite appeal to 'mo charad is mo lao-se an Saesar suairc, an Faraire séimh gan claon, gan cruas' (my friend and darling the cheerful Caesar, the gentle warrior without iniquity or hardness). This can be read as a coded reference to local United Irish hero, Arthur O'Connor, rather than the usual pious invocation of the ghost of the Pretender, if the United Irish tincture of the introduction is fully accepted. More clearly, the expectation of 'an buidhean seo ag taisteal taobh linn' (this troop travelling to be with us) referred to the hope of further French expeditions in the aftermath of Bantry Bay.[8]

The remarkable sequence of political poems that followed features standard Jacobite motifs and language, but they are not *aislingí*. Overall they raise the question whether a successful French landing and campaign in 1796 might have transformed Jacobites into Jacobins, but they can equally be read as confirming French fears that the Irish poor might prove more akin to the vehemently anti-Jacobin Catholic peasantry of the Vendée. However, in Ó Longáin's Wexford poem, 'Beir litir uain do'n Mhumhain' (Carry a letter from us to Munster), even an echo of United Irish language is absent. Written in terms of an appeal by the Wexford rebels to their 'dearbhráithre' (true brothers) in Munster to join them, it was introduced by an interesting summary of the events of 1798, but using traditional terminology. It began:

[281]

Do chuadar drong d'fhearaibh Éireann ar Chnoc na bhFínéigre I Laighnibh san mbli-adhain 1798, i ndóith go n-éireoghadh an Mhumhain agus an chuid eile d'Éirinn do chongnamh leo agus go dtiocfadh Franncaigh dár bhfortacht amhail do ghealladar.

(A group of the men of Ireland went onto Vinegar Hill in Leinster in the year 1798, hoping that the men of Munster would rise, and that the rest of Ireland would help them and that the French would come to help them as they promised.)

This poem categorized the Rebellion in even more traditional anti-colonist terms, 'Gallabhúir do dhíbirt / As fearann dúchais díleas / Ár sinsear go deo (To drive out the foreign boors from our ancestral lands forever).9

The context given by Ó Longáin for the poem, 'Is dubhach liom scéal' ('The story is sad to me') included the arrest of Lord Edward Fitzgerald and Arthur O'Connor, but also local executions in Imokilly and the public flogging of a popular priest. This suggests new meaning for its traditional lament for 'Crú glan éachtach Eibhir Fhinn' ('The pure, heroic native Irish') who are persecuted by 'brúscar bréan do léim thar tuinn' (foul rubbish that leapt across the sea) but who now have 'trúp breágh gléasta réidh dár mbuidhin' (a fine troop of our followers ready) in every district, and the expectation of 'gárda thréan tar sáile ag téacht' (a strong guard coming over the sea). The language of 'Scéal do réab mo chroí ionam' ('A story that broke my heart') was more direct. Written, we are told, 'iar ngabháil Artúir Uí Chonchuir agus iar marú Eadbhard MacGearailt' (after the capture of Arthur O'Connor and the killing of Edward Fitzgerald), it made explicit reference to the two United Irish leaders, and after a traditional lament for Irish disunity and a prayer for victory it ended with a promise of French help and the expression of hope:

> Go bhfeiceam Éire saor gan daoirse
> Is an bhratainn uaithne in uachtar scaoilte
> Gach tíoránach claoincheardach coimhtheach
> In ainm an diabhail is gan Dia dá gcoimhdeacht.

(That I will see Ireland free, without persecution, and the green flag flying high and every foreign tyrant of evil ways pitched to the Devil and without God's protection.)10

After this passing contemporary reference, the remarkable 1799 poem 'Deinidh go súgach a Ghaela' (Be merry, Gaels), written on hearing news of a French fleet leaving Brest and rumours of the Irish Parliament being moved to Britain, harked back to the seventeenth century and transposed the language and perspectives of Ó Bruadair to the 1790s, urging 'Brúighidh, bascaidh réabaidh … Trúip na nOrange mbréana' (Crush, destroy, rend … the foul Orange troop), and eagerly anticipating, in spite of his rags, being able to humiliate the foreign upstarts. The heroic Irish warrior who will accomplish this 'iar theacht mo lao tar toinn' (with the coming of my darling over the sea) was described in traditional terms, 'cú (literally, hound), but also as 'Craipí Gléigeal' (bright croppy – the term for modern French-inspired radicals), and the poet hoped to see Ireland soon 'ag Clanna Gael gan chíos' (in possession of the native Irish without rent). He ended with the first invocation of the *aisling* motif in this series, promising the noble woman / Ireland wine and green silk clothes if she would 'Tair liom féin fén gcoil' (Come with me into the wood, i.e., into an area outside the law).[11]

Clearly Ó Longáin's poems of 1797-9 show how the prospect of help from revolutionary France fulfilled traditional Jacobite hopes of deliverance and fuelled contemporary hopes for social justice. They demonstrate, just as the development of Jacobite verse had done in the late seventeenth century, the remarkable pragmatism, adaptability and sophistication of the Gaelic political tradition. But they do not suggest that such a dynamic was dependent on the absorption of United Irish ideology, which seems to have been superficial in the case of Ó Longáin, whose later writings and those of his circle show virtually no trace of it. In so far as they took on board contemporary French ideas, his 'revolutionary' poems reflect more clearly the heady mixture of traditional and modern that marked Defenderism. And this is their importance for our attempt to understand the mentality of the Irish-speaking countrymen who attacked New Ross, many of them 'dubhsclábhaithe' (menial slaves) as he described himself. Ó Longáin's articulation on the Rebellion in terms of the old dream of driving out the foreign settlers and the Whiteboy agenda of social justice, chimes wells with what we know of their background and their stated objectives. The few surviving contemporary ballads in English from Wexford confirm this interpretation. For the most part stridently sectarian (Father Murphy, for example, 'arose … to shake off heretics and persecutors/and wash them away in a crimson stream'), some of them have the same Defender blend of old and new: 'When the Cross will guide us to victory / And we'll plant the tree of sweet Liberty.'[12] It is unlikely that such a combination would have seemed incongruous to rank-and-file rebels.

APPENDIX B

The Ballads of Thomas Dunne

Even as the Rebellion raged it was being celebrated in ballads, few of which survive in their original form. Those that do, celebrate the deeds of Father Murphy or tell the sad tale of 'The Croppy Boy'. Most simply tell their stories in factual, neutral terms, but the ones that reflect rebel motivation are strongly sectarian:

> Since Father Murphy of the County Wexford
> Has lately arose from a sleeping dream
> To shake off heretics and persecutors
> And wash them away in a crimson stream.

Following the centenary, this had become, in the popular adaptation of P.J. McCall's famous 'Boolavogue':

> 'Arm, Arm,' he cried, 'for I've come to lead you
> For Ireland's freedom we fight or die'[1]

The process of putting a politically correct gloss on the passions of the time had begun almost at once. In *Legends of Mount-Leinster* Patrick Kennedy gave a carefully distanced account of a discussion in his godmother's house, not far from Courtna-cuddy, about 'the scourge of '98'. This was sometime before 1820 and included a non-sectarian rendition of the same ballad, introduced humorously as a 'treason song', with the reassurance, 'you need not fear it will bring about another rising'. And indeed there is no inkling in it of what caused the Rebellion, and when Father Murphy 'lately aroused from his sleeping dream', it is simply to prove himself a great soldier:

> Save Julius Caesar, nor Alexander
> Nor brave King Arthur ever equalled him.

Yet, in Kennedy's account of the discussion that followed, the singer does reflect the perspective of the original:

> It is a curious and sad circumstance, that, though the brave and honest portion that really fought and suffered, thought they were doing it in defence of their religion: the

first contrivers of the insurrection were either men without any spark of religion, or if a sample was amongst them at all, it was not in the Catholic mould it was cast.

Earlier he had justified, 'collecting old ballads … Because they show what the people of the time were much interested about, and besides they preserve things that historians don't think worth notice'. Equally, the more distant they are from 'the people of the time', the more they reflect the politics of their own day.[2]

Indeed ballads (or, more accurately, literary imitations of the ballad form) have long been a common form of propaganda, helping to develop a popular image of the Rebellion as a glorious nationalist struggle. While *The Nation* newspaper is rightly regarded as crucial in this process, the contributors to its ballad collection, *The Spirit of the Nation*, first published in parts in 1843 and 1845 and constantly reprinted in a small cheap volume throughout the nineteenth century, seemed oddly reluctant to engage with the legacy of the Rebellion. Only one ballad (out of 109) even mentions 1798 and that one does so only to ask the revealing rhetorical question, 'Who fears to speak of Ninety-Eight?' One obvious answer is, 'the author does'. John Kells Ingram was the only contributor afraid to attach even a pen-name to his piece, and he was to acknowledge authorship only in 1900, after a lifetime as a pillar of the establishment, ending as vice chancellor of Trinity College, Dublin and president of the Royal Irish Academy – and a staunch opponent of Home Rule. There were considerations of prudence involved, of course, and Ingram's ballad was included in the long bill of indictment drawn up against the editors of *The Nation* for sedition. And from the viewpoint of the Dublin Castle authorities this made sense, because the whole focus of his ballad was the future not the past. Studiously vague about the Rebellion (lacking even one specific reference to it), it was concerned to invoke 'ninety-eight' simply as a catch-cry in an otherwise conventional call to patriotic endeavour. But it was to be a powerful catch-cry to later nationalists who seized upon Ingram's recruitment of the rebels to the Young Ireland cause and claimed:

> They rose in dark and evil days
> To right their native land

As more recently, for Comóradh '98, their memory was:

> For us a guiding light,
> To cheer our strife for liberty
> And teach us to unite![3]

And, perhaps the 'fear' that needed to be overcome related not to official disapproval but to the memory of '98 itself for most bourgeois nationalists, at a time of undisciplined popular insurgency and sectarian atrocity, when 'true men like you men' failed dismally 'to unite' or to control their followers. Thus it is hardly surprising that the rhetorical glorification of war, which was the dominant motif of *The Spirit of the Nation*, dwells instead on a more distant past, and above all on the romantic and chivalric tales of the Irish Brigade in early eighteenth-century France. Intent on ignoring the grim realities of a still vividly remembered war, *The Nation*, above all, feared to speak of '98.

The Spirit of the Nation went through many cheap editions. I have the fiftieth, published in 1874 by Duffy, and it is doubtless similar to the one that Thomas Dunne bought a few years earlier some market day in Enniscorthy. This copy doesn't survive, but it is one of the many historical and patriotic texts referred to in his two journals from this period that do, and that also include extracts, and copies of cartoons from Fenian newspapers. Born in 1848, Thomas was educated at the local National School built by Lord Carew the year before his birth. While his journals indicate the possibility that he had some further education, there is no record or family tradition to support this, and it is more likely that he was largely self-educated, helped no doubt by his younger brother, Father John, to whom he was very close. Even in his twenties he was widely read, articulate and patriotic, an example of the culture and self-confidence that had marked prosperous farmers in Wexford for over a century, and of the generation that was soon to achieve a major social and political revolution through the Land League. Yet while he was active in that campaign, his vision was always romantic rather than practical. Chairing a local meeting of the League in 1885, for example, he 'said their object ... was to carry on the National Movement with more determination, and by meeting oftener to instil more of the National Spirit into the men of the locality'.4 By then he was also a Poor Law Guardian, and like most Wexford Parnellites he became a staunch Redmondite.

Political differences were to be a factor in his ultimate estrangement from his eldest son, my Uncle Jim, prominent in the local IRA and, by his own account, in the burning in 1922 of Castleboro, the great Palladian mansion of their by then former landlords, the Carews. A much-loved uncle, who combined great humour and sweetness of disposition with the most die-hard republican views (he never recognized either the Free State that had betrayed him, or the British state which still held onto the six counties), Jim told me in his old age that he and his friends were in the IRA to right ancient wrongs and to achieve social justice, especially the full redistribution of land – sentiments that connect them directly to the Bantrymen of 1798. When it came to revolution, his father was more in the tradition of Arthur Dunne of Toumallogue, and there is considerable irony in the fact that the violent Young Ireland rhetoric with which his ballads of the 1870s were imbued was to be so unacceptable to him when his son's generation tried to turn it into reality.

Thomas Dunne wrote three ballads about '98 that survive. So far as we know, they were written without any thought of publication. The first, 'A Wexfordian Rally', is dated 1872 and includes a note, 'air: O'Donnell aboo', a reference to M.J. McCann's immensely popular ballad in *The Spirit of the Nation*. It begins:

> Arise men of Wexford your country calls you
> To battle for home and for dear liberty
> Let not the strength of the tyrant appal you
> But onwards like true men and you will be free

Yet the only battle invoked to inspire the 'brave sons of ninety-eight' is that of romantic Fontenoy! His naming of the enemy as the 'Saxon churl' and 'the faithless invader' is also characteristic of *The Nation*, but he also called them 'the Goill' (foreigners), a name more evocative of the Gaelic tradition than the usual romantic antiquarianism of Young Ireland. More interesting is the John Mitchell note of moral contempt for England.

Their proud fleet no longer can conquer tis true
Sunk in debauch and crime.[5]

Grandfather's debt to *The Nation* was also signalled in the first of the two ballads
he wrote in May 1878, the eightieth anniversary of the Rebellion. 'The charge of the
Bantry Men. New Ross A.D. 1798' was prefaced with a quote from Davis, who in turn
was quoting Ingram's ballad: 'Your sons (Wexford) need not fear to speak of ninety-
eight.' But this effort also had some of the immediacy and narrative drive of the
Wexford ballad tradition. It began with the kind of specific detail that was lacking in
Ingram:

'Let Kelly and Cloney their comrades lead on';
Your order scarce given ere these brave men are gone
From their camp, Corbet Hill, driving backward from thence
The foe in confusion o'er field and o'er fence
To the Three Bullet Gate of the old town again,
So fierce the onset of the brave Bantry men.

The ballad was accurate on what it chose to celebrate, the initial remarkable
success of the Bantrymen, and their still more remarkable courage subsequently as 'up,
up to the mouth of the cannon they rush', despite 'grapeshot point blank sweeping
gaps clear and wide':

For over their comrades and right on again
Charge the flower of the rebels, the brave Bantry men.

In this celebration of local pride there was no mention of their ultimate fate in
the battle. Nor was there any explanation for such desperate courage other than, 'What
hate serves each rebel! Like furies they seem', and the description of the enemy poet-
ically as 'the Saxon' and, more accurately, as 'the Yeomen'.[6]

What inspired their 'hate' was explained in Thomas Dunne's longer and more
ambitious ballad of 1878, 'The Battle of Oulart Hill', which again combined the older
ballad tradition with Young Ireland romantic pastiche. It begins:

Upon the crest of Oulart Hill, the s throng
To desperation driven on by cruel and heartless wrong;
They gathered from their plundered homes to stay the tyrants hand,
And raised the green, that grand old flag, for faith and fatherland.'[7]

The final phrase points to an even more direct source, the Reverend Patrick F.
Kavanagh's *A Popular History of the Insurrection of 1798*, published four years earlier and
described by Kevin Whelan as making the Rebellion, 'a crusade of faith and fatherland, devoid of United Irish influence'.[8]

It seems clear that Thomas Dunne would have been delighted to invoke such an
iconic nationalist presence as that of the United Irishmen, had he been aware of it, but
there is nothing in these ballads, pre- or post-Kavanagh, to indicate that he was. As in
Kavanagh (and the early street ballads), the hero of this traditional-style narrative of a
military engagement (cast more in the literary language of *The Nation*) was 'brave
Father Murphy', portrayed as 'this warrior-priest', leading 'the persecuted and pitch-

capped peasantry'. It told how his tactics – 'a plan in Irish genius rich' – gave an improbable victory to 'a motley crowd with pike and scythe against Britain's chosen band'. The likelihood that Grandfather had Kavanagh's book in front of him as he wrote is clear from his account of the fate of Major Lombard:

> Major Lombard ... spurred his steed forward, waving his sword aloft, and calling loudly for his men to follow, exclaiming that 'the course was clear'. The words of ill-timed exultation had scarce passed his lips when a bullet ... pierced his breast ... On beholding their officer fall, the Militia raised a shout of rage and pressed forward at a quickened pace to avenge his death.

(Kavanagh, p. 105)

> Their major waved his sword on high and shouted to his men,
> 'Come on! Come on! The way is clear' now for the sport again.'

> What 'sport' the gallant major had, is part our skills to tell
> For instantly pierced with a ball the helpless leader fell.
> His loyal corps for vengeance nerved pressed madly onward now,
> And hate and rage were plainly stamped upon each knitted brow.

('The Battle of Oulart Hill')

Entirely lacking in Kavanagh, however, was the emotional romantic nationalism of grandfather's ballad.

> Before the sweeping Celtic charge again the Saxon fled,
> And left the green to triumph o'er the often sullied red.

The reference here was clearly to Davis' well-known ballad, 'The Green above the Red', which connected 'our fathers ... in rude but fierce array, with sabre, pike and skian' with the sacrifice of Lord Edward, 'and Wolfe Tone sunk serene', and had the pledge 'our blood to shed / Once and forever more to raise the Green above the Red!'[9] In grandfather's ballad, the enemy were 'aliens', not least 'The North Cork ... the fiercest and basest of them all', and he believed that 'deepest hatred of our race within their bosoms burned'. Clearly he had not absorbed Kavanagh's demonstration of the fact that this militia included many Catholics and Irish-speakers, who used their common race and religion to beg for mercy from the rebels.[10]

For Thomas Dunne, however, Irish Catholic militia and local Protestant yeomanry were all lumped together incongruously as 'the Sassanach', in a manner reminiscent of the Gaelic Jacobite tradition as well as the black and white rhetoric of Young Ireland. He collected local folklore about customs and characters, but when it came to the age-old fight against 'the Sassanach' his local patriotism found expression instead in the satisfying, colourful stereotypes acquired by his reading. He was, as his sons remembered him, 'a great man for the books', something they linked to the fact that he was also 'a useless farmer'. He was a dreamer who lived to see his abstract romanticism challenged by his son's revolutionary generation, a new breed of 'insurgents' who shared some of the more practical concerns of 'the Bantry men'.

ENDNOTES

ABBREVIATIONS

NAI   National Archives of Ireland
NLI   National Library of Ireland
TCD   Trinity College, Dublin
HO   Public Record Office, London: Home Office Papers
IFC   Irish Folklore Commission: Schools Collection

PROLOGUE

1.   S. Heaney, *Door into the Dark* (London 1969).
2.   T. Dunne, 'Popular Ballads, Revolutionary Rhetoric and Politicisation' in H. Gough and D. Dickson (eds), *Ireland and the French Revolution* (Dublin 1993), pp. 139–55.
3.   K. Whelan, *The Tree of Liberty: Radicalism, Catholicism and the Construction of Irish Identity 1760–1830* (Cork 1996), p. 133.
4.   T. Dunne, '1798: Memory, History, Commemoration', *Journal of the Wexford Historical Society*, no. 16, 1996–7, pp. 5–39.
5.   K. Whelan, 'Reinterpreting the 1798 Rebellion in County Wexford' in D. Keogh and N. Furlong (eds), *The Mighty Wave: The 1798 Rebellion in Wexford* (Dublin 1996), p. 35; T. Dunne, 'Dangers Lie in the Romanticising of 1798', *The Irish Times*, 6/1/98.
6.   e.g. *The Irish Times*, 24/3/98, 14/4/98, 4/5/98.
7.   W. Benjamin, 'Theses on the Philosophy of History' in *Illuminations* (London 1970), pp. 259–60.
8.   For an overview, see J.D. Popkin, 'Historians on the Autobiographical Frontier', *The American Historical Review*, 104, no. 3, June 1999, pp. 725–48.

CHAPTER 1

1.   J.V. Gahan, *The Secular Priests of the Diocese of Ferns* (Strasbourg 2000), p. 101.
2.   B. Browne, *Old Ross: The Town that Never Was* (Wexford 1993), pp. 61–2.
3.   S. de Vál, 'Logainmneacha Chontae Loch Garman' in K. Whelan and W. Nolan (eds), *Wexford: History and Society* (Dublin 1987), p. 63.
4.   S. O'Faolain, *An Irish Journey* (London 1940), pp. 25–8.

CHAPTER 2

1. S. O'Faolain, *op. cit.*, p. 28.
2. P.F. Kavanagh, *A Popular History of the Insurrection of 1798* (Dublin 1870).
3. This was collected in M.C. Normoyle, *Memories of Edmund Rice*, published 'for private circulation' by the Christian Brothers in 1979.
4. J.G. Ó Muimhneacháin, *Graiméar Gaeilge na mBráithre Críostaí* (Dublin 1960).
5. L.P. Ó Caithnia, *Scéal na hIomána* (Dublin 1980).
6. See M. Raftery and E. O'Sullivan, *Suffer the Little Children: The Inside Story of Ireland's Industrial Schools* (Dublin 1999), pp. 35, 157, 165, 224–6, 254, 293, 316.

CHAPTER 3

1. A. Clarke, 'Robert Dudley Edwards 1908–88', *Irish Historical Studies*, no. 102, November 1988, pp. 121–7.
2. J.J. Lee, *Ireland 1912–1985* (Cambridge 1989), p. 590.
3. J. McGuire, 'T. Desmond Williams (1921–1987)', *Irish Historical Studies*, XXVI, no. 10, May 1988, pp. 3–7.
4. See T. Dunne, 'Maureen Wall (née McGeehin) 1918–1972: A Memoir' in G. O'Brien (ed.), *Catholic Ireland in the Eighteenth Century: Collected Essays of Maureen Wall* (Dublin 1989).
5. C. Ó Gráda, 'Making History in Ireland in the 1940s and 1950s: The Saga of the Great Famine', *The Irish Review*, no. 12, 1992, pp. 87–107.
6. G.R. Elton, *The Practice of History* (London 1967), pp. vii–viii.
7. R.G. Collingwood, *The Idea of History* (Oxford 1946, revised edn 1994), pp. 231–49, 445.
8. At the Conference of Irish Historians in Britain, held at University of Durham, 18–20 March 1988.
9. M. Wall, 'The Background to the Rising from 1914 until the Issue of the Countermanding Order on Easter Saturday 1916' and 'The Plans and the Countermand: the Country and Dublin', both in K.B. Nowlan (ed.), *The Making of 1916* (Dublin 1969), pp. 235, vii–viii, xii.
10. R. Ellman, *James Joyce* (revised edn, Oxford 1982), p. 83.
11. P.H. Pearse, *The Singer and other Plays* (Dublin 1960 reprint), p. 44.
12. R.D. Edwards and T.W. Moody, preface to the first number of *Irish Historical Studies* (1938–9).
13. B. Bradshaw, 'Nationalism and Historical Scholarship in Modern Ireland', published originally in *Irish Historical Studies*, XXVI (1988–9); reprinted in C. Brady (ed.), *Interpreting Irish History: The Debate on Historical Revisionism* (Dublin 1994), pp. 191–216.
14. S. Deane, 'Wherever Green is Read' in M. Ní Dhonnchadha and T. Dorgan (eds), *Revising the Rising* (Derry 1991), pp. 91–105, 101.
15. H. Butterfield, *The Whig Interpretation of History* (London 1931, 1973), pp. 17, 24, 94.
16. E.H. Carr, *What Is History?* (London 1961, pbk 1964), pp. 36, 44, 139.

17. T. Garvin, 'The Strange Death of Clerical Politics in University College Dublin', *Irish University Review*, spring/summer 1998, pp. 308–14.

18. Collingwood, *op. cit.*, p. 445.

CHAPTER 4

1. See T. Dunne, 'Oliver MacDonagh' in F.B. Smith (ed.), *Ireland, England and Australia: Essays in Honour of Oliver MacDonagh* (Canberra and Cork 1990), pp. 1–13.

2. O. MacDonagh, *Ireland* (New Jersey 1968).

3. O. MacDonagh, *The Nineteenth-Century Novel and Irish Social History: Some Aspects* (Dublin 1970).

4. O. MacDonagh, *A Pattern of Government Growth 1800–1860: The Passenger Acts and their Enforcement* (London 1961).

5. D. Thornley, *Isaac Butt* (London 1964); C.C. O'Brien, *Parnell and his Party* (Oxford 1957); F.S.L. Lyons, *The Fall of Parnell* (London 1960).

6. This culminated in A.B. Cooke and J.R. Vincent, *The Governing Passion: Cabinet Government and Party Politics in Britain, 1865–6* (Brighton 1974).

7. T. Dunne, 'W.E. Gladstone: The Evolution of the Home Rule Policy', MA Thesis, UCC 1971.

8. MacDonagh, *Ireland*, p. viii.

9. R. Fanning, 'The Great Enchantment: Uses and Abuses in Modern Irish History' in Brady (ed.), *Interpreting Irish History*, p. 156.

10. C.C. O'Brien, *States of Ireland* (London 1972, 1974), p. 144.

11. *Ibid.* p. 240.

12. *Ibid.* pp. 248–9.

13. I. d'Alton, 'Southern Irish Unionism: A Study of Cork Unionists 1884–1914' in *Transactions of the Royal Historical Society*, 5th series, 23 (London 1973).

14. G. Steiner, *Errata: An Examined Life* (London 1998), p. 43.

15. R. Cobb, 'Jack Gallagher in Oxford' in his *People and Places* (Oxford 1984), p. 5.

16. R. Guha, 'Dominance without Hegemony and its Historiography' in *Subaltern Studies*, VI (Delhi 1994), p. 305.

17. A. Seal, 'John Andrew Gallagher, 1919–1980' in A. Seal (ed.), *John Gallagher, The Decline, Revival and Fall of the British Empire: The Ford Lectures and Other Essays* (Cambridge 1982), p. xix.

18. Cobb, 'Jack Gallagher', p. 1.

19. T. Dunne, 'Ireland, England and Empire 1868–86: The Ideologies of the British Political Leadership', PhD Thesis, Cambridge 1975.

20. Guha, 'Dominance without Hegemony', pp. 290–305.

21. M. Bentley, 'Prologue: The Retiring Mr. Cowling' in M. Bentley (ed.), *Public and Private Doctrine: Essays in British History Presented to Maurice Cowling* (Cambridge 1993), pp. 1–13.

22. M. Cowling, *Religion and Public Doctrine in Modern England* (Cambridge 1980), pp. xvi, xvii, 444, 49.

23. Bentley, 'The Retiring Mr. Cowling', p. 9.

24. T. Dunne, ' "La trahison des clercs": British Intellectuals and the First Home Rule Crisis', *Irish Historical Studies*, XXIII, November 1982, pp. 134–73.

CHAPTER 5

1. T. Dunne, 'The Gaelic Response to Conquest and Colonisation: The Evidence of the Poetry', *Studia Hibernica*, no. 20, 1980, pp. 7–30.
2. D. Ó Corráin, *Ireland before the Normans;* K. Nicholls, *Gaelic and Gaelicised Ireland in the Middle Ages;* J. Lee, *The Modernisation of Irish Society 1848–1918;* J.A. Murphy, *Ireland in the Twentieth Century* (all Dublin 1972).
3. J.A. Murphy, *The College: A History of Queens/University College Cork* (Cork 1995).
4. L. Gibbons, 'Challenging the Canon: Revisionism and Cultural Criticism' in S. Deane (ed.), *The Field Day Anthology of Irish Writing*, 3 (Derry 1991), pp. 561–79.
5. For an overview, see Brady (ed.), *Interpreting Irish History*.
6. R. Foster, 'We Are All Revisionists Now', *The Irish Review*, no. 1, 1986, p. 2.
7. Bradshaw, 'Nationalism and Historical Scholarship' in Brady (ed.), *Interpreting Irish History*, pp. 207–8.
8. T. Dunne, *Theobald Wolfe Tone: Colonial Outsider* (Cork 1982), p.14.
9. T. Bartlett, 'The Burden of the Present: Theobald Wolfe Tone, Republican and Separatist'; in D. Dickson, D. Keogh and K. Whelan (eds), *The United Irishmen: Republicanism, Radicalism and Rebellion* (Dublin 1993), pp. 1–15, 1–2. See also his *Theobald Wolfe Tone* (Dundalk 1997), pp. 65–7, 88.
10. M. Elliott, *Wolfe Tone: Prophet of Irish Independence* (New Haven 1989).
11. T. Dunne, 'The Gaelic Response'.
12. L. Gibbons, 'Identity Without a Centre: Allegory, History and Irish Nationalism', *Cultural Studies*, 3, October 1992, pp. 358–75, 362–3.
13. T. Dunne, 'Subaltern Voices? Poetry in Irish, Popular Insurgency and the 1798 Rebellion', *Eighteenth Century Life*, 22, N.S. 3, November 1998; ' "Tá Gaedhil Bhocht Cráidhte": Memory, Tradition and the Politics of the Poor in Gaelic Poetry and Song' in L. Geary (ed.), *Rebellion and Remembrance in Modern Ireland* (Dublin 2001).
14. T. Dunne, 'Haunted by History: Irish Romantic Writing 1800–1850' in R. Porter and M. Teich (eds), *Romanticism in National Context* (Cambridge 1988); *Maria Edgeworth and the Colonial Mind* (Dublin 1984); ' "A Gentleman's Estate should be a Moral School": Edgeworthstown in Fact and Fiction' in R. Gillespie and R. Moran (eds), *Longford: Essays in County History* (Dublin 1991), pp. 95–121; 'Fiction as "The Best History of Nations": Lady Morgan's Irish novels' in T. Dunne (ed.), *The Writer as Witness* (Cork 1987), pp. 135–59; 'Murder as Metaphor: Griffin's Portrayal of Ireland in the Year of Catholic Emancipation' in O. MacDonagh and W.F. Mandle (eds), *Ireland and Irish Australia*, (London and Sydney 1986), pp. 64–80; 'The Insecure Voice: A Catholic Novelist in Support of Emancipation' in L.M. Cullen and L. Bergeron (eds), *Culture et Pratiques Politique en France et en Irlande xvi^e–xviii^e siecle* (Paris 1989), pp. 213–34; ' "One of the Tests

of National Character": Britishness and Irishness in Paintings by Barry and Maclise' in B. Stewart (ed.), *Hearts and Minds: Irish Culture and Society under the Act of Union* (Gerrards Cross 2002), pp. 260–90.

15. Bradshaw, 'Nationalism and Historical Scholarship' in Brady (ed.), *Interpreting Irish History*, pp. 212–14.

16. Deane, 'Wherever Green is Read', p. 102.

17. *Ibid.* pp. 96–101.

18. Gibbons, 'Challenging the Canon', pp. 561–8.

19. T. Eagleton, *Crazy John and the Bishop, and other Essays on Irish Culture* (Cork 1998), pp. 308–27.

20. J. Dunn, *Western Political Theory in the Face of the Future* (Cambridge 1979, Canto Edition 1993), p. 36.

21. T. Eagleton, *The Gatekeeper: A Memoir* (London 2001).

22. J. Connolly, *United Irishmen*, 17/4/1900, quoted in R.D. Edwards, *James Connolly* (Dublin 1981), p. 35; W. Shakespeare, 'The Irish Captain' MacMorris in *Henry V*, Act 3, Scene 2; J. Joyce, *Ulysses* (The 1922 text, Oxford 1993), p. 317.

23. See R. Foster, *The Story of Ireland* (Oxford 1995).

24. D. Fennell, 'Against Revisionism', *The Irish Review*, no. 4, 1988, pp. 20–6 (reprinted in Brady [ed.], *Interpreting Irish History*, pp. 183–90).

25. Bradshaw, 'Nationalism and Historical Scholarship' in Brady (ed.), *Interpreting Irish History*, p. 212.

26. H. Butterfield, *An Englishman and His History* (Cambridge 1944), p. 6.

27. Bradshaw, 'Nationalism and Historical Scholarship' in Brady (ed.), *Interpreting Irish History*, p. 201.

28. *Ibid.* pp. 203–4.

29. C. Leighton, *Catholicism in a Protestant Kingdom* (Dublin 1994); S. Connolly, *Religion, Land and Power* (Oxford 1992); J. Hill, *From Patriots to Unionists: Dublin Civic Politics and Irish Protestant Patriotism 1660–1840* (Oxford 1997).

30. L.M. Cullen, *The Emergence of Modern Ireland 1600–1900* (London 1981); J.J. Lee, *The Modernisation of Irish Society* (Dublin 1972).

31. S. Deane, *Strange Country: Modernity and Nationhood in Irish Writing since 1790* (Oxford 1997), p. 193.

32. L. Kennedy, 'Modern Ireland: Post-Colonial Society or Post-Colonial Pretensions?' *The Irish Review*, no. 13, 1992–3, pp. 107–21.

33. See 14 above. For a brilliant overview of these trends in post-colonial studies see E. Said, *Culture and Imperialism* (London 1993).

CHAPTER 6

1. R. Musgrave, *Memoirs of the Different Rebellions in Ireland*, S.W. Myers and D.E. McKnight (eds), with a foreword by D. Dickson (Fort Wayne, Indiana 1995).

2. T. Dunne, 'Subaltern Voices? Poetry in Irish, Popular Insurgency and the 1798 Rebellion', pp. 31–44; also, 'Popular Ballads, Revolutionary Rhetoric and Politicisation'.

3. M. Edgeworth, *Ennui* (London 1809); C.R. Maturin, *The Milesian Chief: A Romance* (London 1812). See T. Dunne, 'Representations of Rebellion: 1798 in Literature' in F.B. Smith (ed.), *Ireland, England and Australia* (Canberra and Cork 1990), pp. 15–40.

4. T. Moore, *Memoirs of Captain Rock* (London 1824).

5. M. McGrath (ed.), *Cinnlae Amhlaoibh Uí Shuíleabháin*, vol. IV (London and Dublin 1928–37), pp. 114–51.

6. E. Hay, *History of the Insurrection of the County of Wexford, AD 1798* (Dublin 1803), pp. i–v; Cullen, 'The 1798 Rebellion in Wexford: United Irish Organization, Membership, Leadership' in K. Whelan and W. Nolan (eds), *Wexford: History and Society* (Dublin 1987), p. 284. See also, M. Ó hÓgartaigh, 'Edward Hay, Wexford Historian of 1798', *Journal of the Wexford Historical Society*, no. 17, 1998–9, pp. 159–75.

7. Whelan, *The Tree of Liberty*, pp. 167–9.

8. T. Bartlett, 'Miles Byrne: United Irishman, Irish Exile and *Beau Sabreur*' in Keogh and Furlong (eds.), *The Mighty Wave*, p. 126.

9. Musgrave, *Memoirs*, vol. 1, pp. 239–40, 138, 155, 83, 94, 227, 7, 110–12.

10. Madden, *The United Irishmen: Their Lives and Times*, vol. 1 (London 1842), p. 401.

11. Madden, *United Irishmen*, 2nd edn, vol. 4 (London 1860), p. 435.

12. *Ibid.* pp. 459–61, 445, footnote.

13. TCD MS 1472; M.V. Ronan (ed.), *Personal Recollections of Wexford and Wicklow Insurgents of 1798 as collected by Rev. Br. Luke Cullen O.D.C.* (Enniscorthy 1959); *Insurgent Wicklow 1798 by Rev. Br. Luke Cullen O.D.C.* (Dublin 1948).

14. Cullen, 'Breakout of the Insurrection in the County of Wexford 1798', TCD MS 1472, f. 10; Ronan (ed.), *Personal Recollections*, pp. 18, 20; *Insurgent Wicklow*, pp. 27–8.

15. For a contrary view, see Whelan, *The Tree of Liberty*, pp. 170–2; see also A. Kinsella, '1798 Claimed for Catholics: Fr. Kavanagh, Fenianism and the Centenary Celebrations' in Keogh and Furlong (eds), *The Mighty Wave*, pp. 139–55.

16. J. Turpin, '1798, 1898 and the Political Implications of Sheppard's Monuments', *History Ireland*, VI, no. 2, 1998, pp. 44–8.

17. See Whelan, *The Tree of Liberty*, pp. 173–4; Rev. James Gordon, *History of the Rebellion in Ireland in the Year 1798* (Dublin 1801).

18. Bartlett, letter to *The Irish Times*, 15/4/1998; W.E.H. Lecky, *A History of Ireland in the Eighteenth Century*, 5 vols, vol. IV (London 1892), pp. 343–95.

19. Gordon, *History of the Rebellion*, p. 103.

20. Lecky, *History*, IV, pp. 344–5, 375–80; see D. McCartney, *W.E.H. Lecky, Historian and Politician 1838–1903* (Dublin 1994).

21. C. Dickson, *The Wexford Rising in 1798: Its Causes and Its Course* (London 1997), pp. 21–4, 15–16; P. Donovan, 'A Commentary on the Commemoration' in *A Military Tattoo Commemorating the Battle of Ross, by the Ross Battalion F.C.A., Barretts Park, New Ross, Saturday and Sunday 5th and 6th June 1948. Souvenir Programme*.

22. D. Gahan, *The People's Rising, Wexford 1798* (Dublin 1995), p. xv.

23. C. Tóibín, 'The Cause that Called You: Notes of a Native Son' in D. Bolger (ed.), *Wexford Through Its Writers* (Dublin 1992), pp. 57–74, 65.

24. T. Pakenham, *The Boer War* (London 1979); S. Heaney, *Door into the Dark* (London 1969).

25. T. Pakenham, *The Year of Liberty: The History of the Great Rebellion of 1798* (London 1969, 1992 edn), pp. 13, 138–41, 143, 198–210.

26. T. Powell, 'The Background to the Rebellion in Co. Wexford: 1790–98', MA Thesis, UCD 1970; Tom Powell, 'An Economic Factor in the Wexford Rebellion of 1798', *Studia Hibernica*, XVI, 1976, pp. 140–57. Both thesis and article are startling omissions from Kevin Whelan's bibliography in *The Tree of Liberty*.

27. Powell, 'Background', p. 195.

28. L.M. Cullen, *Anglo-Irish Trade 1660–1800* (Manchester 1968); L.M. Cullen, *An Economic History of Ireland since 1660* (London 1972).

29. Cullen, *The Emergence of Modern Ireland*.

30. Cullen, *The Emergence of Modern Ireland*, Chapter 10; 'The 1798 Rebellion in its Eighteenth-Century Context' in P.J. Corish (ed.), *Radicals, Rebels and Establishments* (Belfast 1985), pp. 91–113; 'The 1798 Rebellion in Wexford', pp. 248–95.

31. D. Gahan, 'The Estate System of County Wexford 1641–1876' in Whelan and Nolan (eds), *Wexford: History and Society*, pp. 200–21, footnote p. 528.

32. T. Jones-Hughes, 'Continuity and Change in Rural County Wexford in the Nineteenth Century' in Whelan and Nolan (eds), *Wexford: History and Society*, pp. 343, 345, 352–3.

33. K. Whelan, 'The Regional Impact of Irish Catholicism 1700–1850' in W.J. Smyth and K. Whelan (eds), *Common Ground: Essays on the Historical Geography of Ireland presented to T. Jones-Hughes* (Cork 1988), pp. 253–77.

34. K. Whelan, 'The Religious Factor in the 1798 Rebellion' in P. O'Flanagan, P. Ferguson and K. Whelan (eds), *Rural Ireland*, pp. 75, 72, 70, 77–8.

35. Cullen, 'The 1798 Rebellion in Wexford', pp. 248–95.

36. L.M. Cullen, 'The United Irishmen in Wexford' in Keogh and Furlong (eds), *The Mighty Wave*, pp. 48–64, 55; 'The 1798 Rebellion in Wexford', p. 295.

37. T. Powell, 'The United Irishmen and the Wexford Rebellion: The Sources Re-examined', *The Irish Review*, 23, 1998, pp. 127–40.

38. M. Elliott, *Partners in Revolution: The United Irishmen and France* (Yale 1982), pp. xvi, 87, 96, 231.

39. N.J. Curtin, *The United Irishmen: Popular Politics in Ulster and Dublin 1791–1798* (Oxford 1994), pp. 3, 116, 201.

CHAPTER 7

1. See S. Paseta, '1798 in 1898: The Politics of Commemoration', *The Irish Review*, no. 22, summer 1998, pp. 46–53; A. Kinsella, 'The Spirit of '98 Awakened', *Journal of the Wexford Historical Society*, no. 15, 1994–5, pp. 34–42.

2. B. Ringwood, 'Cumann Comórtha 1798: 1798 Bicentenary Association' in *Vinegar Hill Day Enniscorthy, Sunday 21st June 1998. Souvenir Record* (Enniscorthy 1998), pp. 12–13.

3. *The Irish Times*, 28/1/1997.

4.   *The Wexford Echo*, 11/6/1998.
5.   *The Irish Times*, 15/6/1998.
6.   Minute Book, 1994–1998, in Wexford County Library.
7.   F. Hanrahan, 'Making History: Wexford Public Libraries' Contribution to the Bicentennial Commemorations of the Rebellion of 1798', *An Leabharlann: The Irish Library*, 2nd series, 14, nos 3 and 4, 1998, pp. 115–19.
8.   K. Whelan, 'The United Irishmen, the Enlightenment and Popular Culture' in Dickson, Keogh and Whelan (eds), *The United Irishmen*, p. 296.
9.   Minute Book, 10/12/1994.
10. K. Whelan, 'Politicisation in County Wexford and the Origins of the 1798 Rebellion' in H. Gough and D. Dickson (eds), *Ireland and the French Revolution* (Dublin 1990), p. 175.
11. B. Cleary, 'Sowing the Whirlwind', *Journal of the Wexford Historical Society*, no. 13, 1992–3, p. 71.
12. Gahan, *The People's Rising*, Chapter IX, and footnotes pp. 320–1; Dunne, '1798: Memory, History, Commemoration'.
13. R. Musgrave, *Memoirs of the Different Rebellions in Ireland*, 4th edn (London and Dublin 1801), S.W. Myers and D.E. McKnight (eds), (Fort Wayne, Indiana and Enniscorthy 1995), pp. 425, 436. He also printed what was claimed to be an extract from Fr John Murphy's journal for 26 May, which opened, 'Began the republic of Ireland in Boolavogue …', p. 710.
14. Madden, *United Irishmen*, 3rd series, vol. IV, p. 486; Cullen, 'The 1798 Rebellion in Wexford', p. 284; Dunne, 'Ballads, Rhetoric and Politicisation', pp. 150–1.
15. Musgrave, *Memoirs*, pp. 792–5; Hay, *History*, pp. 128, following; Byrne, *Memoirs*, 1, pp. 60–2; Cullen, 'The 1798 Rebellion in Wexford', pp. 283–4; Gahan, *The People's Rising*, pp. 98–100.
16. Whelan, 'Reinterpreting the 1798 Rebellion', p. 25; Gahan, *The People's Rising*, p. 88.
17. G. Taylor, *A History of the Rise, Progress and Suppression of the Rebellion in the County of Wexford in the year 1798. To which is annexed the author's account of his captivity and merciful deliverance* (Dublin 1829), pp. 77–9.
18. *The Irish Times*, 24/4/1998.
19. Roche, *The Irish Times*, 8/4/1998.
20. In C. Póirtéir (ed.), *The Great Irish Rebellion of 1798* (Cork 1998), pp. 101–14, 102, 105, 106.
21. Whelan, 'Reinterpreting the 1798 Rebellion', p. 25; *The Fellowship of Freedom*, pp. 72–3.
22. Whelan, *The Tree of Liberty*, p. ix.
23. *The Irish Times*, 6/5/1996.
24. *Ibid.* 21/1/1998.
25. *Ibid.* 1/6/1998.
26. Meeting of Board of Directors of Comóradh '98, 13/10/1997. Wexford County Library.
27. Wexford County Library.
28. Invitation Leaflet, 'The Wexford Senate 1798–1998'.
29. B. Murray (ed.), *Epitaph of 1798: A Photographic Record of 1798 Memorials on the*

Island of Ireland and Beyond (Carrigbyrne 2002).

30. *The Irish Times*, 6/6/1998.
31. Ibid. 28/1/1997.
32. Ibid. 6/6/1998.
33. *The Guardian*, 24/5/1996.
34. B. Browne, *The Irish Times*, 15/5/1996.
35. S. Cloney, 'South-West Wexford in 1798', *Journal of the Wexford Historical Society*, no. 15, 1994, pp. 84–5.
36. *The Irish Times*, 28/1/1997.
37. Ibid. 22/5/1996.

CHAPTER 8

1. R.F. Foster, *The Irish Story: Telling Tales and Making it up in Ireland* (London 2001), pp. 230–4.
2. Review of *The Irish Story* by Tom Bartlett, *Times Literary Supplement*, 25/1/02.
3. D. Gahan, *The People's Rising*, pp. 8, xi–xii, 88, 315.
4. D. Gahan, 'The Military Planning of the 1798 Rebellion in Wexford' in Keogh and Furlong (eds), *The Mighty Wave*, pp. 100, 103, 108.
5. D. Gahan, *Rebellion! Ireland in 1798* (Dublin 1997), pp. 43, 57. The endorsement is printed on the cover.
6. Gahan, *The People's Rising*, Chapter IX, and footnotes pp. 320–1.
7. Dunne, '1798: Memory, History, Commemoration'.
8. D. Gahan, 'The Scullabogue Massacre, 1798', *History Ireland*, IV, no. 3, 1996, pp. 27–31.
9. *The Irish Times*, Letters Page, 1, 24 April and 4 May 1998.
10. D. Gahan, 'New Ross, Scullabogue and the 1798 Rebellion in South-Western Wexford', *The Past*, no. 21, 1998, pp. 3–37.
11. Whelan, 'Politicisation in County Wexford', p. 156.
12. J. Smyth, 'Interpreting the 1790s', *History Ireland*, VI, no. 2, 1998, pp. 54–8.
13. Whelan, 'Politicisation in County Wexford', pp. 160, 165, 170, 165, 166, 175.
14. Dunne, 'Popular Ballads, Revolutionary Rhetoric and Politicisation', pp. 148, 150–2.
15. K. Whelan, 'Catholics, Politicization and the 1798 Rebellion' in R. Ó Muirí (ed.), *Irish Church History Today* (Armagh 1990), pp. 68, 75.
16. J. Smyth, *The Men of No Property: Irish Radicals and Popular Politics in the Eighteenth Century* (Dublin 1992); 'Popular Politicisation, Defenderism and the Catholic Question' in Gough and Dickson (eds), *Ireland and the French Revolution*, pp. 110, 115.
17. K. Whelan, 'The United Irishmen, the Enlightenment and Popular Culture', pp. 269–96, 271–5, 285.
18. Ibid. pp. 275–84, 294.
19. Ibid. pp. 295, 275.
20. Ibid. pp. 295–6.

21. Whelan, *The Tree of Liberty*, pp. 3, 12, 31, 37–8, 40.
22. Whelan, 'The Religious Factor', pp. 67, 69, 70.
23. Whelan, *The Tree of Liberty*, pp. 99–130, 128.
24. Whelan, 'Reinterpreting the 1798 Rebellion', pp. 10, 35, 25. The criticism of the United Irishmen can be found in Whelan, 'The United Irishmen' in Dickson, Keogh and Whelan (eds), *The United Irishmen*, p. 270.
25. Whelan, 'Politicisation in County Wexford', pp. 174–5, reference 51.
26. Hay, *History*, pp. 128–33; Whelan, 'Reinterpreting the 1798 Rebellion', p. 25.
27. Press release. Wexford County Library.
28. Whelan, *Fellowship of Freedom*, pp. 72–3.
29. *Ibid.* xii, xi.
30. W.A. Maguire (ed.), *The 1798 Rebellion in Ireland: A Bicentenary Exhibition* (Belfast 1998).
31. *The Irish Times*, Weekend Supplement, 13/6/1998.
32. Whelan, *Fellowship of Freedom*, pp. 73–4; K. Whelan (ed.), *A History of Newbawn* (Newbawn 1986), pp. 50–2.
33. Whelan, *Fellowship of Freedom*, p. x.
34. *The Irish Times*, 21/1/1998.
35. Whelan, 'Reinterpreting the 1798 Rebellion', p. 35.
36. Whelan, *Fellowship of Freedom*, p. 74.
37. *Seanad Éireann Debates*, vol. 157, col. 929, 9/12/1998.
38. Letter from Martin Fraser, Head of Corporate Affairs, Department of the Taoiseach, 23/12/02.
39. Cited by R.F. Foster, *The Irish Story*, pp. 225–6.
40. *Seanad Éireann Debates*, vol. 157, cols 928–57.
41. Whelan, 'Reinterpreting the 1798 Rebellion', pp. 34–5.
42. *Dáil Éireann Debates*, vol. 157, cols 928–57, 9/12/98.
43. In briefing material for reply to a parliamentary question by An Taoiseach, 15/12/98.
44. This dominance is continued in the long-awaited conference proceedings, the massive *1798: A Bicentenary Perspective*, published too late to be considered properly in my analysis. Although Kevin Whelan is one of four editors, he was given a 'commission' by the others (Thomas Bartlett, David Dickson and Dáire Keogh) to provide commentaries introducing each of the eight sections into which the thirty-three papers were divided. These commentaries are described carefully in a preface from all four editors as 'an extended personal review' of 1798 studies, and thus 'do not necessarily reflect the views of the editors at large'. This very odd procedure may explain why the book is given the title *A Bicentenary Perspective* rather than one reflecting the very different (and often excellent) 'bicentenary perspectives' which it offers. Once again, Whelan's viewpoint is presented as authoritative, guiding the reader, implying (wrongly) that all of the contributors support his particular position. He repeats many of his old historiographical arguments, but avoids meaningful discussion on the Wexford Rebellion. Indeed, the name 'Wexford' doesn't appear even once in the table of contents, as if it conjures up scenes that can't be accommodated to the Enlightenment

model. (In the 700–page text, which laudably has much on the international dimension, Wexford is covered, once again by Gahan, in less than 17 pages.) Whelan has a brusque, dismissive way with any dissident voice. Predictably, he does not engage with the argument of what he calls my 'plethora of recent articles', but is content to cite one in a footnote as an example of the 'mechanistic, facile or even coarse ways' in which, he believes, 'the vexed issue of sectarianism' is still treated. Such inability or unwillingness to engage meaningfully with opposing viewpoints – a process fundamental to historical writing – is disappointing.

45. Whelan, *The Tree of Liberty*, p. ix.
46. Draft submission to An Taoiseach, January 1994. Wexford County Library.
47. *Dáil Éireann Debates*, vol. 493, cols 1439–40, 3/7/96.
48. *The Irish Times*, 1/8/98.
49. *Dáil Éireann Debates*, vol. 472, cols 21–2, 26/11/96.
50. *Ibid.* vol. 476, cols 499–500, 12/3/97.
51. *Ibid.* vol. 483, cols 995–8, 26/11/97.
52. *Ibid.* vol. 484, cols 217–20, 3/12/97. *Seanad Éireann Debates*, vol. 157, cols 928–57, 9/12/98.
53. *The Irish Times*, 21/5/1996.
54. Minute Book, Historians and Librarians Committee, 7/1/98, County Library.
55. *Dáil Éireann Debates*, vol. 493, cols 1439–40, 3/7/98.

CHAPTER 9

1. See Pakenham, *The Year of Liberty*, especially part II, Chapter III; A.T.Q. Stewart, *The Summer Soldiers: The 1798 Rebellion in Antrim and Down* (Belfast 1995).
2. Musgrave, *Memoirs*, p. 404.
3. J. Alexander, *Some Account of the first Symptoms of the Late Rebellion in the County of Kildare and in the Adjoining Kings County, with a Succinct Narrative of some of the most Remarkable Passages in the Rise and Progress of the Rebellion in the County of Wexford, especially in the Vicinity of Ross* etc. (Dublin 1800), p. 81.
4. J. Alexander, 'To Whom it May Concern', *Walker's Hibernian Magazine*, November 1798, pp. 793–8.
5. T. Bartlett, 'Bearing Witness: Female Evidence in Courts Martial Convened to Suppress the 1798 Rebellion' in D. Keogh and N. Furlong (eds), *Women of 1798* (Dublin 1998).
6. D. Lindsay, 'The Rebellion Papers', *History Ireland*, VI, no. 2, 1998, pp. 18–22, 22.
7. L.M. Cullen, 'The 1798 Rebellion in Wexford', pp. 262–9.
8. Pakenham, *The Year of Liberty*, p. 14.
9. Gahan, *The People's Rising*, p. xv.
10. Fennell, 'Against Revisionism', p. 187.
11. Prim MSS, Irish Folklore Department, UCD Box 4, ND; the text is in D. Ó hÓgáin (ed.), *Duanaire Osraíoch* (Dublin 1980), p. 39.
12. Ó hÓgáin, *Duanaire Osraíoch*, p. 39.

13.   Alexander, *Account*, p. 95.

14.   Dunne, '"Tá Gaedhilch Bhocht Craidhté"', pp. 93–111.

15.   B. Ó Buachalla, 'Irish Jacobite Poetry', *The Irish Review*, no. 12, 1992, pp. 40–9.

16.   Whelan, *The Tree of Liberty*, p. 95; see Smyth, *The Men of No Property*, pp. 31–2 for a different view.

17.   Council Book of the Corporation of New Ross 1732–1841, 29/6/1799.

18.   J. Doran, *A Little History of St Mary's and its Memorials* (New Ross 1997), p. 22.

19.   L.P. Ó Caithnia, 'The Man from Callan' in S.E. Ó Cearbhaill (ed.), *A Man Raised Up: Recollections and Reflections on Venerable Edmund Rice* (Dublin 1994), pp. 13–24, 18; D. Keogh, *Edmund Rice, 1765–1844* (Dublin 1996), pp. 29, 34.

20.   R. Roche (ed.), *Here's their Memory: A Record of the United Irish in Wexford in 1798* (Wexford 1997), p. 83.

CHAPTER 10

1.   P.H. Hore (ed.), *History of the Town and County of Wexford, Vol. 1, Old and New Ross. Compiled principally from the State Papers, the Public Records and Manuscripts of the late Herbert F. Hore, Esq. of Pole House in that County* (London 1900). Reprint Oxford 1978, with an introduction by R.D. Edwards, pp. 42, 50–3. This detailed documentary history is invaluable.

2.   *Ibid.* pp. 42, 44, footnotes.

3.   *Ibid.* pp. 50–5, 120–1.

4.   *Ibid.* pp. 91–7, 55–62.

5.   *Ibid.* pp. 58–60. For a more recent edition and translation of this poem, see H. Shields in *The Long Room*, 12–13 (1975/6), pp. 24–53. A long extract of this can be found in Deane (ed.), *The Field Day Anthology*, vol. 1, pp. 150–2.

6.   A. Thomas, *The Walled Towns of Ireland,* vol. 2 (Dublin 1992), pp. 175–9.

7.   Hore, *History*, pp. 216, 211, 217, 232, 238, 51.

8.   *Cinnlae Amhlaoibh*, IV, pp. 114–151.

9.   Maturin, *The Milesian Chief.* See especially, vol. 111, pp. 50–87.

10.   Hore, *History*, pp. 231–7, 299, 312, 321–4, 331, 336.

11.   *Ibid.* pp. 360–6, 371–3.

12.   *Ibid.* Chapters XVII and XVIII; Powell, 'Background', p. 29.

13.   Hore, *History*, pp. 385, 394–6.

14.   *Ibid.* p. 110.

15.   *Ibid.* p. 117.

16.   A. Young, *A Tour in Ireland with General Observations on the Present State of that Kingdom, made in the Years 1776, 1777, and 1778. And Brought Down to the End of 1779*, 2nd edn, vol. 1 (London 1780), pp. 81–5.

17.   Powell, 'Background', pp. 22, 85–127.

18.   K. Milne (ed.), 'The Elmes Letters', *The Past*, no. 17, 1990, pp. 55–70, 59–60.

19.   Alexander, *Account*, p. 41.

20.   Hore, *History*, p. 112. Charles Tottenham to his daughter Ann, July 1795, Tottenham MSS.

21. P. Luckombe, *A Tour Through Ireland in 1778* (London 1798), p. 40.

22. Rev. James Hall, *Tour through Ireland,* 2 vols (London 1813), pp. 98–111.

23. M. Banim, *The Croppy: A Tale of 1798,* 3 vols, vol. III (London 1828), p. 226.

24. E. Browne and T. Wickham (eds), *Lewis's Wexford* (Enniscorthy 1983), p. 120.

25. Alexander, *Account*, pp. 41–5.

26. *Ibid.* p. 42.

27. Hore, *History*, p. 116, footnote.

28. Alexander, *Account*, pp. 42–3.

29. J.B. Trotter, *Walks through Ireland in the years 1812, 1814 and 1817* (London 1819), pp. 52, 82–99.

30. Wall, *Catholic Ireland*, pp. 77, 88.

31. Whelan, 'The Regional Impact'.

32. K. Whelan, 'The Catholic Community in Eighteenth Century Wexford' in T.P. Power and K. Whelan (eds), *Endurance and Emergence: Catholics in Ireland in the Eighteenth Century* (Dublin 1990), pp. 129–70.

33. Powell, 'Background', pp. 24–5.

34. T.C. Butler, *Near Restful Waters: The Augustinians in New Ross and Clonmines* (Dublin 1975), pp. 99–102.

35. *Ibid.* pp. 102–03.

36. Keogh, *Edmund Rice*, p. 34.

37. T. McGrath, *Religious Renewal and Reform in the Pastoral Ministry of Bishop James Doyle* (Dublin 1999), pp. 1, 2, 242 (footnote 10).

38. Family tradition. A member of the family still occupies the Irishtown house under a Tottenham lease.

39. Alexander, *Account*, p. 47.

40. T. Cloney, *A Personal Narrative of those Transactions in the County of Wexford, in which the Author was Engaged During the Awful Period of 1798* (Dublin 1832), pp. 12, 22.

41. *Ibid.* p. 22.

42. D. Gahan, 'The Estate System of County Wexford', p. 528.

43. Whelan, *The Tree of Liberty*, p. 10.

44. Whelan, 'The Religious Factor', pp. 78, 73.

45. Whelan, 'The Catholic Community', p. 142.

46. Lecky, *History*, IV, pp. 378–9.

47. T. Jones-Hughes, 'Continuity and Change', pp. 342–72; Gahan, 'The Estate System of County Wexford', pp. 200–21.

48. Cloney, *Narrative*, p. 3.

49. Cullen, *The Emergence of Modern Ireland*, p. 216.

50. Whelan, 'The Religious Factor', p. 72.

51. Whelan, 'The Catholic Community', p. 131.

52. Whelan, 'The Religious Factor', pp. 72–75.

53. T. Jones-Hughes, 'Continuity and Change', pp. 355–72.

54. Whelan, 'The Regional Impact'.

55. Whelan, 'The Role of the Catholic Priest in the 1798 Rebellion in County Wexford' in Whelan and Nolan (eds), *Wexford: History and Society*.

56. *The Reply of the Right Rev. Doctor Caulfield, Roman Catholic Bishop, and of the Roman Catholic Clergy of Wexford to the Misrepresentations of Sir Richard Musgrave Bart* (Dublin 1801), pp. 5–6, 33.

57. See G. FitzGerald, 'Estimates for Baronies of Minimum Level of Irish Speaking among Successive Decennial Cohorts 1771–81 to 1861–71', *Proceedings of the Royal Irish Academy*, 84, c. 3, pp. 117–55.

58. 'Bishop Sweetman's Visitation Book, 1753', Appendix no. 6 in W.H. Grattan Flood, *History of the Dioceses of Ferns* (Waterford 1916), pp. 212–14.

59. Trotter, *Walks through Ireland*, pp. 39, 82–3. See also, S. de Vál, 'Oidhreacht Ghaelach Loch Garman', *Irisleabhar Mhá Nuad*, 1992, pp. 75–107, for an important overview.

60. W.S. Mason, *A Statistical Account or Parochial Survey of Ireland, drawn up from the Communication of the Clergy*, vol. 1 (Dublin 1814), pp. 1–9, 456; de Vál, 'Oidhreacht Ghaelach', p. 107.

61. C. Anderson, *Historical Sketches of the Native Irish and their Descendants, Illustrative of their Past and Present State with regard to Literature, Education and Oral Instruction*, 2nd edn (Edinburgh and London 1830), pp. 220, 230.

62. MSS book embossed 'Thomas Dunne Courtnacuddy' on the front and '1875' on the back. Unpaginated. In private possession.

63. de Vál, 'Oidhreacht Ghaelach', pp. 96–100.

64. N. Williams (ed.), *Riocard Bairéad: Amhráin* (Dublin 1978).

65. B. Ó Buachalla, 'Irish Jacobitism and Irish Nationalism: The Literary Evidence' in M. O'Dea and K. Whelan (eds), *Nations and Nationalities: France, Britain, Ireland and the Eighteenth Century Context* (Oxford 1995), pp. 110, 108, 111, 114.

66. Ó Buachalla, *Aisling Ghéar* (Dublin 1996), pp. 631–8.

67. T. Ó Murchú, 'Micheál Óg Ó Longáin (1766–1827)', MA UCC 1940, Poem B1.

68. Ó hÓgáin, *Duanaire Osraíoch*, pp. 36–7, 91–4.

69. Kavanagh, *Popular History*, pp. 303–4; G.F. Handcock, 'Reminiscences of a Fugitive Loyalist in 1798', *The English Historical Review*, 1, 1886, pp. 536–44, 536–7.

70. Prim MSS, Department of Folklore, UCD Box 4, Folder 1.

71. G. Taylor, *A History of the Rise, Progress and Suppression of the Rebellion*, pp. 10–13.

72. Handcock, 'Reminiscences', pp. 536–7.

73. Powell, 'Background', pp. 70–9.

74. *Rambles through Ireland by a French Emigrant. Translated from the French of Monsieur de Latocnaye by an Irishman* (Cork 1798).

75. Lecky, *History*, vol. IV, pp. 343–4.

76. Whelan, 'The Religious Factor', pp. 67–8.

77. Cullen, 'The United Irishmen in Wexford', p. 56.

78. Whelan, 'The Religious Factor', pp. 67–8.

79. *Ibid.* p. 68.

80. J. Barber, 'Recollections of the Summer of 1798', Wexford County Library, Ts.

81. Jane Adams' narrative, dated May 1798, was published as an appendix to T. Crofton Croker's, *Researches in the South of Ireland 1818–1822* (London 1824), pp. 347–85, 355.

82. 'Diary of my grandmother, Elizabeth Richards, copied from the original manu-

script found Huis Ten Duick 1917', NLI microfilm 6486.

83. Smyth, *The Men of No Property*, p. 113.

84. T. Bartlett, 'Defenders and Defenderism in 1795', *Irish Historical Studies*, XXIV, no. 95, May 1985, pp. 373–94, 376–8.

85. See his contribution to T. Bartlett, D. Dickson, D. Keogh and K. Whelan (eds), *1798: A Bicentenary Perspective* (Dublin 2003).

86. P. Hennessy, *Davidstown Courtnacuddy: A Wexford Parish* (1982), pp. 39–40; J.D. Kernan, 'Devereux of the Leap, County Wexford and of Utica, New York', *The Irish Genealogist*, 3, no. 5, November 1972, pp. 23–39.

87. Whelan, 'Politicisation in County Wexford'; Cleary, 'Sowing the Whirlwind', *Journal of the Wexford Historical Society'*, no. 13, 1992–3, pp. 9–80.

88. Hay, *History*, p. vi.

89. Cloney, *Narrative*, p. 8.

90. S. Clark and J. Donnelly (eds), *Irish Peasants: Violence and Political Unrest 1780–1914* (Madison, Wisconsin 1983), p. 16.

91. Cullen, 'The 1798 Rebellion', p. 278; 'The United Irishmen', pp. 54–5.

92. Powell, 'The United Irishmen and the Wexford Rebellion'; 'Background', pp. 140–60.

93. G.H. Binions, 'John Kelly' in G.H. Binions (ed.), *1798–1998. Killanne-Rathnure: A Local History* (Killanne 1997), pp. 1–17.

94. NAI Rebellion Papers 620/31/101; Powell, 'The United Irishmen and the Wexford Rebellion', pp. 132–3; 'Background', pp. 148–9.

95. Handcock, 'Reminiscences', p. 238.

96. Madden, *United Irishmen*, vol. 1 (1847), p. 402; see Cloney, *Narrative*, p. 6; Powell, 'Background', pp. 144–5.

97. Powell, 'Background', pp. 153–8.

98. *Reply*, p. 49.

99. 'The Elmes Letters', p. 61.

100. IFCS 901 and 293.

101. Whelan, 'The Religious Factor', p. 69.

102. Hay, *History*, pp. 59–60; Musgrave, *Memoirs*, pp. 711–3, 716–9; Cloney, *Narrative*, p. 15.

103. Whelan, 'Reinterpreting the 1798 Rebellion', pp. 18, 20.

104. Whelan, 'The Religious Factor', p. 69.

105. Byrne, *Memoirs*, 1, pp. 8–9.

106. Hay, *History*, pp. 59–60, 67–8.

107. Byrne, *Memoirs*, 1, pp. 239–40, 46, 189, 126.

108. Cloney, *Narrative*, pp. 8–11.

CHAPTER 11

1. Cloney, *Narrative*, pp. 8–11.

2. Byrne, *Memoirs*, 1, pp. 49–53.

3. Ronan (ed.), *Personal Recollections*, p. 18.

4. T. Bartlett, K. Dawson and D. Keogh (eds), *Rebellion: A Television History of 1798*

(Dublin 1998), p. 112.

5. C. Tilly, *The Vendée* (London 1964); Powell, 'Background'; Powell, 'The United Irishmen and the Wexford Rebellion', pp. 135–6.

6. J.T. Gilbert, *Documents Relating to Ireland 1795–1804* (1893, IUP reprint, Shannon 1970), p. 171.

7. P.M. Jones, *The Peasantry in the French Revolution* (Cambridge 1988), pp. xiii, 67, 75, 77, 227.

8. D. Sutherland, *The Chouans. The Social Origins of Popular Counter-Revolution in Upper Brittany 1770–1796* (Oxford 1982), p. 6.

9. C. Ramsey, *The Ideology of the Great Fear: The Soissonnais in 1789* (Baltimore and London 1992), pp. xvi–xx.

10. Sutherland, *The Chouans, passim.*

11. Cloney, *Narrative*, pp. 12–16 (my italics).

12. *Ibid.* pp. 15–16.

13. Whelan, 'The Religious Factor', pp. 72–5.

14. NLI MS 25004, fos. 4–5.

15. Taylor, *History*, pp. 105–6.

16. Musgrave, *Memoirs*, pp. 350–1.

17. NLI MS 17,795 (4).

18. Barber, 'Recollections', p. 17.

19. NLI MS 25004, fos. 4–5.

20. Gordon, *History of the Rebellion*, pp. 169–70, 405–6.

21. *Ibid.* p. 167.

22. Cloney, *Narrative*, Appendix, pp. 237–76.

23. NLI MS 25004, f. 5.

24. Cloney, *Narrative*, Appendix.

25. TCD MS 873, f. 811.

26. 'The Elmes Letters', p. 63.

27. J. Ranson (ed.), 'A '98 diary by Mrs. Barbara Newton Lett, Killaligan, Enniscorthy', *The Past*, no. 5, 1949, pp. 117–49, 144, 142.

28. Cloney, *Narrative*, p. 18.

29. Gahan, *The People's Rising*, p. 65.

30. *Ibid.* p. 60.

31. Cloney, *Narrative*, p. 21.

32. *Ibid.* pp. 20–1; Byrne, *Memoirs*, I, p. 94.

33. Gahan, *The People's Rising*, p. 71.

34. Byrne, *Memoirs*, I, pp. 71, 86–90, 93, 95, 138, 121, 131.

35. Gahan, *The People's Rising*, pp. 85–9; Cloney, *Narrative*, pp. 31, 52–4.

36. Hay, *History*, pp. 107–8.

37. *Ibid.* pp. 125–6.

38. Gahan, *People's Rising*, p. 88.

39. Hay, *History*, p. 129.

40. See Dunne, 'Ballads, Rhetoric and Politicisation', pp. 150–2.

41. Dickson, *The Wexford Rising*, p. 77.

42. Hay, *History*, pp. 142–6; 'Diary of Elizabeth Richards', 1 June.

43. Cloney, *Narrative*, pp. 25–7.
44. Cullen, 'The 1798 Rebellion', p. 283.
45. Cloney, *Narrative*, p. 30.
46. Musgrave, *Memoirs*, pp. 362–3; Hay, *History*, p. 123.
47. Gahan, *The People's Rising*, p. 76.
48. *Ibid.* pp. 102–6.
49. *Ibid.* p. 97.
50. Gahan, 'New Ross, Scullabogue and the 1798 Rebellion', pp. 4–5, 25, footnote 14.
51. Whelan, 'The Religious Factor', p. 72.
52. Gahan, 'New Ross, Scullabogue and the 1798 Rebellion', p. 10.
53. Musgrave, *Memoirs*, pp. 775, 779–80, 402, 781–3; NAI Rebellion Papers 620/3/24/2.
54. NAI Rebellion Papers 620/3/24/2. Evidence of Richard Power.
55. *Ibid.*
56. Gahan, 'New Ross, Scullabogue and the 1798 Rebellion', p. 10 and footnotes 102 and 104, p. 28.
57. S. Cloney, 'South West Wexford in 1798', pp. 87–8; Whelan, 'Reinterpreting the 1798 Rebellion', p. 29.
58. NAI Rebellion Papers 620/3/24/2.
59. Gahan, 'New Ross, Scullabogue and the 1798 Rebellion', p. 10.
60. Whelan, 'Reinterpreting the 1798 Rebellion', pp. 28–9.
61. D.W. Goff, *Divine Protection*, pp. 11, 21.
62. NLI MS 17, 795 (3).
63. NAI Rebellion Papers 620/3/24/2, fos. 5–25.
64. NLI MS 17,795 (1), Trial of the Parles.
65. NAI Rebellion Papers 620/3/24/2/, fos. 5–25.
66. *Ibid.*
67. NLI MS 17, 795 (3).
68. NAI Rebellion Papers 620/3/24/2, fos. 5–25.
69. Musgrave, *Memoirs*, pp. 777–8.
70. Caulfield, *Reply*, pp. 47–50.
71. Musgrave, *Memoirs*, pp. 777–8.
72. *Ibid.* pp. 780–2.
73. *Ibid.* p. 778.
74. Cloney, *Narrative*, pp. 31–2.
75. Whelan, 'The Religious Factor', p. 72.
76. Hay, *History*, pp. 140–1.
77. K. Milne, 'The Elmes Letters', pp. 62–3.
78. Alexander, *Account*, pp. 41–5, 27, *passim*.
79. *Ibid.* pp. 20, 26.
80. K. Milne, 'The Elmes Letters', pp. 59–60.
81. Alexander, *Account*, pp. 25–9.
82. Donovan, 'Commentary', p. 9.
83. TCD MS 873, f. 800.
84. W.H. Maxwell, *History of the Irish Rebellion in 1798* (London 1845), p. 119, fn.

85. Alexander, *Account*, pp. 22–3, 31, 53.
86. TCD MS 871, fos. 18–19.
87. Alexander, *Account*, p. 40.
88. *Ibid.* pp. 35–7, 47–9.
89. Pakenham, *The Year of Liberty*, p. 194; Heaney, 'Requiem for the Croppies'.
90. Alexander, *Account*, p. 37.
91. HO 100/77, fos. 23–32; J.F. Maurice (ed.), *The Diary of Sir John Moore*, vol. I (London 1904), pp. 294, 303.
92. Alexander, *Account*, pp. 32–3, 38–9.

CHAPTER 12

1.   Gordon, *History of the Rebellion*, pp. 141–2.
2.   Madden, *United Irishmen*, 3rd series, vol. IV, p. 391.
3.   J. Roche, *Statements and Observations on Cases that Occurred in Cork, Wexford and Wicklow* (Dublin 1799), p. 36.
4.   Taylor, *History*, pp. 56–9.
5.   Cloney, *Narrative*, p. 39.
6.   Alexander, *Account*, pp. 46, 85, 119, 121.
7.   Cloney, *Narrative*, pp. 33–4; Hay, *History*, pp. 148–9.
8.   Musgrave, *Memoirs*, p. 384; Alexander, *Account*, p. 49; TCD MS 871, fos. 18–19.
9.   Musgrave, *Memoirs*, pp. 385, 792.
10. Roche, *Statements and Observations*, pp. 36–9; Cloney, *Narrative*, p. 40; Alexander, *Account*, p. 128.
11. Alexander, *Account*, p. 89.
12. Dickson, *The Wexford Rising*, p. 111; Cloney, *Narrative*, p. 37; Hay, *History*, p. 158.
13. Gahan has 'William Boxwell of Sarshill', a farmer, leading the attack through Priory Gate and still involved with Cloney in trying to meet the counter-attack of General Johnson' *(The People's Rising*, pp. 8, 122, 126, 127, 131, 132). It is difficult to trace this in his references, but Cloney, *Narrative*, p. 41, has no mention of William Boxwell, but says that 'Mr. John Boxwell of Sarshill, a Protestant gentleman of great respectability … was killed early in the day.' In *Rebellion!* (p. 62) Gahan changes to John Boxwell, but depicts him as active throughout the battle. Alexander mentions the death of 'one Boxwell, formerly of the Royal Irish artillery' late in the battle, p. 84.
14. Cloney, *Narrative*, p. 36.
15. Hay, *History*, pp. 150–1.
16. Cloney, *Narrative*, p. 41, *passim*.
17. NAI Rebellion Papers, 620/38/62; 620/38/235.
18. Hay, *History*, pp. 150–1.
19. Cloney, *Narrative*, p. 40 said 13 hours; Major Vesey also had 13 hours, HO 100/77 fos. 82–3; Captain Bloomfield, NLI MS 24,957 had 11 hours; A letter by 'F.R.' from New Ross on 20 July, in J. Jones, *An Impartial Narrative of each Engagement which Took Place between His Majesty's Forces and the Rebels during the Irish Rebellion*

of 1798, 4th edn (Dublin 1800), pp. 38–41, had 12 hours; Taylor, *History*, citing an artillery officer who took part, also had 12 hours; George Hornick likewise, TCD MS 871, fos. 18–19; Alexander said that the real action started at 5 a.m. and ended at 2.30, with a mopping up operation lasting another few hours, *Account*, pp. 54, 64. Gahan, however brought forward all the main phases of the battle, fitting his account of Scullabogue, and had it end at one o'clock. Once again it is difficult to find the basis for this in the cited sources.

20. NLI MS 24,957. HO 100/77 fos. 76, 82–3. J. Tyrell speculates that there may have been 'some light isolated showers' but if so, no-one noticed them in the heat of battle; J. Tyrell, *Weather and Warfare: A Climatic History of the 1798 Rebellion* (Cork 2001), pp. 36–7.

21. Alexander, *Account*, p. 70.

22. Cloney, *Narrative*, p. 34.

23. HO 100/77 fos. 82–3. Johnston, supported by Crawford, claimed to have paraded his men at 2 a.m. and to be preparing an attack when the rebel assault came; *ibid.* fos. 72, 74.

24. Roche, *Statements and Observation*, p. 36; Cloney, *Narrative*, pp. 34–5; Maxwell, *History*, p. 117.

25. Musgrave, *Memoirs*, pp. 382–4; Maxwell, *History*, p. 117.

26. 'Diary of Elizabeth Richards', 19 June. P. Donovan agreed with this. See 'Commentary', p. 26. It is also possible to infer it from Byrne's comments, *Memoirs*, I, p. 126. Cloney claimed that he would have opposed the deposing of Harvey, had he been present, still having 'every confidence' in him, and believing it was important, 'to have a Protestant in command amongst us', *Narrative*, pp. 54–6.

27. Alexander, *Account*, p. 70; Jones, *Impartial Narrative*, p. 39; Roche, *Statements and Observations*, p. 36.

28. HO 100/77 fos. 82–3; NAI Rebellion Papers, 620/38/62; HO 100/77, fos. 126–7.

29. Cloney, *Narrative*, p. 38.

30. Alexander, *Account*, pp. 66, 71–2.

31. Musgrave, *Memoirs*, pp. 391–2.

32. NIA MS 620/70/6.

33. Cloney, *Narrative*, pp. 37–8.

34. Byrne, *Memoirs*, I, p. 76.

35. Roche, *Statements and Observations,* pp. 36–9.

36. 'A '98 diary', p. 144.

37. Cloney, *Narrative*, p. 37.

38. HO 100/77 f. 72.

39. *Ibid.* fos. 82–3; (Vesey 'to a friend', undated).

40. Maxwell, *History*, p. 119, footnote.

41. Alexander, *Account*, pp. 56, 84, 64–5; HO 100/77 fos. 82–3.

42. Alexander, *Account*, pp. 82, 78.

43. NLI MS 24,957.

44. Musgrave, *Memoirs*, p. 385; Taylor, *History*, p. 59; Maxwell, *History*, p. 118 footnote.

45. Pakenham, *The Year of Liberty*, p. 207; Bartlett, Dickson and Keogh, *Rebellion*, p. 119.

46. Alexander, *Account*, p. 83.

47. *Ibid.* pp. 62, 81–2.

48. Gahan, *The People's Rising*, p. 131.

49. *Ibid.* p. 320.

50. Cloney, *Narrative*, pp. 44, 61, 216, 218. In his 1843 letter to Madden, Cloney citing Alexander claimed 'that above seventy persons were thus burned in Ross', but did not claim that they were wounded. Madden, 3rd series, vol. IV, pp. 459–61.

51. Hay, *History*, p. 153.

52. Alexander, *Account*, p. 88.

53. Taylor, *History*, p. 60; Hay, *History*, p. 160.

54. Alexander, *Account*, pp. 73, 86, 111–12, 80–1, 110, *passim*.

55. *Ibid.* pp. 77, 60, 52.

56. *Ibid.* pp. 77–80.

57. *Ibid.* pp. 64, 69, 90.

58. *Ibid.* pp. 58, 93, 99, 119.

59. *Ibid.* pp. 54–5, 61, 119.

60. Cloney, *Narrative*, pp. 31–40; Lecky, *History*, IV, pp. 388–403; 'Zisca', 'Remarks on Street Fighting', *The United Service Journal*, 1835, part III, p. 225; Alexander, *Account*, pp. 56–7.

61. Alexander, *Account*, pp. 63–4.

62. Roche, *Statements and Observations*, pp. 36–9.

63. Cloney, *Narrative*, pp. 38–9.

64. Roche, *Statements and Observations*, pp. 36–9.

65. Alexander, *Account*, pp. 80–1, 53, *passim*; for other evidence that corroborates Alexander's timetable, see references 69 and 71; for Gahan, see *The People's Rising*, pp. 130–1; 'New Ross, Scullabogue and the 1798 Rebellion', p. 12.

66. Alexander, *Account*, p. 41.

67. *Ibid.* p. 37; Musgrave, *Memoirs*, pp. 387–8; Hay, *History*, p. 151. Johnson asked for a general court-martial to charge the five officers who made 'a precipitate retreat'. HO 100/77 fos. 108–13.

68. Alexander, *Account*, pp. 89–90; See also Lecky, *History*, IV, pp. 399–400.

69. At Waterford, 6/8/1799, NAI MS 620/6/70/5.

70. *Ibid.*

71. Hay, *History*, p. 151; Musgrave, *Memoirs*, p. 385; NLI MS 24,957. The same charge is made in the contemporary Gaelic poem, 'An Caol Each Ruadh' in J. O'Daly (ed.), *The Poets and Poetry of Munster*, 3rd edn (Dublin 1860), pp. 64–9.

72. Alexander, *Account*, pp. 65, 63.

73. Cloney, *Narrative*, pp. 39–40.

74. Musgrave, *Memoirs*, p. 385; Maxwell, *History*, p. 118.

75. Alexander, *Account*, p. 80.

76. Taylor, *History*, pp. 56–9.

77. Alexander, *Account*, pp. 61, 81–2.

78. Donovan, 'Commentary', p. 20.

79. Mrs 'H.R. ...' , 'Cursory Remarks on Board the *Friendship*', *The Asiatic Journal*, VIII, 1819, p. 238; 'Zisca', 'Remarks on Street Fighting', p. 225; Cloney, *Narrative*,

pp. 39–40.

80. Alexander, *Account*, pp. 83–4.
81. NLI MS 24,957. Johnson singled out Bloomfield for praise. HO 100/77, fos. 108–13.
82. Cloney, *Narrative*, pp. 40–3; TCD MS 871, fos. 18–19; Alexander, *Account*, pp. 64, 85.
83. Alexander, *Account*, pp. 65–6.
84. Alexander, 'To Whom it May Concern', pp. 793–8.
85. Alexander, *Account*, pp. 47, 56–7, 59–60.
86. Prim MSS, Irish Folklore Department, UCD Box 4; Ó hÓgáin, *Duanaire Osraíoch*, p. 39.
87. *Ibid.* footnote, pp. 95–6. On the seventeenth-century tradition, see Dunne, 'The Gaelic Response'.
88. See Dunne, 'Tá Gaedhil Bhocht Cráidhte'.
89. D. Ó Donnchá (ed.), *Filíocht Mháire Bhuídhe Ní Laoghaire* (Dublin 1931), pp. 37–9, 55–8, *passim*.

CHAPTER 13

1. See N. Ní Shéaghdha, 'Maideann Luain Chíngcíise', *Éigse*, vol. I, part III, pp. 191–5; 'Sliabh na mBan' in T. Ó Concheanainn (ed.), *Nua Dhuanaire, Chuid III* (Dublin 1981), pp. 1–2.
2. Hay, *History*, p. 155.
3. Whelan (ed.), *Newbawn*, pp. 54–5.
4. S. Cloney, 'The Hessians' in *Journal of the Wexford Historical Society*, no. 14, 1992–3, pp. 113–28.
5. Dunne, 'Tá Gaedhil Bhocht Cráidhte'.
6. T.J. Howell, *The Complete Collection of State Trials*, vol. XVII (London 1820), pp. 1138–90.
7. NLI MS 17,795 (1); TCD MS 873, f. 816.
8. Alexander, *Account*, pp. 115–16.
9. Caulfield, *Reply*, pp. 41–2; Musgrave, *Memoirs*, p. 400.
10. NLI MS 17,795 (3). Trial of Michael Quigley, 13 September 1799.
11. TCD MS 871, fos. 18–19.
12. Goff, *Divine Protection*, p. 21.
13. *Nua Dhuanaire, III*, pp. 1–2.
14. Gahan, 'The Scullabogue Massacre, 1798', *History Ireland*, IV, no. 3, 1996, pp. 27–31.
15. NLI MS 17,795 (1).
16. W.J. Fitzpatrick, *The Sham Squire*, 3rd edn (1866), pp. 179–80.
17. Cloney, *Narrative*, p. 44; Cloney, 'South West Wexford in 1798', p. 118.
18. Dickson, *Rising*, p. 122, fn. 1. Citing MS account of Mr Charles Lett, in private hands.
19. Jones, *Impartial Narrative*, pp. 38–41.
20. Musgrave, *Memoirs*, pp. 781–2 (Grandy); NLI MS 17,795 (3) (Mills); 17,795 (1) (James O'Leary and John Keeffe); 17,795 (3) (Patrick Furlong and Michael Quigley); 17,795 (5) (Patrick Kirwan).

21. Hay, *History*, p. 156.
22. Cloney, *Narrative*, p. 44.
23. NLI MS 17,795 (3) (trials of Patrick Furlong and Daniel Sullivan).
24. Musgrave, *Memoirs*, pp. 788–9.
25. NLI MS 17,795 (3).
26. Musgrave, *Memoirs*, p. 786.
27. *Ibid.* pp. 781–3; Madden, *United Irishmen*, 4th series, 2nd edn, vol. 4 (London 1857–60), pp. 491–2.
28. Gahan, 'The Scullabogue Massacre, 1798', p. 30.
29. Jones, *Impartial Narrative*, pp. 291–5.
30. Musgrave, *Memoirs*, pp. 781–3.
31. *Ibid.* pp. 777–8; Caulfield, *Reply*, pp. 47–50.
32. NLI MS 17,795 (1) Patrick Kirwan at the trials of John Keeffe (16/3/99) and James Leary (27/6/99).
33. *Ibid.* Trial of Thomas and Nicholas Parle, 25/4/1799.
34. NLI MS 17,795 (2), trial of Patrick Furlong, 12/8/99; Musgrave, *Memoirs*, pp. 788–9.
35. Jones, *Impartial Narrative*, pp. 296–300; Musgrave, *Memoirs*, p. 400. Cruikshank's etching was published in Maxwell's *History*; see Maguire, *The 1798 Rebellion*, pp. 214, 218.
36. NLI MS 17,795 (1), Patrick Kirwan.
37. Musgrave, *Memoirs*, pp. 788–9.
38. *Ibid.* p. 789.
39. NLI MS 17.795 (3); Jones *Impartial Narrative*, p. 298.
40. Gahan, 'New Ross, Scullabogue and the 1798 Rebellion', pp. 29–32.
41. Musgrave's list is in *Memoirs*, pp. 734–55; Taylor's in *History*, pp. 64–73. The quote is from Musgrave, p. 752. See Gahan, 'New Ross, Scullabogue and the 1798 Rebellion', p. 10, for the targeting of families.
42. Musgrave, *Memoirs*, pp. 734–55.
43. TCD MS 873, f. 815; NLI MS 17,795 (6).
44. Gahan, 'New Ross, Scullabogue and the 1798 Rebellion', p. 28, fn. 104.
45. NLI MS 17,795 (3).
46. *Ibid.*
47. NLI MS 17,795 (1).
48. NLI MS 17,795 (3).
49. *Ibid.* The trial transcript calls him 'Tobrid', but Gahan has 'Tobin', which seems more likely.
50. Gahan, 'New Ross, Scullabogue and the 1798 Rebellion', p. 20.
51. NAI MS 620/6/60/22.
52. Hay, *History*, p. 157.
53. Taylor, *History*, pp. 70–1.
54. Musgrave, *Memoirs*, p. 792.
55. *Ibid.* p. 403.
56. Taylor, *History*, pp. 70–3.
57. Cloney, *Narrative*, p. 44.
58. Musgrave, *Memoirs*, pp. 789–90, 404.

59. *Ibid.* pp. 784–5.
60. 'Diary of Elizabeth Richards', 17 June.
61. Musgrave, *Memoirs*, p. 785.
62. *Ibid.* p. 778.
63. Whelan, *The Tree of Liberty*, p. 138.
64. Musgrave, *Memoirs*, p. 401; Goff, *Divine Protection*, pp. 16–17.
65. Hay, *History*, pp. 156–63.
66. IFC, Schools Collection, 882, fos. 476–7.
67. As related to me by Monsignor John Dunne.

CHAPTER 14

1. Pakenham, *The Year of Liberty*, p. 208.
2. NAI Rebellion Papers 620/38/235. Crawford to Lake, 24 June; see also Moore *Diary*, pp. 244, 295, 302.
3. Gordon, *History of the Rebellion*, p. 269; see also Hay, *History*, pp. 153–4.
4. Madden, *United Irishmen*, 4th series, 2nd edn, vol. 4, p. 445.
5. Donovan, 'Commentary', p. 24.
6. Alexander, *Account*, pp. 91, 92, 96.
7. NAI Rebellion Papers, 620/6/70/5. Trial of Joyce and others.
8. Alexander, *Account*, pp. 91–2; 'A '98 diary', pp. 137–40.
9. Alexander, *Account*, p. 96.
10. *Ibid.* pp. 64–65, 96–97; Taylor, *History*, pp. 61–2.
11. Hall, *Tour*, vol. 1, pp. 98–111.
12. Alexander, *Account*, pp. 96–100, p. 125.
13. Madden, *United Irishmen*, 4th series, 2nd edn, vol. 4, p. 445.
14. Roche, *Statements and Observations*, p. 40.
15. L.M. Cullen, 'Rebellion Mortality in Wexford in 1798', *Journal of the Wexford Historical Society*, no. 17, 1998–9, pp. 7–29.
16. Alexander, *Account*, pp. 85–6.
17. NLI MS 27,957 (Bloomfield); Roche, *Statements and Observations*, p. 39 has a precise 2806 insurgents killed; Butler, *Near Restful Waters*, pp. 98–9.
18. Alexander, *Account*, pp. 86–8, *passim*; HO 100/80 fos. 39–40.
19. Donovan, 'Commentary', p. 24.
20. Ronan (ed.), *Personal Recollections*; IFC Schools Collection, 872, pp. 25–7.
21. Alexander, *Account*, pp. 92–3.
22. B.J. Cantwell, 'Persons Who Died in 1798', parts 1 and 2, *The Past*, nos 17, 18 (1994–5).
23. Doran, *St. Marys*, p. 21.
24. M.C. Normoyle, *A Tree is Planted: The Life and Times of Edmund Rice*, pp. 482–3. A version of this appeared in P.B. Jacob, *Edmund Ignatius Rice* (Dublin 1979), p. 9.
25. Bride's family tree was circulated in manuscript.
26. For Hessian stories see footnote 35 below; Donovan, 'Commentary', pp. 18–20.
27. Jacob, *Rice*, p. 9.

28. Keogh, *Edmund Rice*, p. 34.
29. Alexander, *Account*, p. 32.
30. Cloney, *Narrative*, pp. 39–40; Alexander, *Account*, pp. 72–3. See also Hay, *History*, p. 151. I am grateful to Diarmaid Ó Muirithe for the derivation of the name.
31. NAI Rebellion Papers, 620/6/70.
32. Donovan, 'Commentary', p. 21.
33. Alexander, *Account*, p. 102.
34. S. Cloney, 'The Hessians', *Journal of the Wexford Historical Society*, no. 14, 1992–3, pp. 113–28.
35. IFC Schools Collection, 872, f. 4; Also, e.g. 882, fos. 461–2, fos. 478–9; 898, fos. 54–5; and 899, fos. 32–3.
36. Alexander, *Account*, pp. 92–3.
37. Howell, *State Trials*, xvii, p. 1168; Whelan, 'The Religious Factor', p. 81.
38. NAI Rebellion Papers, 620/38/235.

ENVOI

1. R. Roche (ed.), *Here's their Memory: Record of the United Irishmen in Co. Wexford in 1798* (Wexford 1997), p. 88.
2. Two manuscript versions of this account have been collected and edited by Mons. John Dunne in a privately circulated typescript.
3. *Davidstown – Courtnacuddy Remembers 1798* (1998), p. 60.
4. Whelan, 'Reinterpreting the 1798 Rebellion', p.32.
5. Appendix: The Ballads of Thomas Dunne; Kavanagh, *Insurrection*, pp. 292–303; Cullen, '1798 Rebellion', p. 259.

APPENDIX A

1. R. Ó Donnchadha, *Micheál Óg Ó Longáin: File* (Dublin 1994), pp. 90–2.
2. B. Ó Conchúir, *Scríobhaithe Chorcaí 1700–1850* (Dublin 1982), pp. 91–133; C. Buttimer, 'Gaelic Literature and Contemporary Life in Cork' in P. O'Flanagan and C. Buttimer (eds), *Cork: History and Society* (Dublin 1993); M. Ní Úrdail, *The Scribe in Eighteenth and Nineteenth Century Ireland* (Munster 2000).
3. See Dunne, 'Tá Gaedhil Bhocht Cráiaídhte', p. 96, fn. 11; Ó Conchúir, *Scriobhaithe*, pp. 104–6.
4. Ó Donnchadha, *Ó Longáin*, nos 13–15.
5. Bartlett, 'Defenders and Defenderism', p. 377.
6. Tadhg Ó Murchú, 'Micheál Óg Ó Longáin (1766–1857); a shaoghal agas a shaothar'. MA UCC 1940, Poem B1.
7. *Ibid.* nos B2 B3; Ó Donnchadha, *Ó Longáin*, pp. 70–9. For the Ó Rathaille poems see S. Ó Tuama and T. Kinsella, *An Duanaire: Poems of the Dispossessed* (Mountrath 1981), pp. 150–60.
8. First published in *An Claidheamh Solais*, 17 March 1917, pp. 3–4; see Ó Donn-

chadha, *Ó Longáin*, pp. 80–1.

9.   *Ibid.* pp. 90–2.

10.   *Ibid.* pp. 86–7, 88–9.

11.   *Ibid.* pp. 101–2.

12.   Dunne, 'Popular Ballads', p. 149.

APPENDIX B

1.   Madden, *Literary Remains*, pp. 9–14; McCall's original version can be found in
      G.D. Zimmermann, *Songs of Irish Rebellion* (Dublin 1957), pp. 290–1. The version
      that became the standard one was first published in 1922 and can be found, e.g.
      in P. Galvin, *Irish Songs of Resistance* (London and New York 1962), pp. 28–9; see
      Dunne, 'Ballads, Rhetoric and Politicisation'.

2.   P. Kennedy, *Legends of Mt Leinster: Tales and Sketches* (Dublin and London 1855,
      reprint, Enniscorthy 1989, with a preface by K. Whelan), pp. 130–7.

3.   'The Memory of the Dead' in *The Spirit of the Nation*, 50th edn (Dublin 1874),
      pp. 41–3.

4.   P. Hennessy, *Davidstown Courtnacuddy: A Wexford Parish* (1982), pp. 58–9, extract
      from *The People*, 24 October 1885.

5.   'Borrowed Plumes, gathered by T.J. Dunne Esq. 1872', MS book in my posses-
      sion, pp. 33–4; *The Spirit of the Nation*, pp. 235–7.

6.   'Thomas Dunne, Courtnacuddy, 1875', MS book in possession of Tom Dunne,
      Courtnacuddy.

7.   *Ibid.*

8.   Whelan, 'Reinterpreting the 1798 Rebellion', p. 31.

9.   *The Spirit of the Nation*, pp. 157–9.

10.   Kavanagh, *Insurrection*, p. 299.

BIBLIOGRAPHY

MANUSCRIPT SOURCES

NATIONAL ARCHIVES OF IRELAND, DUBLIN
Rebellion papers
State of the Country papers

NATIONAL LIBRARY, DUBLIN
MS 17,795   Court-martial records
MS 24,957   Letter of Captain Bloomfield
MS 25,004   Anonymous: Account of 1798
MS 3151   Tottenham records
Microfilm 4937   Tottenham records
Microfilm 6486   Diary of Elizabeth Richards

TRINITY COLLEGE, DUBLIN
MS 873   Madden manuscripts
MS 871   Musgrave papers
MS 872   Court-martial records
MS 1472   Cullen manuscripts
MS 3365   Diary of Thomas Prior

UNIVERSITY COLLEGE DUBLIN
Irish Folklore Commission: Schools Collection
Prim MSS

WEXFORD COUNTY LIBRARY
T/s Jane Barber: Recollections
Uncatalogued Comóradh '98 material

PUBLIC RECORDS OFFICE, LONDON
Home Office papers, 100

THE THOLSEL, NEW ROSS
Council Book of the Corporation of New Ross 1732–1841

MANUSCRIPTS IN PRIVATE HANDS
Tottenham papers
Thomas Dunne: journals

PRIMARY PRINTED SOURCES

Alexander, J., 'To whom it may concern', *Walker's Hibernian Magazine*, November 1798, pp. 793–8.

Alexander, J., *Some Account of the First Symptoms of the Late Rebellion in the County of Kildare and in the Adjoining Kings County, with a Succinct Narrative of some of the most Remarkable Passages in the Rise and Progress of the Rebellion in the County of Wexford, especially in the Vicinity of Ross* etc. (Dublin 1800).

Anderson, C., *Historical Sketches of the Native Irish and their Descendants, Illustrative of their Past and Present State with regard to Literature, Education and Oral Instruction*, 2nd edn (Edinburgh and London 1830).

Anon, *History of the Irish Rebellion in the Year 1798* (Dublin 1799).

Auckland, Lord, *Journals and Correspondence*, 4 vols (London 1861–2).

Banim, M., *The Croppy: A Tale of 1798*, 3 vols (London 1828).

Bowden, C.D. A., *Tour through Ireland* (Dublin 1791).

Byrne, M., *Memoirs of Miles Byrne, Chef de Bataillon in the Service of France. Edited by his Widow*, 3 vols (Paris and New York 1863).

Caulfield, Dr, *The reply of the Right Rev. Doctor Caulfield, Roman Catholic Bishop, and of the Roman Catholic Clergy of Wexford to the Misrepresentations of Sir Richard Musgrave Bart* (Dublin 1801).

Cloney, T., *A Personal Narrative of those Transactions in the County of Wexford, in which the Author was Engaged During the Awful Period of 1798* (Dublin 1832).

Croker, T.C., *Researches in the South of Ireland 1818–1822* (London 1824).

Dáil Éireann Debates.

Edgeworth, M., *Ennui* (London 1809).

Fitzpatrick, W.J., *The Sham Squire,* 3rd edn (1866).

Flood, W.H. Grattan, *History of the Dioceses of Ferns* (Waterford 1916), Appendix VI, 'Bishop Sweetman's Visitation Book, 1753'.

Gilbert, J.T., *Documents Relating to Ireland 1795–1804* (1893, IUP reprint Shannon 1970).

Goff, D.W., *Divine Protection through Extraordinary Dangers experienced by Jacob and Elizabeth Goff and their Family during the Irish Rebellion of 1798* (London 1857).

Gordon, Rev. James, *History of the Rebellion in Ireland in the Year 1798* (Dublin 1801).

Hall, Rev. James, *Tour through Ireland,* 2 vols (London 1813).

Handcock, G.F., 'Reminiscences of a Fugitive Loyalist in 1798', *The English Historical Review*, 1, 1886, pp. 536–44.

Hay, E., *History of the Insurrection of the County of Wexford, AD 1798* (Dublin 1803).

Hore, P.H. (ed.), *History of the Town and County of Wexford, vol. 1, Old and New Ross. Compiled principally from the State Papers, the Public Records and Manuscripts of the late Herbert F. Hore, Esq. of Pole House in that County* (London 1900, reprint Oxford 1978, with an introduction by R. Dudley Edwards).

Howell, T.J., *The Complete Collection of State Trials*, vol. XVII (London 1820).

'H.R.', Mrs, 'Cursory Remarks on Board the *Friendship*', *The Asiatic Journal*, VIII, 1819, pp. 223–9.

Irish Times, The.

Jackson, C., *A Narrative of the Sufferings and Escape of Charles Jackson* etc. (Dublin 1798).

Jones, J., *An Impartial Narrative of each Engagement which took place between His Majesty's Forces and the Rebels during the Irish Rebellion of 1798* (Dublin 1800).

Kennedy, P., *Legends of Mt Leinster: Tales and Sketches* (Dublin and London 1855, reprint Enniscorthy 1989).

Lewis, C. and Kernan, J.D. (eds), 'Devereux of the Leap, County Wexford and of Utica, New York', *The Irish Genealogist*, 3, no. 5, November 1972, pp. 23–39.

Luckombe, P., *A Tour Through Ireland in 1778* (London 1798).

McGrath, M. (ed.), *Cinnlae Amhlaoibh Uí Shuíleabháin,* 4 vols (London and Dublin 1928–37).

Madden, R.R., *The United Irishmen: Their Lives and Times,* 7 vols (London 1842–6; 2nd edn, London 1860).

Madden, R.R., *Literary Remains of the United Irishmen* (London 1887).

Maturin, *The Milesian Chief: A Romance* (London 1812).

Maurice, J.F., *The Diary of Sir John Moore,* 2 vols (London 1904).

Milne, K. (ed.), 'The Elmes Letters', *The Past*, no. 17, 1990, pp. 55–70.

Moore, T., *Memoirs of Captain Rock* (London 1824).

Musgrave, R., *Memoirs of the Different Rebellions in Ireland* (London and Dublin 1801), 4th edn, Myers, S.W. and McKnight, D.E. (eds), (Fort Wayne, Indiana and Enniscorthy 1995).

Ní Shéaghdha, N., 'Maideann Luain Chíngcíse', *Éigse*, vol.1, part III, pp. 191–5.

Ó Concheanainn, T. (ed.), *Nua Dhuanaire,* Chuid III (Dublin 1981).

O'Daly, J. (ed.), *The Poets and Poetry of Munster,* 3rd edn (Dublin 1860).

Ó Donnchadha, R., *Micheál Óg Ó Longáin: File* (Dublin 1994).

Ó Donnchú, D. (ed.), *Filíocht Mháire Bhuídhe Ní Laoghaire* (Dublin 1931).

O'Flanagan, M. (ed.), *Ordnance Survey Letters, Wexford* (Dublin 1933).

Ó hÓgáin, D., *Duanaire Osraíoch* (Dublin 1980).

Ó Murchú, T., 'Micheál Óg Ó Longáin (1766–1857); a Shaoghal agas a Shaothar', MA Thesis, University College Cork 1940.

Plowden, F., *An Historical Review of the State of Ireland,* 2 vols (London 1803).

Rambles through Ireland by a French Emigrant. Translated from the French of Monsieur de Latocnaye by an Irishman (Cork 1798).

Ranson, J. (ed.), 'A '98 diary by Mrs. Barbara Newton Lett, Killaligan, Enniscorthy', *The Past*, no. 5, 1949, pp. 117–49.

Richards, E., 'Diary of my grandmother, Elizabeth Richards, copied from the original manuscript, found Huis Ten Duick, 1917' (NLI Ts).

Roche, J., *Statements and Observations on Cases that occurred in Cork, Wexford and Wicklow* (Dublin 1799).

Ronan, M.V. (ed.), *Insurgent Wicklow 1798 by Rev. Br. Luke Cullen O.D.C.* (Dublin 1948).

Ronan, M.V. (ed.), *Personal Recollections of Wexford and Wicklow Insurgents of 1798 as collected by Rev. Br. Luke Cullen, O.D.C.* (Enniscorthy 1959).

Shaw, M.W., *A Statistical Account or Parochial Survey of Ireland, drawn up from the Communication of the Clergy,* 3 vols (Dublin 1814).

Taylor, G., *A History of the Rise, Progress and Suppression of the Rebellion in the County of Wexford in the year 1798. To which is annexed the author's account of his captivity and merciful deliverance* (Dublin 1829).

Trotter, J.B., *Walks through Ireland in the years 1812, 1814 and 1817* (London 1819).

Young, A., *A Tour in Ireland with General Observations on the Present State of that Kingdom, made in the Years 1776, 1777, and 1778. And brought down to the end of 1779*, 2 vols, 2nd edn (London 1780).

SECONDARY SOURCES

Bartlett, T., 'Defenders and Defenderism in 1795', *Irish Historical Studies*, XXIV, no. 95, May 1985, pp. 373–94.

Bartlett, T., 'The Burden of the Present: Theobald Wolfe Tone, Republican and Separatist' in Dickson, D., Keogh, D., and Whelan, K. (eds), *The United Irishmen: Republicanism, Radicalism and Rebellion* (Dublin 1993), pp. 1–15.

Bartlett, T., 'Miles Byrne: United Irishman, Irish Exile and *Beau Sabreur*' in Keogh, D. and Furlong, N. (eds), *The Mighty Wave: The 1798 Rebellion in Wexford* (Dublin 1996).

Bartlett, T., *Theobald Wolfe Tone* (Dundalk 1997).

Bartlett, T., 'Bearing Witness: Female Evidence in Courts Martial Convened to Suppress the 1798 Rebellion' in Keogh, D. and Furlong, N. (eds), *Women of 1798* (Dublin 1998).

Bartlett, T., Dawson, K. and Keogh, D., *Rebellion: A Television History of 1798* (Dublin 1998).

Bartlett, T., Dickson, D., Keogh, D. and Whelan, K., *1798: A Bicentenary Perspective* (Dublin 2003).

Benjamin, W., *Illuminations* (London 1970).

Bentley, M., 'Prologue: The Retiring Mr. Cowling' in Michael Bentley (ed.), *Public and Private Doctrine: Essays in British History Presented to Maurice Cowling* (Cambridge 1993), pp. 1–13.

Binions, G.H., 'John Kelly' in G.H. Binions (ed.), *1798–1998. Killanne-Rathnure: A Local History* (Killanne 1997), pp. 1–17.

Bradshaw, B., 'Nationalism and Historical Scholarship in Modern Ireland', published originally in *Irish Historical Studies*, XXVI (1988–9); reprinted in Brady, C. (ed.), *Interpreting Irish History: The Debate on Historical Revisionism* (Dublin 1994), pp. 191–216.

Browne, B., *Old Ross: The Town that Never Was* (Wexford 1993).

Browne, E. and Wickham, T. (eds), *Lewis's Wexford* (Enniscorthy 1983).

Butler, T.C., *Near Restful Waters: The Augustinians in New Ross and Clonmines* (Dublin 1975).

Butterfield, H., *The Whig Interpretation of History* (London 1931).

Butterfield, H., *An Englishman and his History* (Cambridge 1944).

Buttimer, C., 'Gaelic Literature and Contemporary Life in Cork' in O'Flanagan, P. and Buttimer, C. (eds), *Cork: History and Society* (Dublin 1993).

Cantwell, B.J., 'Persons who died in 1798', parts 1 and 2, *The Past*, nos 17, 18 (1994–5).

Carr, E.H., *What is History?* (London 1961).

Clarke, A., 'Robert Dudley Edwards 1908–88', *Irish Historical Studies*, no. 102, November 1988, pp. 121–7.

Cleary, B., 'Sowing the Whirlwind', *Journal of the Wexford Historical Society*', no. 13, 1992–3.

Cleary, B., 'Wexford in 1798: A Republic Before its Time' in Póirtéir, C. (ed.), *The Great Irish Rebellion of 1798* (Cork 1998), pp. 101–14.

Cloney, S., 'The Hessians', *Journal of the Wexford Historical Society*, no. 14, 1992–3, pp. 113–28.

Cloney, S., 'South West Wexford in 1798', *Journal of the Wexford Historical Society*, no. 15, 1994, pp. 74–97.

Cobb, R., 'Jack Gallagher in Oxford' in *People and Places* (Oxford 1984).

Collingwood, R.G., *The Idea of History* (Oxford 1946, revised edn 1994).

Cooke, A.B. and Vincent, J.R., *The Governing Passion: Cabinet Government and Party Politics in Britain, 1865–6* (Brighton 1974).

Corish, P.J. (ed.), 'The 1798 Rebellion in its Eighteenth-Century Context' in *Radicals, Rebels and Establishments* (Belfast 1985), pp. 91–113.

Cowling, M., *Religion and Public Doctrine in Modern England,* 3 vols (Cambridge 1980–2000).

Cullen, L.M., *The Emergence of Modern Ireland* (London 1981).

Cullen, L.M., 'The 1798 Rebellion in Wexford: United Irish Organisation, Membership, Leadership' in Whelan, K. and Nolan, W. (eds), *Wexford: History and Society* (Dublin 1987), pp. 248–95.

Cullen, L.M., 'The United Irishmen in Wexford' in Keogh, D. and Furlong, N. (eds), *The Mighty Wave: The 1798 Rebellion in Wexford* (Dublin 1996), pp. 48–64.

Cullen, L.M., 'Rebellion Mortality in Wexford in 1798', *Journal of the Wexford Historical Society*, no. 17, 1998–9, pp. 7–29.

Curtin, N.J., *The United Irishmen: Popular Politics in Ulster and Dublin 1791–1798* (Oxford 1994).

d'Alton, I., 'Southern Irish Unionism: A Study of Cork Unionists 1884–1914' in *Transactions of the Royal Historical Society*, 5th series, vol. 23 (London 1973).

Deane, S., 'Wherever Green is Read' in Ní Dhonnchadha, M. and Dorgan, T. (eds), *Revising the Rising* (Derry 1991).

Deane, S., *Strange Country: Modernity and Nationhood in Irish Writing since 1790* (Oxford 1997).

de Vál, S., 'Logainmneacha Chontae Loch Garman' in Whelan, K. and Nolan, W. (eds), *Wexford: History and Society* (Dublin 1987).

de Vál, S., 'Oidhreacht Ghaelach Loch Garman', *Irisleabhar Mhá Nuad*, 1992, pp. 75–107.

Dickson, C., *The Wexford Rising in 1798: Its Causes and Its Course* (London 1997).

Donovan, P., 'A Commentary on the Commemoration' in *A Military Tattoo Commemorating the Battle of Ross, by the Ross Battalion F.C.A., Barretts Park, New Ross, Saturday and Sunday 5th and 6th June 1948. Souvenir Programme.*

Doran, J., *A Little History of St. Mary's and its Memorials* (New Ross 1997).

Doyle, J. and O'Shea, T., *Davidstown–Courtnacuddy Remembers 1798* (Davidstown-Courtnacuddy 1998).

Dunn, J., *Western Political Theory in the Face of the Future* (Cambridge 1979 Canto edn 1993).

Dunne, T., 'W.E. Gladstone: The Evolution of the Home Rule Policy', MA Thesis, University College Cork 1971.

Dunne, T., 'Ireland, England and Empire 1868–86: The Ideologies of the British Political Leadership', PhD Thesis, Cambridge 1975.

Dunne, T., 'The Gaelic Response to Conquest and Colonisation: The Evidence of the Poetry', *Studia Hibernica*, no. 20, 1980, pp. 7–30.

Dunne, T., ' "La trahison des clercs": British Intellectuals and the First Home Rule Crisis', *Irish Historical Studies*, XXIII, November 1982, pp. 134–73.

Dunne, T., *Theobald Wolfe Tone: Colonial Outsider* (Cork 1982).

Dunne, T., *Maria Edgeworth and the Colonial Mind* (Dublin 1984).

Dunne, T., 'Murder as Metaphor: Griffin's Portrayal of Ireland in the year of Catholic Emancipation' in MacDonagh, O. and Mandle, W.F. (eds), *Ireland and Irish Australia* (London and Sydney 1986), pp. 64–80.

Dunne, T., 'Fiction as "The Best History of Nations": Lady Morgan's Irish novels' in Dunne, T. (ed.), *The Writer as Witness* (Cork 1987), pp. 135–59.

Dunne, T., 'Haunted by History: Irish Romantic Writing 1800–1850' in Porter, R. and Teich, M. (eds), *Romanticism in National Context* (Cambridge 1988).

Dunne, T., 'The Insecure Voice: A Catholic Novelist in Support of Emancipation' in Cullen, L.M. and Bergeron, L. (eds), *Culture et Pratiques Politique en France et en Irlande xvie–xviiie siecle* (Paris 1989), pp. 213–34.

Dunne, T., 'Maureen Wall (née McGeehin) 1918–1972: A Memoir' in O'Brien, G. (ed.), *Catholic Ireland in the Eighteenth Century: Collected Essays of Maureen Wall* (Dublin 1989).

Dunne, T., 'Representations of Rebellion: 1798 in Literature' in Smith, F.B. (ed.), *Ireland, England and Australia* (Canberra and Cork 1990).

Dunne, T., 'Oliver MacDonagh' in Smith, F.B. (ed.), *Ireland, England and Australia: Essays in Honour of Oliver MacDonagh* (Canberra and Cork 1990), pp. 1–13.

Dunne, T., 'Popular Ballads, Revolutionary Rhetoric and Politicisation' in Gough, H. and Dickson, D. (eds), *Ireland and the French Revolution* (Dublin 1993).

Dunne, T., '1798: Memory, History, Commemoration', *Journal of the Wexford Historical Society*, no. 16, 1996–7, pp. 5–39.

Dunne, T., 'Dangers Lie in the Romanticising of 1798', *The Irish Times*, 6/1/98.

Dunne, T., 'Subaltern voices? Poetry in Irish Popular Insurgency and the 1798 Rebellion', *Eighteenth Century Life*, 22, N.S. 3, November 1998.

Dunne, T., 'The Memory of the Dead: New Ross and Scullabogue, 5 June 1798', *Journal of the Wexford Historical Society*, no. 17, 1998–9.

Dunne, T., '1798 and the United Irishmen', *The Irish Review*, no. 22, summer 1998.

Dunne, T., 'Rebel Motives and Mentalities: The Battle for New Ross, 5 June 1798', *Eire/Ireland*, XXXIV, summer 1999.

Dunne, T., ' "Tá Gaedhil Bhocht Cráidhte": Memory, Tradition and the Politics of the Poor in Gaelic Poetry and Song' in Geary, L. (ed.), *Rebellion and Remembrance in Modern Ireland* (Dublin 2001).

Dunne, T., ' "One of the Tests of National Character": Britishness and Irishness in Paintings by Barry and Maclise' in Stewart, B. (ed.), *Hearts and Minds: Irish Culture and Society under the Act of Union* (Gerrards Cross 2002).

Eagleton, T., *Crazy John and the Bishop, and Other Essays on Irish Culture* (Cork 1998).

Eagleton, T., *The Gatekeeper: A Memoir* (London 2001).

Edwards, R.D. and Moody, T.W., preface to the first number of *Irish Historical Studies*, 1938–9.

Elliott, M., *Partners in Revolution: The United Irishmen and France* (Yale 1982).

Elliott, M., *Wolfe Tone: Prophet of Irish Independence* (New Haven 1989).

Elton, G.R., *The Practice of History* (London 1967).

Fanning, R., 'The Great Enchantment: Uses and Abuses in Modern Irish History' in Brady, C. (ed.), *Interpreting Irish History: The Debate on Historical Revisionism* (Dublin 1994).

Fennell, D., 'Against Revisionism', *The Irish Review*, no. 4, 1988, pp. 20–6.

FitzGerald, G., 'Estimates for Baronies of Minimum Level of Irish Speaking among Successive Decennial Cohorts 1771–81 to 1861–71', *Proceedings of the Royal Irish Academy*, 84, c. 3, pp. 117–55.

Foster, R.F., 'We Are All Revisionists Now', *The Irish Review*, no. 1, 1986.

Foster, R.F., *The Story of Ireland* (Oxford 1995).

Foster, R.F., *The Irish Story: Telling Tales and Making it up in Ireland* (London 2001).

Gahan, D., 'The Estate System of County Wexford 1641–1876' in Whelan, K. and Nolan, W. (eds), *Wexford: History and Society* (Dublin 1987), pp. 200–21.

Gahan, D., *The People's Rising, Wexford 1798* (Dublin 1995).

Gahan, D., 'The Military Planning of the 1798 Rebellion in Wexford' in Keogh, D. and Furlong, N. (eds), *The Mighty Wave: The 1798 Rebellion in Wexford* (Dublin 1996), pp. 97–108.

Gahan, D., 'The Scullabogue Massacre, 1798', *History Ireland*, iv, no. 3, 1996, pp. 27–31.

Gahan, D., *Rebellion! Ireland in 1798* (Dublin 1997).

Gahan, D., 'New Ross, Scullabogue and the 1798 Rebellion in South-Western Wexford', *The Past*, no. 21, 1998, pp. 3–37.

Gahan, J.V., *The Secular Priests of the Diocese of Ferns* (Strasbourg 2000).

Garvin, T., 'The Strange Death of Clerical Politics in University College Dublin', *Irish University Review*, spring/summer 1998, pp. 308–14.

Gibbons, L. (ed.), 'Challenging the Canon: Revisionism and Cultural Criticism' in *The Field Day Anthology of Irish Writing*, vol. 3 (Derry 1991), pp. 561–79.

Gibbons, L., 'Identity without a Centre: Allegory, History and Irish Nationalism', *Cultural Studies*, 3, October 1992, pp. 358–75.

Guha, R., 'Dominance without Hegemony and its Historiography', in *Subaltern Studies*, vol. VI (Delhi 1994).

Hanrahan, F., 'Making History: Wexford Public Libraries' Contribution to the Bicentennial Commemorations of the Rebellion of 1798', *An Leabharlann: The Irish Library*, 2nd series, 14, nos 3 and 4, 1998, pp. 115–19.

Hennessy, P., *Davidstown Courtnacuddy: A Wexford Parish* (1982).

Jacob, P.B., *Edmund Ignatius Rice* (Dublin 1979).

Jones, P.M., *The Peasantry in the French Revolution* (Cambridge 1988).

Jones-Hughes, T., 'Continuity and Change in Rural County Wexford in the Nineteenth Century' in Whelan, K. and Nolan, W. (eds), *Wexford: History and Society*.

Kavanagh, P.F., *A Popular History of the Insurrection of 1798* (Dublin 1870).

Kennedy, L., 'Modern Ireland: Post-Colonial Society or Post-Colonial Pretensions?', *The Irish Review*, no. 13, 1992–3, pp. 107–21.

Keogh, D., *Edmund Rice 1762–1844* (Dublin 1996).

Keogh, D. and Furlong, N. (eds), *The Mighty Wave: The 1798 Rebellion in Wexford* (Dublin 1996).

Kinsella, A., 'The Spirit of '98 Awakened', *Journal of the Wexford Historical Society*, no. 15, 1994–5, pp. 34–42.

Kinsella, A., '1798 Claimed for Catholics: Fr. Kavanagh, Fenianism and the Centenary Celebrations' in Keogh, D. and Furlong, N. (eds), *The Mighty Wave: The 1798 Rebellion in Wexford* (Dublin 1996), pp. 139–55.

Lecky, W.E.H., *A History of Ireland in the Eighteenth Century,* 5 vols (London 1892).

Lee, J.J., *Ireland 1912–1985* (Cambridge 1989).

Lindsay, D., 'The Rebellion Papers', *History Ireland*, VI, no. 2, 1998, pp. 18–22.

McCartney, D., *W.E.H. Lecky, Historian and Politician 1838–1903* (Dublin 1994).

MacDonagh, O., *Ireland* (New Jersey 1968).

McGrath, T., *Religious Renewal and Reform in the Pastoral Ministry of Bishop James Doyle* (Dublin 1999).

McGuire, J., 'T. Desmond Williams (1921–1987)', *Irish Historical Studies*, XXVI, no. 10, May 1988, pp. 3–7.

Maguire, W.A. (ed.), *The 1798 Rebellion in Ireland: A Bicentenary Exhibition* (Belfast 1998).

Maxwell, W.H., *History of the Irish Rebellion in 1798* (London 1845).

Murray, B. (ed.), *Epitaph of 1798: A Photographic Record of 1798 Memorials on the Island of Ireland and Beyond* (Carrigbyrne 2002).

Normoyle, M.C., *A Tree is Planted: The Life and Times of Edmund Rice* (2nd edn 1976, private printing).

Normoyle, M.C., *Memories of Edmund Rice*, published 'for private circulation' by the Christian Brothers in 1979.

O'Brien, C.C., *States of Ireland* (London 1972, 1974).

Ó Buachalla, B., 'Irish Jacobite Poetry', *The Irish Review*, no. 12, 1992, pp. 40–9.

Ó Buachalla, B., 'Irish Jacobitism and Irish Nationalism: The Literary Evidence' in O'Dea, M. and Whelan, K. (eds), *Nations and Nationalities: France, Britain, Ireland and the Eighteenth Century Context* (Oxford 1995).

Ó Buachalla, B., *Aisling Ghéar* (Dublin 1996).

Ó Caithnia, L.P., *Scéal na hIomána* (Dublin 1980).

Ó Cearbhaill, S.E. (ed.), *A Man Raised Up: Recollections and Reflections on Venerable Edmund Rice* (Dublin 1994).

Ó Conchúir, B., *Scríobhaithe Chorcaí 1700–1850* (Dublin 1982).

O'Faolain, Sean, *An Irish Journey* (London 1940).

Ó Gráda, C., 'Making History in Ireland in the 1940s and 1950s: The Saga of the Great Famine', *The Irish Review*, no. 12, 1992, pp. 87–107.

Ó hÓgartaigh, M., 'Edward Hay, Wexford Historian of 1798', *Journal of the Wexford Historical Society*, no. 17, 1998–9, pp. 159–75.

Pakenham, T., *The Year of Liberty: The History of the Great Rebellion of 1798* (London 1969, 1992 edn).

Paseta, S., '1798 in 1898: The Politics of Commemoration', *The Irish Review*, no. 22, summer 1998, pp. 46–53.

Póirtéir, C. (ed.), *The Great Irish Rebellion of 1798* (Cork 1998).

Popkin, J.D., 'Historians on the Autobiographical Frontier', *The American Historical Review*, 104, no. 3, June 1999, pp. 725–48.

Powell, T., 'The Background to the Rebellion in Co. Wexford: 1790–98', MA Thesis, University College Dublin 1970.

Powell, T., 'An Economic Factor in the Wexford Rebellion of 1798', *Studia Hibernica*, XVI, 1976, pp. 140–57.

Powell, T., 'The United Irishmen and the Wexford Rebellion: The Sources Re-examined', *The Irish Review*, no. 23, 1998, pp. 127–40.

Raftery, M. and O'Sullivan, E., *Suffer the Little Children: The Inside Story of Ireland's Industrial Schools* (Dublin 1999).

Ramsey, C., *The Ideology of the Great Fear: The Soissonnais in 1789* (Baltimore and London 1992).

Ringwood, B., 'Cumann Comórtha 1798: 1798 Bicentenary Association' in *Vinegar Hill Day Enniscorthy, Sunday 21st June 1998. Souvenir Record* (Enniscorthy 1998).

Roche, R. (ed.), *Here's their Memory: A Record of the United Irishmen in Co. Wexford in 1798* (Wexford 1997).

Seal, A., 'John Andrew Gallagher, 1919–1980' in Gallagher, J., *The Decline, Revival and Fall of the British Empire: The Ford Lectures and Other Essays*, ed. Anil Seal (Cambridge 1982).

Smyth, J. *The Men of No Property. Irish Radicals and Popular Politics in the Eighteenth Century* (Dublin 1992).

Smyth, J., 'Popular Politicisation, Defenderism and the Catholic Question' in Gough, H. and Dickson, D. (eds), *Ireland and the French Revolution* (Dublin 1993).

Smyth, J., 'Interpreting the 1790s', *History Ireland*, VI, no. 2, 1998, pp. 54–8.

Steiner, G., *Errata: An Examined Life* (London 1998).

Stewart, A.T.Q., *The Summer Soldiers: The 1798 Rebellion in Antrim and Down* (Belfast 1995).

Sutherland, D., *The Chouans. The Social Origins of Popular Counter-Revolution in Upper Brittany 1770–1796* (Oxford 1982).

Thomas, A., *The Walled Towns of Ireland,* vol. 2 (Dublin 1992).

Thornley, D., *Isaac Butt* (London 1964).

Tilly, C., *The Vendée* (London 1964).

Tóibín, C., 'The Cause that Called You: Notes of a Native Son' in Bolger, D. (ed.), *Wexford Through Its Writers* (Dublin 1992), pp. 57–74.

Turpin, J., '1798, 1898 and the Political Implications of Sheppard's Monuments', *History Ireland*, VI, no. 2, 1998, pp. 44–8.

Tyrell, J., *Weather and Warfare: A Climatic History of the 1798 Rebellion* (Cork 2001).

Wall, M., 'The background to the Rising from 1914 until the issue of the countermanding order on Easter Saturday 1916' and 'The plans and the countermand: the country and Dublin', both in Nowlan, K.B. (ed.), *The Making of 1916* (Dublin 1969).

Wheeler, H.F.B. and Broadley, A.M., *The War in Wexford* (London and New York 1910).

Whelan, K. (ed.), *A History of Newbawn* (Newbawn 1986).

Whelan, K., 'The Religious Factor in the 1798 Rebellion' in O'Flanagan, P., Ferguson, P., and Whelan, K. (eds), *Rural Ireland* (Cork 1987).

Whelan, K. and Nolan, W. (eds), *Wexford: History and Society* (Dublin 1987).

Whelan, K., 'The Role of the Catholic Priest in the 1798 Rebellion in County Wexford' in Whelan, K. and Nolan, W. (eds), *Wexford: History and Society* (Dublin 1987).

Whelan, K., 'The Regional Impact of Irish Catholicism 1700–1850' in Smyth, W.J. and Whelan, K. (eds), *Common Ground: Essays on the Historical Geography of Ireland presented to T. Jones-Hughes* (Cork 1988), pp. 253–77.

Whelan, K., 'Politicisation in County Wexford and the Origins of the 1798 Rebellion' in Gough, H. and Dickson, D. (eds), *Ireland and the French Revolution* (Dublin 1990).

Whelan, K., 'The Catholic Community in Eighteenth Century Wexford' in Power, T.P. and Whelan, K. (eds), *Endurance and Emergence: Catholics in Ireland in the Eighteenth Century* (Dublin 1990), pp. 129–70.

Whelan, K., 'Catholics, Politicization and the 1798 Rebellion' in Ó Muirí, R. (ed.), *Irish Church History Today* (Armagh 1991).

Whelan, K., 'The United Irishmen, the Enlightenment and Popular Culture' in Dickson, D., Keogh, D., and Whelan, K. (eds), *The United Irishmen: Republicanism, Radicalism and Rebellion* (Dublin 1993).

Whelan, K., 'United and Disunited Irishmen: The Discourse of Sectarianism in the 1790s' in O'Dea, M. and Whelan, K. (eds), *Nations and Nationalism: France, Britain and Ireland in the Eighteenth Century Context* (Oxford 1995).

Whelan, K., *The Tree of Liberty: Radicalism, Catholicism and the Construction of Irish Identity 1760–1830* (Cork 1996).

Whelan, K., 'Reinterpreting the 1798 Rebellion in County Wexford' in Keogh, D. and Furlong, N. (eds), *The Mighty Wave: The 1798 Rebellion in Wexford* (Dublin 1996).

Whelan, K., *The Fellowship of Freedom* (Cork 1998).

ACKNOWLEDGMENTS

This book has been 'forthcoming' since 1998 and was originally called *Long Shadows*. It has developed, above all, through dialogue with Clare O'Halloran, who shares my life as well as my fascination with eighteenth-century Ireland. It is dedicated to her and, as it is in part my story, also to our sons, Oisín and Fergus, to my daughters, Fiona and Deirdre, and to my grandson, Seán.

I am grateful to the friends who critiqued the initial draft and encouraged me to persevere; Stefan Collini, Roy Foster, Michael Laffan, John Maguire and my brother John. Louis Cullen made valuable suggestions on an early version of the Scullabogue chapters. Diarmaid Ó Muirithe was my guide to the folklore of the Rebellion. I had help and advice on Gaelic sources from Niall Buttimer, Seán Ó Coileáin and Breandán Ó Conchúir. Brothers Anthony MacDonald and Leo Wright supplied material on Edmund Rice, and Father J. Power on the Augustinians in New Ross.

Roy Foster's advice and his enthusiasm for the project have been crucial throughout, and he did me the great favour of introducing the work to The Lilliput Press. Willy Nolan of Geography Publications had offered to publish it initially, and his encouragement was important. He was also very generous and understanding in facilitating the move to Lilliput when it became clear that it was turning into a different kind of book. Antony Farrell has been the ideal publisher: supportive, professional and unobtrusive. Brendan Barrington has been the ideal editor and contributed greatly to whatever coherence this experimental work now has. I first made the attempt to combine memoir, historiography, commemoration and history in an article in *The Wexford Historical Journal* in 1996, and I am grateful to its then editor, Celestine Murphy, for commissioning it and for much practical help ever since in her other role as librarian in charge of special collections at Wexford County Library. A version of Chapter Two was published in *The Dublin Review*, no. 6, spring 2002. My thanks also to the staff of the National Library, Dublin, especially Gerry Lyne; the National Archives of Ireland, especially Kieran Hoare; the Boole Library, University College Cork; the library at Trinity College Dublin; the Folklore Department, University College Dublin; the Royal Irish Academy; the University Library, Cambridge; the British Library; and the Public Record Office, London. I am grateful to the Tottenham family of Knocknamohill, Co. Wicklow, and especially to Mark Tottenham for access to the family papers.

Friends and colleagues have helped in many ways, particularly Kevin Barry, the late Seán Cloney, Aoife Feeney, Aisling Foster, Tom Garvin, Larry Geary, David Goodall, Michael Hanrahan, Stephen Lalor, Joep Leerssen, Michael and Edna Longley, John A. Murphy, Patrick Maume, Margaret McCurtain, Breandán Ó Buachalla, Diarmaid Ó Catháin, Laura O'Connor, Margaret Ó hÓgartaigh, Tadhg O'Sullivan, Brendan Simms and Helen Skrine. It was a particular pleasure to renew an old friendship with Tom Powell, whose work on 1798 has been a major influence. His death shortly after the bicentenary was a sad loss. Even more so, for me, was the death in 2002 of Oliver MacDonagh, a constant support and inspiration.

I am grateful to Comóradh '98 for invitations to speak at a number of seminars in Wexford, and in particular to its ever-helpful Development Officer, Bernard Browne. I was delighted to be asked to talk to the New Ross Historical Society, and I benefited from the work of its Secretary, Jim Sutton.

I owe a great debt to my cousins, Bride Roe, historian of the Rice family, and Monsignor John Dunne, indefatigable researcher on the Dunnes of Courtnacuddy. My cousin Jack Roe of Tintern made valuable comments on my *Wexford Historical Journal* pieces. My aunt Cathy Rice, who still lives in John Rice's house, was always welcoming and interested, as was Joe Hall of the Irishtown. Tom and Mary Dunne and their family at Courtnacuddy have offered unstinting hospitality and encouragement over many years. Deirdre McGlynn word-processed a series of drafts with great skill and good humour.

Finally, I am grateful for financial support from the Publications Fund of the National University of Ireland and the Arts Faculty of University College Cork.

INDEX

Abban, St, 161
Abbey Theatre, 51
Act of Union, 1801, 101, 103, 165
Adams, Gerry, 5, 127
Adams, Jane, 181
Adamstown, Co. Wexford, 176, 184, 198–9, 205
Agar, James, 202
Ahern, Bertie, 5–6, 124, 125, 126, 142, 145–6, 147
Alexander, Henry, 106, 107
Alexander, James, 131, 152–3, 156, 168, 269
    battle of New Ross, 208–9, 215, 217, 222, 225–33, 235–8, 271
        aftermath, 240–4, 266–8
    on Hessians, 273
    on Irish language, 155, 177
    in New Ross, 169–70, 210–13
    on rebellion, 172–3
    and Tottenham, 208, 233, 234
America, 144
Anderson, Christopher, 176–7
Anglesey, Earl of, 165
Antrim, County, 144
Antrim Militia, 213, 234
Aoife, daughter of Mac Murchadha, 162
Arklow, Co. Wicklow, 105, 194
Armagh, County, 109, 138
Ascherson, Neal, 88
Askin, Michael, 251
Association of Secondary Teachers, Ireland (ASTI), 56, 63
Augustinians, 162, 168, 171, 172
Australia, 144

Bairéad, Riocard, 177
Ballinaboola, Co. Wexford, 22
Ballyanne, Co. Wexford, 17
Ballycullane, Co. Wexford, 273
Ballymacar, Co. Wexford, 14, 16, 221
Ballymorris, Co. Wexford, 250
Ballyraggett, Co. Kilkenny, 178
Ballyshannon, Co. Wexford, 243
Ballyteigue, Co. Wexford, 217
Banim, Michael, 168–9
Bantry, Barony of, 4, 7, 155–6, 172–80, 183, 196
    Irish language, 175–7, 243
    lack of leadership, 197–8
    motivation, 243–6
    New Ross battle, 217–21

sectarianism, 188
Barber, Jane, 181, 190
Barrington, Jonah, 127
Barrow, River, 27–8, 161, 173
Barry, John, 84
Barry, Kevin, 86, 87
Bartlett, Thomas, 90, 103, 106, 127, 142, 143, 147
    on court-martial records, 153
    on Defenders, 133, 136, 181
Battlestown, Co. Wexford, 199
Benjamin, Walter, 8
Bergin, Joe, 67
Birchgrove, Co. Wexford, 182, 190
Blaney, Neil, 62
Bloomfield, Captain, 219, 226, 227, 239, 242, 268
Bond, Oliver, 182
Book of the O'Byrnes, 24
Boolavogue, Co. Wexford, 116, 186
Bórd na Gaeilge, 82
Borris, Co. Carlow, 210
Bosco, St John, 37
Boxwell, John, 217, 225, 242
Bradshaw, Brendan, 51, 52, 79–81, 89, 91, 93–4, 95, 97, 140
Bree, Co. Wexford, 176
Brennan, Seamus, 141, 142–3, 144, 146
Bríd, Sister, 79
Brien, John, 177
Brien, rebel, 250
Brophy, Annie, 26
Browne, Bernard, 116, 118, 326
Browne, Noel, 48
Browne, Vincent, 47
Bruton, John, 123
Bryan, John, 191
'Bualadh Ros Mhic Thriún' (poem), 155
Burke, Edmund, 84, 126
Burke-Roche's Drapery, 17
Butler family, 165
Butler, Hubert, 28, 88
Butler, Richard, Lord Mountgarrett, 164
Butler, Robert, 178
Butt, Isaac, 58
Butterfield, Herbert, 49, 52, 54, 55, 67, 74, 75, 94, 140
Butterfield, Peter, 55, 75
Byrne, Davy, 22

Byrne, Miles, 102, 103–4, 106, 127, 137, 173
    account of, 193, 194–5
    battle of New Ross, 221, 224
    on Orange Order, 186
    on Oulart, 187

Callan, Co. Wexford, 172, 271
Cambridge, University of, 67–77, 79, 80, 97
Camlin Wood, Co. Wexford, 209
Camolin Park, Co. Wexford, 194
Cantwell, Brian, 269
Carew family, 17, 174, 275, 286
Carew, Robert, 183, 275
Carlingford, Lord, 77
Carlisle, victim, 199
Carmelite Order, 171
Carnagh, Co. Wexford, 179, 269
Carnew, Co. Wexford, 186
Carr, E.H., 52–3, 54
Carr, Miss, 211–12
Carr, Mr, 211
Carrigbyrne, Co. Wexford, 116, 207, 215, 243
    rebel camp, 151–2, 196, 202, 212, 250
    witness from, 263–4
Carrigbyrne Pike Group, 124
Carrigbyrne Pikemen, 22
Carty, Robert, 182, 190, 193–4
Cassin, Barry, 37, 41
Castleboro, Co. Wexford, 17, 174, 243, 275
Castlebridge, Co. Wexford, 16
Catholic Committee, 182, 271
Catholic Emancipation, 101
Caulfield, Bishop, 205
Chandler, Raymond, 25
Chesterton, G.K., 25, 35
Christian Brothers, 20, 25–6, 31, 82, 84
    see also Dunne, Thomas
Christian Brothers, Sexton Street, Limerick, 43
Christian Brothers, Synge Street, Dublin, 39–41
Clare Hall, Cambridge, 67
Clare Militia, 216, 243, 271–2, 273–4
Clark, Kitson, 68
Clarke, Philip, 202, 205, 206
Clarke, William, 198, 201, 202–3
Cleary, Brian, 118, 119, 120, 122, 124
Cloney, Sean, 128, 199, 248, 250
Cloney, Thomas, 7, 102, 182, 183, 268, 276
    account of, 103, 104, 111, 173,
        174, 192–4
    battle of New Ross, 131, 195, 214–15,
        217–24, 229–30, 236, 240, 242–3, 271
    battle of Oulart, 106, 187
    chapel burning, 207
    joins rebels, 112, 188–9
    on New Ross, 152
    on Orange Order, 186
    on Scullabogue, 250, 251, 261
    trial of, 191

    and United Irishmen, 184
    on Wexford town, 196
Clongeen, Co. Wexford, 264
Cobb, Richard, 70
Cody, John, 248
Coláiste an Sprid Naoimh, Cork, 55, 56, 62
Coláiste Ciarán, Bray, Co. Wicklow, 33–6
Coláiste Iognáid Rís, Carriglee, 36
Colclough, Caesar, 183–4
Colclough family, 165, 198
Colclough, John Henry, 190, 193, 195, 197, 217
Colfer, Joshua, 198, 199, 201, 206, 248
    court martial, 202–5, 258
Collingwood, R.G., 50, 54
Collins, Gerry, 47
Comité International des Sciences Historiques,
    85
Comóradh '98, 3, 4, 5, 22, 52, 114, 115–29, 136
    political agenda, 132, 145–6
    'Republic of Wexford', 118–24, 130, 139
    Scullabogue memorial, 147
Confederation of Kilkenny, 164–5
Connolly, James, 93
Connolly, Sean, 95
Continuity Army Council, 126
Cooke, A.B., 58, 72–3
Cooke, Robert, 261–2
Cooke, Sir Edward, 268
Corbet Hill, Co. Wexford, 211, 215, 221, 243,
    271
Corkery, Daniel, 83, 137
Cornwallis, Lord, 239
Cosgrave, Art, 49
Costello, M.J., 66
Cotton family, 175
Courtdale, Co. Wexford, 17–18, 21, 22–3
Courtnacuddy, Co. Wexford, 7, 174, 175, 177
Cowling, Maurice, 70, 71, 73–4
Craddock, General, 222
Crawford, Lt Colonel Robert, 221–2, 265,
    273–4
Crawford, Lt William, 218
Crea, weaver, 222
Cromwell, Oliver, 125, 165, 264
Croshee brothers, 191–2
Cruikshank, George, 226, 228, 251, 252
    Scullabogue, 254
Crutched Friars, 162
Cullen, Berchmans, 37
Cullen, Brother Luke, 105, 187, 268
Cullen, Brother W.B., 269, 270, 275
Cullen, Louis, 95, 108, 143, 183, 276
    on archives, 154
    Comóradh '98, 117, 127
    on Defenders, 180
    on Harvey, 196
    heritage centre, 127
    on Oulart, 187

on politicization, 109–10, 132
rebellion mortality, 267–8
on United Irishmen role, 111–12, 114,
118, 130, 133
Cullimore, Mr, 121, 211
Cultural Relations Committee, 134
Cumann Cabhrach, An, 63
Curracloe, Co. Wexford, 16
Curtin, Nancy, 113, 138
Curtis, L.P. Jr, 68
Cushinstown, Co. Wexford, 14, 221, 268–9

Daingean Reformatory, 43
d'Alton, Ian, 66–7, 68
Daly, Sarah, 253
Daly, Sean, 57
Daly, William, 253
Davidstown, Co. Wexford, 175, 179, 180, 185,
189, 191
Davies, Sir John, 69
de Lourdes, Sister, 79
de Rossa, Proinsias, 146
De Vál, Seamus, 24, 177
de Valera, Eamon, 18
de Valera, Síle, 139
Deane, Seamus, 91, 94, 95
Defenderism, 107, 113, 133–4, 135, 136, 157, 179
influence of, 133–8
Whelan on, 137–8, 180–1
Devereux, Edward, 231, 232
Devereux, John, 248
Devereux, Michael, 199, 202, 204
Devereux, Thomas, 182
Devereux, Walter, 182, 259
Dickson, Charles, 106–7, 108, 217
Dickson, David, 134
Dillon, Captain, 237
Dillon, James, 18, 47
Disraeli, Benjamin, 71
Dixon, Captain Thomas, 195–6
Dobbyn, Elizabeth, 205–6, 252, 262
Dobbyn, Patrick, 198–9, 205–6
Donegal Militia, 225, 231
Donnolly, J. and Clarke, S., 183
Donovan, Gerard, 107
Donovan, Patrick, 107, 241–2, 265, 268, 270,
272
Dooge, James, 66
Dormer family, 165
Down, County, 144, 152
Downing Street Declaration, 145
Dowsley family, 222–3, 232, 235, 243
Doyle, Archbishop James, 172
Doyle, Avril, 142, 143–4, 146
Doyle, Father James, 175, 203
Doyle, James, of Carrigbyrne, 263–4
Doyle, Mary, 172
Doyle, Mrs, 243

Drogheda, Co. Louth, 163
Dublin, 144, 167, 197
Dublin Magazine, 166–7
Dublin Militia, 212, 216, 221–2, 230, 231, 235,
244, 265
Catholics in, 266
retreat, 236
Duncannon Fort, Co. Wexford, 198, 199, 202,
209
Dunmain, Co. Wexford, 268–9
Dunne, Arthur, 4, 7, 275, 276
Dunne, Father John (uncle), 16, 18, 19, 20, 25,
32, 35–6
Dunne, Jim, 16, 17, 30
Dunne, Joanna (mother), 1–2, 4, 10, 13, 15–16,
19, 22–3, 28, 30, 32, 33
marriage, 18–21
shop, 64–5
Dunne, John, 14
Dunne, Mary, 46, 64–5, 66
Dunne, May, 16
Dunne, Nick, 16, 19, 30
Dunne, Oisín, 277
Dunne, Peg, 16
Dunne, Rosaleen, 14, 36
Dunne, Thomas (author), 14–15, 20, 21–2, 26,
30, 39, 87, 90
at Cambridge, 67–77
childhood, 21–2, 24–31
in Christian Brothers, 32–44
as historian, 88–97
in Mary Immaculate, 78–81
schooldays, 31
in UCC, 56–67
in UCD, 44–55
Dunne, Thomas (father), 7, 15–22, 19, 29–30,
45–6, 275
death of, 65
shop, 64–5
Dunne, Thomas (grandfather), 16, 177, 221
ballads of, 275, 276, 284–8
Dunphy, Austin, 271
Dwyer, Michael, 107

Eagleton, Terry, 88, 92
Easter Rising, 1916, 5
Echo, The, 16
Edgeworth, Maria, 88, 102, 172
Edmond, Reverend Martin, 176
Edwards, Robin Dudley, 48, 52, 54, 55, 85
Eliot, T.S., 40, 44, 277
Ellard, John, 199, 253, 258, 259
Elliott, Marianne, 90, 112–13, 138, 143
Elmes, Samuel, 167–8, 185, 209
Elmes, Samuel Jr, 192
Elmes, Thomas, 207–8
Elton, Geoffrey, 50
Ely, Earl of, 166, 182

Enniscorthy, Co. Wexford, 1, 7, 16, 117, 173,
    191, 208, 240, 250, 266
    1793 riot, 179
    attack on, 187, 188–9, 197, 221
    heritage centre, 115–16, 125–8
    'hospital' burnt, 229
    Orange Order in, 185
    prisoners, 196
    statue, 105
    United Irishmen in, 184
Enniscorthy District Council, 115
Eustace, General, 211–12
Everett, Catherine, 238, 239

Famine Commemoration Committee, 142, 147
Fanner, victim, 199
Fanning, Ronan, 60, 88
Fardy, Phelim, 252
Farrell, Brian, 53
Father Murphy Centre, 124
Feeney, John, 47
'Fellowship of Freedom' (National Museum),
    139–41
Fenianism, 105
Fennell, Desmond, 88, 93, 154
Ferrier, Kathleen, 40
Fethard, Co. Wexford, 198, 199, 202, 203–4, 207,
    223, 258
Fianna Fáil, 47, 61–2, 126
Field Day, 88–9, 91, 92
Fine Gael, 47
Fitt, Gerry, 86
Fitzgerald, Edward, 193, 195
FitzGerald, Garret, 6, 49, 50
Fitzhenry, Jeremiah, 190
Fitzpatrick, David, 69
Fitzwilliam, Earl, 182
Flaherty, John, 198
Fleming, William, 261–2
Foley, Art, 29
Foley, Mary, 223
Foley, Peter, 187
Foran, Edward, 5, 151, 218
Forth and Bargy, Co. Wexford, 217
Foster, Roy, 87, 91, 130
Foulks Mills, Co. Wexford, 198
Foxe's *Book of Martyrs*, 262
France, 144
    and United Irishmen, 112–13, 115, 117,
        121–2, 132, 134, 137, 155, 157, 246
    Vendée rebellion, 188
Francis, Bridget, 191–2
Francis Street Primary School, 38–42, 45
Franciscans, 162
Freedom of Information Act, 142
French Revolution, 3, 181–2
    bicentenary, 115, 134
Freud, Sigmund, 53

Friends of Comóradh '98, 116, 124
Froude, James Anthony, 69
Furlong, Matthew, 193–4, 216, 224, 259
    death of, 219–20, 260
    trial of, 252, 253
Furlong, Michael
    statue, 218
Furlong, Nicholas, 118, 125, 142, 143
Furlong, Patrick, 253, 258, 259

Gaelic Athletic Association (GAA), 29–30,
    117–18
Gaelic League, 16
Gaffney, M., 238–9
Gahan, Daniel, 107, 110, 130–2, 139, 193, 194,
    197
    on battle of New Ross, 228–9, 236
    on prisoners, 198, 199, 201
    on Scullabogue, 249, 251, 253, 258, 259
    on Wexford government, 195
Gallagher, Jack, 69–72, 73, 75
Galway, Michael, 264
Gantley, James, 15
Garvin, Tom, 54
Gefford, Christopher, 232
Gibbons, Luke, 88, 90, 91
Gill, Valentine, 196
Gilmore, Brother, 39
Gladstone, William Ewart, 56, 58–9, 71–2, 77
Gladwin, gaoler, 196
Glascott, Francis, 260
Glenmore, Co. Wexford, 211, 237–8
Glynn, Jarlath, 118
Goff, Dinah, 201, 262
Goff family, 249
Goff, Mrs, 259
Good Friday Agreement, 145
Gordon, Reverend James, 106, 176, 190, 256
Gorey, Co. Wexford, 196
Gornaghan, 'Captain,' 190
Gowan, Hunter, 185
Graham, Colin, 88
Graham, Tommy, 125
Grandy, Richard, 199, 206, 250, 251, 252
Great Famine, 5–6, 147
Greenberger, A.J., 68
Gregorian chant, 26–7
Grey, Nicholas, 121
Grey, Zane, 25
Grille, 47
Grogan, rebel, 224
Guha, Ranajit, 70, 72

Hall, Reverend James, 168, 266–7
Hammond, J.L., 58
Handcock, Reverend George, 179
Handcock, Reverend Thomas, 184
Hanrahan, Michael, 31

Hardis, William, 203
Harrow, The, Co. Wexford, 186
Harvey, Bagenal, 165, 195, 207, 212, 219, 242–3, 271
    battle of New Ross, 215–17
    execution, 224
    leadership of, 121, 152, 196-8, 240
    letter from, 216
    and Scullabogue, 206, 250, 251, 260–1
Harvie, Christopher, 88
Haughey, Charles, 62
Hay, Edward, 104, 139, 195, 207, 217, 218, 247
    on 1793 riot, 179–80
    account of, 102–3
    burning of 'hospital', 229–30
    on Orange Order, 186
    petition, 182
    on Scullabogue, 103, 260, 263
    on United Irishmen role, 106, 111
Hay, John, 193
Haydon, Mr, 28
Healy, John, 47
Heaney, Seamus, 1, 108, 211
Henry III, King, 162
Henry IV, King, 163
Hessians, 7, 269–70, 273
Hilbert, Lothar, 75
Hill, Jackie, 95
Historians and Librarians Advisory Committee, 118, 119–20, 125, 128
History Ireland, 131
History Society, UCD, 47
Holgan, Pat, 198
Homes, George, 168
Hompesch, General, 273
Hore, H.F., 170
Horetown House, Co. Wexford, 201
Hornick family, 174
Hornick, George, 189–90, 210, 221, 243, 249
Hornick, George Jnr, 190
Hornick, Philip, 189–90, 249
Hornick, Robert, 190
Houghran, John, 198, 199, 201, 204, 205
Houghton Fever Hospital and Dispensary, New Ross, 171
Hume, John, 123
Hussey, Thomas, Bishop of Waterford, 271

Ignatius of Loyola, St, 37
Irish Committee of Historical Sciences, 85–6
Irish Historical Studies, 52
Irish History Students' Association, 48
Irish Manuscripts Commission, 263–4, 268–9
Irish National Liberation Army (INLA), 5
Irish Republican Army (IRA), 5, 52, 60, 61–3, 126–7, 145
Irish Review, The, 86–8, 94–5
Irish Times, The, 5, 6, 47–8, 118, 121, 125, 131,

146–7
Isabella, daughter of Strongbow, 162

Jacobitism, 132
    ballads, 135–6, 158, 245–6
    poetry, 102, 156, 158
James, King, 181
Jefford, Christopher, 269
Jenkins, Hilary, 50
John, King, 161, 162
Johnson, General Henry, 153, 211–12, 216–17, 228, 233, 236, 266
    counter-attack, 240–1, 242
    defence of New Ross, 218–19, 224, 230–2
Jones, John, 201, 262
Jones, P.M., 188
Jones, Samuel, 201, 262
Jones-Hughes, Tom, 110, 174, 175
Jordan, William, 198
Journal of the Wexford Historical Society, 118, 120–1
Joyce, James, 51, 64
Joyce, Thomas, 238

Kant, Immanuel, 53
Kavanagh clan, 162, 164, 165, 173
Kavanagh, Reverend Patrick F., 34–5, 105, 127, 144, 276
Kavanagh, Thomas, 199
Kearney, Alice, 142
Kearney, Hugh, 88
Kearney, Richard, 86, 87
Kearns, Father Mogue, 175, 180, 194
Keeffe, John, 258, 259
Keeffe, Joseph, 239
Kelly, John, 61–2
Kelly, John, of Killanne, 7, 30, 112, 183–4, 191, 193–4, 196
    battle of New Ross, 217, 220, 223–4
Kelly, Joseph, 204
Kemmy, Jim, 79
Kennedy, Dennis, 62
Kennedy, Gus, 45–6, 65
Kennedy, Liam, 88, 96
Kennedy, President John F., 40, 45
Kennedy, rebel, 201
Kennedy, Reverend John, 198
Kenneway, Brian, 146
Keogh, Dáire, 134, 142, 143
Keogh family, 29
Keogh, Matthew, 111, 112, 122
Keogh, Thomas, 168
Kettle, Tom, 47
Kilbride, Co. Wexford, 199
Kilkenny, County, 162, 178, 197, 211, 236
    rebels from, 216, 237, 238
Kilkenny town, 161, 163, 166, 208
Killanne, Co. Wexford, 7, 174, 176, 180, 184, 224
    Hornicks, 189–90

Protestants saved, 190
Killegney, Co. Wexford, 176, 190
King, Colonel, 237–8
King, Mr, 198, 205–6
King, Richard Newton, 191
Knowles, David, 54
Knox, architect, 167
Knox, Ronald, 25

Labour Party, 47
Lacey brothers, 268–9
Laffan, Michael, 74
Lake, General, 197, 221–2, 265
Land League, 16
Lawrence, D.H., 40
Leabhar Branach, 24
Leap, The, 124, 182, 191
Leary, James, 259
Lecky, W.E.H., 105–6, 108, 109, 173, 180
Lee, Augustine, 238–9
Lee, Joe, 67, 81, 84, 95
Leigh family, 165, 249
Leigh, Robert, 166, 174, 199
Leighton, Cadoc, 95
Lemass, Seán, 51
Lennon, Brother 'Matty', 31
Lett, Barbara Newton, 192, 224, 266
Lett, Benjamin, 250
Lett family, 185
Lewis, S., 169
Lindsay, Deirdre, 154
Lloyd, David, 88
Longley, Edna, 86, 87
Loughnageer, Co. Wexford, 249, 250
Lowcay, Standish, 209, 213, 233, 234, 273
Lynch, Anstice, 223
Lynch, Jack, 62–3
Lyons, Leland, 58

Mac Artes, Cahir, 164
McAleese, President Mary, 124
McCabe, William Putnam, 184
McCarthy, M.D., 58
McCartney, Donal, 49
MacConmara, Donnchadh Ruadh, 177
McCormack, Count John, 20
McCormick, Michael, 217, 226, 227–32, 236, 241
MacCurtain, Margaret, 49
McDaniel, John, 223
MacDonagh, Oliver, 55, 56–8, 59, 65–6, 68
McDonnell, Mark, 39
McDonnell, Thomas, 199, 249, 253
Mac Giolla Leith, Caoimhín, 87
McGuire, James, 49
Mac Liammóir, Micheál, 47
MacMahon, Patrick, 166
Mac Muragh, Arthur, 163

Mac Murchadha, Diarmaid, 162
McMurrough Clan, 162
McNeven, William, 188
McQuaid, J.C., Archbishop of Dublin, 53
Madden, Richard Robert, 104–5, 121, 184, 214, 251, 265, 267
Maguire, Leo, 25
Maguire, W.A., 140
Mahony, John, 258–9
Mahony, Thomas, 258, 259
Manning, Maurice, 53
Mansergh, Nicholas, 58, 65, 68–9
Marino College, 36, 38
Mark, Edward, 249
Mark, Francis, 249
Marshall, Earl, 23
Marshall, William, 161–2
Martin, Conor, 53
Martin, John, 239
Marx, Karl, 53, 92
Mary Immaculate College, Limerick, 78–81
Mason, William Shaw, 176
Maturin, Charles Robert, 102, 164
Maxwell, Lt Colonel, 212, 220, 221, 226, 228
Maxwell, W.H., 254
Meath Militia, 193–4
Mercy Order, 78–9
Michael of Kildare, Friar, 163
Militia Act, 1793, 182
Mill, James, 70
Mills, Robert, 199, 250, 251, 252, 253, 258, 259
Misterin, Co. Wexford, 264
Mitchell, Redmond, 259
Monaseed, Co. Wexford, 194
Monasterevin, Co. Kildare, 208
Monastery, The, Tralee, Co. Kerry, 42–3
Moneyhore, Co. Wexford, 7, 189
Moody, Theo, 52
Moore, John, 179, 180
Moore, Sir John, 212
Moore, Thomas, 20, 102
Moran, John, 248, 249, 252
Mountjoy, Lord, 210, 212, 224
Mountnorris, Lord, 194
Murphy, Brother Bonaventure, 56
Murphy, Celestine, 118
Murphy, Christina, 47
Murphy, Father (Taghmon), 251
Murphy, Father John, 13, 103, 104, 105, 106, 117, 187
    biography, 118
    house, 116
Murphy, James, 204–5
Murphy, Jimmy Barry, 56
Murphy, John, 249
    at Scullabogue, 215, 250–1, 252, 258, 259, 261
Murphy, John A., 82–4, 88

Murphy, Margaret, 13
Murphy, Michael, 253, 259
Murphy, Patrick, 201, 203
Murphy, Thomas, 250
Murray, Larry, 31
Musgrave, Sir Richard, 107, 127, 152, 180, 220
    account of, 101–2, 105
    on battle of New Ross, 226
    on drunkenness, 239–40
    on executions, 238
    on Harvey, 196
    list of rebels, 111
    map, 200, 225
    on Scullabogue, 189–90, 205, 206, 247,
        252, 253, 260–1, 262–3
    on 'Wexford Republic' 121, 122, 123

Namier, Sir Lewis B. (Namierite), 54, 58–9, 70,
    71, 74
Napoleon Bonaparte, 156, 245
National 1798 Visitor Centre, 116–17, 125–8,
    132
National Graves Association, 275
National Library of Ireland, 139–40
National Museum of Ireland, 139–40
National University of Ireland (NUI), 78, 85
New Ross, Co. Wexford, 1, 4, 7, 9, 14, 17, 23,
    48, 67, 109, 169, 170, 175, 177, 179, 189, 262
    archive, 8–9
    background to rising, 161–86
    battle of, 107, 108, 126, 180, 183, 194,
        207–8, 211–12, 214–46, 250, 271–2
        aftermath, 265–74
        background to, 172–80, 187–213
        ballads, 244–6
        burials, 105, 266–8
        burning of 'hospital', 126, 131–2,
          227–30
        drunkenness, 239–40
        Harvey leadership, 196–8
        march on, 196
        plan, 216
        rebel motivation, 243–6
        sources for, 151–5, 158–60
    charter, 23
    Dunne family in, 21–9
    enactment, 1948, 29
    fairs, 18
    Irish language, 176
    'Irishtown', 169–70
    Kennedy visit, 45
    map, 200
    Rice's shop, 64–5
    Tholsel, 167, 237
    United Irishmen in, 185
    walls of, 162–3
New Ross Standard, 270
Newbawn, Co. Wexford, 174

Newfort, Co. Wexford, 195
Newlands, Co. Wexford, 271
Newman, Cardinal John Henry, 46
Newman, Jeremiah, Bishop of Limerick, 78–9
Newpark, Co. Wexford, 193
Newtown, Co. Wexford, 211
Newtownbarry, Co. Wexford, 194, 196
Ní Laoghaire, Máire Bhuí, 157, 246
Nicholls, Kenneth, 82
'98 Club, 115
'98 Trail, 115
Nolan, Willy, 110
Norman, Edward, 69, 76
North Cork Militia, 185, 187, 199
Northern Ireland, 5, 47, 55, 60–4, 85–9, 95,
    126–7, 134, 157
    Peace Process, 123, 145–8
Nowlan, Mr, 228

O'Brien, Conor Cruise, 58, 61, 63, 83
O'Brien, Pat, 36
O'Brien, Reverend Michael, 176
O'Brien (Whiteboy), 185
Ó Bruadair, Dáibhí, 245, 246, 248
Ó Buachalla, Breandán, 158, 177–8, 182
Ó Caithnia, Liam, 40
O'Callaghan, Mary, 55
Ó Caoláin, Caoimhghin, 146
Ó Catháin, Conal, 67
O'Connell, Daniel, 103, 138
O'Connor, Arthur, 182
O'Connor, Fergal, 53
Ó Corráin, Donnchadh, 81, 82
Ó Cruaolaoich, Gearóid, 81
Ó Cuív, Éamon, 146
Ó Dálaigh, Cearbhall, 47
Ó Dálaigh, Seán, 247
Ó Doinn, Seán, 155, 156, 244–5
O'Donnell, Nick, 29
O'Faolain, Sean, 28, 29, 33
Ó Gráda, Cormac, 50
O'Halloran, Clare, 87, 97
O'Hehir, Micheál, 30
Ó Longáin, Micheál Óg, 127, 156–7, 245–6
    poetry of, 156, 178, 279–83
Ó Móráin, Donal, 147
Ó Muimhneacháin, J.G., 40
Ó Murchú, Séamus, 177
Ó Rathaille, poet, 156
O'Reilly, Tony, 123
Ó Súilleabháin, Amhlaoibh, 102, 164
Ó Tuathaigh, Gearóid, 66, 68
Ogle, G., 182
Old Conna, Bray, Co. Wicklow, 33–6
Old Ross, Co. Wexford, 128, 161–2, 167–8, 174,
    175, 189, 192, 243
    chapel burned, 207–8
Oldcourt, Co. Wexford, 198–9, 262

Orange Order, 101, 145, 146, 174, 175, 201, 261, 263
    fears of, 102, 104–5, 134, 184–6, 201–3, 206–7, 210, 248–9
    spread of, 180, 182–3
Ormond, Dukes of, 164–5
Oulart, Co. Wexford, 5, 197
    battle of, 105, 106, 187, 194
    memorial, 116

Paine, Thomas, 126
Pakenham, Thomas, 106, 107–8, 154, 211
Palatines, 110–11, 174–5, 189, 191, 207
    dislike of, 232, 248
    in New Ross, 210, 266
Park, Co. Wexford, 250
Parle, Nicholas, 259
Parle, Thomas, 248, 249, 251–2, 259
Parnell, Charles Stewart, 58, 72
Parslow, Shepherd, 262
Parslow, Thomas, 253
Past, The, 131–2
Pearse, James, 27
Pearse, Patrick, 51
Pelham, Henry, Chief Secretary, 106, 173
Perry, Anthony, 112
Peterhouse, Cambridge, 66–77
Plunket, William Conyngham, 34
Politics Society, UCD, 47–8
Poor Law Guardians, 16
Popper, Karl, 53
Porter, John, 204
Portillo, Michael, 74
Poulpeasty, Co. Wexford, 175
Powell, Tom, 47, 108–9, 112, 179–80, 184, 188
Power, Catherine, 198
Power, Miles, 209–10
Power, Pat, 198
Power, Richard, 199, 201, 205
Power, William, 199
Prendergast, Patrick, 199
Prim, John George Augustus, 155

Quakers, 141, 153, 201, 211, 234, 249, 262
Queen, Ellery, 25
Quigley, Michael, 258, 259

Rackard, Bobby, 30
Rackard family, 29, 30
Raftery, poet, 157
Ram estate, Co. Wexford, 174
Ramsey, Clay, 188
Rathgarogue, Co. Wexford, 176
Rathnure, Co. Wexford, 175, 185
Rathsilla, Co. Wexford, 185
Redmond, Nurse, 191–2
Reel, victim, 199
Regan, Michael, 198

'Republic of Wexford', 118–24, 130–1, 132, 139–40
Reynolds, Albert, 123, 145
Rice, Cathy, 22
Rice, Edmund, 271
Rice, Edmund Ignatius, 1, 13, 32, 33, 37–8, 43, 160, 171–2, 269
Rice, Jack, 270
Rice, James, 22
Rice, Joanna; *see* Dunne, Joanna
Rice, John, cousin, 27
Rice, John, of Newlands, 271
Rice, John, rebel, 1, 4–5, 9, 32, 33, 103, 232, 247, 265
    death of, 7, 268, 269–74, 275–7
    gravestone, 159–60
    life of, 171–2
Rice, John (grandfather), 13–15, 274
Rice, Margaret, 269, 270, 275
Rice, Michael, 14
Rice, Nancy, 19
Richard II, King, 163
Richards, Elizabeth, 181, 261
Richards, Reverend John, 189
Rightboys, 101, 178
Ring, Christy, 29
Robinson brothers, 191
Robinson, Francis, 159, 232, 269
Robinson, Ronald, 70, 71, 72, 75
Robinson, Tim, 88
Roche, Edward, 193, 196
Roche, Father Philip, 152, 175, 189, 191, 196, 221, 261
Roche, Richard, 121–3
Roche, Surgeon Jordan, 214, 217, 224, 235–6, 268
Rodriguez, mystic, 37, 38
Roe, Bride, 7, 269–70, 272–3
Roe, Eddie, 270
Roe, Margaret, 269, 270, 275
Roscommon Militia, 237–8
Rosegarland, Co. Wexford, 174, 249, 261
Rossdroit, Co. Wexford, 175, 190
Rossiter, John, 188
Royal Irish Constabulary (RIC), 15, 17
RTÉ, 40
Ryan, Eleanor, 199
Ryan, Elizabeth, 199
Ryan, John, 251, 253
Ryan, Mary, 199
Ryan, Pierce, 238–9
Ryan, Thomas, 204
Ryan, William, 199

Sabourin, Mr and Mrs, 227
St Helen's, Booterstown, 36–8
Salisbury, Lord, 73
Saltmills, Co. Wexford, 198

Scullabogue, massacre of, 7, 103, 104, 184, 192,
    222, 243, 247–64, 268, 273, 274
    background, 196
    burning of barn, 252–3
    Catholic deaths, 199, 253
    Cloney on, 229–30
    commemoration, 6, 126, 128–9, 147
    executions, 259
    Gahan on, 131–2
    Hornick death, 189
    list of dead, 255–7
    motivation for, 201–2, 259–64
    and New Ross defeat, 250–1, 259
    Pakenham on, 108
    sources for, 151–5
    treatment of prisoners, 198, 204–7, 215
    trials, 153–4, 202
    Whelan on, 141
Seal, Anil, 70
Settlement and Explanation, Act of (1666), 165
1798 Commemoration Committee, 141–8, 154
Shallow, Father, John, 184, 205–6, 248–9, 252
Shaw, William, 259
Sheares, Henry, 34
Shee, Patrick, 199
Sheehan, Canon, 35
Shelbourne barony, Co. Wexford, 177
Sheppard, Oliver, 105
Sheridan, John D., 35
Sheridan, Kathy, 140
Sinn Féin, 5, 95, 126, 127, 145, 146
Slaney, River, 173
Sliabh gCua, Co. Waterford, 177
Smith, Bernard, 68
Smith, Sarah, 201, 204
Smyth, Denis, 67
Smyth, Jim, 132, 133, 134, 136, 181
Sodality of the Christian Doctrine, 171
South Africa, 128
South, Sean, 60
Spenser, Edmund, 69, 174
Stanihurst, Richard, 161, 163, 164
Steiner, George, 69–70
Stilman, John, 191
Strongbow (Richard de Clare), 162
Studia Hibernica, 108
Studies in Irish History, 85
Sullivan, Daniel, 258
Sullivan, Patrick, 259
Sutherland, Donald, 188
Sweetman, Bishop, 176
Sylvester, Richard, 249, 250–1, 252
Synott, Richard, 204
Synott, Thomas, 188–9

Taghmon, Co. Wexford, 197, 258, 261
Taoiseach, Department of the, 142
Taylor, Matthew, 238

Taylor, Reverend George, 121–2, 123, 179, 189,
    260–1
    battle of New Ross, 226
    Scullabogue, 253, 260–1
Taylor, Robert, 238
Teeling, C.H., 104
Temple, J., 262
Templescoby, Co. Wexford, 175, 219
Thatcher, Margaret, 74
Thomas, Avril, 163
Thornley, David, 58
Three Rocks camp, 193–4, 195
Tilly, Charles, 188
Tinnerany, Co. Wexford, 238
Tintern, Co. Wexford, 198, 199, 201, 204, 207,
    223
Tobin, John, 259
Tóibín, Colm, 107
Tone, Theobald Wolfe, 3, 89–90, 113, 125
'Tóruigheacht Chailmfhir Mhic Mearcuraidh'
    (Ó Súilleabháin), 164
Tottenham, Charles, 166, 171, 172, 209
    defence of New Ross, 208, 212,
        213, 233–4
    Harvey letter, 216
    and Rice, 271, 273
Tottenham family, 24, 158, 160, 165, 167, 168
Tottenham, Lt-Colonel Charles George, 166
Toumallogue, Co. Wexford, 275, 276
Tour de France, 1998, 117
Trotter, John Bernard, 170–1, 176
Truth and Reconciliation Committee, South
    Africa, 128
Tulach an tSolais, Oulart Hill, 116
Turner, Edward, 195, 196, 199
Turner, John, 258, 259
Turpin, John, 248

Ullmann, Walter, 54
Ulster Museum, 140
United Irishmen, 3, 6, 9, 135, 180
    Catholic support, 182–4
    leadership of, 193–5, 204
    in New Ross, 160
    revolutionary doctrine, 182, 188
    role of, 103–4, 105, 106, 111–14, 118, 124,
        126–7, 130
    Scullabogue, 259
    sectarianism, 136
    use of Irish, 155–7
    Wexford recruitment, 183–4
University Church, Dublin, 19
University College Cork (UCC), 56–67, 81–5
University College Dublin (UCD), 44–55, 57,
    67, 74, 75, 80, 97, 275
    archives department, 85
University of Notre Dame, Indiana, 89
Unsworth, Roger, 227

'Up in Arms' (Ulster Museum), 140

Valloten, Major, 179
Vandelour, Major, 271
Vendée rebellion, France, 188
Vesey, Major, 219, 221, 224, 225–6, 231, 265
Vincent, John, 58, 71, 72–3, 74, 77
Vinegar Hill, Co. Wexford, 1, 2–3, 4, 189, 193
    atrocities, 190, 192, 196, 222, 229, 230
    battle of, 126
    memorial, 115, 118
    prisoners, 190, 191, 198, 203, 209–10
    trials, 251
Vinegar Hill Day, 116
Volunteer Corps, 183, 194

Walker, Brian, 87, 88
Walker's Hibernian Magazine, 153
Wall, Maureen, 49–50, 51, 61, 171
Walsh, Martin, 268–9
Waterford, County, 9, 162, 177, 197, 236
Waterford town, 161, 167, 172, 208, 211, 212,
    237, 271
    trade war, 163–4
Westmoreland, Earl of, 182
Wexford County Council, 115
Wexford Echo, The, 117–18, 120
Wexford Rebellion; *see also* 'Republic of
    Wexford'
        commemorations of, 115–29
        Comóradh '98, 115–29
        historiography of, 101–14
        political influences on, 130–48
        politicization, 132–9
        sectarianism, 102, 108–11, 133–4, 136–9,
            182–6, 189–92, 195–6, 198–207;
            see also Scullabogue, massacre of
        'Senate', 119–24, 195–6
Wexford town, 103, 107, 111, 133, 161, 175,
    240, 250
        1793 riot, 179
        atrocities, 222, 229, 230
        executions, 192, 224
        Irish language, 176
        march on, 193–4, 195, 197
        prisoners, 198, 203
        rebel government, 195–6
        'Republic of Wexford', 118–24, 139–40
        riot, 1793, 109
Wheeler, Ned, 29
Whelan, Catherine, 222–3

Whelan, Kevin, 88, 108, 118, 158, 207
    on Catholicism, 171, 173, 175
    and commemorations, 5–6, 118, 127,
        132–47
    on Defenders, 180–1
    on politicization, 132–9
    on prisoners, 198, 199, 201
    repression of memory, 276
    'Republic' claim, 119, 121, 123, 132,
        139–40
    Scullabogue memorial, 128
    on sectarianism, 110–11, 114, 185, 189
Whelan, Mary, 266, 272
White, Hawtry, 105
Whiteboyism, 111, 133, 174, 177–80, 185, 192,
    210, 249
    revenge, 189–90
Whyte, John, 53
Williams, T. Desmond, 48–9, 50, 55, 67, 74
Wiseman, James, 191
Wolfe Tone, Theobald, 88
Wormwold, Brian, 67
Wright, G.N., 170

Yale, University of, 66, 76
Young, Arthur, 167
Young Irelanders, 276